Collins

REAL-TIME SYSTEMS
Design Principles for Distributed Embedded Applications

THE KLUWER INTERNATIONAL SERIES
IN ENGINEERING AND COMPUTER SCIENCE

REAL-TIME SYSTEMS
Consulting Editor
John A. Stankovic

REAL-TIME SYSTEMS
Design Principles for Distributed Embedded Applications

by

Hermann Kopetz
Technische Universität Wien

KLUWER ACADEMIC PUBLISHERS
Boston / Dordrecht / London

Distributors for North America:
Kluwer Academic Publishers
101 Philip Drive
Assinippi Park
Norwell, Massachusetts 02061 USA

Distributors for all other countries:
Kluwer Academic Publishers Group
Distribution Centre
Post Office Box 322
3300 AH Dordrecht, THE NETHERLANDS

Library of Congress Cataloging-in-Publication Data

A C.I.P. Catalogue record for this book is available
from the Library of Congress.

Printed on acid-free paper.

Printed in the United States of America

for Renate
Pia, Georg, and Andreas

Table of Contents

Preface

The primary objective of this book is to serve as a textbook for a student taking a senior undergraduate or a first-year graduate one-semester course on real-time systems. The focus of the book is on hard real-time systems, which are systems that must meet their temporal specification in all anticipated load and fault scenarios. It is assumed that a student of computer engineering, computer science or electrical engineering taking this course already has a background in programming, operating systems, and computer communication. The book stresses the system aspects of distributed real-time applications, treating the issues of real-time, distribution, and fault-tolerance from an integral point of view. The selection and organization of the material have evolved from the annual real-time system course conducted by the author at the Technische Universität Wien for more than ten years. The main topics of this book are also covered in an intensive three-day industrial seminar entitled *The Systematic Design of Embedded Real-Time Systems*. This seminar has been presented many times in Europe, the USA and Asia to professionals in the industry. This cross fertilization between the academic world and the industrial world has led to the inclusion of many insightful examples from the industrial world to explain the fundamental scientific concepts in a real-world setting. These examples are mainly taken from the emerging field of embedded automotive electronics that is acting as a catalyst for technology in the current real-time systems market.

The secondary objective of this book is to provide a reference book that can be used by professionals in the industry. An attempt is made to explain the relevance of the latest scientific insights to the solution of everyday problems in the design and implementation of distributed and embedded real-time systems. The demand of our industrial sponsors to provide them with a document that explains the present state of the art of real-time technology in a coherent, concise, and understandable manner has been a driving force for this book. Because the cost/effectiveness of a method is a major concern in an industrial setting, the book also looks at design decisions from an economic viewpoint. The recent appearance of cost-effective powerful system chips has a momentous influence on the architecture and economics of future distributed system solutions. The composability of an architecture, i.e., the capability to build dependable large systems out of pre-tested components with minimal integration effort, is one of the great challenges for designers of the next generation of real-time systems. The topic of composability is thus a recurring theme throughout the book.

The material of the book is organized into three parts comprising a total of fourteen Chapters, corresponding to the fourteen weeks of a typical semester. The first part from Chapters 1 to 6, provides an introduction and establishes the fundamental concepts. The second part from Chapters 7 to 12, focuses on techniques and methods. Finally, the third part from Chapters 13 and 14, integrates the concepts developed throughout the book into a coherent architecture.

The first two introductory chapters discuss the characteristics of the real-time environment and the technical and economic advantages of distributed solutions. The concern over the temporal behavior of the computer is the distinctive feature of a real-time system. Chapter 3 introduces the fundamental concepts of time and time measurement relevant to a distributed computer system. It covers intrinsically difficult material and should therefore be studied carefully. The second half of this Chapter (Section 3.4 and 3.5) on internal and external clock synchronization can be omitted in a first reading. Chapters 4 and 5 present a conceptual model of a distributed real-time system and introduce the important notions of temporal accuracy, permanence, idempotency, and replica determinism. Chapter 6 introduces the field of dependable computing as it relates to real-time systems and concludes the first part of the book.

The second part of the book starts with the topic of real-time communication, including a discussion about fundamental conflicts in the design of real-time communication protocols. Chapter 7 also briefly introduces a number of event-triggered real-time protocols, such as CAN, and ARINC 629. Chapter 8 presents a new class of real-time communication protocols, the time-triggered protocols, which have been developed by the author at the Technische Universität Wien. The time-triggered protocol TTP is now under consideration by the European automotive industry for the next generation of safety-critical distributed real-time applications onboard vehicles. Chapter 9 is devoted to the issues of input/output. Chapter 10 discusses real-time operating systems. It contains a case study of a new-generation operating system, ERCOS, for embedded applications, which is used in modern automotive engine controllers. Chapter 11 covers scheduling and discusses some of the classic results from scheduling research. The new priority ceiling protocol for scheduling periodic dependent tasks is introduced. Chapter 12 is devoted to the topic of validation, including a section on hardware- and software-implemented fault injection.

The third part of the book comprises only two chapters: Chapter 13 on "System Design" and Chapter 14 on the "Time-Triggered Architecture". System design is a creative process that cannot be accomplished by following the rules of a "design rule book". Chapter 13, which is somewhat different from the other chapters of the book, takes a philosophical interdisciplinary look at design from a number of different perspectives. It then presents a set of heuristic guidelines and checklists to help the designer in evaluating design alternatives. A number of relevant real-time architecture projects that have been implemented during the past ten years are discussed at the end of Chapter 13. Finally, Chapter 14 presents the "Time-Triggered Architecture" which has been designed by the author at the Technische Universität Wien. "Time-Triggered Architecture" is an attempt to integrate many of the concepts and techniques that have been developed throughout the text.

The Glossary is an integral part of the book, providing definitions for many of the technical terms that are used throughout the book. A new term is highlighted by *italicizing* it in the text at the point where it is introduced. If the reader is not sure about the meaning of a term, she/he is advised to refer to the glossary. Terms that are considered important in the text are also italicized.

At the end of each chapter the important concepts are summarized in the section "Points to Remember". Every chapter closes with a set of discussive and numerical problems that cover the material presented in the chapter.

ACKNOWLEDGMENTS

Over a period of a decade, many of the more than 1000 students who have attended the "Real-Time Systems" course at the Technische Universität Wien have contributed, in one way or another, to the extensive lecture notes that were the basis of the book.

The insight gained from the research at our Institut für Technische Informatik at the Technische Universität Wien formed another important input. The extensive experimental work at our institute has been supported by numerous sponsors, in particular the ESPRIT project PDCS, financed by the Austrian FWF, the ESPRIT LTR projects DEVA, and the Brite Euram project X-by-Wire. We hope that the recently started ESPRIT OMI project TTA (Time Triggered Architecture) will result in a VLSI implementation of our TTP protocol.

I would like to give special thanks to Jack Stankovic, from the University of Massachusetts at Amherst, who encouraged me strongly to write a book on "Real-Time Systems", and established the contacts with Bob Holland, from Kluwer Academic Publishers, who coached me throughout this endeavor.

The concrete work on this book started about a year ago, while I was privileged to spend some months at the University of California in Santa Barbara. My hosts, Louise Moser and Michael Melliar-Smith, provided an excellent environment and were willing to spend numerous hours in discussions over the evolving manuscript— thank you very much. The Real-Time Systems Seminar that I held at UCSB at that time was exceptional in the sense that I was writing chapters of the book and the students were asked to correct the chapters.

In terms of constructive criticism on draft chapters I am especially grateful to the comments made by my colleagues at the Technische Universität Wien: Heinz

Appoyer, Christian Ebner, Emmerich Fuchs, Thomas Führer, Thomas Galla, Rene Hexel, Lorenz Lercher, Dietmar Millinger, Roman Pallierer, Peter Puschner, Andreas Krüger, Roman Nossal, Anton Schedl, Christopher Temple, Christoph Scherrer, and Andreas Steininger.

Special thanks are due to Priya Narasimhan from UCSB who carefully edited the book and improved the readability tremendously.

A number of people read and commented on parts of the book, insisting that I improve the clarity and presentation in many places. They include Jack Goldberg from SRI, Menlo Park, Cal., Markus Krug from Daimler Benz, Stuttgart, Stefan Poledna from Bosch, Vienna, who contributed to the section on the ERCOS operating system, Krithi Ramamritham from the University of Massachusetts, Amherst, and Neeraj Suri from New Jersey Institute of Technology.

Errors that remain are, of course, my responsibility alone.

Finally, and most importantly, I would like to thank my wife, Renate, and our children, Pia, Georg, and Andreas, who endured a long and exhausting project that took away a substantial fraction of our scarce time.

Hermann Kopetz

Vienna, Austria, January 1997

Chapter 1

The Real-Time Environment

OVERVIEW

The purpose of this introductory chapter is to describe the environment of real-time computer systems from a number of different perspectives. A solid understanding of the technical and economic factors which characterize a real-time application helps to interpret the demands that the system designer must cope with. The chapter starts with the definition of a real-time system and with a discussion of its functional and metafunctional requirements. Particular emphasis is placed on the temporal requirements that are derived from the well-understood properties of control applications. The objective of a control algorithm is to drive a process so that a performance criterion is satisfied. Random disturbances occurring in the environment degrade system performance and must be taken into account by the control algorithm. Any additional uncertainty that is introduced into the control loop by the control system itself, e.g., a non-predictable jitter of the control loop, results in a degradation of the quality of control.

In the Sections 1.2 to 1.5 real-time applications are classified from a number of viewpoints. Special emphasis is placed on the fundamental differences between hard and soft real-time systems. Because soft real-time systems do not have catastrophic failure modes, a less rigorous approach to their design is often followed. Sometimes resource-inadequate solutions that will not handle the rarely occurring peak-load scenarios are accepted on economic arguments. In a hard real-time application, such an approach is unacceptable because the safety of a design in all specified situations, even if they occur only very rarely, must be demonstrated *vis-a-vis* a certification agency. In Section 1.6, a brief analysis of the real-time system market is carried out with emphasis on the field of embedded real-time systems. An embedded real-time system is a part of a self-contained product, e.g., a television set or an automobile. In the future, embedded real-time systems will form the most important market segment for real-time technology.

1.1   WHEN IS A COMPUTER SYSTEM REAL-TIME?

A *real-time computer system* is a computer system in which the correctness of the system behavior depends not only on the logical results of the computations, but also on the physical instant at which these results are produced.

A real-time computer system is always part of a larger system–this larger system is called a *real-time system*. A real-time system changes its state as a function of physical time, e.g., a chemical reaction continues to change its state even after its controlling computer system has stopped. It is reasonable to decompose a real-time system into a set of subsystems called *clusters* (Figure 1.1) e.g., the *controlled object* (the *controlled cluster*), the real-time computer system (the *computational cluster*) and the *human operator* (the *operator cluster*). We refer to the controlled object and the operator collectively as the *environment* of the real-time computer system.

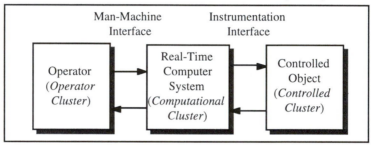

Figure 1.1: Real-time system.

If the real-time computer system is *distributed*, it consists of a set of (computer) *nodes* interconnected by a real-time communication network (see also Figure 2.1).

The interface between the human operator and the real-time computer system is called the *man-machine interface,* and the interface between the controlled object and the real-time computer system is called the *instrumentation interface.* The man-machine interface consists of input devices (e.g., keyboard) and output devices (e.g., display) that interface to the human operator. The instrumentation interface consists of the sensors and actuators that transform the physical signals (e.g., voltages, currents) in the controlled object into a digital form and *vice versa.* A node with an instrumentation interface is called an *interface node.*

A real-time computer system must react to stimuli from the controlled object (or the operator) within time intervals dictated by its environment. The instant at which a result must be produced is called a *deadline.* If a result has utility even after the deadline has passed, the deadline is classified as *soft,* otherwise it is *firm.* If a catastrophe could result if a firm deadline is missed, the deadline is called *hard.* Consider a railway crossing a road with a traffic signal. If the traffic signal does not change to "red" before the train arrives, a catastrophe could result. A real-time computer system that must meet at least one hard deadline is called a *hard real-time computer system* or a *safety-critical real-time computer system*. If no hard real-time deadline exists, then the system is called a *soft real-time computer system*.

The design of a hard real-time system is fundamentally different from the design of a soft real-time system. While a hard real-time computer system must sustain a guaranteed temporal behavior under all specified load and fault conditions, it is permissible for a soft real-time computer system to miss a deadline occasionally. The differences between soft and hard real-time systems will be discussed in detail in the following sections. The focus of this book is on the design of hard real-time systems.

1.2   FUNCTIONAL REQUIREMENTS

The functional requirements of real-time systems are concerned with the functions that a real-time computer system must perform. They are grouped into data collection requirements, direct digital control requirements, and man-machine interaction requirements.

1.2.1   Data Collection

A controlled object, e.g., a car or an industrial plant, changes its state as a function of time. If we freeze time, we can describe the current state of the controlled object by recording the values of its state variables at that moment. Possible state variables of a controlled object "car" are the position of the car, the speed of the car, the position of switches on the dash board, and the position of a piston in a cylinder. We are normally not interested in *all* state variables, but only in the *subset* of state variables that is *significant* for our purpose. A significant state variable is called a *real-time (RT) entity*.

Every RT entity is in the *sphere of control (SOC)* of a subsystem, i.e., it belongs to a subsystem that has the authority to change the value of this RT entity. Outside its sphere of control, the value of an RT entity can be observed, but cannot be modified. For example, the current position of a piston in a cylinder of the engine of a controlled car object is in the sphere of control of the car. Outside the car, the current position of the piston can only be observed.

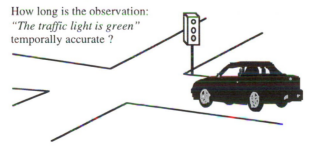

How long is the observation:
"The traffic light is green"
temporally accurate ?

Figure 1.2: Temporal accuracy of the traffic light information.

The first functional requirement of a real-time computer system is the observation of the RT entities in a controlled object and the collection of these observations. An observation of an RT entity is represented by a *real-time (RT) image* in the computer system. Since the state of the controlled object is a function of real time, a given RT image is only *temporally accurate* for a limited time interval. The length of this time interval depends on the dynamics of the controlled object. If the state of the controlled object changes very quickly, the corresponding RT image has a very short *accuracy interval*.

Example: Consider the example of Figure 1.2, where a car enters an intersection controlled by a traffic light. How long is the observation "the traffic light is green" temporally accurate? If the information "the traffic light is green" is used outside its accuracy interval, i.e., a car enters the intersection after the traffic light has switched to red, a catastrophe may occur. In this example, an upper bound for the accuracy interval is given by the duration of the yellow phase of the traffic light.

The set of all temporally accurate real-time images of the controlled object is called the *real-time database*. The real-time database must be updated whenever an RT entity changes its value. These updates can be performed periodically, triggered by the progression of the real-time clock by a fixed period (*time-triggered (TT) observation*), or immediately after a change of state, which constitutes an event, occurs in the RT entity (*event-triggered (ET) observation*). A more detailed analysis of event-triggered and time-triggered observations will be presented in Chapter 5.

Signal Conditioning: A physical sensor, like a thermocouple, produces a *raw data* element (e.g., a voltage). Often, a sequence of raw data elements is collected and an averaging algorithm is applied to reduce the measurement error. In the next step the raw data must be calibrated and transformed to standard measurement units. The term *signal conditioning* is used to refer to all the processing steps that are necessary to obtain meaningful *measured data* of an RT entity from the raw sensor data. After signal conditioning, the measured data must be checked for plausibility and related to other measured data to detect a possible fault of the sensor. A data element that is judged to be a correct RT image of the corresponding RT entity is called an *agreed data element*.

Alarm Monitoring: An important function of a real-time computer system is the continuous monitoring of the RT entities to detect abnormal process behaviors. For example, the rupture of a pipe in a chemical plant will cause many RT entities (diverse pressures, temperatures, liquid levels) to deviate from their normal operating ranges, and to cross some preset alarm limits, thereby generating a set of correlated alarms, which is called an *alarm shower*. The computer system must detect and display these alarms and must assist the operator in identifying a *primary event* which was the initial cause of these alarms. For this purpose, alarms that are observed must be logged in a special alarm log with the exact time the alarm occurred. The exact time order of the alarms is helpful in eliminating the secondary alarms, i.e., all alarms that are consequent to the primary event. In complex industrial plants, sophisticated knowledge-based systems are used to assist the operator in the alarm analysis. The predictable behavior of the computer system during peak-load alarm situations is of major importance in many application scenarios.

A situation that occurs infrequently but is of utmost concern when it does occur is called a *rare-event* situation. The validation of the rare-event performance of a real-time computer system is a challenging task.

Example: The sole purpose of a nuclear power plant monitoring and shutdown system is reliable performance in a peak-load alarm situation (rare event). Hopefully, this rare event will never occur.

1.2.2   Direct   Digital   Control

Many real-time computer systems must calculate the *set points* for the actuators and control the controlled object directly (*direct digital control–DDC*), i.e., without any underlying conventional control system.

Control applications are highly regular, consisting of an (infinite) sequence of control periods, each one starting with sampling of the RT entities, followed by the execution of the control algorithm to calculate a new set point, and subsequently by the output of the set point to the actuator. The design of a proper control algorithm that achieves the desired control objective, and compensates for the random disturbances that perturb the controlled object, is the topic of the field of control engineering. In the next section on temporal requirements, some basic notions in control engineering will be introduced.

1.2.3   Man-Machine   Interaction

A real-time computer system must inform the operator of the current state of the controlled object, and must assist the operator in controlling the machine or plant object. This is accomplished via the man-machine interface, a critical subsystem of major importance. Many catastrophic computer-related accidents in safety-critical real-time systems have been traced to mistakes made at the man-machine interface [Lev95].

Most process-control applications contain, as part of the man-machine interface, an extensive data logging and data reporting subsystem that is designed according to the demands of the particular industry. For example, in some countries, the pharmaceutical industry is required by law to record and store all relevant process parameters of every production batch in an archival storage so that the process conditions prevailing at the time of a production run can be reexamined in case a defective product is identified on the market at a later time.

Man-machine interfacing has become such an important issue in the design of computer-based systems that a number of courses dealing with this topic have been developed. In the context of this book, we will introduce an abstract man-machine interface in Section 4.3.1, but we will not cover its design in detail. The interested reader is referred to standard textbooks, such as the books by Ebert [Ebe94] or by Hix and Hartson [Hix93], on man-machine interfacing.

1.3   TEMPORAL REQUIREMENTS

1.3.1   Where Do Temporal Requirements Come From?

The most stringent temporal demands for real-time systems have their origin in the requirements of the control loops, e.g., in the control of a fast mechanical process such as an automotive engine. The temporal requirements at the man-machine interface are, in comparison, less stringent because the human perception delay, in the range of *50-100* msec, is orders of magnitudes larger than the latency requirements of fast control loops.

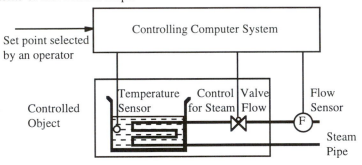

Figure 1.3: A simple control loop.

A Simple Control Loop: Consider the simple control loop depicted in Figure 1.3 consisting of a vessel with a liquid, a heat exchanger connected to a steam pipe, and a controlling computer system. The objective of the computer system is to control the valve (*control variable*) determining the flow of steam through the heat exchanger so that the temperature of the liquid in the vessel remains within a small range around the *set point* selected by the operator.

The focus of the following discussion is on the temporal properties of this simple control loop consisting of a controlled object and a controlling computer system.

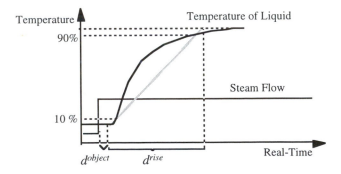

Figure 1.4: Delay and rise time of the step response.

The Controlled Object: Assume that the system is in equilibrium. Whenever the steam flow is increased by a step function, the temperature of the liquid in the vessel will change according to Figure 1.4 until a new equilibrium is reached. This *response function* of the temperature depends on the amount of liquid in the vessel and the flow of steam through the heat exchanger, i.e., on the dynamics of the controlled object. (In the following section, we will use d to denote a duration and t, a point in time).

There are two important temporal parameters characterizing this elementary step response function, the *object delay* d^{object} after which the *measured variable* temperature begins to rise (caused by the initial inertia of the process, called the *process lag*) and the *rise time* d^{rise} of the temperature until the new equilibrium state has been reached. To determine the *object delay* d^{object} and the *rise time* d^{rise} from a given experimentally recorded shape of the step-response function, one finds the two points in time where the response function has reached *10%* and *90%* of the difference between the two stationary equilibrium values. These two points are connected by a straight line (Figure 1.4). The significant points in time that characterize the *object delay* d^{object} and the *rise time* d^{rise} of the step response function are constructed by finding the intersection of this straight line with the two horizontal lines that extend the two liquid temperatures that correspond to the stable states before and after the application of the step function.

Controlling Computer System: The controlling computer system must sample the temperature of the vessel periodically to detect any deviation between the intended value and the actual value of the controlled variable. The constant duration between two sample points is called the sampling period d^{sample} and the reciprocal $1/d^{sample}$ is the sampling frequency, f^{sample}. A rule of thumb is that, in a digital system which is expected to behave like a quasi-continuous system, the sampling period should be less than one-tenth of the rise time d^{rise} of the step response function of the controlled object, i.e. $d^{sample} < (d^{rise}/10)$. The computer compares the measured temperature to the temperature set point selected by the operator and calculates the *error term*. This error term forms the basis for the calculation of a new value of the control variable by a *control algorithm*. A given time interval after each sampling point, called the *computer delay* $d^{computer}$, the controlling computer will output this new value of the control variable to the control valve, thus closing the control loop. The delay $d^{computer}$ should be smaller than the sampling period d^{sample}.

The difference between the maximum and the minimum values of the delay is called the *jitter* of the delay, $\Delta d^{computer}$. This jitter is a sensitive parameter for the quality of control, as will be discussed in Section 1.3.2.

The *dead time* of the open control loop is the time interval between the observation of the RT entity and the start of a reaction of the controlled object due to a computer action based on this observation. The dead time is the sum of the controlled object delay d^{object}, which is in the sphere of control of the controlled object and is thus determined by the controlled object's dynamics, and the computer delay $d^{computer}$, which is determined by the computer implementation. To reduce the dead time in a control loop and to improve the stability of the control loop, these delays should be as small as possible.

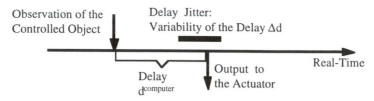

Figure 1.5: Delay and delay jitter.

The computer delay $d^{computer}$ is defined by the time interval between the *sampling point,* i.e., the observation of the controlled object, and the *use* of this information (see Figure 1.5), i.e., the output of the corresponding actuator signal to the controlled object. Apart from the necessary time for performing the calculations, the computer delay is determined by the time required for communication.

Symbol	Parameter	Sphere of Control	Relationships
d^{object}	controlled object delay	controlled object	physical process
d^{rise}	rise time of step response	controlled object	physical process
d^{sample}	sampling period	computer	$d^{sample} \ll d^{rise}$
$d^{computer}$	computer delay	computer	$d^{computer} < d^{sample}$
$\Delta d^{computer}$	jitter of the computer delay	computer	$\Delta d^{computer} \ll d^{computer}$
$d^{deadtime}$	dead time	computer and controlled object	$d^{computer} + d^{object}$

Table 1.1: Parameters of an elementary control loop.

Parameters of a Control Loop: Table 1.1 summarizes the temporal parameters that characterize the elementary control loop depicted in Figure 1.3. In the first two columns we denote the symbol and the name of the parameter. The third column denotes the sphere of control in which the parameter is located, i.e., what subsystem determines the value of the parameter. Finally, the fourth column indicates the relationships between these temporal parameters.

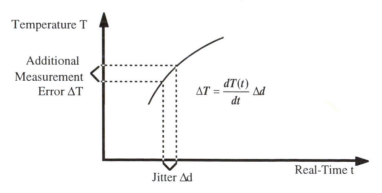

Figure 1.6: The effect of jitter on the measured variable *T*.

1.3.2 Minimal Latency Jitter

The data items in control applications are state-based, i.e., they contain images of the RT entities. The computational actions in control applications are mostly time-triggered, e.g., the control signal for obtaining a sample is derived from the progression of time within the computer system. This control signal is thus in the sphere of control of the computer system. It is known in advance when the next control action must take place. Many control algorithms are based on the assumption that the delay jitter $\Delta d^{computer}$ is very small compared to the *delay $d^{computer}$*, i.e., the delay is close to constant. This assumption is made because control algorithms can be designed to compensate a *known* constant delay. Delay jitter brings an additional uncertainty into the control loop that has an adverse effect on the quality of control. The jitter Δd can be seen as an uncertainty about the instant the RT-entity was observed. This jitter can be interpreted as causing an additional value error ΔT of the measured variable temperature T as shown in Figure 1.6. Therefore, the delay jitter should always be a small fraction of the delay, i.e., if a delay of 1 msec is demanded then the delay jitter should be in the range of a few μsec [SAE95].

1.3.3 Minimal Error-Detection Latency

Hard real-time applications are, by definition, safety-critical. It is therefore important that any error within the control system, e.g., the loss or corruption of a message or the failure of a node, is detected within a short time with a very high probability. The required *error-detection latency* must be in the same order of magnitude as the sampling period of the fastest critical control loop. It is then possible to perform some corrective action, or to bring the system into a safe state, before the consequences of an error can cause any severe system failure. Jitterless systems will always have a shorter error-detection latency than systems that allow for jitter, since in a jitterless system, a failure can be detected as soon as the expected event fails to occur [Lin96].

1.4 DEPENDABILITY REQUIREMENTS

The notion of dependability covers the metafunctional attributes of a computer system that relate to the quality of service a system delivers to its users during an extended interval of time. (A user could be a human or another technical system.) The following measures of dependability attributes are of importance [Lap92]:

1.4.1 Reliability

The *Reliability R(t)* of a system is the probability that a system will provide the specified service until time *t*, given that the system was operational at $t = t_0$. If a system has a constant *failure rate* of λ *failures/hour*, then the reliability at time *t* is given by

$$R(t) = \exp(-\lambda(t-t_o)),$$

where $t - t_O$ is given in hours. The inverse of the failure rate $1/\lambda = MTTF$ is called the *Mean-Time-To-Failure MTTF* (in hours). If the failure rate of a system is required to be in the order of 10^{-9} failures/h or lower, then we speak of a system with an *ultrahigh reliability* requirement.

1.4.2 Safety

Safety is reliability regarding *critical failure modes*. A critical failure mode is said to be *malign*, in contrast with a noncritical failure, which is *benign*. In a malign failure mode, the cost of a failure can be orders of magnitude higher than the utility of the system during normal operation. Examples of malign failures are: an airplane crash due to a failure in the flight-control system, and an automobile accident due to a failure of a computer-controlled intelligent brake in the automobile. Safety-critical (hard) real-time systems must have a failure rate with regard to critical failure modes that conforms to the *ultrahigh reliability* requirement. Consider the example of a computer-controlled brake in an automobile. The failure rate of a computer-caused critical brake failure must be lower than the failure rate of a conventional braking system. Under the assumption that a car is operated about one hour per day on the average, one safety-critical failure per million cars per year translates into a failure rate in the order of 10^{-9} failures/h. Similar low failure rates are required in flight-control systems, train-signaling systems, and nuclear power plant monitoring systems.

Certification: In many cases the design of a safety-critical real-time system must be approved by an independent certification agency. The certification process can be simplified if the certification agency can be convinced that:

(i)   The subsystems that are critical for the safe operation of the system are protected by stable interfaces that eliminate the possibility of error propagation from the rest of the system into these safety-critical subsystems.

(ii)   All scenarios that are covered by the given load- and fault-hypothesis can be handled according to the specification without reference to probabilistic arguments. This makes a resource adequate design necessary.

(iii)   The architecture supports a constructive certification process where the certification of subsystems can be done independently of each other, e.g., the proof that a communication subsystem meets all deadlines is independent of the proof of the performance of a node. This requires that subsystems have a high degree of autonomy and clairvoyance (knowledge about the future).

[Joh92] specifies the required properties for a system that is "designed for validation":

(i)   A complete and accurate reliability model can be constructed. All parameters of the model that cannot be deduced analytically must be measurable in feasible time under test.

(ii)   The reliability model does not include state transitions representing design faults; analytical arguments must be presented to show that design faults will not cause system failure.

(iii) Design tradeoffs are made in favor of designs that minimize the number of parameters that must be measured and simplify the analytical argument.

1.4.3 Maintainability

Maintainability is a measure of the time required to repair a system after the occurrence of a benign failure. Maintainability is measured by the probability $M(d)$ that the system is restored within a time interval d after the failure. In keeping with the reliability formalism, a constant repair rate μ (repairs per hour) and a *Mean-Time to Repair (MTTR)* is introduced to define a quantitative maintainability measure.

There is a fundamental conflict between reliability and maintainability. A maintainable design requires the partitioning of a system into a set of *smallest replaceable units* (*SRUs*) connected by serviceable interfaces that can be easily disconnected and reconnected to replace a faulty *SRU* in case of a failure. A serviceable interface, e.g., a plug connection, has a significantly higher physical failure rate than a non-serviceable interface, e.g., a solder connection. Furthermore, a serviceable interface is more expensive to produce. These conflicts between reliability and maintainability are the reasons why many mass-produced consumer products are designed for reliability at the expense of maintainability.

1.4.4 Availability

Availability is a measure of the delivery of correct service with respect to the alternation of correct and incorrect service, and is measured by the fraction of time that the system is ready to provide the service. Consider the example of a telephone switching system. Whenever a user picks up the phone, the system should be ready to provide the telephone service with a very high probability. A telephone exchange is allowed to be out of service for only a few minutes per year.

In systems with constant failure and repair rates, the reliability *(MTTF)*, maintainability *(MTTR)*, and availability *(A)* measures are related by

$$A = MTTF/ (MTTF+MTTR).$$

The sum *MTTF+MTTR* is sometimes called the *Mean Time Between Failures (MTBF)*. Figure 1.7 shows the relationship between *MTTF, MTTR, and MTBF.*

System State:

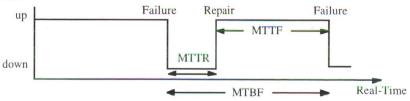

Figure 1.7: Relationship between *MTTF, MTBF* and *MTTR*.

A high availability can be achieved either by a long *MTTF* or by a short *MTTR*. The designer has thus some freedom in the selection of her/his approach to the construction of a high-availability system.

1.4.5 Security

A fifth important attribute of dependability–the *security attribute*–is concerned with the ability of a system to prevent unauthorized access to information or services. There are difficulties in defining a quantitative security measure, e.g., the specification of a *standard burglar* that takes a certain time to intrude a system. Traditionally, security issues have been associated with large databases, where the concerns are confidentiality, privacy, and authenticity of information. During the last few years, security issues have also become important in real-time systems, e.g., a cryptographic theft-avoidance system that locks the ignition of a car if the user cannot present the specified access code.

1.5 CLASSIFICATION OF REAL-TIME SYSTEMS

In this section we classify real-time systems from different perspectives. The first two classifications, hard real-time versus soft real-time (on-line), and fail-safe versus fail-operational, depend on the characteristics of the application, i.e., on factors *outside* the computer system. The second three classifications, guaranteed-timeliness versus best-effort, resource-adequate versus resource-inadequate, and event-triggered versus time-triggered, depend on the design and implementation, i.e., on factors *inside* the computer system.

1.5.1 Hard Real-Time System versus Soft Real-Time System

The design of a hard real-time system, which must produce the results at the correct instant, is fundamentally different from the design of a soft-real time or an on-line system, such as a transaction processing system. In this section we will elaborate on these differences. Table 1.2 compares the characteristics of hard real-time systems versus soft real-time systems.

characteristic	hard real-time	soft real-time (on-line)
response time	hard–required	soft–desired
peak-load performance	predictable	degraded
control of pace	environment	computer
safety	often critical	non-critical
size of data files	small/medium	large
redundancy type	active	checkpoint–recovery
data integrity	short-term	long-term
error detection	autonomous	user assisted

Table 1.2: Hard real-time versus soft real-time systems.

Response Time: The demanding response time requirements of hard real-time applications, often in the order of milliseconds or less, preclude direct human intervention during normal operation and in critical situations. A hard real-time system must be highly autonomous to maintain safe operation of the process. In contrast, the response time requirements of soft real-time and on-line systems are often in the order of seconds. Furthermore, if a deadline is missed in a soft real-time system, no catastrophe can result.

Peak-load Performance: In a hard real-time system, the peak-load scenario must be well-defined. It must be guaranteed by design that the computer system meets the specified deadlines in all situations, since the utility of many hard real-time applications depends on their predictable performance during rare event scenarios leading to a peak load. This is in contrast to the situation in a soft-real time system, where the *average* performance is important, and a degraded operation in a rarely occurring peak load case is tolerated for economic reasons.

Control of Pace: A hard real-time computer system must remain synchronous with the state of the environment (the controlled object and the human operator) in all operational scenarios. It is thus paced by the state changes occurring in the environment. This is in contrast to an on-line system, which can exercise some control over the environment in case it cannot process the offered load. Consider the case of a transaction processing system, such as an airline reservation system. If the computer cannot keep up with the demands of the operators, it just extends the response time and forces the operators to slow down.

Safety: The safety criticality of many real-time applications has a number of consequences for the system designer. In particular, error detection must be autonomous so that the system can initiate appropriate recovery actions within the time intervals dictated by the application.

Size of Data Files: Real-time systems have small data files, which constitute the *real-time database* that is composed of the temporally accurate images of the RT-entities. The key concern in hard real-time systems is on the *short-term* temporal accuracy of the real-time database that is invalidated due to the flow of real-time. In contrast, in on-line transaction processing systems, the maintenance of the *long-term* integrity of large data files is the key issue.

Redundancy Type: After an error has been detected in an on-line system, the computation is rolled back to a previously established checkpoint to initiate a recovery action. In hard real-time systems, roll-back/recovery is of limited utility for the following reasons:

(i)   It is difficult to guarantee the deadline after the occurrence of an error, since the roll-back/recovery action can take an unpredictable amount of time.

(ii)   An irrevocable action (see Section 5.5.1) which has been effected on the environment cannot be undone.

(iii) The temporal accuracy of the checkpoint data is invalidated by the time difference between the checkpoint time and the instant *now*.

The topic of data integrity is discussed at length in Section 5.4 while the issues of error detection and types of redundancy are dealt with in Chapter 6.

1.5.2 Fail-Safe versus Fail-Operational

For some hard real-time systems one or more safe states which can be reached in case of a system failure, can be identified. Consider the example of a railway signaling system. In case a failure is detected, it is possible to stop all the trains and to set all the signals to red to avoid a catastrophe. If such a safe state can be identified and quickly reached upon the occurrence of a failure, then we call the system *fail-safe*. Fail-safeness is a characteristic of the controlled object, not the computer system. In fail-safe applications the computer system must have a *high error-detection coverage*, i.e., the probability that an error is detected, provided it has occurred, must be close to one.

In many real-time computer systems a special external device, a *watchdog*, is provided to monitor the operation of the computer system. The computer system must send a periodic life-sign (e.g., a digital output of predefined form) to the watchdog. If this life-sign fails to arrive at the watchdog within the specified time interval, the watchdog assumes that the computer system has failed and forces the controlled object into a safe state. In such a system, timeliness is needed only to achieve high availability, but is not needed to maintain safety since the watchdog forces the controlled object into a safe state in case of a timing violation.

There are, however, applications where a safe state cannot be identified, e.g., a flight control system aboard an airplane. In such an application the computer system must provide a minimal level of service to avoid a catastrophe even in the case of a failure. This is why these applications are called *fail-operational*.

1.5.3 Guaranteed-Response versus Best-Effort

If we start out with a specified fault- and load-hypothesis and deliver a design that makes it possible to reason about the adequacy of the design without reference to probabilistic arguments, then, even in the case of a peak load and fault scenario, we can speak of a system with a *guaranteed response*. The probability of failure of a perfect system with guaranteed response is reduced to the probability that the assumptions about the peak load and the number and types of faults hold in reality (see Section 4.1.1 on *assumption coverage*). Guaranteed response systems require careful planning and extensive analysis during the design phase.

If such an analytic response guarantee cannot be given, we speak of a *best-effort* design. Best-effort systems do not require a rigorous specification of the load- and fault-hypothesis. The design proceeds according to the principle "best possible effort taken" and the sufficiency of the design is established during the test and integration phases. It is very difficult to establish that a best-effort design operates correctly in rare-event scenarios. At present, many non safety-critical real-time systems are designed according to the best-effort paradigm.

1.5.4   Resource-Adequate versus Resource-Inadequate

Guaranteed response systems are based on the principle of resource adequacy, i.e., there are enough computing resources available to handle the specified peak load and the fault scenario [Law92]. Many non safety-critical real-time system designs are based on the principle of resource inadequacy. It is assumed that the provision of sufficient resources to handle every possible situation is not economically viable, and that a dynamic resource allocation strategy based on resource sharing and probabilistic arguments about the expected load and fault scenarios is acceptable.

It is expected that, in the future, there will be a paradigm shift to resource-adequate designs in many applications. The use of computers in important volume-based applications, e.g., in cars, will raise both the public awareness, as well as concerns about computer-related incidents, and will force the designer to provide convincing arguments that the design will function properly under *all* stated conditions. Hard real-time systems must be designed according to the guaranteed response paradigm that requires the availability of adequate resources.

1.5.5   Event-Triggered versus Time-Triggered

The flow of real time can be modeled by a directed time line that extends from the past into the future. Any occurrence that happens at a cut of this time line is called an *event*. Information that describes an event (see also Section 5.2.4 on event observation) is called *event information*. The present point in time, *now,* is a very special event that separates the past from the future (the presented model of time is based on Newtonian physics and disregards relativistic effects). An *interval* on the time line is defined by two events, the *start event* and the *terminating event.* The *duration* of the interval is the time of the terminating event minus the time of the start event. Any property of an RT entity or an object that remains valid during a finite duration, is called a *state attribute,* the corresponding information *state information.* A change of state is thus an event. An *observation* is an event that records the state of an RT entity at a particular instant, the *point of observation.* A digital clock partitions the time line into a sequence of equally-spaced durations, called the *granules* of the clock which are bounded by special periodic events, the *ticks* of the clock.

A *trigger* is an event that causes the start of some action, e.g., the execution of a task or the transmission of a message. Depending on the triggering mechanisms for the start of communication and processing activities in each node of a computer system, two distinctly different approaches to the design of real-time computer applications can be identified [Kop93b, Tis95]. In the *event-triggered (ET)* approach, all communication and processing activities are initiated whenever a significant change of state, i.e., an event other than the regular event of a clock tick, is noted. In the *time-triggered (TT)* approach, all communication and processing activities are initiated at predetermined points in time.

In an ET system, the signaling of significant events is realized by the well-known interrupt mechanism, which brings the occurrence of a significant event to the attention of the CPU. ET systems require a dynamic scheduling strategy to activate the appropriate software task that services the event.

In a time-triggered (TT) system, all activities are initiated by the progression of time. There is only one interrupt in each node of a distributed TT system, the periodic clock interrupt, which partitions the continuum of time into the sequence of equally spaced granules. In a distributed TT real-time system, it is assumed that the clocks of all nodes are synchronized to form a global notion of time, and that every observation of the controlled object is timestamped with this synchronized time. The granularity of the global time must be chosen such that the time order of any two observations made anywhere in a distributed TT system can be established from their time-stamps [Kop92]. The topics of global time and clock synchronization will be discussed at length in Chapter 3.

1.6   THE REAL-TIME SYSTEMS MARKET

In a market economy, the cost/performance relation is a decisive parameter for the market success of any product. There are only a few scenarios where cost arguments are not the major concern. The total life-cycle cost of a product can be broken down into three rough categories: development cost, production cost, and maintenance cost. Depending on the product type, the distribution of the total life-cycle cost over these three cost categories can vary significantly. We will examine this life-cycle cost distribution by looking at two important examples of real-time systems, embedded systems and plant-automation systems.

1.6.1   Embedded Real-Time Systems

The ever decreasing price/performance ratio of microcontrollers makes it economically attractive to replace the conventional mechanical or electronic control system within many products by an embedded real-time computer system. There are numerous examples of products with embedded computer systems: engine controllers in cars, heart pacemakers, FAX machines, cellular phones, computer printers, television sets, washing machines, even some electric razors contain a microcontroller with some thousand instructions of software code [Ran94]. Because the external interfaces of the product, and in particular, the man-machine interface, often remain unchanged relative to the previous product generation, it is often not visible from the outside that a real-time computer system is controlling the product behavior.

Characteristics: An embedded real-time computer system is always part of a well-specified larger system, which we call an *intelligent product*. An intelligent product consists of a mechanical subsystem, the controlling embedded computer, and, most often, a man-machine interface. The ultimate success of any intelligent product depends on the relevance and quality of service it can provide to its users. A focus on the genuine user needs is thus of utmost importance.

Embedded systems have a number of distinctive characteristics that influence the system development process:

(i)   Mass Production: embedded systems are designed for a mass market and consequently for mass production in highly automated assembly plants. This implies that the production cost of a single unit must be as low as possible, i.e., efficient memory and processor utilization are of concern.

(ii)   Static Structure: the computer system is embedded in an intelligent product of given functionality and rigid structure. The known *a priori* static environment can be analyzed at design time to simplify the software, to increase the robustness, and to improve the efficiency of the embedded computer system. In an embedded system there is little need for flexible dynamic software mechanisms that increase the resource requirements, reduce the error-detection coverage, and lead to unnecessary complexity of the implementation.

(iii)   Man-Machine Interface: if an embedded system has a man-machine interface, it must be specifically designed for the stated purpose and must be easy to operate. Ideally, the use of the intelligent product should be self-explanatory, and not require any training or reference to an operating manual.

(iv)   Minimization of the Mechanical Subsystem: to reduce the manufacturing cost and to increase the reliability of the intelligent product, the complexity of the mechanical subsystem is minimized.

(v)   Functionality Determined by Software in Read-Only Memory: the functionality of an intelligent product is determined by the integrated software that resides in read-only memory. Because there is hardly any possibility to modify the software after its release, the quality standards for this software are high.

(vi)   Maintenance Strategy: many intelligent products are designed to be non maintainable, because the partitioning of the product into replaceable units is too expensive. If, however, a product is designed to be maintained in the field, the provision of an excellent diagnostic interface and a self-evident maintenance strategy is of importance.

(vii)   Ability to communicate: although most intelligent products start out as stand-alone units, many intelligent products are required to interconnect with some larger system at a later stage. The protocol controlling the data transfer should be simple and robust. An optimization of the transmission speed is seldomly an issue.

By far, the largest fraction of the life-cycle cost of an intelligent product is in the production, i.e., in the hardware, whereas the development cost and software cost are only a small part, sometimes less than 5 % of the life-cycle cost. The known *a priori* static configuration of the intelligent product can be used to reduce the resource requirements, and thus the production cost, and also to increase the robustness of the embedded computer system. Maintenance cost can become significant, particularly if an undetected design fault (software fault) requires a recall of the product, and the replacement of a complete production series.

Example: In [Neu96] we find the following laconic one-liner (see also Problem 1.19):

General Motors recalls almost 300 K cars for engine software flaw.

The Four Phases: During the short history of embedded real-time systems, a characteristic pattern has emerged for the deployment of computer technology within a product family [Bou95]. In the first phase, an *ad hoc* stand-alone computer implementation on a microcomputer without an operating system realizes the given function of the conventional control system. The software is developed by engineers who understand the application and have little training in computer technology. To be cost competitive with the conventional control system, this first implementation tries to minimize resource requirements (e.g., memory) at the expense of software structure. In the second phase, the functionality of the product is augmented by adding software functions to improve the utility of the intelligent product. The increasing software complexity leads to reliability problems and forces the system designer to step back and to introduce a software architecture and an operating system in the third phase. This third phase requires a fundamental redesign of the software, which produces additional development cost without any significant increase in visible functions. It is thus a critical phase for the organization that is developing a product. Finally, in the fourth phase, the intelligent product is seen as part of a larger system that needs to communicate with its environment. Communication interfaces are first developed within a company, and then standardized across an industrial sector. This standardization makes it possible to define standard subsystems that can be implemented cost-effectively by application-specific VLSI solutions with large production numbers, for the entire industrial sector.

Different industries have started this transition process from conventional technology to computer technology, at different times. Therefore, at present, some industries are already further along in this transition than others.

Future Trends: During the last few years, the variety and number of embedded computer applications have grown to the point that, now, this segment is by far the most important one in the real-time systems market. The embedded systems market is driven by the continuing improvements in the cost/performance ratio of the semiconductor industry that makes computer-based control systems cost-competitive relative to their mechanical, hydraulic, and electronic counterparts. Among the key mass markets are the fields of consumer electronics and automotive electronics. The automotive electronics market is of particular interest, because of stringent timing, dependability, and cost requirements that act as "technology catalysts".

After a conservative approach to computer control during the last ten years, a number of automotive manufacturers now view the proper exploitation of computer technology as a key competitive element in the never-ending quest for increased vehicle performance and reduced manufacturing cost. While some years ago, the computer applications on board a car focused on non-critical body electronics or comfort functions, there is now a substantial growth in the computer control of core vehicle functions, e.g., engine control, brake control, transmission control, and suspension control. In the not-too-distant future we will observe an integration of many of these functions with the goal of increasing the vehicle stability in critical driving maneuvers. Obviously, an error in any of these core vehicle functions has severe safety implications.

At present the topic of computer safety in cars is approached at two levels. At the basic level a mechanical system provides the proven safety level that is considered sufficient to operate the car. The computer system provides optimized performance on top of the basic mechanical system. In case the computer system fails cleanly, the mechanical system takes over. Consider, for example, an Antilock Braking System (ABS). If the computer fails, the conventional mechanical brake system is still operational. Soon, this approach to safety may reach its limits for two reasons:

(i)   If the computer controlled system is further improved, the magnitude of the difference between the performance of the computer controlled system and the performance of the basic mechanical system is further increased. A driver who is used to the high performance of the computer controlled system might consider the fallback to the inferior performance of the mechanical system a safety risk.

(ii)   The improved price/performance of the microelectronic devices will make the implementation of fault-tolerant computer systems cheaper than the implementation of mixed computer/mechanical systems. Thus, there will be an economical pressure to eliminate the redundant mechanical system and to replace it with a computer system using active redundancy.

The automotive industry operates in a highly competitive worldwide market under an extreme economical pressure. Although the design of a new automotive model is a major effort requiring the cooperation of thousands of engineers over a period of three to four years, it is important to realize that more than 95% of the cost of delivering a car lies in manufacturing and marketing, and only 5 % of the cost is related to development. The cost-effective and highly dependable computer solutions that are being developed for the automotive market will thus be adopted in many other real-time system applications. It is expected that the automotive market will be the driving force for the real-time systems market.

The embedded system market is expected to grow significantly during the next ten years. Compared to other information technology markets, this market will offer–according to a recent study [Ran94]–the best employment opportunities for the computer engineers of the future.

1.6.2 Plant Automation Systems

Characteristics: Historically, industrial plant automation was the first field for the application of real-time digital computer control. This is understandable since the benefits that can be gained by the computerization of a sizable plant are much larger than the cost of even an expensive process control computer of the late 1960's. In the early days, industrial plants were controlled by human operators who were placed in close vicinity to the process. With the refinement of industrial plant instrumentation and the availability of remote automatic controllers, plant monitoring and command facilities were concentrated into a central control room, thus reducing the number of operators required to run the plant. In the late 1960's, the next logical step was the introduction of central process control computers to monitor the plant and assist the operator in her/his routine functions, e.g., data logging and operator guidance. In the early days, the computer was considered an "add-on" facility that was not fully trusted. It was the duty of the operator to judge whether a set point calculated by a computer made sense and could be applied to the process (*open-loop control*). With the improvement of the process models and the growth of the reliability of the computer, control functions have been increasingly allocated to the computer and gradually, the operator has been taken out of the control loop (*closed-loop control*). Sophisticated control techniques, which have response time requirements beyond human capabilities, have been implemented.

A plant automation system is normally unique. There is an extensive amount of engineering and software effort required to adapt the computer system to the physical layout, the operating strategy, the rules and regulations, and the reporting system of a particular plant. To reduce these engineering and software efforts, many process control companies have developed a set of modular building blocks, which can be configured individually to meet the requirements of a customer. Compared to the development cost, the production cost (hardware cost) is of minor importance. Maintenance cost can be an issue if a maintenance technician must be on-site for 24 hours in order to minimize the downtime of a plant.

Future Trends: The market of industrial plant automation systems is limited by the number of plants that are newly constructed or are refurbished to install a computer control system. During the last twenty years, many plants have already been automated. This investment must pay off before a new generation of computer and control equipment is installed.

Furthermore, the installation of a new generation of control equipment in a production plant causes disruption in the operation of the plant with a costly loss of production that must be justified economically. This is difficult if the plant's efficiency is already high, and the margin for further improvement by refined computer control is limited.

The size of the plant automation market is too small to support the mass production of special application-specific components. It is thus expected that the special VLSI components that are developed for other application domains, such as automotive electronics, will be taken up by this market to reduce the system cost. Examples of such components are sensors, actuators, real-time local area networks and processing nodes. Already several process-control companies have announced a new generation of process-control equipment that takes advantage the of low-priced mass produced components that have been developed for the automotive market, such as the chips developed for the Control Area Network (CAN–see Section 7.5.3).

1.6.3 Multimedia Systems

Characteristics: The multimedia market is an emerging mass market for specially designed soft real-time systems. Although the deadlines for many multimedia tasks, such as the synchronization of audio and video streams, are firm, they are not hard deadlines. An occasional failure to meet a deadline results in a degradation of the quality of service, but will not cause a catastrophe. The processing power required to transport and render a continuous video stream is very large and difficult to bound, because it is often possible to improve a good picture even further. The resource allocation strategy in multimedia applications is thus quite different from that of hard real-time applications; it is not determined by the given application requirements, but by the amount of available resources. A fraction of the given computational resources (processing power, memory, bandwidth) is allocated to a user domain. Quality of service considerations at the end user determine the detailed resource allocation strategy. For example, if a user reduces the size of a window and enlarges the size of another window on his multimedia terminal, then the system can reduce the bandwidth and the processing allocated to the first window to free the resources for the other window that has been enlarged. Other users of the system should not be affected by this local reallocation of resources.

Future Trends: The marriage of the Internet with multimedia personal computers is expected to lead to many new volume applications. At present many companies invest heavily into the multimedia market that is expected to become an important market of the future. The focus of this book is not on multimedia systems, because these systems belong to the class of soft real-time applications.

1.7   EXAMPLES OF REAL-TIME SYSTEMS

In this section, three typical examples of real-time systems are introduced and these will be used throughout the text to explain the evolving concepts. We start with an example of a very simple system for flow control to demonstrate the need for end-to-end protocols in process input/output.

1.7.1   Controlling the Flow in a Pipe

It is the objective of the simple control system depicted in Figure 1.8 to control the flow of a liquid in a pipe. A given flow set point determined by a client should be maintained despite changing environmental conditions. Examples for such changing conditions are the varying level of the liquid in the vessel or the temperature sensitive viscosity of the liquid. The computer interacts with the controlled object by setting the position of the control valve. It then observes the reaction of the controlled object by reading the flow sensor F to determine whether the desired effect, the intended change of flow, has been achieved. This is a typical example of the necessary *end-to-end protocol* [Sal84] that must be put in place between the computer and the controlled object (see also Section 7.1.4). In a well-engineered system, the effect of any control action of the computer must be monitored by one or more independent sensors. For this purpose, many actuators contain a number of sensors in the same physical housing. For example, the control valve in Figure 1.8 might contain a sensor, which measures the mechanical position of the valve in the pipe, and two limit switches, which indicate the firmly closed and the completely open positions of the valve. A rule of thumb is that there are about three to seven sensors for every actuator.

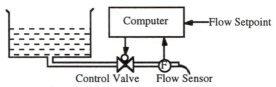

Figure 1.8: Flow of liquid in a pipe.

The dynamics of the system in Figure 1.8 is essentially determined by the speed of the control valve. Assume that the control valve takes *10* seconds to open or close from *0%* to *100%*, and that the flow sensor *F* has a precision of *1%*. If a sampling interval of *100* msec is chosen, the maximum change of the valve position within one sampling interval is *1%*, the same as the precision of the flow sensor. Because of this finite speed of the control valve, an output action taken by the computer at a given time will lead to an effect in the environment at some later time. The observation of this effect by the computer will be further delayed by the given latency of the sensor. All these latencies must either be derived analytically or measured experimentally, before the temporal control structure for a stable control system can be designed.

1.7.2   Engine   Control

The task of an engine controller in an automobile engine is the calculation of the proper amount of fuel, and the exact moment at which the fuel must be injected into the combustion chamber of each cylinder. The amount of fuel and the timing depend on a multitude of parameters: the intentions of the driver, articulated by the position of the accelerator pedal, the current load on the engine, the temperature of the engine, the condition of the cylinder, and many more. A modern engine controller is a complex piece of equipment. Up to 100 concurrently executing software tasks must cooperate in tight synchronization to achieve the desired goal, a smoothly running and efficient engine with a minimal output of pollutants.

The up- and downward moving piston in each cylinder of a combustion engine is connected to a rotating axle, the *crankshaft*. The intended start point of fuel injection is relative to the position of the piston in the cylinder, and must be precise within an accuracy of about *0.1* degree of the measured angular position of the crankshaft. The precise angular position of the crankshaft is measured by a number of digital sensors that generate a rising edge of a signal at the instant when the crankshaft passes these defined positions. Consider an engine that turns with *6000* rpm (revolutions per minute), i.e., the crankshaft takes *10* msec for a *360* degree rotation. If the required precision of *0.1* degree is transformed into the time domain, then a temporal accuracy of *3* μsec is required. The fuel injection is realized by opening a solenoid valve that controls the fuel flow from a high-pressure reservoir into the cylinder. The latency between giving an "open" command to the valve and the actual point in time when the valve opens is in the order of hundreds of μsec, and changes considerably depending on environmental conditions (e.g., temperature). To be able to compensate for this latency jitter, a sensor signal indicates the point in time when the valve has actually opened. The duration between the execution of the output command by the computer and the start of opening of the valve is measured during every engine cycle. The measured latency is used to determine when the output command must be executed during the next cycle so that the intended effect, the start of fuel injection, happens at the proper point in time.

This example of an engine controller has been chosen because it demonstrates convincingly the need for extremely precise temporal control. For example, if the processing of the signal that measures the exact position of the crankshaft in the engine is delayed by a few μsec, the quality of control of the whole system is compromised. It can even happen that the engine is mechanically damaged if the valve is opened at an incorrect moment.

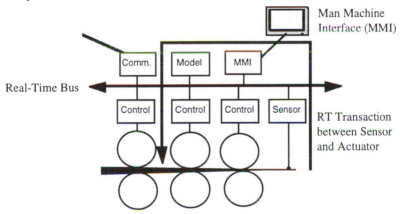

Figure 1.9: An RT transaction.

1.7.3   Rolling Mill

A typical example of a distributed plant automation system is the computer control of a rolling mill. In this application a slab of steel (or some other material, such as paper) is rolled to a strip and coiled. The rolling mill of Figure 1.9 has three drives and some instrumentation to measure the quality of the rolled product. The distributed computer-control system of this rolling mill consists of seven nodes connected by a real-time communication system. The most important sequence of actions–we call this a *real-time (RT) transaction*–in this application starts with the reading of the sensor values by the sensor computer. Then, the RT transaction passes through the model computer that calculates new set points for the three drives, and finally reaches the control computers to achieve the desired action by readjusting the rolls of the mill.

The duration of the real-time transaction between the sensor node and the drive nodes (bold line in Figure 1.9) must be considered by the control algorithms because it is an important parameter for the quality of control. The shorter the delay of this transaction, the better the control quality, since this transaction contributes to the *dead time* of the critical control loop. The other important term of the dead time is the time it takes for the strip to travel from the drive to the sensor. A jitter in the deadtime that is not compensated for will reduce the quality of control significantly. It is evident from Figure 1.9 that the latency jitter is the sum of the jitter of all processing and communication actions that form the critical real-time transaction.

Note that the communication pattern among the nodes of this control system is *multicast*, not *point-to-point*. This is typical for most distributed real-time control systems. Furthermore, the communication between the model node and the drive nodes has an *atomicity requirement*. Either all of the drives are changed according to the output of the model, or none of them is changed. The loss of a message, which may result in the failure of a drive to readjust to a new position, may cause mechanical damage to the drive.

POINTS TO REMEMBER

- A real-time computer system must react to stimuli from the controlled object (or the operator) within time intervals *dictated* by its environment. If a catastrophe could result in case a firm deadline is missed, the deadline is called *hard*.

- In a hard real-time computer system, it must be guaranteed by design that the computer system will meet the specified deadlines in all situations because the utility of many hard real-time applications can depend on predictable performance during a peak load scenario.

- A hard real-time system must maintain synchrony with the state of the environment (the controlled object and the human operator) in all operational scenarios. It is thus paced by the state changes occurring in the environment.

- Because the state of the controlled object changes as a function of real-time, an observation is *temporally accurate* only for a limited time interval.

- Real-time systems have only small data files, the *real-time database* that is formed by the temporally accurate images of the RT-entities. The key concern is on the *short-term* temporal accuracy of the real-time database that is invalidated by the flow of real-time.

- A *trigger* is an event that causes the start of some action, e.g., the execution of a task or the transmission of a message.

- The real-time database must be updated whenever an RT entity changes its value. This update can be performed periodically, triggered by the progression of the real-time clock by a fixed period (*time-triggered observation*), or immediately after a change of state, an event, occurs in the RT entity (*event-triggered observation*).

- The most stringent temporal demands for real-time systems have their origin in the requirements of the control loops.

- The temporal behavior of a simple controlled object can be characterized by *process lag* and *rise time* of the *step-response function*.

- The *dead time* of a control loop is the time interval between the observation of the RT entity and the start of a reaction of the controlled object as a consequence of a computer action based on this observation.

- Many control algorithms are based on the assumption that the delay jitter is a very small fraction of the *delay* since control algorithms are designed to compensate a known constant delay. Delay jitter brings an additional uncertainty into the control loop that has an adverse effect on the quality of control.

- The term *signal conditioning* is used to refer to all processing steps that are needed to get a meaningful RT image of an RT entity from the raw sensor data.

- The *Reliability R(t)* of a system is the probability that a system will provide the specified service until time t, given that the system was operational at $t = t_o$.

- If the failure rate of a system is required to be about 10^{-9} failures/h or lower, then we are dealing with a system with an *ultrahigh reliability* requirement.

- Safety is reliability regarding *critical failure modes*. In a malign failure mode, the cost of a failure can be orders of magnitude higher than the utility of the system during normal operation.

- *Maintainability* is a measure of the time it takes to repair a system after the last experienced benign failure, and is measured by the probability $M(d)$ that the system is restored within a time interval d seconds after the failure.

- *Availability* is a measure of the correct service delivery regarding the alternation of correct and incorrect service, and is measured by the probability $A(t)$ that the system is ready to provide the service at time t.

- The probability of failure of a perfect system with guaranteed response is reduced to the probability that the assumptions concerning the peak load and the number and types of faults are valid in reality.

- If we start out from a specified fault- and load-hypothesis and deliver a design that makes it possible to reason about the adequacy of the design without reference to probabilistic arguments, then, even in the case of the extreme load and fault scenarios, we can speak of a system with a *guaranteed response.*

- An embedded real-time computer system is part of a well-specified larger system, an *intelligent product*. An intelligent product normally consists of a mechanical subsystem, the controlling embedded computer, and a man-machine interface.

- The static configuration, known *a priori*, of the intelligent product can be used to reduce the resource requirements and increase the robustness of the embedded computer system.

- An industrial plant automation system is normally unique. Compared to development cost, the production cost (hardware cost) of a plant automation system is less important.

- The embedded system market is expected to grow significantly during the next ten years. Compared with other information technology markets, this market will offer the best employment opportunities for the computer engineers of the future.

BIBLIOGRAPHIC NOTES

In the well-publicized paper "Misconceptions about Real-Time Computing" [Sta88, p.14] Stankovic discusses the key requirements and common misconceptions about real-time computing, and highlights many open research issues. A number of tutorials on real-time systems have been published in the last few years: Stankovic and Ramamritham edited two tutorials; "Hard Real-Time Systems" [Sta88] and "Advances in Real-Time Systems" [Sta92] that contain carefully selected research papers on the topic of real-time systems. Other recent collections of research papers are contained in the book "Real-Time Systems, Abstractions, Languages and Design Methodologies" edited by Kavi [Kav92] and the book "Advances in Real-Time Systems", edited by Son [Son94]. The tutorial "Advances in Ultradependable Distributed Systems" [Sur95], edited by Suri, Walter and Hugue, focuses on research papers relevant to ultra-dependable systems. The textbook by Burns [Bur89] on "Real-Time Systems and their Programming Languages" gives a good introduction to real-time systems programming. The Handbook of the Society of Automotive Engineers [SAE95] contains an excellent description of the requirements of onboard safety-critical computer systems in vehicles. It provides a benchmark example of a typical distributed real-time control system in a car. A solution to this benchmark example has been published in [Kop94].

REVIEW QUESTIONS AND PROBLEMS

1.1   What makes a computer system a *real-time* computer system?

1.2   What are typical functions that a real-time computer system must perform?

1.4   Where do the *temporal requirements* come from? What are the parameters that describe the temporal characteristics of a controlled object?

1.5   Give a "rule of thumb" that relates the *sampling period* in a quasi-continuous system to the *rise time* of the step-response function of the controlled object.

1.6   What are the effects of delay and delay jitter on the quality of control? Compare the error-detection latency in systems with and without jitter.

1.3   What does *signal conditioning* mean?

1.7   Consider an RT entity that changes its value periodically according to $v(t) = A_o \sin(2\pi t/T)$ where T, the period of the oscillation, is *100* msec. What is the maximum change of value of this RT entity within a time interval of *1* msec? (express the result in percentage of the amplitude A_o).

1.8   Consider an engine that rotates with *3000* rpm. By how many degrees will the crankshaft turn within *1* msec?

1.9   Give some examples where the predictable rare-event performance determines the utility of a hard real-time system.

1.10   What is a *critical failure mode*? Give examples.

1.11   Consider a fail-safe application. Is it necessary that the computer system provides guaranteed timeliness to maintain the safety of the application? What is the level of error-detection coverage required in an ultrahigh dependability application?

1.12   What is the difference between availability and reliability? What is the relationship between maintainability and reliability?

1.13   When is there a simple relation between the MTTF and the failure rate?

1.14   Assume you are asked to certify a safety-critical control system. How would you proceed?

1.15   What are the main differences between a soft real-time system and a hard real-time system?

1.16   Why is an *end-to-end protocol* required at the interface between the computer system and the controlled object?

1.17   What is the fraction *development cost/production cost* in embedded systems and in plant automation systems? How does this relation influence the system design?

1.18   Assume that an automotive company produces *2 000 000* electronic engine controllers of a special type. The following design alternatives are discussed:

(i) Construct the engine control unit as a single SRU with the application software in Read Only Memory (ROM).The production cost of such a unit is *250* $. In case of an error, the complete unit has to be replaced.

(ii) Construct the engine control unit such that the software is contained in a ROM that is placed on a socket and can be replaced in case of a software error. The production cost of the unit without the ROM is *248* $. The cost of the ROM is *5*$.

(iii) Construct the engine control unit as a single SRU where the software is loaded in a Flash EPROM that can be reloaded. The production cost of such a unit is *255* $.

The labor cost of repair is assumed to be *50* $ for each vehicle. (It is assumed to be the same for each one of the three alternatives). Calculate the cost of a software error for each one of the three alternative designs if *300 000* cars have to be recalled because of the software error (example in Section 1.6.1).

Which one is the lowest cost alternative if only *1 000* cars are affected by a recall?

1.19   Estimate the relation (development cost)/(production cost) in an embedded application and in a plant automation system.

Chapter 2

Why a Distributed Solution?

OVERVIEW

From the functional point of view, it makes little difference whether a given specification is implemented using a centralized architecture or a distributed architecture. In this chapter, a number of arguments are presented in favor of a distributed approach for the implementation of a hard real-time system. The chapter starts with an overview of a distributed real-time system architecture, which consists of a set of nodes and a communication network that interconnects these nodes. The interface between the communication network and the host computer within a node is discussed at length, and the concept of event message and state message is introduced. The semantics of state messages facilitates the exchange of state information among the nodes, and enforces a high degree of autonomy of the nodes and the communication system.

The next sections argue for a distributed architecture as the preferred alternative for the implementation of a hard real-time system. The first and most important argument is that of composability. In a composable architecture, system properties follow from subsystem properties. In such an architecture, a constructive approach to system building and to system validation is supported. In the context of real-time systems, composability requires that the communication network interface between the host computer in a node and the communication network is fully specified, not only in the value domain, but also in the time domain. Scalability requires that there exist no limits on the extensibility of a system, and that the complexity of reasoning about the proper operation of any system function be independent of the system size. It is shown that the economics of VLSI production favor the distributed approach for building a scalable large real-time system. Dependability arguments advocate a distributed approach because such an approach makes it possible to implement well-defined error-containment regions, and to achieve fault tolerance by replicating nodes.

2.1   SYSTEM ARCHITECTURE

2.1.1   Form Follows Function

It is an established architectural principle that the function of an object should determine its physical form [Vit60,p.13]. Distributed computer architectures enable the application of this proven architectural principle to the design of computing systems. In a distributed system, it is feasible to encapsulate a logical function and the associated computer hardware into a single unit, a node. The advances in the field of microelectronics have made it possible to implement nodes of considerable computational power cost effectively on a single silicon die. Well-designed distributed systems utilize many instances of the same hardware node type, and can thus take advantage of the tremendous economy of scale in VLSI mass production.

Viewed from a higher level, a node can be replaced by an understandable abstraction that captures the essential functional and temporal properties of the node and hides the irrelevant details of the implementation behind a simple and stable external node interface. The layout and the placement of these external node interfaces are significant design activities that determine the structure and the properties of the system as a whole.

It is a major advantage of such an approach that the extracted abstractions hold also in the case of failures. Abstractions that cannot be maintained in case of a fault in one of the subsystems are of limited utility when designing large systems. If there is a one-to-one mapping between functions and nodes, then, the cause for a malfunction can be readily diagnosed, and the node that has failed can be pinpointed. Vice versa, it is possible to foresee what functions will be affected in case of an error in a node. In a centralized computer system, where such a one-to-one mapping between system resources (hardware, operating system, etc.) and application functions is not possible, the problems of fault diagnosis and the analysis of the effects of a subsystem failure can become formidable.

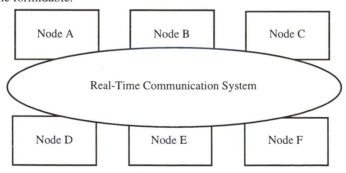

Figure 2.1: Distributed computer system.

2.1.2   Hardware Structure

Figure 1.1 shows that a distributed application can be decomposed into a set of clusters, the operator cluster, the computational cluster, and the controlled object cluster. If the computational cluster is implemented as a distributed computer system, it has the general structure of Figure 2.1. A set of nodes is interconnected by a real-time communication system.

A node can be partitioned into at least two subsystems, the local communication controller, and the host computer (Figure 2.2). The set of all the communication controllers of the nodes within a cluster, along with the physical interconnection medium, forms the real-time communication system of the cluster. The interface between the communication controller within a node and the host computer of the node is called the *communication-network interface* (CNI). The CNI is located at the transport level of the OSI reference model [Tan88], and is considered to be the most important interface of a distributed real-time architecture.

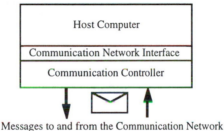

Messages to and from the Communication Network

Figure 2.2: Structure of a node.

2.1.3   The Communication-Network Interface

The purpose of the real-time communication system is to transport messages from the CNI of the sender node to the CNI of the receiver node within a predictable time interval, with a small latency jitter, and with high reliability. The communication system must ensure that the contents of the messages are not corrupted. Faults specified in the fault hypothesis must be handled correctly. From the point of view of the host computer, the details of the protocol logic and the physical structure of the communication network are hidden behind the CNI.

Data Semantics: Depending on whether the information contained in a message relates to the occurrence of an event or to the value of a state, two types of message processing are distinguished at the CNI of the receiver.

Since *every event is significant*, the loss of a single event can lead to a loss of synchronization in state between the sender and the receiver. Messages containing *event information* must be queued at the receiver and be removed on reading to ensure that every event is processed *exactly once*. The order in the queue should be the temporal order of event occurrence, and not the often unpredictable order in which the messages are delivered by the communication system, such as the FIFO order of message arrival.

If the message contains *state information*, e.g., the current temperature, it is reasonable to overwrite the old version of a state value by a new version because the receiver is normally interested in the latest version of the state. State values are not disposed of on reading because many readers may be interested in the same state value, e.g., the current value of the particular temperature sensor. In real-time systems, state semantics is needed much more frequently than event semantics.

Control Strategy: The decision when a message must be sent can reside either within the sphere of control of the host computer (*external control*) or within the sphere of control of the communication system (*autonomous control*). The most common temporal control strategy used in computer networks is external control. The execution of a "send" command in the host computer causes the transfer of a control signal across the CNI and initiates the transmission of a message by the communication system. When a message arrives at the receiver, a control signal (interrupt) from the communication system crosses the CNI and unblocks a "receive" command in the receiving host computer.

In the case of autonomous control, the communication system decides autonomously when to send the next message, and when to deliver the message at the CNI of the receiver. The receiving host is not interrupted when a new message arrives because this would compromise the autonomy of the receiver. Autonomous control is normally time-triggered. The communication system contains a transmission schedule, a table of points in time that determine which message must be transmitted next. If the control of the communication system is autonomous, no control signals must cross the CNI. In this case the CNI is used strictly for sharing data.

The Design Space: The sixteen different combinations of data semantics and control strategies, at the CNI of the sender and at the CNI of the receiver, are listed in Table 2.1. Some of these combinations make no sense, and this is indicated by a "no" in the appropriate field. Of these sixteen combinations, the beginning and the end of the table are of special significance. They represent *event messages* and *state messages*.

Sender Receiver	Event Inf. Ext.Control	Event Inf. Aut.Control	State Inf. Ext.Control	State Inf. Aut.Control
Event Information/ External Control	Event Message	maybe	yes	yes
Event Information/ Autonomous Control	no	maybe	yes	yes
State Information/ External Control	yes	maybe	yes	yes
State Information/ Autonomous Control	no	maybe	yes	State Message

Table 2.1: Possible combinations of data semantics and control strategy.

Event Message: An event message combines event semantics with external control. Every arriving event message is queued at the receiver and disposed of on processing. Event messages require one-to-one synchronization between the sender and the receiver; otherwise the queue will overflow, or the receiver will be blocked. Event-message semantics corresponds to the classic message semantics that is used in most non real-time communication systems, such as transaction-processing systems.

State Message: A state message combines state-value semantics with autonomous control. State-message semantics is closely related to the semantics of a global variable with two notable differences; with state message semantics

(i)   The communication system guarantees the atomicity of a message write operation, and

(ii)   There is only a single sender (writer) process.

There is no need for one-to-one synchronization between the sender process and the receiver processes, because the receivers can read a state value many times or not at all, thereby leading to a looser coupling between the nodes. In a distributed system based on state messages, the CNI can be implemented as a dual-ported RAM with no control signals crossing the interface. State-message semantics corresponds naturally to the requirements of control applications and is thus well-suited for the implementation of distributed control systems. Recently, operating systems [Pol96a, Rei95] have been developed to support state-message semantics at the level of the basic interprocess communication primitives.

2.1.4   The Communication System

There are a number of different alternatives available for the design and implementation of the communication service: a single channel system, such as a bus or ring, or a multiple channel system, such as a mesh network. Communication reliability can be increased by message retransmission in case of a failure, or by always replicating messages so that a loss of a message is immediately masked. The permanent loss of a complete channel can be tolerated if the communication channels are replicated.

The communication system is a critical resource of a distributed system, since the loss of communication results in the loss of all global system services. Therefore, the reliability of the communication system should be an order of magnitude higher than the reliability of the individual nodes. The topic of real-time communication systems is treated in detail in Chapter 7.

2.1.5   Gateways

The purpose of a gateway is to exchange relative views between two interacting clusters. A gateway node must have either an instrumentation interface and a communication interface (interface node), or two communication interfaces (two CNIs), each interfacing to one of the interacting clusters. An interface node is thus a special type of gateway node. The gateway host must pass the relevant information from the CNI of the sending cluster to the CNI of the receiving cluster. In most cases, only a small subset of the information of one cluster is relevant to the other cluster. In general, it cannot be assumed that the structure of the messages and the representation of the information is identical in both clusters. Thus, the gateway host must transform the data formats of one cluster to those expected by the other cluster.

In a time-triggered (TT) architecture, a gateway has data-sharing interfaces. There are no control signals passing through a gateway component, i.e., in a TT architecture a gateway does not reduce the autonomy of control of the interconnected clusters.

Many large real-time systems are not designed from scratch according to a single master plan, but evolve gradually over many years, using different generations of hardware and software technology. Gateways are important for designing interfaces to such *legacy* systems with reasonable effort. One CNI can be designed to conform to the data representation and protocol conventions of the legacy architecture, while the other CNI can be designed according to the rules of the newly-implemented extension to this legacy system. The gateway thus encapsulates and hides the internal features of the legacy system and provides a clean and flexible interface.

2.2 COMPOSABILITY

In many engineering disciplines, large systems are built by integrating a set of well-specified and tested subsystems. It is important that properties that have been established at the subsystem level are maintained during system integration. Such a constructive approach to system design is only possible if the architecture supports *composability*.

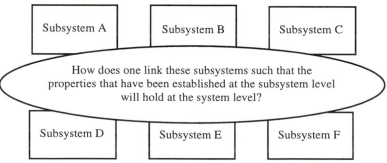

Figure 2.3: The composability problem.

2.2.1 Definition

An architecture is said to be *composable* with respect to a specified property if the system integration will not invalidate this property once the property has been established at the subsystem level. Examples of such properties are timeliness or testability. In a composable architecture, the system properties follow from the subsystem properties.

Example: In a car, different engines may be combined with different transmissions and different braking and suspension systems. The composability of an architecture guarantees that all these combinations of subsystems will work correctly without a need for redesign or retesting of any of the already validated subsystems.

In a distributed real-time system, the integration effect is achieved by interactions among the different nodes. Therefore, the communication system has a central role in determining the composability of a distributed architecture with respect to the temporal properties.

2.2.2 Event-Triggered Communication Systems

If a communication system transports event messages (we call such a communication system *event-triggered–ET*), the temporal control is external to the communication system. It is within the sphere of control of the host computers (see Figure 2.2) to decide when a message must be sent. Consider the case where a number of nodes decide to send a message to a particular receiving node at the same instant. If the communication system has dedicated channels between any two nodes, all messages will arrive simultaneously at the receiver, and overload the receiver. On the other hand, if the communication system uses a single shared channel that serializes the traffic, then a conflict for gaining access to this channel is unavoidable. Different shared-channel ET protocols resolve such an access conflict by different techniques which include random access techniques (Ethernet), introducing a predefined order of access (a token protocol), and message priority (Control Area Network, CAN–see Section 7.5.3). This does not solve the fundamental problem, namely that the temporal control at the CNI is not defined by an ET protocol. Temporal control in an ET system is thus a global issue, depending on the behavior of the application software in all nodes of the distributed system. From the point of view of temporal behavior, ET systems are not composable. The basic capability to talk to each other does not ensure a disciplined conversation.

In a number of proposals, the (sometimes fuzzy) notion of *real-time network management* is suggested to solve this fundamental problem of node coordination in the time domain. The following quote, taken from the minutes of a meeting of the SAE (Society of Automotive Engineers) Multiplexing Committee (March 2, 1995) concerning the SAE J1850 single channel communication protocol for automotive applications, paints a vivid picture of this issue (bolds added):

*SAE J1850 is a complete document. However, its content is not sufficient to guarantee that devices designed and built to its requirements will communicate, as intended, to perform some operational function. The reason for this is that SAE J1850 does not provide a network management framework to manage total network traffic. SAE J1850, and its companion J2178, establish how a device A, can report a parameter X, to another device B, during normal vehicle operation. However, neither of these documents provides a framework for agreement on **why** and **when** A shall report X. Agreement on this is necessary so that devices which communicate to* *cooperatively accomplish some function know what to expect from the other devices. Without this agreement, the* **interoperability** *of designs cannot be ensured.*

2.2.3   Time-Triggered   Communication   Systems

In a *time-triggered (TT)* communication system, temporal control resides within the communication system, and is not dependent on the application software in the nodes. State messages are transported from the sender CNI to the receiver CNI at predetermined points in time which are stored in message scheduling tables within the communication controllers. The host computers have no opportunity to influence the temporal behavior of the communication system. The CNI is strictly a data-sharing interface without any control signals crossing the interface. It thus acts as a temporal firewall, isolating the temporal behavior of the host computer from the temporal behavior of the communication system. There is no possibility for control-error propagation from the host to the communication system, and *vice versa.*

The temporal properties of the CNI between a node and the communication system are fully defined at design time. It is thus possible to test each node individually with respect to the CNI. Since system integration will not change the temporal properties of the CNI, a TT architecture is composable with respect to communication timeliness.

2.3   SCALABILITY

Almost all large systems evolve over an extended period of time, i.e., over many years or even decades of years. A successful computer system changes its environment and this changed environment brings about new requirements on the computer system itself. Only unsuccessful systems, which are obviously never used, will not undergo changes. Evolving requirements are thus not an exception, but the rule. Existing functions have to be modified, and many new functions have to be added over the lifetime of the system. A scalable architecture is open to such changes, and does not limit the extensibility of a system by some predefined upper limit.

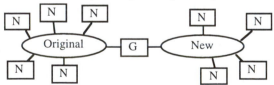

Figure 2.4: Transparent expansion of a node into a new cluster.

2.3.1   Extensibility

A scalable architecture must not have any central bottleneck, neither in processing capacity nor in communication capacity. Only distributed architectures provide the necessary framework for unlimited growth since:

(i)   Nodes can be added within the given capacity of the communication channel. This introduces additional processing power to the system.

(ii) If the communication capacity within a cluster is fully utilized, or if the processing power of a node has reached its limit, a node can be transformed into a gateway node to open a way to a new cluster. The interface between the original cluster and the gateway node can remain unchanged (Figure 2.4).

This transformation of a node into a gateway supporting a new cluster requires the proper design of the *name space*. This issue is discussed in Section 8.4.1.

2.3.2   Complexity

Large systems can only be built if the effort required to understand the system operation, i.e., the complexity of the system, remains under control as the system grows. The *complexity* of a system relates to the number of parts, and the number and types of interactions among the parts, that must be considered to understand a particular function of the system. The effort required to understand *any particular function* should remain constant, and *independent* of the system size. Of course, a large system provides *many more different* functions than does a small system. Therefore the effort needed to understand *all functions* of a large system grows with the system size.

As indicated before, the complexity of a large system can be reduced if the inner behavior of the subsystems can be encapsulated behind stable and simple interfaces. Only those aspects of the behavior of a subsystem that are relevant to the function under consideration must be examined to understand the particular function.

The partitioning of a system into subsystems, the encapsulation of the subsystem, the preservation of the abstractions in case of faults, and most importantly, a strict control over the interaction patterns among the subsystems, are thus the key mechanisms for controlling the complexity of a large system.

In a time-triggered architecture, the structure depicted in Figure 2.4 encapsulates the inner operation of one cluster from that of other clusters via the data-sharing gateway interfaces. When reasoning about a particular function in a given cluster, the only knowledge that is needed about the behavior of the other clusters is contained in the temporal and value attributes of the data at the gateway interface. Because every TT cluster exercises autonomous control, there are no control signals passing through these gateway interfaces. In essence, the momentary values of the state variables at the gateway CNIs to the other clusters form a sufficient abstraction of the environment for the function under investigation. Such an architecture is scalable, because the complexity of reasoning about the correctness of any system function is determined by the cluster under investigation, and does not depend on the number of clusters in the total system, i.e., on the system size.

2.3.3 Silicon Cost

The expected further advances of microelectronics technology will make the design of large distributed systems even more competitive when compared with the implementation of the same functionality using a centralized system.

The implementation of a given specification with a distributed architecture requires more hardware (i.e., silicon area) than that with a centralized architecture. The additional hardware is needed for the realization of the communication system among the nodes, the replicated implementation of certain system functions (e.g., the operating system in each node), and the additional packaging cost. This extra hardware causes a higher initial investment for a distributed solution than for a centralized one.

Example: Assume that the implementation of the communication system requires about *100,000* transistors. If the transistor count in a single-chip node is just *400,000*, this amounts to *25%* of the silicon area of a node. However if a node contains *10,000,000* transistors—a size that is within the reach of today's technology—then, the implementation of the same communication system requires only *1%* of the silicon area of the node (Figure 2.5).

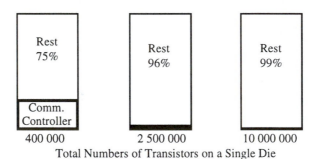
Total Numbers of Transistors on a Single Die

Figure 2.5: Fraction of the silicon real-estate of the communication controller in a node.

Example: The next generation of microcomputers for engine control, which will be mass produced by the year 2000, will consist of a 32-bit CPU, about *512* kB of memory, dedicated I/O processors, and a communication controller on a single chip. On such a chip the communication controller will only require a few percent of the available silicon area. To be competitive, the production cost of such a chip must be about US $ *10*.

According to Patterson [Pat90, p.60], the approximate cost for manufacturing a chip is proportional to the third power of the die area:

$$Cost = K \cdot (Die\ area)^3$$

The proportionality factor K depends on the process technology and the production parameters.

Although a centralized system with a powerful single CPU starts with a lower initial cost, the growth curve of the cost, as a function of system size, rises with a larger gradient for a centralized system than for a distributed system (Figure 2.6).

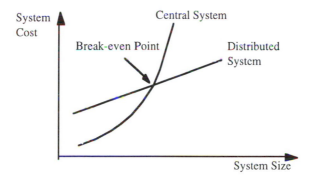

Figure 2.6: Cost growth of centralized versus distributed architectures.

As the size of a system increases, there exists a break-even point beyond which the hardware for a distributed system is cheaper than that for the corresponding centralized solution (Figure 2.6). At the present time, the VLSI field is developing at such a rapid pace that the break-even point itself is moving to the right as a consequence of a continuing reduction in the VLSI feature size.

Since the transition from a centralized implementation to a distributed implementation requires substantial redesign of the system, it is important to determine which of the cost curves of Figure 2.6 applies to an implementation. Using a centralized system might provide a short-term cost advantage, but can lead to a significant long-term cost disadvantage, as the functionality and size of a system grows beyond the break-even point.

2.4   DEPENDABILITY

Implementing a dependable real-time service requires distribution of functions to achieve effective fault containment, error containment, and fault tolerance so that the service can continue despite the occurrence of faults. The term *responsive system* has been introduced to denote a system that has all of the three attributes: distribution, fault tolerance, and real-time performance [Mal94].

2.4.1   Error-Containment Regions

A fault-tolerant system must be structured into partitions that act as *error-containment regions* in such a way that the consequences of faults that occur in one of these partitions can be detected and corrected or masked before these consequences corrupt the rest of the system. An error-containment region must implement a well-specified service. This service is provided across a small interface to the outside world so that an error in the service can be detected at this interface. We call the probability that an error that occurs within an error-containment region is detected at one of the interfaces of this error-containment region the *error-containment coverage.*

An error-containment region can be introduced at different levels, e.g., at the level of a functional hardware block, or at the level of the task. In a distributed computer system, it is reasonable to regard a complete node as an error-containment region and to perform the error detection at the node's message interface to the communication system. At this interface, error detection must be performed in the value domain and in the time domain.

It is difficult to implement clean error-containment regions in a centralized architecture because many system resources are multiplexed over many services. For example, it is not possible to predict the consequences of an error in the hardware of a central processor on a particular service because such an error can lead to a failure of any one of the system services that use the central processor.

2.4.2 Replication

In a distributed system, a node must represent a unit of failure, preferably with a simple failure mode, e.g., *fail-silence.* All inner failure modes of a node are mapped into a single external failure mode–*silence* (see Section 6.1.1). The implementation of the node must guarantee that such a failure hypothesis stipulated on the architectural level will remain valid during the operation with a high probability.

Given that this failure hypothesis holds, node failures can be masked by providing actively replicated nodes. The replicas must show deterministic behavior. The issue of *replica determinism*, i.e., replicated nodes "visit" the same states at about the same time, requires careful hardware/software design. It is close to impossible to implement a deterministic behavior in a large system that supports many concurrent tasks and relies on asynchronous preemptive scheduling. The topic of replica determinism is discussed at length in Section 5.6.

2.4.3 Certification Support

Frequently the design of a safety critical system must be approved by an independent certification agency. The certification agency bases its assessment of the system on the analysis of the safety case presented by the designer. A *safety case* is the accumulation of credible analytic and experimental evidence that convinces the certification agency that the system is fit for its purpose, i.e., is safe to deploy. What constitutes a sufficient safety case for the operation of a safety-critical computer system is a topic of current discussion and varies among the different industrial sectors (see also Section 12.1).

Not all of the faults in a large real-time computer system are equally critical. For example, the aircraft industry is recommending a fault categorization according to the following criteria [ARI92]:

(i)   *Catastrophic:* Fault that prevents continued safe operation of the system and can be the cause of an accident.

(ii)   *Hazardous:* Fault that reduces the safety margin of the redundant system to an extent that further operation of the system is considered critical.

(iii) *Major:* Fault that reduces the safety margin to an extent that immediate maintenance must be performed.

(iv)   *Minor:* Fault that has only a small effect on the safety margin. From the safety point of view, it is sufficient to repair the fault at the next scheduled maintenance.

(v)   *No Effect:* Fault that has no effect on the safety margin.

The key concern in this categorization is the remainder of the safety margin after the occurrence of a primary fault. The safety case must present trustworthy arguments that the occurrence of a catastrophic or hazardous fault is extremely unlikely. The classification of a fault into one of the listed categories is based on rational arguments relating to the probability of the fault under investigation causing a catastrophic failure.

The consequence of a fault is an error, i.e., a damage of the system state. An error in a non-safety critical subsystem must be detected before it can propagate into a safety critical subsystem. The issue of error containment thus plays a crucial role. If it is not possible to demonstrate that the error-containment coverage is very close to one, i.e., that the consequences of a particular error in a non safety-critical function do not have an adverse effect on a safety-critical system function, then, the error in the non safety-critical function must be classified as catastrophic. It is of utmost importance to present an architecture that rules out by design any unintended interactions among subsystems of differing criticality. This reverts to the issue of composability.

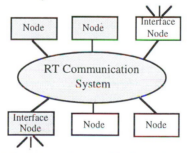

Figure 2.7: Critical (shaded) and non-critical (unshaded) system functions.

The distributed architecture of Figure 2.7 supports both critical (shaded) and non-critical (unshaded) system functions. The architecture must ensure that a fault in a non-critical node cannot affect the correct operation of a critical system function. Evidently, the communication system itself is a critical resource that must be certified. The software in the unshaded nodes can be excluded from the certification if it is possible to demonstrate that there is no way that a fault in such software could have any impact on the communication between the critical nodes.

In our opinion, it is very difficult to define independent error-containment regions in a centralized architecture. As a consequence, the total amount of real-time software that is contained in the central node must be subjected to the certification requirements–a very expensive endeavor if one considers that the design and validation of safety-critical software is 2-10 times more expensive than the design and validation of non safety-critical software.

2.5   PHYSICAL INSTALLATION

There are many good arguments for the physical integration of a small micro-controller into a mechanical subsystem to build a compact component of given functionality with a simple and small external interface to the outside world:

(i)   The electromechanical parts can interface directly with the microcontroller, avoiding error-prone and expensive cabling and connections.

(ii)   The component becomes self-contained and achieves a high degree of autonomy. The functions of the component can be performed and tested without the need to interconnect the component to a distant control system.

(iii)   The communication to and from this component can be serialized and accomplished by a single wire or twisted-pair field bus, thus simplifying the installation of the component.

The field of *mechatronics* treats this integration of electromechanical and control functions into a single unit as a primary design objective to reduce the manufacturing and installation cost and to increase the reliability of the device. The microcontroller in such a device can be considered as a node of a distributed system.

POINTS TO REMEMBER

- It is an established architectural principle that the function of an object should determine its physical form. Distributed computer architectures enable the application of this proven architectural principle to the design of computing systems.

- The interface between the communication controller within a node and the host computer of the node, the communication-network interface (CNI), is the most important interface within a distributed architecture.

- An event message combines event semantics with external control and requires one-to-one synchronization between the sender and the receiver.

- A state message combines state-value semantics with autonomous control. State-message semantics corresponds naturally to the requirements of control applications.

- The purpose of a gateway is to implement the relative views of two interacting clusters. In most cases, only a small subset of the information in one cluster is relevant to the other cluster.

- In a time-triggered architecture, a gateway consists of a strictly data-sharing interface. There are no control signals passing through a gateway component.

- The communication system is a critical resource of a distributed system, because the loss of communication results in the loss of all global system services. Therefore the reliability of the communication system should be an order of magnitude higher than the reliability of the individual nodes.

- An architecture is called *composable* with respect to a specified property if system integration will not invalidate a property that has been established at the subsystem level.

- Temporal control in an ET system is a global issue, depending on the behavior of all nodes in the system. From the point of view of temporal behavior, ET systems are not composable.

- In a time-triggered communication system that transports only state messages, temporal control resides within the communication system. Since system integration will not change the temporal properties of the CNI, a TT architecture is composable with respect to temporal properties.

- The *complexity* of a system relates to the number of parts and the number and types of interactions among the parts that must be considered in order to understand a particular function of the system.

- The effort required to understand *any particular function* of a large system should remain constant, and *independent* of the system size.

- The partitioning of a system into subsystems, the encapsulation of the subsystem, the preservation of the abstractions in case of faults, and most importantly, a strict control over the interaction patterns among the subsystems, are the key mechanisms for controlling the complexity of a large system.

- In a time-triggered architecture, the momentary values of state variables at the gateway CNIs to the other clusters form a sufficient abstraction of the environment of the cluster under investigation.

- The approximate cost of producing a chip is proportional to the third power of the die area. Although a centralized system starts with a lower initial cost, the growth curve of the cost as a function of system size rises with a larger gradient for a centralized system than for a distributed system.

- A fault-tolerant system must be structured into partitions that act as *error-containment regions* in such a way that the consequences of faults that occur in one of these partitions can be detected and corrected or masked before these consequences corrupt the rest of the system.

- If it cannot be demonstrated that the consequences of a particular fault in a non safety-critical function will not affect any safety-critical system function, then the fault in the non safety-critical function must be classified as catastrophic as well.

- The field of *mechatronics* treats the integration of electromechanical and control functions into a single unit as a primary design objective to reduce the manufacturing and installation cost, and to increase the reliability of the device.

BIBLIOGRAPHIC NOTES

The International Federation of Automatic Control (IFAC) periodically organizes a workshop on Distributed Computer Control Systems. The 13th of these workshops was held in Toulouse, France in September 1995 [IFA95]. The proceedings of these workshops are a valuable source of information. Similarly, the IEEE Distributed Systems Symposium, organized annually by the IEEE Computer Society, contains a number of relevant papers covering important topics of distributed real-time systems. A good survey of the conceptual and theoretical foundations of Distributed Systems is contained in [Mul95].

REVIEW QUESTIONS AND PROBLEMS

2.1   What are the advantages of an architecture where every logical function is implemented in a self-contained hardware unit? What are the disadvantages?

2.2   Why is it important to have stable and testable interfaces among the subsystems of a large system? What is the cost associated with such interfaces?

2.3   What are the differences between *event-message semantics* and *state-message semantics*?

2.4   Discuss each one of the sixteen combinations of data semantics and control strategy at the CNI (Table 2.1).

2.5   Why is it not possible to specify the temporal properties of the CNI in event-triggered communication systems? What are the consequences of the missing temporal specifications of the CNI on the temporal composability?

2.6   Discuss the responsiveness of a CNI that is supporting state-messages. Compare this responsiveness to that of a CNI that supports event messages.

2.7   What are the economic effects of a further increase in the integration density of VLSI devices on the field of distributed systems?

2.8   Give an estimate of the relationship between the silicon die area and the production cost of a VLSI chip. Investigate these dependencies further by studying the respective section in [Pat90, p.60].

2.9   Why is it difficult to define error-containment regions in a centralized architecture?

2.10   What is a "safety case"?

2.11   Give examples of faults of different criticality in a control system of an airplane.

2.12   How can an architecture support the certification of safety-critical real-time systems?

2.13   Discuss the advantages/disadvantages of distributed real-time systems from the point of view of physical installation.

2.14   What is "mechatronics"?

Chapter 3

Global Time

OVERVIEW

This chapter starts with a general discussion on time and order. The notions of causal order, temporal order, and delivery order and their interrelationships are elaborated. The parameters that characterize the behavior and the quality of a digital clock are investigated. Section 3.2 proceeds along the positivist tradition by introducing an omniscient external observer with an absolute reference clock that can generate precise timestamps for all relevant events. These absolute timestamps are used to reason about the precision and accuracy of a global time base, and to expose the fundamental limits of time measurement in a distributed real-time system.

In Section 3.3 the idea of a sparse time base is introduced to establish a consistent view of the order of computer-generated events in a distributed real-time system without having to execute an agreement protocol.

The topic of internal clock synchronization is covered in Section 3.4. First, the notions of convergence function and drift offset are introduced to express the synchronization condition that must be satisfied by any synchronization algorithm. Then, the simple central-master algorithm for clock synchronization is presented, and the precision of this algorithm is analyzed. Section 3.4.3 deals with the more complex issue of fault-tolerant distributed clock synchronization. The jitter of the communication system is a major limiting factor that determines the precision of the global time base.

The topic of external synchronization is studied in Section 3.5. The role of a time gateway and the problem of faults in external synchronization are discussed. Finally, the network time protocol (NTP) time format of the Internet is presented.

3.1   TIME AND ORDER

The notion of time is fundamental to our existence. We can reflect on past events and on possible future events, and thus reason about events in the domain of time. In many models of natural phenomena (e.g., Newtonian mechanics), time is an independent variable that determines the sequence of states of a system. The basic constants of physics are defined in relation to the standard of time, the physical second. This is why the global time base in a distributed real-time system should be based on the metric of the physical second.

In a typical real-time application, the distributed computer system performs a multitude of different functions concurrently, e.g., the monitoring of real-time (RT) entities (both their value and rate of change), the detection of alarm conditions, the display of the observations to the operator, and the execution of control algorithms to find new setpoints. These different functions are normally executed at different nodes. In addition, replicated nodes are introduced to provide fault tolerance by active redundancy. To guarantee a consistent behavior of the entire distributed system, it must be ensured that all nodes process all events in the same consistent order, preferably in the same temporal order in which the events occurred (see also the example in Section 5.5). A global time base helps to establish such a consistent temporal order on the basis of the timestamps of the events.

3.1.1   Different Orders

Temporal Order: The continuum of real time can be modeled by a *directed timeline* consisting of an infinite set {T} of *instants* with the following properties [Whi90,p.208]:

(i)   {T} is an ordered set, that is, if p and q are any two instants, then either p is simultaneous with q, or p precedes q, or q precedes p, where these relations are mutually exclusive. We call the order of instants on the timeline the *temporal order*.

(ii)   {T} is a dense set. This means that there is at least one q between p and r iff p *is not the same instance as* r, where $p,q,$ and r are instants.

A section of the time line is called a *duration*. An *event* takes place at an instant of time. An event does not have a duration. If two events occur at an identical instant, then the two events are said to occur *simultaneously*. Instants are totally ordered; however, events are only partially ordered, since simultaneous events are not in the order relation. Events can be totally ordered if another criterion is introduced to order events that occur simultaneously, e.g., in a distributed computer system, the number of the node at which the event occurred can be used to order events that occur simultaneously [Lam78].

Causal Order: In many real-time applications, the causal dependencies among events are of interest. Consider a nuclear reactor equipped with many sensors that monitor different RT entities (e.g., the values of pressures and the values of flows in the various pipes). If a pipe ruptures, a number of RT entities will deviate outside their normal operating ranges. Whenever the value of an RT entity leaves its normal operating range and enters an alarm region, an alarm event is signaled to the operator. At first, the pressure in the ruptured pipe changes abruptly, thereafter the flow changes, causing many other RT entities to react and generate alarms. Such a set of correlated alarms is called an *alarm shower*. The event that triggers the alarm shower is called the *primary event*. The computer system must assist the operator in identifying this primary event. Knowledge of the exact temporal order of the events is helpful in identifying this primary event. If an event $e1$ occurs after an event $e2$, then $e1$ cannot be the cause of $e2$. If, however, $e1$ occurs before $e2$, then it is possible, but not certain, that $e1$ is the cause of $e2$. The *temporal* order of two events is necessary, but not sufficient, for their *causal* order. Causal order is *more* than temporal order.

Reichenbach [Rei57,p.145] defined causality by a *mark method* without reference to time: "If event $e1$ is a cause of event $e2$, then a small variation (a *mark*) in $e1$ is associated with small variation in $e2$, whereas small variations in $e2$ are not necessarily associated with small variations in $e1$."

Example: Suppose there are two events $e1$ and $e2$:

$e1$ Somebody enters a room.

$e2$ The telephone starts to ring.

Consider the following two cases

(i) $e2$ occurs after $e1$.

(ii) $e1$ occurs after $e2$.

In both cases the two events are temporally ordered. However, while it is unlikely that there is a causal order between the two events of case (i), it is likely that such a causal order exists between the two events of case (ii), since the person might enter the room to answer the telephone.

If the (partial) temporal order between alarm events has been established, it is possible to exclude an alarm event from being the primary event if it *definitely occurred later* than another alarm event. Subsequently, we will show that a precise global time base helps to determine the event set that is in this *definitely-occurred-later-than* relation.

Delivery Order: A weaker order relation that is often provided by distributed communication systems is a consistent *delivery order*. The communication system guarantees that all host computers in the nodes see the sequence of events in the same delivery order. This delivery order is not necessarily related to the temporal order of event occurrences or the causal relationship between events.

3.1.2   Clocks

In ancient history, the measurement of durations between events was mainly based on subjective judgment. With the advent of modern science, objective methods for measuring the progression of time by using *physical clocks* have been devised.

Physical Clock: A *(physical) clock* is a device for measuring time. It contains a *counter,* and a *physical oscillation mechanism* that periodically generates an event to increase the counter. The periodic event is called the *microtick* of the clock. (The term *tick* is introduced in Section 3.2.1 to denote the events generated by the global time).The duration between two consecutive microticks is the *granularity* of the clock. The granularity of any digital clock leads to a digitalization error in time measurement.

In subsequent definitions, we use the following notation: clocks are identified by natural numbers *1, 2, . , n.* If we express properties of clocks, the property is identified by the clock number as a superscript with the microtick or tick number as a subscript. For example, microtick *i* of clock *k* is denoted by $microtick_i^k$.

Reference Clock: Assume an *omniscient external observer* who can observe all events that are of interest in a given context (relativistic effects are disregarded). This observer possesses a *unique reference clock z* with frequency f^z which is in perfect agreement with the international standard of time. The counter of the reference clock is always the same as that of the international time standard. We call $1/f^z$ the *granularity* g^z of clock *z.* Let us assume that f^z is very large, say 10^{15} microticks/second, so that the granularity g^z is *1* femtosecond (10^{-15} seconds). Since the granularity of the reference clock is so small, the digitalization error of the reference clock is disregarded in the following analysis.

Whenever the omniscient observer perceives the occurrence of an event *e*, she/he will instantaneously record the current state of the reference clock as the time of occurrence of this event *e,* and, will generate a *timestamp* for *e. Clock(event)* denotes the timestamp generated by the use of a given *clock* to timestamp an *event.* Because *z* is the single reference clock in the system, *z(e)* is called the *absolute timestamp* of the event *e.*

The *duration* between two events is measured by counting the microticks of the reference clock that occur in the interval between these two events. The *granularity* g^k of a given clock *k* is given by the nominal number n^k of microticks of the reference clock *z* between two microticks of this clock *k.*

The temporal order of events that occur between any two consecutive microticks of the reference clock, i.e., within the granularity g^z, cannot be reestablished from their absolute timestamps. This is a fundamental limit in time measurement.

Clock Drift: The *drift* of a physical clock *k* between microtick *i* and microtick *i+1* is the frequency ratio between this clock *k* and the reference clock, at the instant of microtick *i*. The drift is determined by measuring the duration of a granule of clock *k* with the reference clock *z* and dividing it by the nominal number n^k of reference clock microticks in a granule:

$$drift_i^k = \frac{z(microtick_{i+1}^k) - z(microtick_i^k)}{n^k}$$

Because a good clock has a drift that is very close to 1, for notational convenience the notion of a *drift rate* ρ_i^k is introduced as

$$\rho_i^k = \left| \frac{z(microtick_{i+1}^k) - z(microtick_i^k)}{n^k} - 1 \right|.$$

A perfect clock will have a drift rate of 0. Real clocks have a varying drift rate that is influenced by environmental conditions, e.g., a change in the ambient temperature, a change in the voltage level that is applied to a crystal resonator, or aging of the crystal. Within specified environmental parameters, the drift rate of a resonator is bounded by the *maximum drift rate* ρ_{max}^k, which is documented in the data sheet of the resonator. Typical maximum drift rates ρ_{max}^k are in the range of 10^{-2} to 10^{-7} sec/sec, or better, depending on the quality (and price) of the resonator. Because every clock has a non-zero drift rate, *free-running* clocks, i.e., clocks that are never resynchronized, leave any bounded relative time interval after a finite time, even if they are fully synchronized at startup.

Example: During the Gulf war on February 25, 1991 a Patriot missile defense system failed to intercept an incoming scud rocket. The clock drift over a 100 hour period (which resulted in a tracking error of 678 meters) was blamed for the Patriot missing the scud missile that hit an American military barracks in Dhahran, killing 29 and injuring 97. The original requirement was a 14 hour mission. The clock drift during a 14 hour mission could be handled [Neu95, p.34].

Failure Modes of a Clock: A physical clock can exhibit two types of failures. The counter could be mutilated by a fault so that the counter value becomes erroneous, or the drift rate of the clock could depart from the specified drift rate (the shaded area of Figure 3.1) because the clock starts ticking faster (or slower) than specified.

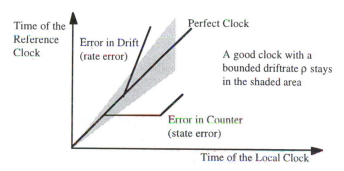

Figure 3.1: Failure modes of a physical clock.

3.1.3   Precision and Accuracy

Offset: The *offset* at microtick i between two clocks j and k with the same granularity is defined as

$$offset_i^{jk} = \left| z(microtick_i^j) - z(microtick_i^k) \right|$$

The offset denotes the time difference between the respective microticks of the two clocks, measured in the number of microticks of the reference clock.

Precision: Given an ensemble of clocks $\{1, 2, \ldots, n\}$, the maximum offset between any two clocks of the ensemble

$$\Pi_i = \max_{\forall 1 \le j, k \le n} \{offset_i^{jk}\}$$

is called the *precision* Π_i of the ensemble at microtick i. The maximum of Π_i over an *interval of interest* is called the *precision* Π of the ensemble. The precision denotes the maximum offset of respective microticks of any two clocks of the ensemble during the period of interest. The precision is expressed in the number of microticks of the reference clock.

Because of the drift rate of any physical clock, the clocks of an ensemble will drift apart if they are not resynchronized periodically (i.e., brought closer together). The process of mutual resynchronization of an ensemble of clocks to maintain a bounded precision is called *internal synchronization*.

Accuracy: The offset of clock k with respect to the reference clock z at microtick i is called the $accuracy_i^k$. The maximum offset over all microticks i that are *of interest* is called the $accuracy^k$ of clock k. The accuracy denotes the maximum offset of a given clock from the external time reference during the time interval of interest.

To keep a clock within a bounded interval of the reference clock, it must be periodically resynchronized with the reference clock. This process of resynchronization of a clock with the reference clock is called *external synchronization*.

If all clocks of an ensemble are externally synchronized with an accuracy A, then the ensemble is also internally synchronized with a precision of at most $2A$. The converse is not true. An ensemble of internally synchronized clocks will drift from the external time if the clocks are never resynchronized with the external time base.

3.1.4 Time Standards

In the last decades a number of different time standards have been proposed to measure the time difference between any two events and to establish the position of an event relative to some commonly agreed origin of a time base, the *epoch*. Two of these time bases are relevant for the designer of a distributed real-time computer system, the International Atomic Time (TAI) and the Universal Time Coordinated (UTC).

International Atomic Time (TAI–Temps Atomique Internationale): The need for a time standard that can be generated in a laboratory gave birth to the International Atomic Time (TAI). TAI defines the second as the duration of 9 192 631 770 periods of the radiation of a specified transition of the cesium atom 133. The intention was to define the duration of the TAI second so that it agrees with the second derived from astronomical observations. TAI is a *chronoscopic* timescale, i.e., a timescale without any discontinuities.

Universal Time Coordinated (UTC): UTC is a time standard that has been derived from astronomical observations of the rotation of the earth relative to the sun. It is the basis for the time on the "wall-clock". However, there is a known offset between the local wall-clock time and UTC determined by the timezone and by the political decisions about when daylight savings time must be used. The UTC time standard was introduced in 1972, replacing the Greenwich Mean Time (GMT) as an international time standard. Because the rotation of the earth is not smooth, but slightly irregular, the duration of the GMT second changes slightly over time. In 1972, it was internationally agreed that the duration of the second should conform to the TAI standard, and that the number of seconds in an hour would have to be modified occasionally by inserting a *leap second* into the UTC to maintain synchrony between the UTC (wall-clock time) and astronomical phenomena, like day and night. Because of this leap second, the UTC is not a chronoscopic time scale, i.e., it is not free of discontinuities. It was agreed that on January 1, 1958 at midnight, both the UTC and the TAI had the same value. Since then the UTC has deviated from TAI by about *30* seconds. The point in time when a leap second is inserted into the UTC is determined by the Bureau International de l'Heure and publicly announced, so that the current offset between the UTC and the TAI is always known.

Example: In *Software Engineering Notes* of March 1996 [Pet96, p.16] was the following story:

Ivan Peterson reported on a problem that occurred when a leap second was added at midnight on New Year's Eve 1995. The leap second was added, but the date inadvertently advanced to Jan. 2. Ivars heard from a source at AP radio that the synchronization of their broadcast networks depends on the official time signal, and this glitch affected their operation for several hours until the problem was corrected. You can't even count on the national timekeepers to get it right all the time.

Bob Huey responded (R 17 63) that making corrections at midnight is obviously risky: (1) The day increments to January 1, 1996, 00:00:00. (2) You reset the clock to 23:59:59, back one second. (3) The clock continues running. (4) The day changes again, and it's suddenly, January 2, 1996, 00:00:00. No wonder they had problems.

3.2   TIME MEASUREMENT

If the real-time clocks of all nodes of a distributed system were perfectly synchronized with the reference clock z, and all events were timestamped with this reference time, then it would be easy to measure the interval between any two events or to reconstruct the temporal order of events, even if variable communication delays generated differing delivery orders. In a loosely coupled distributed system where every node has its own local oscillator, such a tight synchronization of clocks is not possible. A weaker notion of a universal time reference, the concept of *global time*, is therefore introduced into a distributed system.

3.2.1 Global Time

Suppose a set of nodes exists, each one with its own local physical clock c^k that ticks with granularity g^k. Assume that all of the clocks are internally synchronized with a precision Π, i.e., for any two clocks j,k and all microticks i

$$\mid z(microtick_i^j) - z(microtick_i^k) \mid < \Pi.$$

(In Section 3.4, a number of methods for the internal synchronization of the clocks is presented). It is then possible to select a *subset of the microticks* of each local clock k for the generation of the local implementation of a global notion of time. We call such a selected local microtick i a *macrotick* (or a *tick*) of the global time. For example, every tenth microtick of a local clock k may be interpreted as the global tick, the *macrotick* t_i^k, of this clock (see Figure 3.2). If it does not matter at which clock k the (macro)tick occurs, we denote the tick t_i without a superscript. A global time is thus an *abstract notion* that is *approximated* by properly selected microticks from the synchronized local physical clocks of an ensemble.

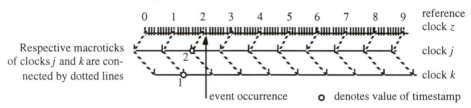

Figure 3.2: Timestamps of a single event.

Reasonableness Condition: The global time t is called *reasonable*, if all local implementations of the global time satisfy the condition

$$g > \Pi$$

the *reasonableness condition* for the global granularity g. This reasonableness condition ensures that the synchronization error is *bounded* to less than one *macrogranule*, i.e., the duration between two ticks. If this reasonableness condition is satisfied, then for a single event e, that is observed by any two different clocks of the ensemble,

$$\mid t^j(e) - t^k(e) \mid \le 1,$$

i.e., the global timestamps for a single event can differ by at most one tick. *This is the best we can achieve.* Because of the impossibility of synchronizing the clocks perfectly, and the denseness property of real time, there is always the possibility of the following sequence of events: clock j ticks, event e occurs, clock k ticks. In such a situation, the single event e is timestamped by the two clocks j and k with a difference of one tick (Figure 3.2).

One Tick Difference–What does it mean? What can we learn about the temporal order of two events, observed by different nodes of a distributed system with a reasonable global time, given that the global timestamps of these two events differ by one tick?

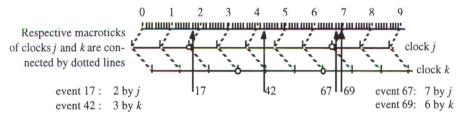

Figure 3.3: Temporal order of two events with a difference of one tick.

In Figure 3.3, four events are depicted, *event 17, event 42, event 67* and *event 69* (timestamps from the reference clock). Although the duration between *event 17* and *event 42* is *25* microticks, and the duration between *event 67* and *event 69* is only two microticks, both durations lead to the *same* measured difference of one macrogranule. The global timestamp for *event 69* is *smaller* than the global timestamp for *event 67*, although *event 69* occurred *after event 67*. Because of the accumulation of the synchronization error and the digitalization error, it is not possible to reconstruct the temporal order of two events from the knowledge that the global timestamps differ by one tick. However, if the timestamps of two events differ by two ticks, then the temporal order can be reconstructed because the sum of the synchronization and digitalization error is always less than 2 granules.

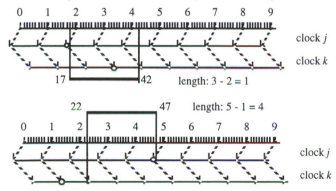

Figure 3.4: Errors in interval measurement.

3.2.2   Interval Measurement

An interval is delimited by two events, the start event of the interval and the terminating event of the interval. The measurement of these two events relative to each other can be affected by the synchronization error and the digitalization error. The sum of these two errors is *less than 2g* because of the reasonableness condition, where g is the granularity of the global time. It follows that the true duration d_{true} of an interval is bounded by

$$(d_{obs} - 2g) < d_{true} < (d_{obs} + 2g)$$

where d_{obs} is the observed difference between the start event and the terminating event of the interval. Figure 3.4 depicts how the observed duration of an interval of length 25 microticks can differ, depending on which node observes the start event and the terminating event. The global tick, assigned by an observing node to an event delimiting the interval is marked by a small circle in Figure 3.4.

3.2.3 π/Δ-Precedence

Consider a distributed system that consists of three nodes j, k, and m. Every node is to generate an event at the times *1, 5,* and *9.* An omniscient outside observer will see the scenario depicted in Figure 3.5.

All events that are generated locally at the same global clock tick will occur within a small interval π, where $\pi \leq \Pi$, the precision of the ensemble. Events that occur at different ticks will be at least Δ apart (Figure 3.5). The omniscient outside observer should not order the events that occur within π, because these events are *supposed* to occur at the same instant. Events that occur at different ticks should be ordered. How many granules of silence must exist between the event subsets so that an outside observer or another cluster will always recover the temporal order intended by the sending cluster? Before we can answer this question (in Section 3.3.2) we must introduce the notion of π/Δ precedence.

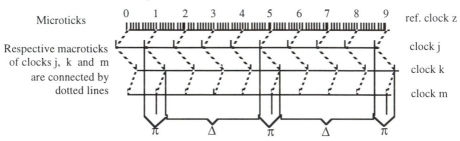

Figure 3.5: π/Δ precedence.

Given a set of events {E} and two durations π and Δ where $\pi << \Delta$, such that for any two elements e_i and e_j of this set, the following condition holds:

$$[|z(e_i) - z(e_j)| \leq \pi] \vee [|z(e_i) - z(e_j)| > \Delta]$$

where z is the reference clock. Such an event set is called π/Δ-*precedent.* π/Δ-*precedence* means that a subset of the events that happen at about the same time (and that are therefore close together within π) is separated by a substantial interval (at least Δ) from the elements in another subset. If π is zero, then any two events of the *0/Δ-precedent* event set occur either at the same instant or are at least a duration Δ apart.

Assume a global time base with granularity g and two events, *e1* and *e2*, that are observed by two different nodes of the distributed system. Table 3.1 gives the minimum differences of the observed timestamps for differing $0/\Delta$-precedence [Ver94].

Event Set	Observed timestamps of two non-simultaneous events are always greater or equal to	Temporal order of the events can always be reestablished
0/1g precedent	$\left\| t^j(e1) - t^k(e2) \right\| \geq 0$	no
0/2g precedent	$\left\| t^j(e1) - t^k(e2) \right\| \geq 1$	no
0/3g precedent	$\left\| t^j(e1) - t^k(e2) \right\| \geq 2$	yes
0/4g precedent	$\left\| t^j(e1) - t^k(e2) \right\| \geq 3$	yes

Table 3.1: Temporal order of observed events.

Because an observed difference of at least two ticks is necessary to establish the temporal order of events from their timestamps, a *0/3g* precedent event set is required to be able to establish the temporal order from the timestamps generated by a global clock.

3.2.4   Fundamental Limits of Time Measurement

The above analysis leads to the following four fundamental limits of time measurement in distributed real-time systems with a reasonable global time base with granularity g:

(i)   If a single event is observed by two different nodes, there is always the possibility that the timestamps differ by one tick. A one-tick difference in the timestamps of two events is not sufficient to reestablish the temporal order of the events from their timestamps.

(ii)   If the observed duration of an interval is d_{obs}, then the true duration d_{true} is bounded by

$$(d_{obs} - 2g) < d_{true} < (d_{obs} + 2g)$$

(iii) The temporal order of events can be recovered from their timestamps, if the difference between their timestamps is equal to or greater than 2 ticks.

(iv)   The temporal order of events can *always* be recovered from their timestamps, if the event set is at least *0/3g* precedent.

3.3   DENSE TIME VERSUS SPARSE TIME

Example: It is known *a priori* that a particular train will arrive at a train station every hour. If the train is always on time and all clocks are synchronized, it is possible to uniquely identify each train by its time of arrival. Even if the train is slightly off, say, by 5 minutes, and the clocks are slightly out of synchronization, say, by one minute, there will be no problem in uniquely identifying a train by its time of arrival. What are the limits within which a train can still be uniquely identified by its time of arrival?

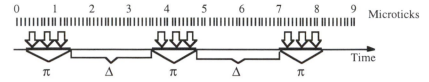

Events ⇩ are only allowed to occur within the intervals π.

Figure 3.6: Sparse time-base.

Assume a set {E} of events that are of interest in a particular context. This set {E} could be the ticks of all clocks, or the events of sending and receiving messages. If these events are allowed to occur at any instant of the timeline, then, we call the time base *dense*. If the occurrence of these events is restricted to some *active intervals* of duration ε, with an interval of silence of duration Δ between any two active intervals, then we call the time base *ε/Δ-sparse,* or simply *sparse* for short (Figure 3.6). If a system is based on a sparse time base, there are time intervals during which no significant event is allowed to occur.

It is evident that the occurrences of events can only be restricted if the given system has the authority to control these events, i.e., these events are in the sphere of control of the computer system [Dav79]. For example, within a distributed computing system the sending of messages can be restricted to some intervals of the timeline and can be forbidden at some other intervals. The occurrence of events outside the sphere of control of the computer system cannot be restricted. These external events are based on a dense time base.

3.3.1   Dense Time-base

Suppose that we are given two events *e1* and *e2* that occur on a dense time base. If these two events are closer together than *3g*, where g is the granularity of the global time, then, it is not always possible to establish the temporal order, or even a consistent order of these two events on the basis of the timestamps generated by the different nodes if no *agreement protocol* (see below) is applied.

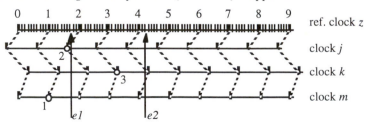

Figure 3.7: Different observed order of two events *e1* and *e2*.

Example: Consider the scenario of Figure 3.7 with two events, *e1* and *e2*, which are *2.5* granules apart. Event *e1* is observed by node j at time *2* and by node m at time *1*, while *e2* is only observed by node *k* that reports its observation "*e2* occurred at *3*" to node *j* and node *m*. Node *j* calculates a timestamp difference of one tick and concludes that the events occurred at about the same time and *cannot* be ordered. Node *m* calculates a timestamp difference of *2* ticks and concludes that *e1 has definitely occurred* before *e2*. The two nodes *j* and *m* have an *inconsistent* view about the order of event occurrence.

Agreement Protocol: To arrive at a consistent view (which does not necessarily reflect the temporal order of event occurrence) of the order of the events, the nodes must execute an *agreement protocol*. The first phase of an agreement protocol requires an information interchange among the nodes of the distributed system with the goal that every node acquires the differing local views about the state of the world from every other node. At the end of this first phase, every node possesses exactly the same information as every other node. In the second phase of the agreement protocol, each node applies a deterministic algorithm to this consistent information to reach the same conclusion–the commonly agreed value. In the fault-free case, an agreement algorithm requires an additional round of information exchange as well as the resources for executing the agreement algorithm (see also Section 9.2).

Agreement algorithms are costly, both in terms of communication requirements, processing requirements, and–worst of all–in terms of the additional delay they introduce into a control loop. It is therefore expedient to look for solutions to the ordering problem that do not require these additional overheads.

3.3.2 Sparse Time-Base

Consider a distributed system that consists of two clusters: cluster *A* generates events, and cluster *B* observes these generated events. Each one of the clusters has its own cluster-wide synchronized time with a granularity *g*, but these two cluster-wide time bases are not synchronized with each other. Under what circumstances is it possible for the nodes in the observing cluster to reestablish the *intended temporal order* of the generated events without the need to execute an agreement protocol?

If two nodes, nodes *j* and *k* of cluster *A*, generate two events at the same cluster-wide tick t_i, i.e., at tick t_i^j and at tick t_i^k, then these two events can be a distance Π apart from each other, where $g > \Pi$, the granularity of the cluster-wide time. Because there is no intended temporal order among the events that are generated at the same cluster-wide tick of cluster *A*, the observing cluster *B* should *never* establish a temporal order among the events that have been sent at about the same time. On the other hand, the observing cluster *B* should *always* reestablish the temporal order of the events that have been sent at different cluster-wide ticks. Is it sufficient if cluster *A* generates a *1g/3g* precedent event set, i.e., after every cluster-wide tick at which events are allowed to be generated there will be silence for at least three granules?

If cluster *A* generates a *1/3g* precedent event set, then it is possible that two events that are generated at the same cluster-wide tick at cluster *A* will be timestamped by cluster *B* with timestamps that differ by 2 ticks. The observing cluster *B* should not order these events (although it could), because they have been generated at the same cluster-wide tick. Events that are generated by cluster *A* at different cluster-wide ticks (*3g* apart) and therefore should be ordered by cluster *B,* could also obtain timestamps that differ by 2 ticks. Cluster *B* cannot decide whether or not to order events with a timestamp difference of 2 ticks. To resolve this situation, cluster *A* must generate a *1/4g* precedent event set. Cluster *B* will not order two events if their timestamps differ by ≤ 2 ticks, but will order two events if their timestamps differ by ≥ 3 ticks, thus reestablishing the temporal order that has been intended by the sender.

3.3.3 Space-Time Lattice

The ticks of the global clock can be seen as generating a space-time lattice, as depicted in Figure 3.8. A node is allowed to generate an event (e.g., send a message) at the filled dots and must be silent at the empty dots. This rule makes it possible for the receiver to establish a consistent temporal order of events without executing an agreement protocol. Although a sender might have to wait for four ticks before generating an event, this is still much faster than executing an agreement protocol, provided a global time base of sufficient precision is available.

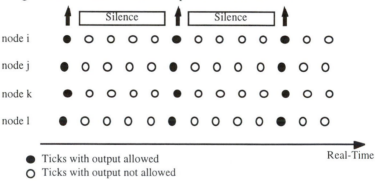

Figure 3.8: *1/4g* precedent event set.

Events that occur outside the sphere of control of the computer system cannot be confined to a sparse time base: they happen on a dense time base. To generate a consistent view of events that occur in the controlled object, and that are observed by more than one node of the distributed computer system, the execution of an agreement protocol is unavoidable at the instrumentation inerface (i.e., the interface between the computer system and the controlled object).

Node failures also occur on a dense time base. In a TT architecture, it is possible to restrict to a sparse time base the points in time when node failures are recognized by the other nodes of the distributed computer system. This avoids the need to execute an agreement protocol for the consistent detection of node failures. This issue will be discussed further in Chapter 8 on the Time-Triggered Protocol TTP.

3.4   INTERNAL CLOCK SYNCHRONIZATION

The purpose of internal clock synchronization is to ensure that the global ticks of all correct nodes occur within the specified precision Π, despite the varying drift rate of the local real-time clock of each node. Because the availability of a proper global time base is crucial for the operation of a distributed real-time system, the clock synchronization should be fault-tolerant.

Every node of a distributed system has a local oscillator that (micro)ticks with a frequency determined by the physical parameters of the oscillator. A subset of the local oscillator's microticks called the ticks (or macroticks–see Section 3.2.1), are interpreted as the global time ticks at the node. These global time ticks increment the node's local global time counter.

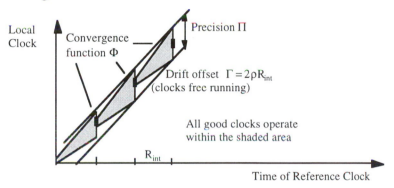

Figure 3.9: Synchronization condition.

3.4.1   The Synchronization Condition

The global time ticks of each node must be periodically resynchronized within the ensemble of nodes to establish a global time base with specified precision. The period of resynchronization is called the *resynchronization interval*. At the end of each resynchronization interval, the clocks are adjusted to bring them into better agreement with each other. The *convergence function* Φ denotes the offset of the time values immediately after the resynchronization. Then, the clocks again drift apart until they are resynchronized at the end of the next resynchronization interval R_{int} (Figure 3.9). The *drift offset* Γ indicates the maximum divergence of any two good clocks from each other during the resynchronization interval R_{int}, where the clocks are free running. The drift offset Γ depends on the length of the resynchronization interval R_{int} and the maximum specified drift rate ρ of the clock:

$$\Gamma = 2\rho \; R_{int}$$

An ensemble of clocks can only be synchronized if the following *synchronization condition* between the *convergence function* Φ, the *drift offset* Γ and the *precision* Π holds:

$$\Phi + \Gamma \leq \Pi$$

Assume that at the end of the resynchronization interval, the clocks have diverged so that they are at the edge of the precision interval Π (Figure 3.9). The synchronization condition states that the synchronization algorithm must bring the clocks so close together that the amount of divergence during the next free-running resynchronization interval will not cause a clock to leave the precision interval.

Byzantine Error: The following example explains how, in an ensemble of three nodes, a malicious node can prevent the other two nodes from synchronizing their clocks since they cannot satisfy the synchronization condition. Assume an ensemble of three nodes, and a convergence function where each of the three nodes sets its clock to the average value of the ensemble. Clocks A and B are good, while clock C is a malicious "two-faced" clock that disturbs the other two good clocks in such a manner that neither of them will ever correct their time value (Figure 3.10), and will thus eventually violate the synchronization condition.

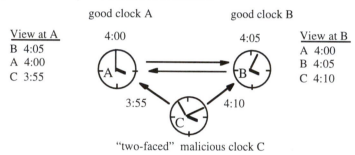

good clock A   good clock B

View at A   4:00   4:05   View at B
B 4:05   A 4:00
A 4:00   B 4:05
C 3:55   C 4:10

3:55   4:10

"two-faced" malicious clock C

Figure 3.10: Behavior of a malicious clock.

Such a malicious, "two-faced" manifestation of behavior is sometimes called a *malicious error* or a *Byzantine error*. During the exchange of the synchronization messages, a Byzantine error can lead to inconsistent views of the state of the clocks among the ensemble of nodes. A special class of algorithms, the *interactive-consistency algorithms* [Pea80], inserts additional rounds of information exchanges to agree on a consistent view of the time values at all nodes. These additional rounds of information exchanges increase the quality of the precision at the expense of additional communication overhead. Other algorithms work with inconsistent information, and establish bounds for the maximum error introduced by the inconsistency. An example of such an algorithm is the Fault-Tolerant-Average algorithm, described later in this section. It can be shown [Lam85] that clock synchronization can only be guaranteed in the presence of Byzantine errors if the total number of clocks $N \geq (3k + 1)$, where k is the number of Byzantine faulty clocks.

3.4.2 Central Master Synchronization

A unique node, the central master, periodically sends the value of its time counter in synchronization messages to all other nodes, the slave nodes. As soon as a slave node receives a new time value from the master, the slave records the state of its local-time counter as the time of message arrival. The difference between the master's time, contained in the synchronization message, and the recorded slave's time of message arrival, corrected by the latency of the message transport, is a measure of the deviation of the two clocks. The slave then corrects its clock by this deviation to bring it into agreement with the master's clock.

The convergence function Φ of the central master algorithm is determined by the difference between the fastest and slowest message transmission to the slave nodes of the ensemble, i.e., the *latency jitter* ε between the event of reading the clock value at the master and the events of message arrival at all slaves.

Applying the synchronization condition, the precision of the central master algorithm is given by:

$$\Pi_{central} = \varepsilon + \Gamma$$

The central master synchronization is often used in the startup phase of a distributed system. It is simple, but not fault tolerant, since a failure of the master ends the resynchronization, causing the free-running clocks of the slaves to leave the precision interval soon thereafter. In a variant of this algorithm, a multi-master strategy is followed: if the active master fails and the failure is detected by a local time-out at a "shadow" master, one of the shadow masters assumes the role of the master and continues the resynchronization.

3.4.3   Distributed Synchronization Algorithms

Typically, distributed fault-tolerant clock resynchronization proceeds in three distinct phases. In the first phase every node acquires knowledge about the state of the global time counters in all the other nodes by exchange of messages among the nodes. In the second phase, every node analyzes the collected information to detect errors, and executes the convergence function to calculate a correction value for the local global time counter. A node must deactivate itself if the correction term calculated by the convergence function is larger than the specified precision of the ensemble. Finally, in the third phase, the local time counter of the node is adjusted by the calculated correction value. Existing algorithms differ in the way in which the time values are collected from the other nodes, in the type of convergence function used, and in the way in which the correction value is applied to the time counter.

Reading the Global Time: In a local-area network the most important term affecting the precision of the synchronization is the jitter of the time messages that carry the current time values from one node to all the other nodes. The known minimal delay for the transport of a time message between two nodes can be compensated by an *a priori* known delay-compensation term [Kop87] that compensates for the delay of the message in the transmission channel and in the interface circuitry. The delay jitter depends more than anything else on the system level at which the synchronization message is assembled and interpreted. If this is done at a high level of the architecture, e.g., in the application software, all random delays caused by the scheduler, the operating system, the queues in the protocol software, the message retransmission strategy, the media-access delay, the interrupt delay at the receiver, and the scheduling delay at the receiver, accumulate and degrade the quality of the time values, thus deteriorating the precision of the clock synchronization. Table 3.2 gives approximate value ranges for the jitter that can be expected at the different levels [Kop87]:

synchronization message assembled and interpreted	approximate range of jitter
at the application software level	500 μsec to 5 msec
in the kernel of the operating system	10 μsec to 100 μsec
in the hardware of the communication controller	less than 10 μsec

Table 3.2: Approximate jitter of the synchronization message.

Since a small jitter is important to achieve high precision in the global time, a number of special methods for jitter reduction have been proposed. Christian [Cri89] proposed the reduction of the jitter at the application software level using a probabilistic technique: a node queries the state of the clock at another node by a query-reply transaction, the duration of which is measured by the sender. The received time value is corrected by the synchronization message delay that is assumed to be half the round-trip delay of the query-reply transaction (assuming that the delay distribution is the same in both directions). A different approach is taken in the MARS system [Kop89]. A special clock synchronization unit has been implemented to support the segmentation and assembly of synchronization messages at the hardware level, thereby reducing the jitter to a few microseconds.

Impossibility Result: The important role of the latency jitter ε for internal synchronization is emphasized by an impossibility result by Lundelius and Lynch [Lun84]. According to this result, it is not possible to internally synchronize the clocks of an ensemble consisting of N nodes to a better precision than

$$\Pi = \varepsilon\left(1 - \frac{1}{N}\right)$$

(measured in the same units as ε) even if it is assumed that all clocks have perfect oscillators, i.e., the drift rates of all the local clocks are zero.

The Convergence Function: The construction of a convergence function is demonstrated by the example of the distributed Fault-Tolerant-Average (FTA) algorithm in a system with N nodes where k Byzantine faults should be tolerated. The FTA algorithm is a one-round algorithm that works with inconsistent information and bounds the error introduced by the inconsistency. At every node, the N measured time differences between the node's clock and the clocks of all other nodes are collected (the node considers itself a member of the ensemble with time difference zero). These time differences are sorted by size. Then the k largest and the k smallest time differences are removed (assuming that an erroneous time value is either larger or smaller than the rest). The remaining N-$2k$ time differences are, by definition, within the precision window. The average of these remaining time differences is the correction term for the node's clock.

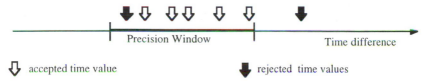

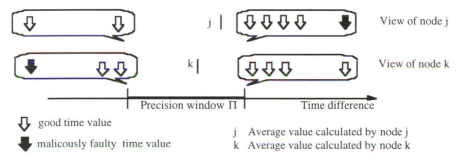

Figure 3.11: Accepted and rejected time values.

Example: Figure 3.11 shows an ensemble of 7 nodes and one tolerated Byzantine fault. The FTA takes the average of the five accepted time values shown.

Figure 3.12: Worst possible behavior of a malicious (Byzantine) clock.

The worst-case scenario occurs if all good clocks are at opposite ends of the precision window Π, and the Byzantine clock is seen at different corners by two nodes. In the example of Figure 3.12, node j will calculate an average value of $4\Pi/5$ and node k will calculate an average value of $3\Pi/5$; the difference between these two terms, caused by the Byzantine fault, is thus $\Pi/5$.

Precision of the FTA: Assume a distributed system with N nodes, each one with its own clock (all time values are measured in seconds). At most k out of the N clocks behave in a Byzantine manner.

A single Byzantine clock will cause the following difference in the calculated averages at two different nodes in an ensemble of N clocks:

$$E_{byz} = \Pi / (N - 2k).$$

In the worst case a total of k Byzantine errors will thus cause an error term of

$$E_{k-byz} = k\Pi / (N - 2k).$$

Considering the jitter of the synchronization messages, the convergence function of the FTA algorithm is given by

$$\Phi(N, k, \varepsilon) = (k\Pi / (N - 2k)) + \varepsilon.$$

Combining the above equation with the synchronization condition (Section 3.4.1) and performing a simple algebraic transformation, we have the precision of the FTA algorithm to be:

$$\Pi(N, k, \varepsilon, \Gamma) = (\varepsilon + \Gamma)\frac{N - 2k}{N - 3k} = (\varepsilon + \Gamma)\mu(N, k).$$

where $\mu(N, k)$ is called the *Byzantine error term* and is tabulated in Table 3.3.

Faults	Number of nodes in the ensemble							
	4	5	6	7	10	15	20	30
1	2	1.5	1.33	1.25	1.14	1.08	1.06	1.03
2				3	1.5	1.22	1.14	1.08
3					4	1.5	1.27	1.22

Table 3.3: Byzantine error term $\mu(N,k)$.

The Byzantine error term $\mu(N,k)$ indicates the loss of quality in the precision due to the inconsistency arising from the Byzantine errors. In a real environment, at most one Byzantine error is expected to occur in a synchronization round (and even this will happen very, very infrequently), and thus, the consequences of a Byzantine error in a properly-designed synchronization system are not serious.

The drift offset Γ is determined by the quality of the selected oscillator and the length of the resynchronization interval. If a standard quartz oscillator with a nominal drift rate of 10^{-4} sec/sec is used, and the clocks are resynchronized every second, then Γ is about 100 μsec. Because the stochastic drift rate of a crystal is normally two orders of magnitude smaller than the nominal drift rate that is determined by the systematic error of the quartz oscillator, it is possible to reduce the drift offset Γ by two orders of magnitude using systematic error compensation [Sch96].

Many other convergence functions for the internal synchronization of the clocks have been proposed and analyzed in the literature [Sch88].

3.4.4 State Correction versus Rate Correction

The correction term calculated by the convergence function can be applied to the local-time value immediately (*state correction*), or the rate of the clock can be modified so that the clock speeds up or slows down during the next resynchronization interval to bring the clock into better agreement with the rest of the ensemble (*rate correction*).

State correction is simple to apply, but it has the disadvantage of generating a discontinuity in the time base. If clocks are set backwards and the same nominal-time value is reached twice, then, pernicious failures can occur within the real-time software (see the example in Section 3.1.4). It is therefore advisable to implement rate correction with a bound on the maximum value of the clock drift so that the error in interval measurements is limited. The resulting global time base then maintains the chronoscopy property despite the resynchronization. Rate correction can be implemented either in the digital domain by changing the number of microticks in some of the (macro)ticks, or in the analog domain by adjusting the voltage of the crystal oscillator. To avoid a common-mode drift of the complete ensemble of clocks, the average of the rate correction terms among all clocks in the ensemble should be close to zero.

3.5   EXTERNAL CLOCK SYNCHRONIZATION

External synchronization links the global time of a cluster to an external standard of time. For this purpose it is necessary to access a *time server*, i.e., an external time source that periodically broadcasts the current reference time in the form of a *time message*. This time message must raise a synchronization event (such as the beep of a wrist watch) in a designated node of the cluster and must identify this synchronization event on the agreed time scale. Such a time scale must be based on a constant measure of time, e.g., the physical second, and must relate the synchronization event to a defined origin of time, the *epoch*. The interface node to a time server is called a *time gateway*.

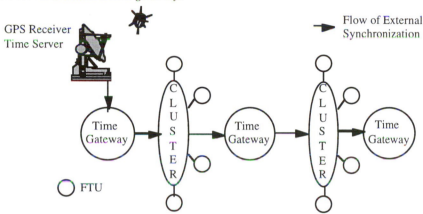

Figure 3.13: Flow of external synchronization.

3.5.1   Principle of Operation

Assume that the time gateway is connected to a GPS (Global Positioning System) receiver. This UTC time server periodically broadcasts time messages containing a synchronization event, as well as information to place this synchronization event on the TAI scale. The time gateway must synchronize the global time of its cluster with the time received from the time server. This synchronization is unidirectional, and therefore asymmetric, as shown in Figure 3.13.

If another cluster is connected to this "primary" cluster by a secondary time gateway, then, the unidirectional synchronization functions in the same manner. The secondary time gateway considers the synchronized time of the primary cluster as its time reference, and synchronizes the global time of the secondary cluster.

While internal synchronization is a cooperative activity among all the members of a cluster, external synchronization is an authoritarian process: the time server forces its view of external time on all its subordinates. From the point of view of fault tolerance, such an authoritarian regime introduces a problem: if the authority sends an incorrect message, then all its "obedient" subordinates will behave incorrectly. However, for external clock synchronization, the situation is under control because of the "inertia" of time. Once a cluster has been synchronized, the fault-tolerant global time base within a cluster acts as a *monitor* of the time server. A time gateway will only accept an external synchronization message if its content is sufficiently close to its view of the external time. The time server has only a limited authority to correct the drift rate of a cluster. The enforcement of a maximum common-mode drift rate–we propose less than 10^{-4} sec/sec–is required to keep the error in relative time-measurements small. The maximum correction rate is checked by the software in each node of the cluster.

The implementation must guarantee that it is impossible for a faulty external synchronization to interfere with the proper operation of the internal synchronization, i.e., with the generation of global time within a cluster. The worst possible failure scenario occurs if the external time server fails maliciously. This leads to a common-mode deviation of the global time from the external time base with the maximum permitted correction rate. The internal synchronization within a cluster will, however, not be affected by this controlled drift from the external time base.

3.5.2   Time   Formats

Over the last few years, a number of external-time formats have been proposed for external clock synchronization. The most important one is the standard for the time format proposed in the Network Time Protocol (NTP) of the Internet [Mil91]. This time format (Figure 3.14) with a length of eight bytes contains two fields: a four byte full seconds field, where the seconds are represented according to UTC, and a fraction of a second field, where the fraction of a second is represented as a binary fraction with a resolution of about *232* picosecond. On January 1, 1972, at midnight the NTP clock was set to *2,272,060,800.0* seconds, i.e., the number of seconds since January 1, 1900 at 00:00h.

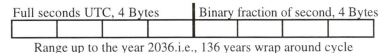

Range up to the year 2036.i.e., 136 years wrap around cycle

Figure 3.14: Time format in the Network Time Protocol (NTP).

The NTP time is not chronoscopic because it is based on UTC. The occasional insertion of a leap second into UTC can disrupt the continuous operation of a time-triggered real-time system.

3.5.3   Time   Gateway

The time gateway must control the timing system of its cluster in the following ways:

(i)   It must initialize the cluster with the current external time.

(ii)   It must periodically adjust the rate of the global time in the cluster to bring it into agreement with the external time and the standard of time measurement, the second.

(iii) It must periodically send the current external time in a time message to the nodes in the cluster so that a reintegrating node can reinitialize its external time value.

The time gateway achieves this task by periodically sending a time message with a rate-correction byte. This rate-correction byte is calculated in the time gateway's software. First, the difference between the occurrence of a significant event, e.g., the exact start of the full second in the time server, and the occurrence of the related significant event in the global time of the cluster, is measured by using the local time base (microticks) of the gateway node. Then, the necessary rate adjustment is calculated, bearing in mind the fact that the rate adjustment is bounded by the agreed maximum rate correction. This bound on the rate correction is necessary to keep the maximum deviation of relative time measurements in the cluster below an agreed threshold, and to protect the cluster from faults of the server.

POINTS TO REMEMBER

- An event happens at an *instant*, i.e., at a point of the timeline. A *duration* is a section of the timeline delimited by two instants.

- A consistent delivery order of a set of events in a distributed system does not necessarily reflect the temporal or causal order of the events.

- A *physical clock* is a device for time measurement that contains a counter and a physical oscillation mechanism that periodically generates an event to increase the counter.

- Typical maximum drift rates ρ of physical clocks are in the range from 10^{-2} to 10^{-7} sec/sec, or lower, depending on the quality (and price) of the resonator.

- The *precision* denotes the maximum offset of respective ticks of any two clocks of an ensemble during the time interval of interest.

- The *accuracy* of a clock denotes the maximum offset of a given clock from the external time reference during the time interval of interest.

- TAI is a *chronoscopic* timescale, i.e., a timescale without any discontinuities, that is derived from the frequency of the radiation of a specified transition of the cesium atom 133.

- UTC is a non-chronoscopic timescale that is derived from astronomical observations of the rotation of the earth in relation to the sun.

- A *global time* is an abstract notion that is approximated by properly selected microticks from the synchronized local physical clocks of an ensemble.

- The *reasonableness condition* ensures that the synchronization error is always less than one granule of the global time.

- If the difference between the timestamps of two events is *equal to or larger than 2 ticks*, then that temporal order of events can be recovered, provided the global time is reasonable.

- The temporal order of events can *always* be recovered from their timestamps, if the event set is at least 0/3g precedent.

- If events happen only at properly selected points of a *sparse time base*, then it is possible to recover the temporal order of the events without the execution of an agreement protocol.

- The *convergence function* Φ denotes the offset of the time values immediately after the resynchronization.

- The *drift offset* Γ indicates the maximum divergence of any two good clocks from each other during the resynchronization interval R_{int}, in which the clocks are free running.

- The synchronization condition states that the synchronization algorithm must bring the clocks so close together that the amount of divergence during the next free-running resynchronization interval will not cause a clock to leave the precision interval.

- Clock synchronization is only possible if the total number of clocks N is larger or equal to *(3k +1)*, if k is the number of clocks behaving *maliciously* faulty.

- The most important term affecting the precision of the synchronization is the *latency jitter* of the synchronization messages that carry the current time values from one node to all other nodes of an ensemble.

- When applying the fault-tolerant average algorithm, the *Byzantine error factor* $\mu(N,k)$ indicates the loss of quality in the precision caused by the Byzantine errors.

- *State correction* of a clock has the disadvantage of generating a discontinuity in the time base.

- While internal synchronization is a cooperative activity among all members of a cluster, external synchronization is an authoritarian process: the timeserver forces its view of external time on all its subordinates.

- The *NTP time*, based on UTC, is not chronoscopic. The occasional insertion of a leap second can disrupt the continuous operation of a time-triggered real-time system.

- The *time gateway* maintains the external synchronization by periodically sending a time message with a rate correction byte to all the nodes of a cluster.

BIBLIOGRAPHIC NOTES

The problem of generating a global time base in a distributed system has first been analyzed in the context of the SIFT [Wen78] and FTMP [Hop78] projects. The problem was investigated again in the mid-eighties by a number of research groups. Lundelius and Lynch [Lun84] established theoretical bounds on the achievable synchrony in 1984. Lamport and Melliar Smith [Lam85] and Schneider [Sch86] investigated the synchronization of clocks in the presence of Byzantine faults, and compared a number of different synchronization algorithms. A VLSI chip for clock synchronization in distributed systems was developed by Kopetz and Ochsenreiter [Kop87]. Probabilistic clock synchronization, i.e., clock synchronization in systems where no upper bound on the jitter is known, has been studied by Cristian [Cri89], and Olson and Shin [Ols91]. Shin also investigated the problem of clock synchronization in large multiprocessor systems [Shi87]. The Network Time Protocol of the Internet was published in 1991 by Mills [Mil91]. The concept of a sparse time was first presented by Kopetz [Kop92]. The issue of establishing a global time base among a set of nodes with differing oscillators is covered in [Kop95d]. Schedl [Sch96] developed a detailed simulation model to simulate the effects of many parameters that determine the precision and accuracy of a global time base. A compendium of papers on clock synchronization can be found in the tutorial by Yang and Marsland [Yan93]. For a more philosophical treatment of the problem of time, the reader is advised to study the excellent book by Withrow [Whi90] entitled "The Natural Philosophy of Time".

REVIEW QUESTIONS AND PROBLEMS

3.1   What is the difference between an *instant* and an *event*?

3.2   What is the difference between *temporal* order, *causal* order and a consistent *delivery* order of messages? Which of the orders implies another?

3.3   How can clock synchronization assist in finding the *primary* event of an alarm shower?

3.4   What is the difference between UTC and TAI? Why is TAI better suited as a time base for distributed real-time systems than UTC?

3.5   Define the notions of *offset, drift, drift rate, precision* and *accuracy*.

3.6   What is the difference between *internal* synchronization and *external* synchronization?

3.7   What are the fundamental limits of time measurement?

3.8   When is an event set π/Δ-*precedent*?

3.9   What is an *agreement protocol*? Why should we try to avoid agreement protocols in real-time systems? When is it impossible to avoid agreement protocols?

3.10   What is a *sparse time base*? How can a sparse time base help to avoid agreement protocols?

3.11   Give an example that shows that, in an ensemble of three clocks a Byzantine clocks, can disturb the two good clocks such that the synchronization condition is violated.

3.12   Given a clock synchronization system that achieves a precision of *90* microseconds, what is a reasonable granularity for the global time? What are the limits for the observed values for a time interval of *1.1* msec?

3.13   What is the role of the *convergence function* in internal clock synchronization?

3.14   Given a latency jitter of *20* µsec, a clock drift rate of 10^{-5}sec/sec, and a resynchronization period of *1* second, what precision can be achieved by the central master algorithm?

3.15   What is the effect of a Byzantine error on the quality of synchronization by the FTA algorithm?

3.16   Given a latency jitter of *20* µsec, a clock drift rate of 10^{-5}sec/sec and a resynchronization period of *1* second, what precision can be achieved by the FTA algorithm in a system with *10* clocks where *1* clock could be malicious?

3.17   Discuss the consequences of an error in the external clock synchronization. What effect can such an error have on the internal clock synchronization in the worst possible scenario?

Chapter 4

Modeling Real-Time Systems

OVERVIEW

In this chapter, a conceptual model of a distributed real-time system is developed. The focus of the model is on the system structure and on the temporal aspects of its behavior. After a short section on the essence of model building, a clear distinction is made between the relevant properties that must be part of the conceptual model, and the irrelevant details that can be neglected at the conceptual level. The structural elements of the model are tasks, nodes, fault-tolerant units, and clusters. The important issues of interface placement and interface layout between the structural elements are analyzed in detail. Correctly designed external interfaces provide understandable abstractions to the interfacing partners, and capture the essential properties of the interfacing subsystems while hiding the irrelevant details.

It is important to distinguish clearly between temporal control and logical control in the design of a real-time system. Temporal control determines when a task must be executed or a message must be sent, while logical control is concerned with the control flow within a sequential task. The merging of temporal control and logical control adds to the complexity of a design, as shown by a convincing example in Section 4.4.1.

A deadline for the completion of an RT transaction can only be guaranteed if the worst-case data-independent execution times of all application and communication tasks that are part of the transaction are known *a priori*. Modern microprocessors with caches and pipelines make the worst-case execution time analysis challenging. In these modern microprocessors, the context switches caused by interrupts can increase the administrative overhead significantly.

The final section is devoted to an analysis of the internal state or history state (h-state) of a node.

4.1   APPROPRIATE ABSTRACTIONS

4.1.1   The Purpose of the Model

The limited information processing capacity of the human mind–compared to the large amount of information in the real world–requires a goal-oriented information reduction strategy to develop a reduced representation of the world (*a model*) that helps in understanding the problem posed. New concepts emerge and take shape if mental activity is focused on solving a particular problem. Reality can be represented by a variety of models: a physical-scale model of a building, a simulation model of a technical process, a mathematical model of quantum physics phenomena, or a formal logical model of the security in a computer system. All these models are different abstractions of reality, but should not be mistaken for reality itself. A model that introduces a set of well-defined concepts and their interrelationships is called a *conceptual model*. When proceeding from informal to formal modeling, a certain order must be followed: a sound and stable conceptual model is a necessary prerequisite for any more formal model. Formal models have the advantage of a precise notation and rigorous rules of inference that support the automatic reasoning about selected properties of the modeled system.

This section is aimed at developing a conceptual model to understand the temporal behavior of a distributed real-time computer system. We introduce quantitative measures about temporal properties where necessary.

Assumption Coverage: The essence of model building lies in accuracy for the stated purpose, simplification and understandability. Given a set of models that describe a given phenomenon, the model that requires the smallest number of concepts and relationships to explain the issue involved is the preferred one. There is, however, the danger of oversimplification, or of omitting a relevant property. *Information reduction, or abstraction, is only possible if the goal of the model-building process has been well defined.* Otherwise, it is hopeless to distinguish between the relevant information that must be part of the model, and the irrelevant information that can be discarded. All assumptions that are made during modeling in order to achieve simplification, must be stated clearly as they define the range of validity of the emerging model. The probability that the assumptions made in the model building process hold in reality is called the *assumption coverage* [Pow95]. The assumption coverage limits the probability that conclusions derived from a model are valid in the real world.

Two important assumptions must be made while designing a model of a fault-tolerant real-time computer system: the *load hypothesis* and the *fault hypothesis*. Every computer system has only a finite processing capacity. Statements on the response time of a computer system can only be made under the assumption that the load offered to the computer system is below a maximum load, called the *peak load*. We call this important assumption the *load hypothesis*. A fault-tolerant computer system is designed to tolerate all faults that are covered by the *fault hypothesis*, i.e., a statement about the assumptions that relate to the type and frequency of faults that the computer system is supposed to handle. If the faults that occur in the real world are not covered by the fault hypothesis, then, even a perfectly designed fault-tolerant computer system will fail.

4.1.2   What is Relevant?

In this section, we discuss those temporal properties of the world that must be part of the model of a distributed real-time computer system.

Notion of Physical Time: The progression of physical time is of central importance in any real-time computer system. As mentioned before, many constants of the laws of physics, e.g., the speed of light, are defined with respect to the physical time TAI. If a different time-base is selected for the real-time system model, then all these physical constants may become meaningless or must be redefined. We assume that the omniscient external observer, with the precise reference clock z that was introduced in Chapter 3, is present and that the real-time clocks within all nodes are synchronized to a precision Π that is sufficient for the given purpose, i.e., the granularity is fine enough for the temporal attributes of the application under consideration to be described correctly.

Durations of Actions: The execution of a statement constitutes an *action*. The duration (or *execution time*) of a computational or communication action on a given hardware configuration between the occurrence of the stimulus and the occurrence of the associated response, is an important measure in the domain of time. Given an action a, we distinguish the following four quantities that describe its temporal behavior:

(i)   *Actual duration*: (or *actual execution time*): given a concrete input data set x we denote by $d_{act}(a,x)$ the number of time units of the reference clock z that occur between the start of action a and the termination of action a.

(ii)   *Minimal duration*: the minimal duration $d_{min}(a)$ is the smallest time interval it takes to complete the action a, quantified over all possible input data.

(iii)   *Worst-case execution time (WCET)*: the worst-case execution time $d_{wcet}(a)$ is the maximum duration it may take to complete the action a under the stated load and fault hypothesis, quantified over all possible input data.

(iv)   *Jitter:* the jitter for an action a is the difference between the worst-case execution time $d_{wcet}(a)$ and the minimal duration $d_{min}(a)$.

In a later section of this chapter, the worst-case execution times and the jitter of data-transformation and communication actions will be analyzed.

Frequency of Activations: We call the maximum number of activations of an action per unit of time the *frequency of activations*. Every computational resource, e.g., a node computer or a communication system, has a finite capacity determined by the physical parameters of the resource. A resource can only meet its temporal obligations if the frequency and the temporal distribution of the activations of the resource are strictly controlled.

4.1.3   What Is Irrelevant?

Which attributes of reality can be discarded without jeopardizing the purpose of the model? Since a model is a reduced representation of reality, a clear description of the attributes of the real world that are not relevant for the given purpose is of paramount importance in model building. Introducing irrelevant details into a model complicates the representation and the analysis of the given problem unnecessarily.

Issues of Representation: The focus of the conceptual model of a distributed real-time system is on the temporal properties and on the meaning of real-time variables, and not on their syntactic appearance, i.e., the representation of the values. Consider, for instance, the example of a temperature measurement: at the *physical interface* between the computer system and the temperature sensor, the temperature can be represented by a 4-20 mA current signal, by a particular bit pattern generated by an analog-to-digital (A/D) converter, or by a floating-point number within the computer. We ignore all these low-level representational issues and assume an *abstract interface* that provides an agreed standard representation that is uniform within an entire subsystem, e.g., *degrees Celsius* for any temperature. *Different representations of the same value only matter at an interface between two different subsystems.* These representational differences can be hidden within a gateway component that transforms the representation used in one subsystem to the representation used in the other subsystem without changing the meaning, i.e., the semantics, of the value under consideration.

Details of the Data Transformations: In a real-time system, there are many programs that compute a desired result from given input data. Examples of such programs are control algorithms, and the algorithms for the transformation of one representation of information into another. These programs can be described on a level of abstraction that considers the following aspects in the data domain along with the functional intent of the program:

(i)   The given input data,

(ii)   The internal state of the program,

(iii)   The intended results,

(iv)   The modifications to the internal state of the program, and

(v)   The resource requirements of the program, e.g., the memory size.

In the time domain, the worst-case execution time to derive the results from the input data and the control signal that initiates the computation are considered relevant. The internal program logic and the intermediate results of the program are treated as irrelevant detail at the level of a conceptual model.

4.2   THE STRUCTURAL ELEMENTS

Viewed externally, a distributed fault-tolerant real-time application can be decomposed into a set of communicating clusters (see also Figure 1.1). A computational cluster can be further partitioned into a set of fault-tolerant units (FTUs) connected by a real-time local area network. Each FTU consists of one or more node computers. Within a node computer, a set of concurrently executing tasks performs the intended functions. In the following section, we explain these building blocks of the model, starting at the task level.

4.2.1   Task

A task is the execution of a sequential program. It starts with reading of the input data and of the internal state of the task, and terminates with the production of the results and updating the internal state. The control signal that initiates the execution of a task must be provided by the operating system. The time interval between the start of the task and its termination, given an input data set x, is called the actual duration $d_{act}(task,x)$ of the task on a given target machine. A task that does not have an internal state at its point of invocation is called a *stateless task*; otherwise, it is called a *task with state*.

Simple Task (S-task): If there is no synchronization point within a task, we call it a *simple task (S-task)*, i.e., whenever an S-task is started, it can continue until its termination point is reached. Because an S-task cannot be blocked within the body of the task, the execution time of an S-task is not directly dependent on the progress of the other tasks in the node, and can be determined *in isolation*. It is possible for the execution time of an S-task to be extended by indirect interactions, such as by task preemption by a task with higher priority.

Complex Task (C-Task): A task is called a *complex task (C-Task)* if it contains a blocking synchronization statement (e.g., a semaphore operation "wait") within the task body. Such a "wait" operation may be required because the task must wait until a condition outside the task is satisfied, e.g., until another task has finished updating a common data structure, or until input from a terminal has arrived. If a common data structure is implemented as a protected shared object, only one task may access the data at any particular moment (mutual exclusion). All other tasks must be delayed by the "wait" operation until the currently active task finishes its critical section. The worst-case execution time of a complex task in a node is therefore a *global* issue because it depends directly on the progress of the other tasks within the node, or within the environment of the node.

4.2.2   Node

A *node* is a self-contained computer with its own hardware (processor, memory, communication interface, interface to the controlled object) and software (application programs, operating system), which performs a set of well-defined functions within the distributed computer system. *A node is the most important abstraction in a distributed real-time system because it binds software resources and hardware resources into a single operational unit with observable behavior in the temporal domain and in the value domain.* A node that operates correctly accepts input messages and produces the intended and timely output messages via the communication network interface (CNI) introduced in Chapter 2. From the point of view of the network, the function and timing of the node is characterized by the messages it sends to, and receives from, the communication channels.

Structure of a Node: The node hardware consists of a host computer, a communication network interface (CNI), and a communication controller as depicted in Figure 2.2. The host computer comprises the CPU, the memory and the real-time clock that is synchronized with the real-time clocks of all other nodes within the cluster. The host computer shares the CNI with the communication controller. The node software, residing in the memory of the host, can be divided into two data structures: the *initialization state (i-state)* and the *history state (h-state)*. The *i-state* is a static data structure that comprises the reentrant program code and the initialization data of the node, and can be stored in Read-Only Memory (ROM). The *h-state* is the dynamic data structure of the node that changes its contents as the computation progresses, and must be stored in read/write memory (RAM). In an embedded real-time system, it is important to distinguish between the data structures that can be stored in ROM and those that must be allocated to RAM, because the VLSI implementation of a ROM memory cell requires considerably less silicon die area than that of a RAM memory cell. Furthermore, storage of a data element in a ROM cell is more robust with respect to disturbances caused by transient faults than is the storage of a data element in a RAM cell.

In many applications, a node of a distributed computer system is the *smallest replaceable unit* (SRU) that can be replaced in case of a fault. It is therefore important that the interfaces of a node be precisely specified, both in the temporal domain and in the value domain, so that any malfunction of the node can be diagnosed promptly.

The execution of the concurrently executing tasks within a node is controlled by the node operating system. If a node supports an event-triggered communication system, then the control of the communication system, i.e., the decisions as to when a message must be sent, is determined by the host software. If a node supports a time-triggered communication system, then the communication system acts autonomously. The data structure that specifies when a message must be sent is stored in the memory of the communication controller.

4.2.3   Fault-Tolerant Unit (FTU)

A *fault-tolerant unit (FTU)* is an abstraction that is introduced for implementing fault tolerance by active replication. An FTU consists of a set of replicated nodes that are intended to produce *replica determinate* result messages, i.e., the same results at approximately the same points in time. The issue of replica determinism is discussed in detail in Section 5.6.

In case one of the nodes of the FTU produces an erroneous result, a judgment mechanism which is provided detects the erroneous result, and ensures that only correct results are delivered to the client of the FTU. For example, a *voter* that takes three independently computed results as inputs and delivers as output a result that is the majority (two) of the input messages, can detect and mask one error in the value domain. From the logical and temporal point of view, an FTU acts as a single node.

4.2.4   Computational Cluster

A computational cluster comprises a set of FTUs that cooperate to perform the intended fault-tolerant service for the cluster environment. The cluster environment consists of the controlled object, the operator, and other computational clusters. The interfaces between a cluster and its environment are formed by the *gateway nodes* of the cluster. Computational clusters can be interconnected by the gateway nodes in the form of a mesh network. The model does not require a hierarchical relationship among the clusters, although a hierarchy of clusters can be introduced, if desired. A uniform representation of the information within a cluster simplifies the application software within the nodes.

4.3   INTERFACES

The most important activity in the design of a large real-time system architecture is the layout and the placement of the interfaces, since *architecture design* is primarily *interface design.* An interface is a common boundary between two subsystems. A correctly designed interface provides understandable abstractions, to the interfacing partners, which capture the essential properties of the interfacing subsystems and hide the irrelevant details. An interface between two subsystems of a real-time system can be characterized by:

(i)   The *control properties*, i.e., the properties of the control signals crossing the interface, e.g., which task must be activated if a particular event happens.

(ii)   The *temporal properties*, i.e., the temporal constraints that must be satisfied by the control signals and by the data that cross the interface.

(iii) The *functional intent*, i.e., the specification of the intended functions of the interfacing partner.

(iv)   The *data properties*, i.e., the structure and semantics of the data elements crossing the interface.

Example: The *functional intent* of a node in a plant automation system is to determine whether the exhaust fumes in a smokestack meet the environmental standards. If the environmental standards change (perhaps because a new law has been passed), the parameters in the node, i.e., the concrete function implemented by the node, must be changed. The functional intent of the node, however, remains unchanged. The *functional intent* is thus at a higher level of abstraction than a *function.*

In many cases, the interfacing partners use differing syntactic structures and incompatible coding schemes to represent the information that must cross the interface. In such situations an *intelligent* interface component must be placed between the interfacing partners to transform the differing representations of the information. An intelligent interface component is sometimes called a *resource controller* (Figure 4.1). A resource controller has two interfaces to the two interacting subsystems. The resource controller transforms the information from the representation used in one subsystem to that used in the other subsystem. In a computer network, a gateway acts like a resource controller.

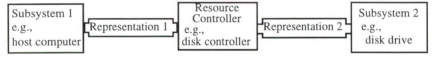

Figure 4.1: Resource controller transforming information.

Example: Consider the interface between a host computer (subsystem one) and a storage subsystem, such as a disk (subsystem two). The disk controller acts as a resource controller with two interfaces. At interface one, the disk controller accepts/delivers data from the host in a standard format via direct memory access (DMA). At interface two, the disk controller controls the specific electro-mechanical devices within the given disk system, generates and checks the parity of the data, and executes the input/output commands at precise moments in time.

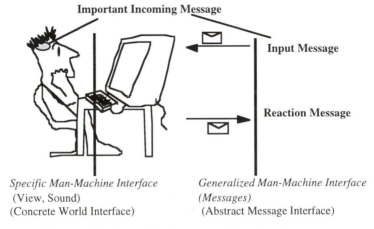

Figure 4.2: Generalized man-machine interface versus specific man-machine interface.

4.3.1 World and Message Interfaces

Example: Let us look at another important example of an interface, the man-machine interface (MMI), in order to learn to distinguish between a *concrete world interface* and an *abstract message interface*. In a distributed computer system, we can assume that the man-machine subsystem is an encapsulated dedicated subsystem with two interfaces: one, the *specific man-machine interface (SMMI* –concrete world interface), between the machine and the human operator, the other, the *generalized man-machine interface (GMMI*–abstract message interface), the interface between the man-machine subsystem and the rest of the distributed computer system (Figure 4.2). From the point of view of the conceptual modeling of an architecture, we are only interested in the temporal properties of the messages at the GMMI. An important message is sent to the GMMI of the man-machine subsystem, and is somehow relayed to the operator's mind (across the SMMI in Figure 4.2). A response message from the operator (via the SMMI) is expected within a given time interval at the GMMI. All intricate issues concerning the representation of the information contained in the important message at the SMMI are irrelevant from the point of view of conceptual modeling of the temporal interaction patterns between the operator and the cluster. The encapsulated man-machine subsystem can thus be seen as a resource controller transforming the information that is exchanged between two different subsystems. If the purpose of our model were the study of human factors governing the specific man-machine interaction, then the form and attributes of the information representation at the SMMI (e.g., shape and placement of symbols, color, and sound) would be relevant, and could not be disregarded.

Table 4.1 compares the characteristics of world- and message interfaces:

Characteristic	Concrete World Interface	Abstract Message Interface
Information Representation	unique, determined by the given device	uniform within the whole cluster
Coupling	tight, determined by the specific I/O protocol of the connected device	weaker, determined by the message communication protocol
Coding	analog or digital, unique	digital, uniform codes
Time-base	dense	possibly sparse
Interconnection Pattern	one-to-one	one-to-many
Freedom in Design	determined by the format and timing of the physical I/O devices	determined by the uniform standards of the architecture

Table 4.1: Concrete world interface versus abstract message interface.

It is important to verify that subsystems do not interact via *hidden* interfaces. Uncontrolled interactions among subsystems via such hidden interfaces can invalidate the arguments which are the basis for reasoning about the correctness of a composition. An example of a hidden interface is given in Section 5.5.1.

The information representation within a computational cluster should be uniform at the message interfaces within a cluster. This may require that a resource controller be placed between the external world interface of a cluster and the internal message interface (Figure 4.3). The resource controller hides the concrete world (physical) interface of the real-world devices from the standardized message formats within the computational cluster.

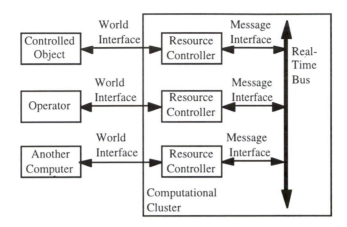

Figure 4.3: World and message interface in a distributed system.

Standardized Message Interfaces

To improve the compatibility between systems designed by different manufacturers, and to enhance the interoperability of I/O devices, some international standard organizations have attempted to standardize message interfaces. Two such standardization efforts are the MAP Manufacturing Message Specification and the SAE J 1587 Message Specification.

MAP Manufacturing Message Specification (MAP MMS): The MAP MMS [Rod89, p.83] is an example of a standardized message interface for shop floor equipment in a manufacturing environment. In the MMS, standard virtual manufacturing devices, such as a virtual drill, are specified, and a set of messages that are required to control these devices and to collect the shop floor information produced by these devices are defined. Any real device that conforms to this standard can be controlled by standard MMS messages. The manufacturer of a real device must implement a resource controller that transforms the standard MMS messages to the format required by the interfacing hardware.

SAE J 1587 Message Specification: The Society of Automotive Engineers (SAE) has standardized the message formats for heavy duty vehicle applications in the J 1587 Standard [SAE94]. This standard defines message names and parameter names for many data elements that occur in the application domain of heavy vehicles. Besides data formats, the range of the variables and the update frequencies are also covered by the standard.

4.3.2 Temporal Obligation of Clients and Servers

Let us now analyze the temporal performance of an interaction across an interface by making use of the client-server model [Kop96]. In the client-server model, a request (a message) from a client to a server causes a response from the server at a later time. This response could be a state change of the server and/or the transmission of a response message to the client. Three temporal parameters characterize such a client-server interaction:

(i)   The maximum response time, RESP, that is expected by the client, and stated in the specification,

(ii)   The worst-case execution time, WCET, of the server that is determined by the implementation of the server, and

(iii) The minimum time, MINT, between two successive requests by the client.

It is important to note that the WCET is in the sphere of control of the server, and that the minimum time between two successive requests, MINT, is in the sphere of control of the client. In a hard real-time environment, the implementation must guarantee that the condition

$$WCET < RESP$$

holds, under the assumption that the client respects its obligation to keep a minimum temporal distance MINT between two successive requests.

If the condition *WCET<<RESP* holds, then, in the given execution environment the performance of the server is orders of magnitude faster than required by the particular application under worst-case conditions, i.e., the hardware is "over dimensioned"; in such a case performance concerns are not an issue. However, this situation is exceptional in embedded systems because of the cost pressure in a market economy. If WCET is in the same order of magnitude as RESP, then careful analysis of the temporal properties of the server object is required. It must be ensured that the server will always meet the temporal requirements, provided the client observes its obligation to issue requests only at a rate less than *1/MINT*.

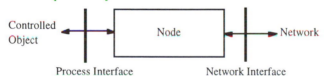

Figure 4.4: Interfaces of a node.

Typically, a node of a distributed computer system has two interfaces (Figure 4.4). It provides services to the network across the network interface, and to the controlled object across the process interface. If the service activation at these interfaces is not in the sphere of control of the node, timely operation of the node is only possible if the clients fulfill their obligations concerning frequency of service activations. The failure of a client to meet its obligation, e.g., by the generation of too many interrupts at the process interface, can result in the consequent failure of the node.

4.4   TEMPORAL CONTROL VERSUS LOGICAL CONTROL

4.4.1   The Rolling Mill Example Revisited

Let us reconsider the rolling mill example of Figure 1.9 of Chapter 1, and specify a condition between measured variables that must be monitored by the alarm monitoring node. Assume that pressures p_1, p_2, and p_3, between the rolls of the three drives are measured by the three controller nodes and is sent to the man-machine interface (MMI) node for checking the following alarm condition:

$$\textbf{when } ((p_1 < p_2) \wedge (p_2 < p_3))$$

$$\textbf{then } \textit{everything ok}$$

$$\textbf{else } \textit{raise pressure alarm};$$

At a first glance, this looks like a reasonable specification. Whenever the pressure between the rolls does not satisfy the specified condition, a pressure alarm must be raised.

During the implementation of this specification, four different S-tasks in four different nodes must be designed. The following questions concerning the activation of these tasks arise:

(i)   What is the maximum tolerable time difference between the occurrence of the alarm condition in the controlled object and the triggering of the alarm at the MMI? Because the communication among the nodes takes a finite amount of time, some time difference is unavoidable!

(ii)   What are the maximum tolerable time differences between the three pressure measurements in the different controller nodes? If these time differences are not properly controlled, false alarms will be generated or important alarms will be missed.

(iii)   When do we have to activate the pressure measurement tasks at the drive controller nodes?

(iv)   When do we have to activate the alarm monitoring task at the alarm monitoring node (the MMI node in Figure 1.9)?

Because these questions are not answered by the given specification, it is evident that this specification lacks precise information concerning the requirements in the time domain. The temporal dimension is buried in the ill-specified semantics of the **when** statement. The **when** statement is intended to serve two purposes: it is required to specify

(i)   The point in time when the alarm condition must be raised, and

(ii)   The conditions in the value domain that must be monitored.

It thus intermingles two separate issues, the behavior in the value domain and the behavior in the time domain. A clean distinction between these two issues requires a careful definition of the concepts of logical and temporal control.

Logical control is concerned with the control flow *within* a task that is determined by the given program structure and the particular input data, in order to achieve the desired data transformation. In the above example, the evaluation of the branch condition and the consequent selection of one of the two alternatives is an example of logical control.

Temporal control is concerned with determining the points in time when a task must be activated, or when a task must be blocked, because some conditions *outside* the task are not satisfied at a particular moment. In the above example, the decision regarding the instant at which the alarm monitoring task is activated is an issue for temporal control.

The only temporal control issue in an S-task is the determination of the moment when this S-task must be activated. Once it has been activated, it will run till its completion within its WCET.

A C-task blends issues of logical control with issues of temporal control. An explicit synchronization statement, such as a "wait" on a semaphore variable, can delay the program execution until a temporal condition outside the task under consideration is satisfied. As mentioned before, it is impossible to calculate the WCET of a C-task without analyzing the temporal properties of the complete system of interacting tasks.

Synchronous real-time languages, such as LUSTRE [Hal92], ESTEREL [Ber85], and SL [Bou96] distinguish cleanly between logical control and temporal control. Their computational model assumes that a task, once activated by an external event that can be the tick of a clock (temporal control), finishes its computation immediately, i.e., that program outputs are synchronous with the inputs. This model presupposes that the WCET is smaller than the minimum time interval between external events.

4.4.2   Event-Triggered versus Time-Triggered

In the following subsection the concepts of event-triggered and time-triggered activation that were introduced in Section 2.2, are refined and extended beyond the communication system. A temporal control signal for the activation of a task in a node can arise from one of the following two sources:

(i)   The control signal is derived from a significant state change, an event, in the environment or within the computer system. Examples of such significant state changes are the depressing of a push button by an operator, the activation of a limit switch, the arrival of a new message at a node, or the completion of a task within a node. We call a control signal that is derived from a significant state change an *event trigger*. A system where all the control signals are derived from event triggers is called an *event-triggered (ET) system*.

(ii) The control signal is derived from the progression of real-time. Whenever the real-time clock within a node reaches a preset value specified in a scheduling table, a temporal control signal is generated. We call such a control signal that is derived from the progression of time a *time trigger*. A system where all the control signals are derived from time triggers is called a *time-triggered (TT) system*.

Example: The design of a computer system controlling a set of elevators in a high-rise building can be event-triggered or time-triggered. In an event-triggered implementation, every press of the lift-call button causes an interrupt in the computer system, and activates a task that reschedules the lifts to service the request. In a time-triggered implementation, every press of the lift-call button sets a local memory element in the lift-call button. The memory elements of all the lift-call buttons are periodically sampled with a sampling period of, say, 500 msec and then reset by the computer system. After a complete sampling cycle, the lift scheduler is activated to calculate a new schedule to service all requests. If a user becomes impatient if the lift does not arrive and presses the lift-call button again, the different implementations will handle the redundant call-button pushes differently. The event-triggered implementation will relay additional interrupts to the computer system, while the time-triggered implementation will not recognize the redundant call-button signals as long as the memory elements are set.

There are many real-time systems that use time triggers as well as event triggers. However, most real-time system architectures tend to favor either on one or the other: control signals are either predominantly event triggers or predominantly time triggers. The main advantage of ET systems is their flexibility. The main advantage of TT systems is their predictability.

4.4.3   Interrupts

In an ET system, the significant external event triggers are often relayed to the computer system by means of the interrupt mechanism. An *interrupt* is an asynchronous hardware-supported request for a specific task activation caused by an event *external* (i.e., outside the node) to the currently active computation. This definition of an interrupt does not include an exception, i.e., a synchronous break in the control flow caused by a condition *within* the task.

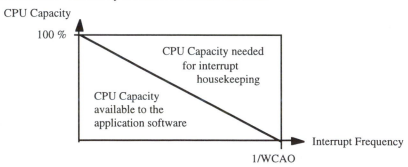

Figure 4.5: Worst case CPU capacity needed for interrupt housekeeping.

Overhead of an Interrupt: Whenever the interrupt mechanism is enabled, and an interrupt occurs, the execution of the current task is preempted, and a context switch to the interrupt handler is enforced by the hardware. To reduce the size of the hardware context that must be saved after an interrupt, the interrupt condition, i.e., the voltage level of an external signal line, is only checked at well-defined points during a hardware instruction, or at the end of the hardware instruction. After the termination of the interrupt handler, another context switch is initiated to either continue the preempted task, or to hand control over to an interrupt service task. These context switches require a *worst-case administrative overhead, WCAO*. Every interrupt reduces the CPU capacity that is available to the application by an amount up to the size of the WCAO, as shown in Figure 4.5. The administrative overhead is required even if the interrupt handler decides that the interrupt was erroneous, and no application task needs to be activated.

If the interrupt frequency reaches the value *1/WCAO*, then, no CPU capacity may be left over for the application tasks. It is therefore of paramount importance to limit the frequency of interrupts, particularly if the interrupts could be erroneous. This can be difficult, because the source of the interrupt is outside the *sphere of control, SOC*, of the considered node. Hence, it cannot be known *a priori* whether a pending interrupt is in error, or whether it carries relevant event information that must not be lost.

Characteristic	Interrupt	Trigger Task
Factors affecting latency	interrupt response	sampling period
Source of control	external to node	internal
Scanning Overhead	none	WCET(trigger task)/laxity
Processing Overhead	variable	constant
Preemption	any time	controlled
Memory Element	internal	external
Trigger Condition	simple	complex
Predictability	low	high

Table 4.2: Task activation by interrupt versus trigger task.

4.4.4   Trigger Task

In a TT system, control always remains within the computer system. To recognize significant state changes outside the computer, a TT system must regularly capture the state of the environment by a trigger task (Table 4.2). A *trigger task* is a periodic time-triggered task that evaluates a trigger condition on a set of temporally accurate real-time variables. The result of a trigger task can be a control signal that activates another application task. Since the states, either external or internal, are sampled at the frequency of the trigger task, only those states with a duration greater than the sampling period of the trigger task are guaranteed to be observed. Short-lived states, e.g., the push of a button, must be stored in a memory element outside the computer (e.g., in the interface) for a duration that is longer than the sampling period of the trigger task (see also Section 9.3 on sampling).

Overhead of a Trigger Task: The periodic trigger task generates an administrative overhead in a TT system. The period of the trigger task must be smaller than the laxity (i.e., the difference between deadline and execution time) of an RT transaction that is activated by an event in the environment. If the laxity of the RT transaction is very small (<1msec), then, the overhead associated with a trigger task can become intolerable [Pol95b].

4.5   WORST-CASE EXECUTION TIME

A deadline for completing an RT transaction can only be guaranteed if the worst-case execution times (WCET) of all the application tasks that are part of the transaction are known *a priori*. The WCET of a task is an upper bound for the time between task activation and task termination. It must be valid for all possible input data and execution scenarios of the task, and should be a tight bound.

In addition to the knowledge about the WCET of the application tasks, we must find an upper bound for the delays caused by the administrative services of the operating system, the worst-case administrative overhead (WCAO). The WCAO includes all administrative delays that affect an application task but are not under the direct control of the application task (e.g., those caused by context switches, scheduling, cache reloading because of task preemption by interrupts or blocking, and direct memory access).

This section starts with an analysis of the WCET of a nonpreemptive simple task. We then proceed to investigate the WCET of a preemptive simple task before looking at the WCET of complex tasks and, finally, we discuss the state of the art regarding the timing analysis of real-time programs.

4.5.1   WCET of S-Tasks

The simplest task we can envision is a single sequential task that runs on dedicated hardware without preemption and without requiring any operating system services. The WCET of such a task depends on

(i)   the source code of the task,

(ii)   the properties of the object code generated by the compiler, and

(iii)   the characteristics of the target hardware.

In this section, we investigate the analytical construction of a tight worst-case execution time bound of such a simple task.

Source Code Analysis: The first problem concerns the calculation of the WCET of a program written in a higher-level language, under the assumption that the maximum execution times of the basic language constructs are known. In general, the problem of determining the WCET of an arbitrary sequential program is unsolvable and is equivalent to the halting problem for Turing machines. Consider, for example, the simple statement that controls the entry to a loop:

S: **while** (*exp*)
     do *loop*;

It is not possible to determine *a priori* after how many iterations, if at all, the Boolean expression *exp* will evaluate to the value FALSE, and when statement S will terminate. In order that the determination of the WCET be a tractable problem there are a number of restrictions that must be met by a real-time program, and these are listed by Puschner and Koza [Pus89] as follows:

(i)   Absence of unbounded control statements at the beginning of a loop,

(ii)   Absence of recursive function calls, and

(iii) Absence of dynamic data structures.

The WCET analysis concerns only the temporal properties of a program. The temporal characteristics of a program can be abstracted into a WCET bound for every program statement using the known WCET bound of the basic language constructs. For example, the WCET bound of a conditional statement

$$S: \textbf{if } (exp)$$
$$\textbf{then } S_1$$
$$\textbf{else } S_2;$$

can be abstracted as

$$T(S) = max \, (\, T(exp) + T(S_1), T(exp) + T(S_2) \,)$$

where $T(S)$ is the maximum execution time of statement S, with $T(exp)$, $T(S_1)$, and $T(S_2)$ being the WCET bounds of the respective constructs. Such a formula for reasoning about the timing behavior of a program is called a *timing schema* [Sha89].

The WCET analysis of a program which is written in a high-level language must determine which program path, i.e., which sequence of instructions, will be executed in the worst-case scenario. The longest program path is called the *critical path*. Because the number of program paths normally grows exponentially with the program size, the search for the critical path can become intractable if the search is not properly guided and the search space is not reduced by excluding infeasible paths.

The WCET analysis problem can be transformed into an integral linear-programming problem [Pus93, Li95] to find the maximum execution time of a task, under the constraints dictated by the program structure and by additional semantic information about the problem domain expressed by the programmer. The *program structure constraints* can be derived automatically from the program control flow graph. The *program functionality constraints* that help to tighten the WCET bound must be provided by the programmer, and can be expressed in the form of annotations to the source program that can be processed by a worst-case execution-time analysis tool.

Compiler Analysis: The next problem concerns the determination of the maximum execution time of the basic language constructs of the source language under the assumption that the maximum execution times of the machine language commands are known. For this purpose, the code generation strategy of the compiler must be analyzed, and the timing information that is available at the source code level must be mapped into the object code representation of the program so that an object-code timing analysis tool can make use of this information. Vrchoticky [Vrc94] proposes the construction of a *timing tree* during compilation. This timing tree contains all the information necessary to calculate the WCET of the compiled program, and presents the results of the analysis to the programmer as statement-level annotations of the source program. The effects of register allocation, code optimization, and other decisions made during the compilation process must be considered in the WCET analysis.

Microarchitecture Timing Analysis: The final problem concerns the determination of the worst-case execution time of the commands of the target hardware. If the processor of the target hardware has fixed instruction execution times, then, the duration of the hardware instructions can be found in the hardware documentation and can be retrieved by an elementary table look-up. Such a simple approach does not work if the target hardware is a modern RISC processor with pipelined execution units and instruction/data caches [Lim94]. While these architectural features result in significant performance improvements, they also introduce a high level of unpredictability. Dependencies among instructions can cause pipeline hazards, and cache misses will lead to a significant delay of the instruction execution. To make things worse, these two effects are not independent.

[Hea95] has published a method (Figure 4.6) for the *a priori* analysis of the WCET of code segments that are executed on machines with pipelines and instruction caches.

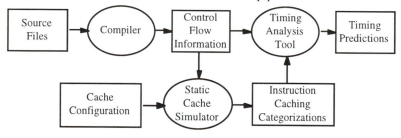

Figure 4.6: Microarchitecture timing analysis.

The relevant control-flow information of the program is assembled during the compilation and used to classify each instruction's caching behavior. This information is then used by the timing analysis tool to arrive at a WCET for each program segment, with due consideration of the integrated effects of caching and pipelining. An experimental validation of this method on a number of test programs executing on a SPARC architecture has shown that the WCET bound calculated by this method is at most 100% above the measured bound. The worst deviation between the measured and the estimated WCET execution times is shown by a sort program that contains many data-dependent loop iterations. If the program does not contain data-dependent loop iterations, as in a typical control algorithm, then, the calculated WCET bound is in closer agreement with the measured value. Similar results have been published by [Lim94] who investigated the WCET of the Intel i960KB processor.

4.5.2 Preemptive S-Tasks

If a simple task (S task) is preempted by another independent task, e.g., a higher priority task that must service a pending interrupt, then, the execution time of the S-task under consideration is extended by three terms:

(i)   The WCET of the interrupting task (task B in Figure 4.7),

(ii) The WCET of the operating system required for context switching, and

(iii) The time required for reloading the instruction cache and the data cache of the processor whenever the context of the processor is switched.

We call the sum of the worst-case delays caused by the context switch (ii), and the cache reloading (iii) the Worst-Case Administrative Overhead (WCAO) of a task preemption. The WCAO is an unproductive administrative overhead that is avoided if task preemption is forbidden.

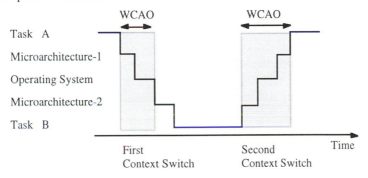

Figure 4.7: Worst-case administrative overhead (WCAO) of a task preemption.

The additional delay caused by the preemption of task A by task B is the WCET of the independent task B and the sum of the two WCAOs for the two context switches (shaded area in Figure 4.7). The times spent in Microarchitecture-1 and Microarchitecture-2 are the delays caused by cache reloading. The Microarchitecture-2 time of the first context switch is part of the WCET of task B, because task B is assumed to start on an empty cache. The second context switch includes the cache reload time of task A, because in a nonpreemptive system, this delay would not occur. In many applications with modern processors, the microarchitecture delays can be the most significant terms determining the cost of a task preemption because the WCET of the interrupting task is normally quite short.

4.5.3 WCET of Complex Tasks

We now turn to the WCET analysis of a preemptive complex task (C-task) that accesses protected shared objects. The WCET of such a task depends not only on performance of the task itself, but also on the behavior of other tasks and the operating system within a node. WCET analysis of a C-task is therefore not a local problem of a single task, but a global problem involving all the interacting tasks within a node.

In addition to the delays caused by the task preemption (which was analyzed in the previous section), an additional delay that originates from the direct interactions caused by the intended task dependencies (mutual exclusion, precedence) must be considered. In the last few years, progress has been made in coping with the direct interactions caused by the intended task dependencies–e.g., access to protected shared objects controlled by the priority ceiling protocol [Sha94]. This topic will be investigated in Section 11.3.3 on the scheduling of dependent tasks.

4.5.4 State of Practice

The previous discussion establishes that the analytic calculation of a tight WCET bound of an S-task which does not make use of operating system services is possible only under restricting assumptions. It requires an annotated source program that contains programmer-supplied application-specific information to ensure that the program terminates, and to achieve a tight WCET bound. Furthermore, the compiler must map this application-specific information into the object code so that a WCET analysis of the object code is possible. At present, the systematic analysis of all the effects that determine the WCET of C-tasks is still in its infancy. The analytic determination of a tight WCET bound between a stimulus to, and a response from, a node with a RISC processor is beyond the present state of the practice.

However, since bounds for the WCET of the tasks are *needed* in almost all hard real-time applications, this important problem is solved by the current practice of combining a number of diverse techniques:

(i)   The measurement of an implementation (tasks, operating system service times) to gather experimental WCET data.

(ii)   Use of a restricted architecture that reduces the interactions among the tasks and facilitates the *a priori* analysis of the control structure. The number of explicit synchronization actions that require context switches and operating system services is minimized.

(iii) The analysis of subproblems (e.g., the maximum execution time analysis of the source program) so that an effective set of test cases biased towards the worst-case execution time can be generated mechanically.

(iv)   The extensive testing of the complete implementation to validate the assumptions and to measure the safety margin between the assumed WCET and the actual measured execution times.

The state of current practice is not satisfactory, because it is difficult to ascertain that the *assumed* WCET is a guaranteed upper bound of the *actual* WCET. Further work is needed in all areas of timing analysis to come to tight analytical bounds of the WCET.

4.6   THE HISTORY STATE (H-STATE)

In the Section 4.2.2, the concept of the h-state was introduced as "the dynamic data structure of the node that undergoes change as the computation progresses". In this section, this important concept of the h-state is analyzed in further detail.

4.6.1   The Pocket Calculator Example

Let us introduce the example of a pocket calculator to investigate the concept of the h-state. An operand, i.e., a number of keyboard digits, must be entered into the calculator before the selected operator, e.g., a key for the trigonometric function *sine*, can be pressed to initiate the computation of the selected function. As soon as the computation terminates, the result is shown on the calculator display. If we consider the process of computation to be an atomic operation, and observe the system immediately before or after the execution of this atomic operation, then, the h-state of this simple calculator device is empty at the selected points of observation.

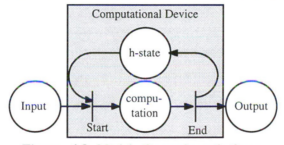

Figure 4.8: Model of a pocket calculator.

Let us now observe the device (shaded box in Figure 4.8) during the interval between the *start* of the computation and the *end* of the computation. If the device is equipped with the appropriate sensors, a number of intermediate results that are stored in the local memory of the pocket calculator can be observed during the series expansion of the *sine* function. If the computation is halted at a point between *start* and *end*, the contents of the program counter and all memory cells that hold the intermediate results form the h-state at this chosen moment. At the end of the computation, the contents of these intermediate memory cells are no longer relevant, and the h-state becomes empty again.

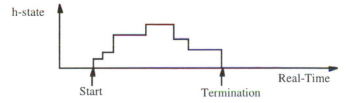

Figure 4.9: Expansion and contraction of the h-state during a computation.

The h-state at any point of interruption can be defined as the contents of the program counter and of all data structures that must be loaded into a "virgin" hardware device to resume the operation at the point of interruption. Figure 4.9 depicts a typical expansion and contraction of the h-state during a computation.

Let us now analyze the h-state of a pocket calculator used to sum up a set of numbers. When entering a new number, the sum of the previously entered numbers must be stored in the device. If we interrupt the work after having added a subset of numbers and continue the addition with a new calculator, we first have to input the intermediate result of the previously added numbers. At the user level, the h-state consists of the intermediate result of the previous additions. At the end of the operation, we receive the final result and clear the calculator. The h-state is empty again.

From this simple example we can conclude that the size of the h-state depends on the level of abstraction, and the associated point in time chosen for the observation of the system. If the granularity of observations is increased, and if the observation points are selected immediately before or after an atomic operation at the chosen level of abstraction, then, the size of the h-state can be reduced. A small h-state at the reintegration point simplifies the reintegration of a failed component.

4.6.2 Ground State

We define the *ground state* of a node in a distributed system at a given level of abstraction as a state where no task is active and where all communication channels are flushed, i.e., there are no messages in transit [Ahu90]. Consider a node that contains a number of concurrently executing S-tasks that exchange messages with each other and with the environment of the node. Let us choose a level of abstraction that considers the execution of an S-task as an *atomic action*. If the execution of the tasks is asynchronous, then, the situation depicted in the upper section of Figure 4.10, can arise; at every point in real time, there is at least one active task, thus implying that there is no point in real time when the ground state of the node can be defined.

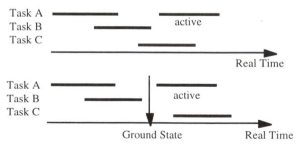

Figure 4.10: Task executions: without (above), and with (below) ground state.

In the lower part of Figure 4.10, there is a point in time where no task is active and all the channels are empty, i.e., where the system is in the *ground state*. If a node is in the ground state, then the h-state of the node is contained in the visible data structures and the program counter. The reintegration of a node after a failure is simplified if a node periodically visits a ground state that can be used as a reintegration point.

POINTS TO REMEMBER

- A model that introduces a set of well-defined concepts and their interrelationships is called a *conceptual model.*

- The probability that the assumptions made in the model building process hold in reality is called the *assumption coverage.* The assumption coverage limits the probability that conclusions derived from a model are valid in the real world.

- Statements about the response time of a computer system can only be made under the assumption that the load offered to the computer system is below a maximum load, called the *peak load* (load hypothesis).

- If the faults that occur in the real world are not covered by the *fault-hypothesis*, then, even a perfectly designed fault-tolerant computer system will fail.

- Different representations of the same value only matter at *an interface* between two different subsystems.

- If there is no synchronization point within a task, we call it a *simple task (S-task)*, i.e., whenever an S-task is started, it can continue until its termination point is reached.

- A task is called a *complex task (C-Task)* if it contains a blocking synchronization statement (e.g., a semaphore operation "wait") within the task body.

- A node is the most important abstraction in a distributed real-time system because it binds software resources and hardware resources into a single operational unit with observable behavior in the temporal domain and in the value domain.

- An interface is a common boundary between two subsystems. It provides understandable abstractions to the interfacing partners. These abstraction capture the essential properties of the interfacing subsystems and hide the irrelevant details.

- The information representation within a computational cluster should be uniform at the message interfaces within a cluster.

- If the service activation at an interface is not in the sphere of control of the node, i.e., it is in the sphere of control of the client outside the node, then, a timely service of the node is only possible if the client fulfills its obligations concerning the frequency of service activations.

- *Logical control* is concerned with the control flow *within* a task that is determined by the given program structure and the particular input data to achieve the desired data transformation.

- *Temporal control* is concerned with the determination of the points in time when a task must be activated or when a task must be blocked, because some conditions *outside* the task are not satisfied at a particular moment.

- A system where all control signals are derived from event triggers is called an *event-triggered (ET) system.*

- A system where all control signals are derived from time triggers is called a *time-triggered (TT) system.*

- If the interrupt frequency reaches the value *1/WCOA* then no CPU capacity may be left for the application tasks. It is therefore of paramount importance to limit the frequency of interrupts, particularly if they can be erroneous.

- A *trigger task* is a periodic time-triggered task that evaluates a trigger condition on a set of temporally accurate real-time variables.

- The WCET of an S-task depends on the source code of the task, the properties of the object code generated by the compiler, and the characteristics of the target hardware.

- The WCET of a C-task depends not only on performance of the task itself, but also on the behavior of other tasks and the operating system within a node.

- The h-state at any point of interruption can be defined as the contents of the program counter and of all data structures that must be loaded into a "virgin" hardware device to continue the operation at the point of interruption.

- The *ground state* of a node in a distributed system at a given level of abstraction is a state where no task is active and where all communication channels are flushed, i.e., there are no messages in transit.

BIBLIOGRAPHIC NOTES

The following two books, dealing with topics outside the field of computing, contain a wealth of information on modeling and design: "Design Methods" by Jones [Jon78] and "Systems Architecting" by Rechtin [Rec91]. Powell has investigated the important problem of assumption coverage [Pow95]. The question as to whether hard real-time systems should be event-triggered or time-triggered has been a topic of intense debate over the past ten years [Lam84], [Lel90], [Agn91], [Xu90], [Loc92], [Kop93b], and [Tis95]. The WCET of programs has been investigated by [Kli86] in the context of the EUCLID project. Puschner [Pus89] tried to improve the execution bounds by using programmer-supplied information and continued the work in the context of his thesis [Pus93], where he transformed the WCET problem into a linear programming problem. A similar approach has been followed independently by [Li95]. The problem of investigating the effects of the microarchitecture (caching, pipelining) is a topic of extensive research by a number of people [Vrc94], [Li95], [Hea95].

REVIEW QUESTIONS AND PROBLEMS

4.1   What is *assumption coverage?* How can you determine a quantitative value for the assumption coverage? What do we mean by *load hypothesis* and *fault hypothesis?*

4.2   List the properties that must be part of an architectural model of a real-time system and the properties that can be disregarded in such a model?

4.3   Describe the structure of a *node?* Why is it important to distinguish between the *i-state* and the *h-state* of a node in an embedded system?

4.4   Describe the elements of an *interface.* What is the difference between *functional intent* and *function?* What are the characteristics of *world interfaces* and *message interfaces?* Give examples of standardized message interfaces.

4.5   In a real-time application the information is represented in many different syntactic forms, e.g., as a 4-20 mA signal on a wire, in the form of an icon on a computer screen or in the from of a particular bit pattern within the computer. How can we arrive at a uniform information representation within a cluster?

4.6   What are the temporal obligations of clients and servers at a client-server interface in a real-time system?

4.7   What is the difference between *temporal control* and *logical control?*

4.8   Assume that the pressures p_1 and p_2 between the first two pairs of rolls in Figure 1.9 are measured by the two controller nodes and sent to the man-machine interface (MMI) node for verifying the following alarm condition:

$$\textbf{when } \left(p_1 < p_2 \right)$$
$$\textbf{then } everything\ ok$$
$$\textbf{else } raise\ pressure\ alarm;$$

The rolling mill is characterized by the following parameters: maximum pressure between the rolls of a stand=1000 kp cm^{-2} [kp is kilopond], absolute pressure measurement error in the value domain=5 kp cm^{-2}, maximum rate of change of the pressure=200 kp cm^{-2} sec^{-1}. It is required that the error due to the imprecision of the points in time when the pressures are measured at the different rolls should be of the same order of magnitude as the measurement error in the value domain, i.e., 0.5% of the full range. The pressures must be *continuously* monitored, and the first alarm must be raised by the alarm monitor within 200 msec (at the latest) after a process has possibly left the normal operating range. A second alarm must be raised within 200 msec after the process has definitely entered the alarm zone.

(a) Assume an event-triggered architecture where each node contains a local real-time clock, but where no global time is available. The minimum time d_{min} for the transport of a single message by the communication system is 1 msec. Derive the temporal control signals for the three tasks.

(b) Assume a time-triggered architecture where the clocks are synchronized with a precision of 10 μsec. The time-triggered communication system is characterized by a TDMA round of 10 msec. The time for the transport of a single message by the communication system is 1 msec. Derive the temporal control signals for the three time-triggered tasks.

(c) Compare the solutions of 4.8.(a) and 4.8.(b) with respect to the generated computational load and the load on the communication system. How sensitive are the solutions if the parameters, e.g. the jitter of the communication system or the length of the TDMA round, are changed?

4.9 Calculate the overhead of a trigger task if the WCET of the trigger task is 200 μsec and the laxity of an RT transaction is 10 msec. Discuss the advantages and disadvantages of an application-task activation by an interrupt versus that by a trigger task.

4.10 What are the effects of pipelining and caching on the WCET? Assume that an interrupt must be serviced during the execution of a task. How is the WCET of the task affected?

4.11 Assume that there is a large difference between the experimentally observed WCET and the analytically calculated WCET. What can you learn from this difference? How can you reduce the difference? What are the problems with the experimental measurement of the WCET?

4.12 Assume that an instruction cache has a cycle time of 20 nsec. If an instruction resides in the cache the access time is one cycle, while the penalty of a cache miss is 8 extra cycles. The cache size is 256 instructions. What is the worst-case variability of the microarchitecture delay caused by cache reloading?

Assume that a processor has an instruction "Perform the operation without using the cache" and that the time for the two context switches and the interrupt service by task B (Figure 4.7) is 50 μsec if the caches are bypassed. What would be the effect of such a microarchitecture on the WCET?

Chapter 5

Real-Time Entities and Images

OVERVIEW

In this chapter, the notions of a real-time (RT) entity and a real-time (RT) image are refined. The new concept of a real-time (RT) object is introduced. An RT object is a container that holds the current version of the RT image of the associated RT entity. The temporal validity of the RT image (and consequently that of the RT object) can be extended by state estimation. This technique uses the knowledge about a past state as well as the regularity of the RT entity to predict the state of the RT entity at a future point of use. A real-time clock is associated with every RT object. The object's clock provides periodic temporal control signals for the execution of the object procedures, particularly for state estimation procedures. The granularity of the RT object's clock is determined by the dynamics of the RT entity in the controlled object that is associated with the RT object.

The issue of temporal accuracy, which is a relation between an RT entity and its associated RT image, is investigated in detail. The notions of parametric and phase-sensitive observations of RT entities are introduced, and the concept of permanence of an observation is discussed. The duration of the action delay, which is the time interval between the transmission of a message and the point in time when this message becomes *permanent*, is estimated.

The final section of this chapter is devoted to an elaboration of the problem of replica determinism. A set of replicated RT objects is *replica determinate* if the objects visit the same state at approximately the same time. Replica determinism is needed for the implementation of fault tolerance by active redundancy. The main causes for replica non-determinism are the digitalization error in the process inputs, the drift of the local clocks, non-deterministic language constructs, and the use of preemptive dynamic scheduling.

This chapter is divided into two major parts. In the first part (Section 5.1 to Section 5.3), the set of structural units introduced in Chapter 1, including the *real-time (RT) entity*, the *observation*, the *RT image*, and the *RT object* is refined. The second part (Section 5.4 to Section 5.6) analyzes the relationships between these structural units:

(i)   *Temporal accuracy* is a relation between an RT entity and its associated RT images and RT objects.

(ii)   *Permanence* and *Idempotency* are relations among a set of messages arriving at the same RT object.

(iii) *Replica determinism* is a relation among a set of replicated RT objects.

5.1   REAL-TIME ENTITIES

A *real-time (RT) entity* is a state variable of relevance for the given purpose, and is located either in the environment or in the computer system. Examples of RT entities are the flow of a liquid in a pipe, the setpoint of a control loop that is selected by the operator, and the intended position of a control valve. An RT entity has static attributes that do not change during the lifetime of the RT entity, and has dynamic attributes that change with time. Examples of static attributes are the name, the type, the value domain, and the maximum rate of change. The value set at a particular point in time is the most important dynamic attribute. Another example of a dynamic attribute is the rate of change at a chosen point in time.

5.1.1   Sphere of Control

Every RT entity is in the sphere of control (SOC) of a subsystem that has the authority to set the value of the RT entity [Dav79]. Outside its SOC, the RT entity can only be observed, but not modified. At the chosen level of abstraction, syntactic transformations of the representation of the value of an RT entity that do not change its semantic content are disregarded.

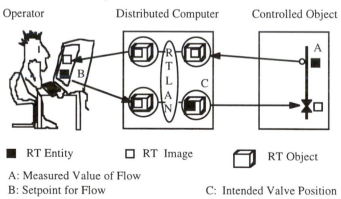

Figure 5.1: RT entities, RT images, and RT objects.

Figure 5.1 shows another view of Figure 1.8, and represents the small control system that controls the flow of a liquid in a pipe according to a setpoint selected by the operator. In this example, there are three RT entities: the flow in the pipe is in the SOC of the controlled object, the setpoint for the flow is in the SOC of the operator, and the intended position of the control valve is in the SOC of the distributed system.

5.1.2   Discrete and Continuous Real-Time Entities

An RT entity can have a discrete value set (*discrete RT entity*) or a continuous value set (*continuous RT entity*). The value set of a discrete RT entity is defined and remains constant between a left event (*L_event*) and a right event (*R_event*)–see Figure 5.2.

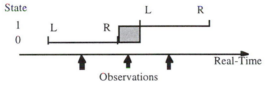

Figure 5.2: Discrete RT entity.

In the interval between an R_event and the next L_event, the set of values of a discrete RT entity is undefined. In contrast, the set of values of a continuous RT entity is always defined.

Example: Consider a garage door. Between the defined states specified by "door closed" and "door open", there are many intermediate states that can be classified neither as "door open" nor as "door closed".

5.2   OBSERVATIONS

The information about the state of an RT entity at a particular point in time is captured by the notion of an *observation*. An observation is an *atomic data structure*

$$Observation = <Name, t_{obs}, Value>$$

consisting of the name of the RT entity, the point in real time when the observation was made (t_{obs}), and the observed value of the RT entity. A continuous RT entity can be observed at any point in time while a discrete RT entity can only be observed between a L_event and an R_event (see Figure 5.2).

We assume that a local microprocessor (a *field bus node* as introduced in Section 7.3.3) is associated with a sensor to perform the observation. An observation should be transported in a single message from this field bus node to the rest of the system because the message concept provides for the atomicity of the observation message.

5.2.1 Untimed Observation

In a distributed system without global time, a timestamp can only be interpreted within the scope of the node that created the timestamp. The timestamp of a sender that made an observation is thus meaningless at the receiver of the observation message. Instead, the time of arrival of an untimed observation message at the receiver node is often taken to be the time of observation t_{obs}. This timestamp is imprecise because of the delay and the jitter between the actual point of observation and the arrival time of the message at its destination. In a system with a significant jitter of the execution time of the communication protocol (in comparison to the median execution time) and without access to a global time-base it is not possible to determine the time of observation of an RT entity precisely. This imprecision of time measurement can reduce the quality of the state estimation, as will be shown in Section 5.4.

5.2.2 Indirect Observation

In some situations, it is not possible to observe the value of an RT entity directly. Consider, for example, the measurement of the temperature within a slab of steel. This internal temperature (the value of the RT entity) must be measured indirectly.

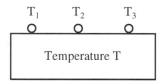

Figure 5.3: Indirect measurement of an RT entity.

The three temperature sensors T_1, T_2, and T_3 measure the change of temperature of the surface (Figure 5.3) over a period of time. The value of the temperature T within the slab and the point in time of its relevance must be inferred from these surface measurements by using a mathematical model of heat transfer.

5.2.3 State Observation

An observation is a *state observation* if the value of the observation contains the state of the RT entity. The time of the state observation refers to the point in real-time when the RT entity was sampled. Every reading of a state observation is self-contained because it carries an *absolute value*. Many control algorithms require a sequence of equidistant state observations, a service provided by periodic time-triggered readings.

The semantics of state observations matches well with the semantics of the state messages introduced in Chapter 2. A new reading of a state observation replaces the previous readings because clients are normally interested in only the most recent value of a state variable.

5.2.4   Event Observation

An *event* is an occurrence (a state change) that happens at a point in time. Because an observation is also an event, it is not possible to observe an event in the controlled object directly. It is only possible to observe the consequences of the controlled object's event (Figure 5.4), i.e., the subsequent state. An observation is an *event observation* if it contains the *change in value* between the "old" and the "new" states. The time of the event observation denotes the best estimate of the point in time of this event. Normally, this is the time of the L-event of the new state.

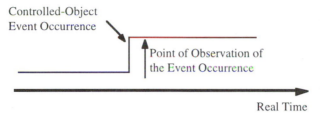

Figure 5.4: Observation of an event.

There are a number of problems with event observations:

(i)   Where do we get the precise time of the event occurrence? If the event observation is event-triggered, then, the time of event occurrence is assumed to be the rising edge of the interrupt signal. Any delayed response to this interrupt signal will cause an error in the timestamp of the event observation. If the event observation is time-triggered, then, the time of the event occurrence can be at any point within the sampling interval.

(ii) Since the value of an event observation contains the *difference* between the old state and the new state (and no absolute state), the loss or duplication of a single event observation causes the loss of state synchronization between the state of the observer and the state of the receiver. From the point of view of reliability, event observations are more fragile than state observations.

(iii) An event observation is only sent if the RT entity changes its value. The latency for the detection of a failure of the observer node cannot be bounded because the receiver assumes that the RT entity has not changed its value if no new message arrives.

On the other hand, event observations are more efficient than state observations in the case where the RT entity does not change frequently.

5.3   REAL-TIME IMAGES AND REAL-TIME OBJECTS

5.3.1   Real-Time Images

A real-time (RT) image is a *current* picture of an RT entity. An RT image is valid at a given point in time if it is an accurate representation of the corresponding RT entity, both in the value and the time domains. The notion of *temporal accuracy* of an RT image will be discussed in detail in the next Section. While an observation records a fact that remains valid forever (a statement about an RT entity that has been observed at a particular point in time), the validity of an RT image is *time-dependent* and thus invalidated by the progression of real-time. RT images can be constructed from up-to-date state observations or from up-to-date event observations. They can also be estimated by a technique called "state estimation" that will be discussed in Section 5.4.3. RT images are stored either inside the computer system or in the environment (e.g., in an actuator).

5.3.2   Real-Time Objects

A real-time (RT) object is analogous to a container within a node of the distributed computer system holding an RT image or an RT entity [Kop90b]. A real-time clock with a specified granularity is associated with every RT object. Whenever this object clock ticks, a temporal control signal is relayed to the object to activate an object procedure [Kim94]. If there is no other way to activate an object procedure than by this periodic clock tick, we call the RT object a *synchronous RT object*.

Distributed RT Objects: In a distributed system, an RT object can be replicated in such a manner that every local site has its own version of the RT object to provide the specified service to the local site. The quality of service of a distributed RT object must conform to some specified consistency constraints.

Example: A good example of a distributed RT object is global time; every node has a local clock object which provides a synchronized time service with a specified precision Π (quality of service attribute of the internal clock synchronization). Whenever a process reads its local clock, it is guaranteed that a process, in another node, that reads its local clock at the same point in real-time will get a time value that differs by at most one tick.

Membership Service: Another example of a distributed RT object is a membership service in a distributed system. A *membership service* generates consistent information about the state (operational or failed) of all nodes of the system at agreed points in time (*membership points*). The length and the jitter of the interval between a membership point and the point in time when the consistent membership information is known at the other nodes, are quality of service parameters of the membership service. A responsive membership service has a small maximum delay between the point in time of a relevant state change of a node (failure or join), and the moment at which all other nodes have been informed of this state change, in a consistent manner.

5.4   TEMPORAL ACCURACY

Temporal accuracy is the relationship between an RT entity and its associated RT image. Because an RT image is stored in an RT object, the temporal accuracy can also be looked upon as a relation between an RT entity and an RT object.

5.4.1 Definition

The temporal accuracy of an RT image is defined by referring to the *recent history* of observations of the related RT entity. A recent history RH_i at time t_i is an ordered set of time points $\{t_i, t_{i-1}, t_{i-2}, \dots t_{i-k}\}$, where the length of the recent history, $d_{acc} = z(t_i) - z(t_{i-k})$, is called the *temporal accuracy interval* or the *temporal accuracy*. ($z(e)$ is the timestamp of event e generated by the reference clock z; see Section 3.1.2). Assume that the RT entity has been observed at every time point of the recent history. An RT image is temporally accurate at the present time t_i if

$$\exists\, t_j \in RH_i\colon Value\,(RT\,image\,at\,t_i) = Value\,(\,RT\,entity\ at\ t_j)$$

The present value of a temporally accurate RT image is a member of the set of values that the RT entity had in its recent history. Because the transmission of an observation message from the observing node to the receiving node takes some amount of time, the RT image lags behind the RT entity (See Figure 5.5).

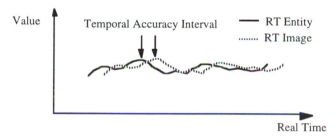

Figure 5.5: Time lag between RT entity and RT image.

Temporal Accuracy Interval: The size of the admissible temporal accuracy interval is determined by the dynamics of the RT entity in the controlled object. The delay between the observation of the RT entity and the use of the RT image causes an error, *error(t)*, of the RT image that can be approximated by the product of the gradient of the value *v* of the RT entity multiplied by the length of the interval between the observation and its use (see also Figure 1.6):

$$error(t) \;=\; \frac{dv(t)}{dt}\,(z(t_{use}) - z(t_{obs}))$$

If a temporally valid RT image is used, the worst-case error,

$$error \;=\; \left(\max_{\forall t}\frac{dv(t)}{dt}\,d_{acc}\right),$$

is given by the product of the maximum gradient and the temporal accuracy d_{acc}. In a balanced design, this worst-case error caused by the temporal delay is in the same order of magnitude as the worst-case measurement error in the value domain, and is typically a fraction of a percentage point of the full range of the measured variable.

If the RT entity changes its value quickly, a short accuracy interval must be maintained. Let us call t_{use} the point in time when the result of a computation using an RT image is applied to the environment. For the result to be accurate, it must be based on a temporally accurate RT image, i.e.,:

$$z(t_{obs}) \le z(t_{use}) \le (z(t_{obs}) + d_{acc})$$

where d_{acc} is the accuracy interval of the RT image. If this important condition is transformed. it follows that:

$$(z(t_{use}) - z(t_{obs})) \le d_{acc}.$$

Example: On September 14, 1993, a Lufthansa Airbus A 320 overran the runway after landing at Warsaw Airport, killing a crew member and a passenger, and injuring 54. The A320 control logic required the airplane to be settled on both main landing gears before the brakes, ground spoilers and thrust reversers can be activated. The airplane did not settle onto its second main landing gear for nine seconds, at which point it was still traveling at 154 knots--20 knots above normal landing speed--with only 1000 m of runway left [Neu95,p.46]. In this example the information "the plane is still in the air and therefore the brakes, ground spoilers and trust reversers cannot be activated" was temporally invalid because of an improper instrumentation logic.

Phase-Aligned Transaction: Consider the case of an RT transaction consisting of the following tightly synchronized tasks: the computational task at the sender (observing node) with a worst-case execution time $WCET_{send}$, the message transmission with a worst-case communication delay $WCCOM$, and the computational task at receiver (actuator node) with a worst-case execution time $WCET_{rec}$ (Figure 5.6). Such a transaction is called a *phase-aligned transaction*.

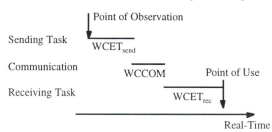

Figure 5.6: Synchronized actions.

In such a transaction, the worst-case difference between the point of observation and the point of use,

$$(t_{use} - t_{obs}) = WCET_{send} + WCCOM + WCET_{rec},$$

is given by the sum of the worst-case execution time of the sending task, the worst-case communication delay, and the worst-case execution time of the receiving task that uses the data in the output of a setpoint to the actuator in the controlled object. If the temporal accuracy d_{acc} that is required by the dynamics of the application is smaller than this sum, the application of a new technique, *state estimation,* is inevitable in solving the temporal accuracy problem. The technique of state estimation is discussed in Section 5.4.3.

RT Image within Computer	Max.Change	Accuracy	d_{acc}
Position of piston within cylinder	6000 rpm	0.1°	3 μsec
Position of accelerator pedal	100%/ sec	1 %	10 msec
Engine load	50 % / sec	1 %	20 msec
Temperature of the oil and the coolant	10 % /minute	1 %	6 seconds

Table 5.1: Temporal accuracy intervals in engine control.

Example: Let us analyze the required temporal accuracy intervals of the RT images that are used in a controller of an automobile engine (Table 5.1) with a maximum rotational speed of 6000 revolutions per minute (rpm).

There is a difference of more than six orders of magnitude in the temporal accuracy intervals of these RT images. It is evident that the d_{acc} of the first data element, namely the position of the piston within the cylinder, requires the use of state estimation.

5.4.2   Classification of Real-Time Images

Parametric RT Image: Assume that an RT image is updated periodically, by a state observation message from the related RT entity, with an update period d_{update}. (Figure 5.7) and that the transaction is phase aligned at the sender. If the temporal accuracy interval d_{acc} satisfies the condition

$$d_{acc} > (d_{update} + WCET_{send} + WCCOM + WCET_{rec}),$$

then, we call the RT image *parametric* or *phase insensitive*.

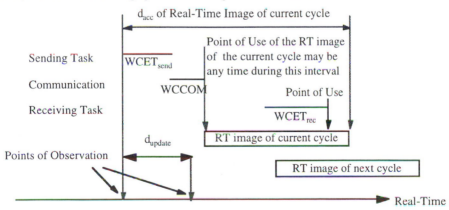

Figure 5.7: Parametric Real-time image

A parametric RT image can be accessed at the receiver at any time without having to consider the phase relationship between the incoming observation message and the point of use of the data

Example: The RT transaction that handles the position of the accelerator pedal (observation and preprocessing at sender, communication to the receiver, processing at the receiver and output to the actuator) takes an amount of time

$$WCET_{send} + WCCOM + WCET_{rec} = 4\ msec.$$

Because the accuracy interval of this observation is 10 msec (Table 5.1), messages sent with periods less than 6 msec will make this RT image parametric.

Phase-Sensitive RT Image: Assume a RT transacation that is phase aligned at the sender. The RT image at the receiver is called *phase sensitive* if

$$d_{acc} \le (d_{update} + WCET_{send} + WCCOM + WCET_{rec})\ \text{and}$$

$$d_{acc} > (WCET_{send} + WCCOM + WCET_{rec})$$

In this case, the phase relationship between the moment at which the RT image is updated, and the moment at which the information is used, must be considered. In the above example, an update period of more than 6 msec, e.g., 8 msec, would make the RT image phase sensitive.

Every phase-sensitive RT image imposes an additional constraint on the scheduling of the real-time task that uses this RT image. The scheduling of a task that accesses phase-sensitive RT images is thus significantly more complicated than the scheduling of tasks using parametric RT images. It is good practice to minimize the number of RT images that are phase-sensitive. This can be done, within the limits imposed by d_{update}, by either increasing the update frequency of the RT image, or by deploying a state-estimation model to extend the temporal accuracy of the RT image. While an increase in the update frequency puts more load on the communication system, the implementation of a state-estimation model puts more load on the processor. A designer is at liberty to find a tradeoff between utilizing communication resources or processing resources.

5.4.3   State   Estimation

State estimation involves the building of a model of an RT entity inside an RT object to compute the probable state of an RT entity at a selected future point in time, and to update the corresponding RT image accordingly. The state estimation model is executed periodically within the RT object that stores the RT image. The control signal for the execution of the model is derived from the tick of the real-time clock that is associated with the RT object (see Section 5.3.2). The most important future point in time where the RT image must be in close agreement with the RT entity is t_{use}, the point in time where the value of the RT image is used to deliver an output to the environment. State estimation is a powerful technique to extend the temporal accuracy interval of an RT image, i.e., to bring the RT image into better agreement with the RT entity.

Example: Assume that the crankshaft in an engine rotates with a rotational speed of 3000 revolutions per minute, i.e., 18 degrees per millisecond. If the time interval between the point of observation, t_{obs}, of the position of the crankshaft and the point of use, t_{use}, of the corresponding RT image is 500 microseconds, we can update the RT image by 9 degrees to arrive at an estimate of the position of the crankshaft at t_{use}. We could improve our estimate if we also consider the angular acceleration or deceleration of the engine during the interval $[t_{obs}, t_{use}]$.

An adequate state estimation model of an RT entity can only be built if the behavior of the RT entity is governed by a known and regular process, i.e., a well-specified physical or chemical process. Most technical processes, such as the above-mentioned control of an engine, fall into this category. However, if the behavior of the RT entity is determined by chance events, then, the technique of state estimation is not applicable.

Input to the State Estimation Model: The most important dynamic input to the state estimation model is the precise length of the time interval $[t_{obs}, t_{use}]$. Because t_{obs} and t_{use} are normally recorded at different nodes of a distributed system, a communication protocol with minimal jitter or a global time-base with a good precision is a prerequisite for state estimation. This prerequisite is an important requirement in the design of a field bus.

If the behavior of an RT entity can be described by a continuous and differentiable function $v(t)$, the first derivative dv/dt is sometimes sufficient in order to obtain a reasonable estimate of the state of the RT entity at the point t_{use} in the neighborhood of the point of observation:

$$v(t_{use}) \approx v(t_{obs}) + (t_{use} - t_{obs}) dv / dt$$

If the precision of such a simple approximation is not adequate, a more elaborate series expansion around t_{obs} can be carried out. In other cases a more detailed mathematical model of the process in the controlled object may be required. The execution of such a mathematical model can demand considerable processing resources.

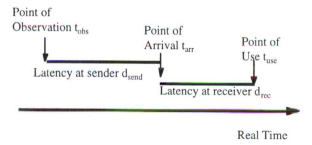

Figure 5.8: Latency at sender and receiver.

5.4.4 Composability Considerations

Assume a time-triggered distributed system where an RT entity is observed by the sensor node, and the observation message is then sent to one or more nodes that interact with the environment. The length of the relevant time interval $[t_{obs}, t_{use}]$ is thus the sum of the delay at the sender, given by the length $[t_{obs}, t_{arr}]$, and the delay at the receiver, given by the length $[t_{arr}, t_{use}]$, (the communication delay is subsumed in the sender delay). In a time-triggered architecture, all these intervals are static and known *a priori* (Figure 5.8).

If the state estimation is performed in the RT object at the receiver, then any modification in the delay at the sender will cause a modification of the time interval that must be compensated by the state estimation of the receiver. The receiver software must be changed if a latency change takes place inside the sender node. To decrease this coupling between the sender and the receiver, the state estimation can be performed in two steps: the sender performs a state estimation for the interval $[t_{obs}, t_{arr}]$ and the receiver performs a state estimation for the interval $[t_{arr}, t_{use}]$. This gives the receiver the illusion that the RT entity has been observed at the point of arrival of the observation message at the receiver. The point of arrival is then the implicit timestamp of the observation, and the receiver is not affected by a schedule change at the sender. Such an approach helps to unify the treatment of sensor data that are collected via a field bus, as well as sensor data that are collected directly by the receiving node.

5.5   PERMANENCE AND IDEMPOTENCY

5.5.1   Permanence

Permanence is a relation between a particular message arriving at a node and the set of all messages that have been sent to this node before this particular message. A particular message becomes *permanent* at a given node at that point in time when the node knows that all the messages that have been sent to it prior to the send time of this message, have arrived (or will never arrive) [Ver94].

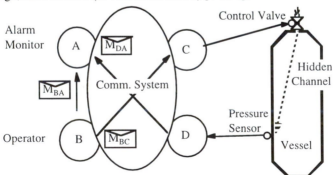

Figure 5.9: Hidden channel in the controlled object.

Example: Consider the example of Figure 5.9, where the pressure in a vessel is monitored by a distributed system. The alarm monitoring node (node A) receives a message M_{DA} from the pressure sensor node (node D) whenever there is a pressure change.

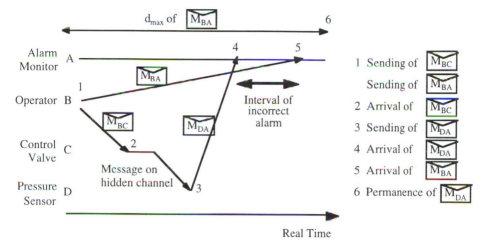

Figure 5.10: Permanence of messages.

If the pressure changes abruptly for no apparent reason, the alarm monitoring node A should raise an alarm. Suppose that the operator node B sends a message M_{BC} to node C to open the control valve in order to release the pressure. At the same time, the operator node B sends a message M_{BA} to node A, to inform node A about the opening of the valve, so that node A will not raise an alarm due to the anticipated drop in pressure.

Assume that the communication system has a minimum protocol execution time d_{min}, and a maximum protocol execution time d_{max}, i.e., a jitter $d_{jit} = d_{max} - d_{min}$. Then the situation depicted in Figure 5.10 could occur. In this figure, the message M_{DA} from the pressure sensor node arrives at the alarm monitoring node A before the arrival of the message M_{BA} from the operator (that informs the alarm monitoring node A of the anticipated drop in pressure). The transmission delay of the *hidden channel* in the controlled object between the opening of the valve and the changing of the pressure sensor is shorter than the maximum protocol execution time. Thus, to avoid raising any false alarms, the alarm monitoring node should delay any action until the alarm message M_{DA} has become *permanent*.

Action Delay: The time interval between the start of transmission of a given message and the point in time when this message becomes permanent at the receiver, is called the *action delay*. The receiver must delay any action on the message until *after* the action delay has passed to avoid an incorrect behavior.

Irrevocable Action: An *irrevocable action* is an action that cannot be undone. An irrevocable action causes a lasting effect in the environment. An example of an irrevocable action is the activation of the firing mechanism on a firearm. It is particularly important that an irrevocable action is triggered only after the action delay has passed.

Example: The pilot of a fighter aircraft is instructed to eject from the airplane (irrevocable action) immediately after a critical alarm is raised. Consider the case where the alarm has been raised by a message that has not become permanent yet (e.g., event *4* in Figure 5.10). In this example, the hidden channel, which was not considered in the design, is the cause for the loss of the aircraft.

5.5.2 Duration of the Action Delay

The duration of the action delay depends on the jitter of the communication system and the temporal awareness of the receiver [Kop89]. Let us assume the position of the omniscient outside observer who can see all significant events.

Systems with a Global Time: In a system with global time, the send time t_{send} of the message, measured by the clock of the sender, can be part of the message, and can be interpreted by the receiver. If the receiver knows that the maximum delay of the communication system is d_{max}, then, the receiver can infer that the message will become permanent at $t_{permanent} = t_{send} + d_{max} + 2g$, where g is the granularity of the global time-base (see Section 3.2.4 to find out where the $2g$ comes from).

Systems without a Global Time: In a system without global time, the receiver does not know when the message has been sent. To be on the safe side, the receiver must wait $d_{max} - d_{min}$ time units after the arrival of the message, even if the message has already been d_{max} units in transit. In the worst case, as seen by the outside observer, the receiver thus has to wait for an amount of time

$$t_{permanent} = t_{send} + 2d_{max} - d_{min} + g_l$$

before the message can be safely acted on (where g_l is the granularity of the local time-base). Since $(d_{max} - d_{min} + g_l)$ is normally much larger than $2g$, where g is the granularity of the global time, a system without a global time-base is *slower* than a system with a global time-base.

5.5.3 Accuracy Interval versus Action Delay

An RT image may only be used if the message that transported the image is permanent, and the image is temporally accurate. In a system without state estimation, both conditions can only be satisfied in the time window $(t_{permanent}, t_{obs}+d_{acc})$. The temporal accuracy d_{acc} depends on the dynamics of the control application while $(t_{permanent}-t_{obs})$ is an implementation-specific duration. If an implementation cannot meet the temporal requirements of the application, then, state estimation may be the only alternative left in order to design a correct real-time system.

5.5.4 Idempotency

Idempotency is the relationship among the members of a set of replicated messages arriving at the same receiver. A set of replicated messages is *idempotent* if the effect of receiving more than one copy of a message is the same as receiving only a single copy. If messages are idempotent, the implementation of fault tolerance by means of replicating messages is simplified. No matter whether the receiver receives one or more of the replicated messages, the result is always the same.

Example: Let us assume that we have a distributed system without synchronized clocks. In such a system, only untimed observations can be exchanged among nodes, and the time of arrival of an observation message is taken as the time of observation. Assume a node observes an RT entity, e.g., a valve, that changes its value between $0°$ and $180°$, and reports this observation to other nodes in the system. The receivers use this information to construct an updated version of the local RT image of the RT entity in their RT objects. A state observation might contain the absolute value "position of valve at $45°$", and will replace the old version of the image. An event message might contain the relative value "valve has moved by $5°$". The contents of this event message are added to the previous contents of the state variable in the RT object to arrive at an updated version of the RT image. While the state message is idempotent, the event message is not. A loss or duplication of the event message results in a permanent error of the RT image.

5.6   REPLICA DETERMINISM

Replica determinism is a desirable relation among replicated RT objects. A set of replicated RT objects is *replica determinate* if all the members of this set have the same *externally visible h-state,* and produce the same output messages at points in time that are at most an interval of d time units apart (as seen by the omniscient outside observer with the reference clock z). A set of nodes is *replica determinate*, if all the nodes in this set contain the same *externally visible h-state* at their ground state, and produce the same output messages at points in time that are at most an interval of d time units apart.

In a fault-tolerant system, the time interval d determines the time it takes to replace a missing message or an erroneous message from a node by a correct message from redundant replicas. This time interval must be derived from the dynamics of the application. If, in a time-triggered system, the objects (nodes) contain the same h-state and produce the same output messages at the same global ticks of their local clocks, then an upper bound for the time interval d is given by the precision of the global time.

Why Do We Need Replica Determinism? Replica determinism is needed to:

(i)   Implement fault-tolerance by active redundancy [Sch90]: If the replicated nodes proceed along significantly different computational trajectories, then, the switchover from the result of one replica to that of the other will upset the controlled object, and may even lead to a serious error. The voter in a fault-tolerant system based on majority voting may reach an erroneous result if the inputs to the voter are not replica determinate (see Figure 5.11).

(ii) Facilitate the system test: A replica determinate system always produces identical results, in the value domain and the time domain, from the same input data presented at exactly the same relative points in time. A non-determinate system may produce different results from identical input data, thus complicating the regression test and the debugging of the system.

5.6.1 Major Decision Point

A *major decision* point is a decision point in an algorithm that provides a choice between a set of significantly different courses of action. If the replicated nodes select different computational trajectories at a major decision point, then, the h-states of the replicas will start to diverge. It then becomes impossible to replace the result of one replicated node by that of another in the case a replicated node crashes in a fault-tolerant system.

Example: Consider an airplane with a three-channel flight-control system and a majority voter. Each channel has its own sensors and computers to minimize the possibility of a common-mode error. Within a specified time interval after the event "start of take-off", the control system must check whether the plane has attained the take-off speed. In case the take-off speed has been attained, the lift-off procedure is initiated, and the engines are further accelerated. In case the take-off speed has not been reached within this specified time interval, the take-off must be aborted, and the engines must be stopped (Figure 5.11). The decision whether or not to take off occurs at a major decision point.

Channel	Decision	Action
Channel 1	Take off	Accelerate Engine
Channel 2	Abort	Stop Engine
Channel 3	Abort	*Accelerate Engine (Fault)*
Majority	*Abort*	*Accelerate Engine*

The faulty channel wins!

Figure 5.11: The need for replica determinism.

Assume that the speed of the plane at the major decision point is *about* the same as the specified limit of the take-off speed. Because of random effects (deviation in the sensor calibration, digitalization error, slightly different points in the time of speed measurement), channels 1 and 2 reach different conclusions: channel 1 decides that the take-off speed has been reached and that the plane should take off. Channel 2 decides that the take-off speed has not been reached and the take-off should be aborted. Both channels take the *correct* decisions, although the decisions are *not replica determinate*. Channel 3 is faulty and decides to abort, and to accelerate the engine. In the majority vote, the faulty channel wins, because the correct channels are not replica determinate.

Not all the decisions within the software are major decisions. A loop iteration that is terminated after a different number of iterations at the two replicas does normally not lead to significantly different computational trajectories. The occurrence of a major decision point is determined by the semantics of an application, and not by syntactic properties of an algorithm. For example, the application-specific decision as to whether a process should continue or be shut down because of some irregularity, is always a major decision point.

5.6.2 Basic Causes of Replica Non-determinism

The basic causes of replica non-determinism are: differing inputs, a difference between the progress of the computation and that of the local clocks in the replicas, differing oscillator drifts caused by the physical variations of the resonators, and algorithmic peculiarities[Pol95a].

Differing Inputs: Whenever a value that is defined over a continuous value domain is mapped onto a discrete value domain, a digitalization error occurs. The physical RT entities in the controlled object, e.g., temperature and pressure, are defined over continuous value domains. The analog-to-digital transformation at the computer interfaces maps these values into discrete domains, causing a potential digitalization error of one bit. The same phenomenon occurs in the temporal domain: external time is dense, while internal time within a computer is discrete. If events that occur on a dense time-base are observed in a different order by two replicas, then, significantly different computational trajectories could develop.

Example: Consider a man-machine interface where two operators work on two replicated operator consoles. Assume that the delivery order of two significant events is different at these two consoles. The two operators could come to different conclusions about the cause-effect relationship between these two events and start to act inconsistently.

Deviations of Computational Progress Relative to Physical Time: In many computers, the CPU is driven by the same resonator as the real-time clock. One would therefore assume that the progress of the local physical time is in synchrony with the progress of the computation. This assumption is not generally valid, since, to correct a randomly occurring transient error, many processors provide hardware-controlled instruction-retry mechanisms that take physical time without resulting in computational progress. If, in two replicas, a different number of instruction retries are executed, the computational progress can diverge from the progress of the local physical time. If different resonators are used for the real-time clock and the CPU, then, a different relationship between local physical time and computational progress in replicated nodes is unavoidable.

The differences in the progress between the physical time and the computational time lead to consequences whenever a program reads the local clock. The two replicas read different clock values at the same point of the computation, and could thus make different decisions.

Oscillator Drift: The control signals for the CPU originate from a physical oscillator, a quartz crystal. Because the mechanical dimensions of any two physical quartz crystals are slightly different, no two physical oscillators have the same drift. These slight differences in the drift of the oscillators of replicated nodes can lead to an non-determinate outcome for those decisions that involve, in one way or another, the local time. A prime example is the local use of time-outs. The same time-out value that is defined abstractly by a time-out value in a replicated program will lead to time-out intervals of slightly differing physical lengths at the replicas. If a significant event, e.g., the expected arrival of an acknowledgment message that is monitored by a local time-out, occurs after the local time-out event in one replica, but before the same time-out event in another replica, then, remarkably different computational trajectories may develop in the two replicas (see also Fig. 5.12).

Preemptive Scheduling: If dynamic preemptive scheduling is used (see Section 11.3), then, the points in the computations where an external event (interrupt) is recognized may differ at the different replicas. Consequently, the interrupting processes see different states at the two replicas at the point of interruption. They may reach different results at the next major decision point.

Nondeterministic Language Features: The use of a programming language with nondeterministic language constructs, such as the SELECT statement in an ADA program, can lead to the loss of replica determinism. Since the programming language does not define which alternative is to be taken at a decision point, it is left up to the implementation to decide the course of action to be taken. Two replicas may take different decisions.

Race Conditions: The wait statement in a C-task (see Section 4.2.1) can also give rise to non-determinism, because of the uncertain outcome regarding the process which will win the race for a semaphore. Communication protocols that resolve a media-access conflict by reference to a random number generator, such as the Ethernet protocol, also suffer from replica non-determinism. The same argument applies to communication protocols that resolve the access conflict by relying on the outcome of non-determinate temporal decisions, such as ARINC 629 or CAN (see Section 7.5).

Consistent Comparison Problem: If different software versions are deployed in the replicas with the goal of tolerating design faults in the software, then, the *consistent comparison problem* [Bri89] must be addressed. If an application uses inexact algorithms, such as those for floating-point arithmetic, then, a different order of the operations can lead to a difference in the results. If, however, all floating-point operations are performed in the same order in the replicated software versions, then, the diversity of the versions is significantly reduced.

5.6.3   Building a Replica Determinate System

The construction of replica determinate nodes requires careful design of the software system so that all the causes of replica non-determinism that have been discussed in the previous Section are properly addressed.

Sparse Time-base: A sparse global time-base makes it possible to assign a significant event to the same global clock tick at all the replicas without the execution of an agreement protocol (see Section 3.3). Any reference to the local real-time clock of a node (without the execution of an agreement protocol) can lead to replica non-determinism. This means that no local time-outs may be used in any part of the software, including the application software, the operating system and the communication software.

Example: Consider a situation where a message is transmitted from a sending FTU (consisting of two nodes, node A and B) to a receiving FTU, where the receiving FTU responds with an acknowledgment message. This acknowledgment message is monitored at both nodes, node A and B, of the sending FTU by a local time-out at each node, as shown in Figure 5.12.

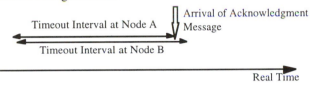

Figure 5.12: The effect of local time-outs at an FTU.

Because the frequency of any two oscillators is slightly different, node A may encounter its time-out before the arrival of the acknowledgment message, while node B may see the acknowledgment message before its time-out. This will result in differing computational trajectories at the two replicas.

Agreement on Input: Whenever a redundant observation of an RT entity outside the sphere of control (SOC) of a fault-tolerant computer system is performed, an agreement protocol must be executed among all replicas of the observing FTU to reach a common view of the exact digital value of an observation, and the exact point in time on the sparse time-base when the observation was taken. The agreement on the time is the basis for establishing a consistent system-wide order of all observation events (see also Section 9.2).

Static Control Structure: The implementation of a data-independent static control structure that can be validated independently of the data inputs is a safe choice for the implementation of replica determinate software. All inputs from the control object are periodically sampled by a trigger task, and no interrupt from the controlled object is allowed to occur. If the application timing requirements are so stringent (less than 1 msec response time) that a process interrupt causing a dynamic task preemption cannot be avoided, then all the possibilities of task preemption must be statically analyzed in the application context to ensure that replica determinism is maintained. Nonpreemptive dynamic scheduling avoids the problems of unpredictable task interference.

Deterministic Algorithms: In the algorithmic section of an implementation, all constructs that could lead to non-determinate results must be avoided. Special attention must be paid to any dynamic synchronization construct that relies on the unpredictable resolution of a race condition, such as a semaphore "wait" operation. If software diversity is implemented, exact arithmetic must be performed to avoid the consistent comparison problem.

5.6.4   Leader-Follower Protocol

The above mentioned guidelines for the implementation of replica determinate systems are so stringent that some researchers have looked for other methods to maintain replica determinism. One such method that was investigated in the DELTA 4 project [Pow91] is the *leader-follower* protocol. In this protocol one replica, the leader, takes all the major decisions, and forces the followers, who must be slightly behind the leader, to take the same decisions. The leader-follower protocol requires a fair amount of inter-replica coordination that entails additional bandwidth requirements. Furthermore, it has a window of vulnerability between the point in time when a leader takes a major decision, and the point in time when the followers learns about this decision.

If at all possible, inter-replica coordination should be avoided for the following reasons:

(i)   It compromises the independence of the replicas, and thus weakens the boundaries of the error-containment regions.

(ii)   It requires additional time, and has thus a negative impact on the temporal accuracy of the observation.

(iii)   It requires additional communication bandwidth between the nodes.

POINTS TO REMEMBER

- An observation of an RT entity is an atomic triple *<Name, t_{obs}, Value>* consisting of the name of the RT entity, the point in real time when the observation was made (t_{obs}), and the observed value of the RT entity. A continuous RT entity can be observed at any point in time, whereas a discrete RT entity can only be observed between the L_event and the R_event

- An observation is a *state observation* if the value of the observation contains the absolute state of the RT entity. The time of the state observation refers to the point in real time when the RT entity was sampled.

- An observation is an *event observation* if it contains information abaout the *change of value* between the "old state" and the "new state". The time of the event observation denotes the best estimate of the point in time of this event.

- A real-time (RT) image is a *current* picture of an RT entity. An RT image is valid at a given point in time if it is an accurate representation of the corresponding RT entity, both in the value domain and time domain.

- A real-time (RT) object is analogous to a container within a node of the distributed computer system holding an RT image or an RT entity. A real-time clock with a specified granularity is associated with every RT object.

- The present value of a temporally accurate RT image is a member of the set of values that the RT entity had in its recent history.

- The delay between the observation of the RT entity and the use of the RT image can cause, in the worst-case, a maximum error *error(t)* of the RT image that can be approximated by the product of the maximum gradient of the value *v* of the RT entity multiplied by the length of the accuracy interval.

- Every phase-sensitive RT image imposes an additional constraint on the scheduling of the real-time task that uses this RT image.

- *State estimation* involves the building of a model of an RT entity inside an RT object to compute the probable state of an RT entity at a selected future point in time, and to update the corresponding RT image accordingly.

- If the behavior of an RT entity can be described by a continuous and differentiable variable *v(t)*, the first derivative *dv/dt* is sometimes sufficient to get a reasonable estimate of the state of the RT entity at the point t_{use} in the neighborhood of the point of observation.

- To decrease the coupling between sender and receiver the state estimation can be performed in two steps: the sender performs a state estimation for the interval $[t_{obs},t_{arr}]$, and the receiver performs a state estimation for the interval $[t_{arr},t_{use}]$.

- A particular message becomes *permanent* at a given node at that point in time when the node knows that all the messages that were sent to it, prior to the send time of this message, have arrived (or will never arrive).

- The time interval between the start of transmission of a message and the point in time when this message becomes permanent at the receiver, is called the *action delay*. To avoid incorrect behavior, the receiver must delay any action on the message until *after* the action delay has passed.

- An RT image may only be used if the message that transported the image has become permanent, and the image is temporally accurate. In a system without state estimation, both conditions can be satisfied only in the time window $[t_{permanent}, t_{obs}+d_{acc}]$.

- No matter whether the receiver receives one or more out of set of replicated *idempotent* messages, the result will always be the same.

- A set of nodes is *replica determinate*, if all nodes of this set contain the same externally visible h-state at their ground state and produce the same output messages at points in time that are at most an interval of *d* time units apart.

- The basic causes of replica non-determinism are: differing inputs, a difference between the computational progress and the progress of the physical time in the replicas, differing oscillator drifts caused by the physical variations of the resonators, and algorithmic peculiarities.

- If at all possible, inter-replica coordination should be avoided because it compromises the independence of the replicas, and requires additional time and additional communication bandwidth.

BIBLIOGRAPHIC NOTES

The concept of *temporal accuracy* of a real-time object has been introduced in the real-time object model presented in [Kop89]. Kim has extended this model and analyzed the temporal properties of real-time applications using this model [Kim94]. The problem of replica determinism has been extensively studied in the context of the MARS project [Kop89] and the DELTA 4 project [Pow91]. An excellent treatment of this problem is contained in [Pol95a].

REVIEW QUESTIONS AND PROBLEMS

5.1   Give examples of RT entities that are needed to control an automotive engine. Specify the static and dynamic attributes of these RT entities, and discuss the temporal accuracy of the RT images associated with these RT entities.

5.2   What is the difference between a *state observation* and an *event observation*? Discuss their advantages and disadvantages.

5.3   What are the problems with event observations?

5.4   Give an informal and a precise definition of the concept of *temporal accuracy*. What is the *recent history*?

5.5   What is the difference between a *parametric* RT image and a *phase-sensitive* RT image? How can we create parametric RT images?

5.6   What are the inputs to a state estimation model? Discuss state estimation in a system with and without a global time-base.

5.7   Discuss the interrelationship between state estimation and composability.

5.8   What is a *hidden* channel? Define the notion of *permanence.*

5.9   Calculate the action delay in a distributed system with the following parameters: $d_{max} = 20$ msec, $d_{min} = 1$ msec,

(a) no global time available, and the granularity of the local time is 10 μsec,

(b) granularity of the global time 20 μsec.

5.10   What is the relationship between *action delay* and *temporal accuracy*?

5.11   Define the notion of *replica determinism*. Give an example of a major decision point that can be found in almost any application.

5.12   Give an example that shows that a local time-out can lead to replica non-determinism. Why can dynamic preemptive scheduling cause replica non-determinism?

5.13   What mechanisms may lead to replica non-determinism?

5.14   How can we build a replica-determinate system?

5.15   Why should explicit inter-replica coordination be avoided?

Chapter 6

Fault Tolerance

OVERVIEW

Fault tolerance is important in safety-critical real-time systems because otherwise a single component failure may lead to a catastrophic system failure. This chapter starts with an explanation of the concepts of failure, error, and fault. It then proceeds to investigate the topic of error detection. Error detection requires knowledge about the intended behavior of a system. This knowledge can stem either from *a priori* established regularity constraints and known properties of the correct behavior of a computation, or from the comparison of the results that have been computed by two redundant channels. Different error detection techniques for the detection of timing errors and value errors are discussed.

In a distributed system, a node is an appropriate unit of failure. A node implements a self-contained function so that the established architectural principle "form follows function" can be maintained even in a failure scenario. The node implementation must map all internal node failures into simple external failure modes. The problem of node failure detection and membership in event-triggered and time-triggered architectures is elaborated. A set of replica-determinate nodes is grouped together to form a fault-tolerant unit (FTU) that masks a failure of one of its nodes. Two different types of fault-tolerant units are introduced, and the problem of the reintegration of a node into an operating cluster is taken up. The key issue is to find a reintegration point where the h-state of the node is minimal. Different techniques for h-state minimization are discussed.

The final section is devoted to a discussion about the utility of design diversity in the implementation of safety-critical systems. An industrial example of a fail-safe system that uses design diversity to increase the safety of the application is described.

6.1 FAILURES, ERRORS, AND FAULTS

In this section, a short overview of the basic concepts that have been established in the field of fault-tolerant computing are given. The Working Group 10.4 on Fault-Tolerant Computing of the International Federation of Information Processing (IFIP) has published a five-language book [Lap92] where these concepts are explained in more detail. The core of this document details the three terms: fault, error and failure (Figure 6.1).

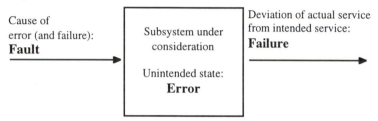

Faults and Errors are States,   Failures are Events

Figure 6.1: Faults, errors, and failures.

Computer systems are installed to provide dependable service to system users. A user can be a human user or another (higher level) system. Whenever the service of a system, as seen by the user of the system, deviates from the agreed specification of the system, the system is said to have *failed*.

6.1.1 Failures

A *failure* is an event that denotes a deviation between the actual service and the specified or intended service, occurring at a particular point in real time.

The following classifications of failures can be made:

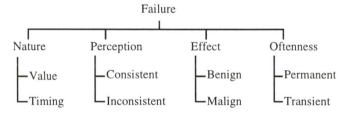

Figure 6.2: Classification of failures [Lap92].

Failure Nature: According to the nature of the failure, we distinguish between *value failures* and *timing failures*. A value failure means that an incorrect value is presented at the system-user interface. A timing failure means that a value is presented outside the specified interval of real-time. Timing failures only exist if the system specification contains information about the expected temporal behavior of the system.

Failure Perception: In a system with more than one user, we can distinguish between *consistent failures* and *inconsistent failures*. In a consistent failure scenario, all users see the same (possibly wrong) result. If a subsystem either produces correct results or no results at all, i.e., it is quiet in case it cannot deliver the correct service, we call this special consistent failure a *fail-silent failure*. If a system stops operating after the first fail-silent failure, the failure is called a *crash failure*. A crash failure is the simplest failure mode a system can exhibit. A crash failure that is made known to the rest of the system is a *fail-stop failure* [Sch83]. In an *inconsistent failure situation*, different users may perceive different false results. A malicious subsystem can disturb correctly operating subsystems by showing contradictory faces of a failure to each of the correctly operating subsystems. This is why inconsistent failures are sometimes called *two-faced failures*, *malicious failures*, or *Byzantine failures* (see Figure 3.10). Theoretical results [Pea80] have been published concerning the minimum number of components needed to tolerate a specific type of failure. To tolerate k failures of a certain type, we need:

(i) $k+1$ components if the failures are *fail-silent*,

(ii) $2k+1$ components if the failures are *fail-consistent*, and

(iii) $3k+1$ components if the failures are *malicious*.

It is therefore wise to provide enough error-detection logic inside a component to guarantee fail-silent behavior at the system level. This approach is followed in many commercial fault-tolerant systems, e.g., in Stratus [Web91].

Failure Effect: Depending on the effect a failure has on its environment, we distinguish between *benign* and *malign* failures. A benign failure can only cause failure costs that are of the same order of magnitude as the loss of the normal utility of the system, whereas a malign failure can cause failure costs that are orders of magnitude higher than the normal utility of a system, e.g., a malign failure can cause a catastrophe such as the crash of an airplane. We call applications where malign failures can occur, *safety-critical* applications. The characteristics of the application the computer system is controlling determine whether a failure is benign or malign.

Failure Oftenness: Within a given time interval, a failure can occur only once or a repeated number of times. If it occurs only once, it is called a *single* failure. A special case of a single failure is a *permanent* one, i.e., a failure after which the system ceases to provide a service until an explicit repair action has eliminated the cause of the failure. If a system continues to operate after the failure, we call the failure a *transient failure*. A frequently occurring transient failure is sometimes called an *intermittent* failure.

Permanent Failures: The failure rate (permanent failures) of a typical VLSI device changes over time as depicted in Figure 6.3. After an initial period of a few hundred hours of early failures, the failure rate of a high quality chip stabilizes in a range between $10-100$ FITS (1 FIT means *1* failure per 10^9 hours, i.e., an MTTF of about *115 000* years). The failure rate of a chip is not very sensitive to the number of transistors on the chip; rather it depends on physical parameters, such as the number of pins and the packaging. The period of high early failure rate can be reduced by burn-in, i.e., the operation of the chip at elevated temperatures. Cabling constitutes a significant source of failure in distributed systems. Even a high quality connection is expected to fail with a failure rate of *0.1 – 1* FIT/per wiring.

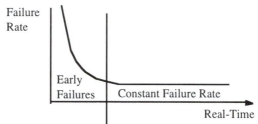

Figure 6.3: Typical failure rate over time.

Transient Failures: At the chip level, transient failures are much more likely to occur than permanent failures. The transient chip failure rate can be *10 - 100 000* times higher than the permanent chip failure rate, depending on the physical environment of the installation. The most common causes of transient failures are electromagnetic interference (EMI), disturbances in the power supply, and high-energy particles (e.g., α-particles).

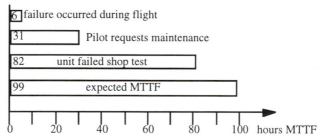

Figure 6.4: Transient failures in the F16 fire-control radar.

Example: The system-level transient failure rate in the fire-control radar of 150 F-16 fighter planes was observed during a six months period from June - December 1984 [Geb88]. The results of this observation are depicted in Figure 6.4. According to the data, pilots noticed malfunctions about every 6 flight hours, and requested maintenance about every 31 hours. However, only every third malfunction that led to a maintenance request could be reproduced in the maintenance shop. Altogether, less than 10% of the transient failures that were observed during operation (uppermost bar in Figure 6.4) could be reproduced in the shop's controlled test environment. Such a failure pattern can be observed in many of today's real-time systems.

6.1.2   Errors

Most computer system failures can be traced to an incorrect *internal state* of the computer, e.g., a wrong data element in the memory or a register. We call such an incorrect internal state an *error*. An error is thus an unintended state. If the error exists only for a short interval of time, and disappears without an explicit repair action, it is called a *transient* error. If the error persists permanently until an explicit repair action removes it, we call it a *permanent* error. In a fault-tolerant architecture, every error must be confined to a particular error containment region to avoid the propagation of the error throughout the system. The boundaries of the error containment regions must be protected by error detection interfaces.

Transient Errors: Transient errors form the predominant error class in many computer systems. There are a number of applications, particularly in the field of small real-time systems, where the system behavior can be characterized by periodic duty cycles (e.g., control loops). A cycle starts with the sampling of the input data, continues with the computation using a given control algorithm, and terminates after the output of the results to an actuator in the environment. If, at the beginning of each cycle, all internal data structures are initialized, i.e., the h-state is empty, then, the result of the previous cycle cannot affect the current cycle. In such a system, a transient data error that occurs in one of the duty cycles cannot have a direct impact on any of the subsequent duty cycles. In many control applications, a failure of a single control cycle has no serious effect on the environment (there is only a finite amount of energy to move the actuator in a single cycle). Such systems are, by design, tolerant to transient errors.

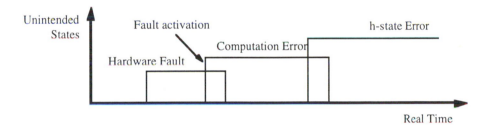

Figure 6.5: A transient hardware fault leading to a permanent h-state error.

Permanent Errors: In a large database, there is a large number of h-state data elements that are stored in the database. An error in any one of these data elements is very likely to be permanent–i.e., the error remains in the system until an explicit repair action is invoked to repair the state. If a database transaction is disturbed by a transient fault, and the resulting error is not immediately detected, then, a wrong value will be written into the database (Figure 6.5), and remains as a permanent error in the database. This mechanism shows how a transient fault can lead to a permanent error. Since the data elements of the database act as inputs to future database transactions, an erroneous data element causes the subsequent transaction to produce an incorrect output as well, and to store another erroneous data element into the database [Kop82]. We call such a steady increase in the number of errors in the database *database erosion*. Utmost care must be taken to detect any transaction failure before the results of this transaction are permanently stored in the database.

In a system without an h-state, such an "h-state erosion" is not possible. Every new computation starts with an empty (and therefore correct) h-state. This is why "stateless" systems are much more robust regarding transient faults than systems with h-state.

6.1.3 Faults

The cause of an error, and thus the indirect cause of a failure, is called a *fault*. Faults can be classified as follows:

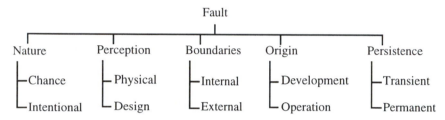

Figure 6.6: Classification of faults.

Fault Nature: A fault that has its origin in a chance event, e.g., the random break of a wire, is called a *chance fault*. If the fault can be traced to an intentional action by someone, e.g., the introduction of a Trojan horse by a programmer in order to break the security of a system, then, the fault is called an *intentional fault*.

Fault Perception: A fault can be caused either by some physical phenomenon, e.g., the breakdown of a computer chip, or by an error in the design, such as a programmer's mistake or an error in the system specification. In the field of fault-tolerant computing, a number of techniques have been developed that are effective in handling *random physical faults*, such as the provision of active hardware redundancy by replication of the hardware components [Lee90].

No comparable progress has been achieved to handle design faults: subtle design faults in large systems are difficult to avoid, and it is nearly hopeless to diagnose them by testing, within a reasonable period of time [Lit95]. The most promising approach tries to limit the complexity of a design by providing a clear structure and understandable behavior, e.g., by partitioning a large system into a set of composable autonomous subsystems that are interconnected by small, stable, and testable interfaces.

Fault Boundaries: It is very useful to distinguish whether a fault is caused by a deficiency within the system or by some external disturbance, e.g., a lightning stroke causing spikes in the power supply line. Care must be taken to avoid that a single external fault causes correlated errors in disjoint error-containment regions.

Fault Origin: Faults that have their origin in the incorrect development of the system must be distinguished from faults that are related to system operation, e.g., a wrong input by the operator.

Fault Persistence: Finally, it is important to distinguish between faults that occur only once and disappear by themselves (e.g., the mentioned lightning stroke), and faults that remain in a system until they are removed by an explicit repair action. In a system with h-state, even a transient fault can cause a permanent error (Figure 6.5).

A more detailed description of the different types of failures and faults can be found in the above mentioned book by Lapric [Lap92].

Fault Tolerance Aspects	Systematic Mechanism	Application-Specific Mechanism
Main error detection mechanisms	Replication of computations (temporal, spatial) Error detecting codes	Application-specific reasonableness checks
Application know-how	Not required	Required
Replica determinism	Required	Not required
Distinction between correct and erroneous	Exact	Gray zone
Overhead for fault tolerance	Replication of hardware units (or time) More complex architecture	Increase of application software complexity Error processing at application level
Cost	Additional hardware	Additional application software
Main Advantage	Transparent application-independent mechanism	Little extra hardware overhead
Main Disadvantage	Significant additional hardware costs	Significant increase in the application software complexity

Table 6.1: Systematic versus application-specific fault tolerance [Pol96b].

6.1.4   Systematic versus Application-Specific Fault Tolerance

No complex system will survive for an extended period of time without fault tolerance [Avi78, Avi96]. The designer of a safety-critical system has two options to implement the necessary fault tolerance:

(i) At the architecture level, transparent to the application code. We call this type of fault tolerance *systematic fault tolerance*. The architecture must provide replica determinism so that fault tolerance can be achieved by the temporal or spatial replication of computations to detect and mask the faults specified in the fault hypothesis.

(ii)   At the application level, within the application code. We call this type of fault tolerance *application-specific fault tolerance*. Application-specific fault tolerance intertwines the normal processing functions with the error-detection and fault-tolerance functions at the application level.

In systematic fault tolerance, the fault-tolerance mechanisms can be implemented and tested independently of the application code. Systematic fault tolerance avoids an increase in the application software complexity at the expense of additional hardware costs (Table 6.1). Technological developments, such as the significant decrease of hardware costs, favor the implementation of systematic fault tolerance.

In practice, there is always some compromise between systematic and application-specific mechanisms. For example, even if systematic fault tolerance is implemented, the error-detection coverage can be increased by using application-specific reasonableness checks.

6.2   ERROR DETECTION

An *error* is a discrepancy between the *intended correct state* and the *current state* of a system. It is the goal of the fault-tolerant computing effort to detect and mask or repair errors before they show up as failures at the system-user service interface. Error detection requires that, along with the information about the current state, knowledge about the intended state of a system is available. This knowledge about the intended correct state can arise from two different sources: either from *a priori* knowledge about the intended properties of states and behaviors of the computation, or from the comparison of the results of two redundant computational channels. In either case, error detection is based on redundancy.

6.2.1   Error Detection Based on *A priori* Knowledge

The more is known *a priori* about the properties of correct states and the temporal patterns of correct behavior of a computation, the more effective are the error detection techniques that are based on *a priori* knowledge. If a subsystem is to be flexible in the temporal domain and in the value domain, i.e., there are no known regularity assumptions that restrict the system behavior beforehand, then, error detection based on *a priori* knowledge is hardly possible. There is a fundamental conflict between the requirement for flexibility and the requirement to provide a good *error-detection coverage,* i.e., to detect errors with a high probability.

Syntactic Knowledge about the Code Space: Consider the scenario where each symbol of an alphabet of 128 symbols is encoded using a single byte. Because only seven bits ($2^7=128$) are needed to encode a symbol, the eighth bit can be used as a parity bit to be able to distinguish a *valid codeword* from an *invalid codeword* of the 256 codewords in the code space. This *a priori* knowledge about the syntactic structure of valid codewords can be used for error detection. The code space is subdivided into two partitions, one partition encompassing syntactically correct values, with the other containing detectably erroneous codewords. One plus the maximum number of bit errors that can be detected in a codeword is called the *Hamming Distance* of the code. Examples of the use of error-detecting codes are: parity bits and error-detecting codes in memory, CRC polynomials in data transmission, and check digits at the man-machine interface. Such codes are very effective in detecting the corruption of a value stored in memory or the transmission of a value over a computer network.

Assertions and Acceptance Tests: Application-specific knowledge about the restricted ranges and the known interrelationships of the values of RT entities can be used to detect additional errors that are undetectable by syntactic methods. Sometimes these application-specific error-detection mechanisms are called *plausibility checks.* For example, the constraints that are imposed on the speed of change of the RT entities by the inertia of a technical process form a basis for very effective plausibility checks. Plausibility checks can be expressed in the form of assertions within a program, or can be used to check for the plausibility of a result at the end of a program by applying an *acceptance test* [Ran75]. Assertions and acceptance tests are effective to detect errors that occur in the value domain during the processing of information.

Activation Patterns of Computations: Knowledge about the regularity in the activation pattern of a computation can be used to detect errors in the temporal domain. If it is known that a result message must arrive every second, then, the non-arrival of such a message can be detected within one second. If it is known that the result message must arrive *exactly at every full* second, then, the error-detection latency is given by the precision of the clock synchronization. Systems that tolerate jitter do have a longer error-detection latency than systems without jitter. This extra time gained from an earlier error detection can be significant in a safety-critical real-time system [Lin96].

Type of Redundancy	Implementation	Type of Detected Errors
Time redundancy	The same software is executed on the same hardware during two different time intervals	Errors caused by transient physical faults in the hardware with a duration of less than one execution time slot
Hardware redundancy	The same software executes on two independent hardware channels	Errors caused by transient and permanent physical hardware faults
Diverse software on the same hardware	Different software versions are executed on the same hardware during two different time intervals	Errors caused by independent software faults and transient physical faults in the hardware with a duration of less than one execution time slot
Diverse software on diverse hardware	Two different versions of the software are executed on two independent hardware channels	Errors caused by independent software faults and by transient and permanent physical hardware faults

Table 6.2: Error-detection by redundant computations.

Worst-Case Execution Time of Tasks: In a real-time system, the worst-case execution time (WCET) of the hard real-time tasks must be known *a priori* for the calculation of the schedules. This WCET information can also be used by the operating system at run time to detect task errors in the temporal domain. Similarly, *a priori* information about the minimum execution time of a task can be used for error detection as.

6.2.2 Error Detection Based on Redundant Computations

There are many different possible combinations of hardware, software, and time redundancy that can be used to detect different types of errors by performing the computations twice [Lap95]. Of course, both computations must be replica determinate; otherwise, many more discrepancies are detected between the redundant channels those actually caused by faults. The problems in implementing replica determinate fault-tolerant software have already been discussed in Section 5.6.

Table 6.2 presents a number of combinations of redundant computations, and explains the types of errors that can be detected.

6.2.3 Duplicate Execution of Tasks

Fault-injection experiments [Kar95] have shown that the duplicate execution of application tasks at different times is an effective technique for the detection of transient hardware errors (see also Section 12.4). This technique can be applied to increase the error-detection coverage, even if it cannot be guaranteed that *all* task instances can be completed twice in the available time interval.

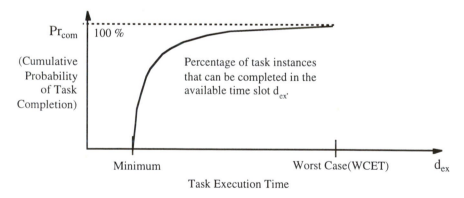

Figure 6.7: Execution time distribution of tasks.

Figure 6.7 depicts a typical cumulative distribution $Pr_{com}(d_{ex})$ of the percentages of task instances that can be completed in a time slot of given length d_{ex}. $Pr_{com}(d_{ex})$ can be experimentally measured on the target architecture. No task instance can complete if the allocated execution time slot is less than the minimum execution time, while all task instances can complete if this time slot exceeds the WCET (worst-case execution time of a task–see Section 4.5). To guarantee the termination of the task, the execution time slot must have at least the length of WCET.

Due to the shape of the distribution in Figure 6.7, the probability that two instances of the task can complete within the WCET is fairly high. Assume that the error-detection coverage of duplicate executions for the detection of a transient fault is E_{double}. Given the shape of the distribution of Figure 6.7, the probability that two instances of the task can complete in a given slot time, d_{slot}, can be calculated by statistical techniques. Let us call this probability $Pr_{double}(d_{ex})$. The probability that a transient error is detected by double execution with a given execution slot d_{ex} is then given by:

$$E_{double} \, Pr_{double}(d_{ex})$$

It is thus possible to select an execution time slot with a length between *WCET* and 2·*WCET*, such that the intended error-detection coverage is realized. If the time slot is 2·*WCET,* then the error-detection coverage corresponds to the term E_{double} which, according to the experiments described in Section 12.4, is better than 99.9 %.

6.3   A NODE AS A UNIT OF FAILURE

In a distributed real-time system, a node is considered to be an appropriate unit of failure. A node is a self-contained unit that provides a function across a small well-defined external interface. A failure of a node thus corresponds to the failure of the function of the node in such a way that the architectural principle "form follows function" can be maintained.

The implementation of fault tolerance in a distributed real-time system must proceed on two levels. At the architectural level, the behavior of a complete node is considered. At this level, a node should display simple failure modes. In the optimal case, a node exhibits only fail-silent failures, i.e., a node is either operational or not. In this case, the fault-tolerance mechanisms at the architecture level must perform two major tasks:

(i)   Membership service: to detect a node failure, and to report this node failure consistently to all operating nodes of the cluster within a short latency.

(ii)   Redundancy management: to mask the node failure by active redundancy, and to reintegrate repaired nodes into the cluster as soon as they become available again.

At the node level, the node implementation must ensure that the failure assumption that has been made at the architectural level holds with a high probability.

6.3.1 Minimum Service Level of a Node

Large systems have many operational states between fully operational and non-operational. Consider, for example, a man-machine interface equipped with two displays. In a normal situation, both displays operate to give the operator a good overview of what is happening in the process. If one display fails, the operator can still control the process with the other display, though in a degraded mode. If both displays fail, the industrial plant must be shut down because it cannot be observed anymore. The state where only one display is working is considered to be the *minimum level of service*. Every level of service at and above this minimum level is considered *operational*. Every level of service below this minimum level is considered a *failure*.

The system specification must contain precise statements about the minimum level of service of all major system functions. As long as a node provides this minimum level of service it is classified as operational. If it can no longer provide this minimum level of service, it is considered non-operational. The membership service classifies nodes according to this binary scheme: operational versus non-operational. A further differentiation of the service capability of a node at the architectural level adds to the complexity of the architecture level without corresponding rewards.

6.3.2   Error Detection within a Node

A node must detect all internal failures within a short latency, and must map these failures to a single external failure mode, a *fail-silent* node failure. The error detection in the node must be concerned with value failures and timing failures. The techniques for error detection were detailed in the previous section.

Error detection in the temporal domain is of major importance in a distributed real-time system that uses a shared communication channel. A faulty node that monopolizes the common channel by sending high-priority messages at erroneous points in time disrupts the communication between all properly operating nodes, and can thus cause a complete system failure. A node that sends messages at the wrong moment is called a *babbling idiot*. A babbling idiot timing failure is the most serious failure of a node in a system with a shared communication channel, such as in a bus system.

Error detection in the temporal domain at the external node interface, e.g., below the CNI of a node, can only be performed if *a priori* knowledge is available about the intended instants of time when a node is allowed to send a message. In a TT architecture, this information is static and is stored in the communication system, independent of the application software in the host. It can be used to construct effective mechanisms for detecting timing failures of the host. In an ET architecture, the application software decides dynamically when to send a message. It is thus difficult to devise an error-detection scheme for the detection of timing failures of a host in an ET architecture.

6.3.3   Exception Handling

Exception handling is a well-known technique for handling errors that are detected within a task. After an exception has been raised, either by the software (e.g., invalid range of a variable) or by the hardware (e.g., arithmetic overflow), control is transferred to an exception handler. After the exception handler has terminated, control is either resumed from the point of exception, or the task is terminated. A number of programming languages support exception handling by providing appropriate programming constructs [Bur89, p.125].

In real-time systems, exception handling must be used with care. The WCET of a task is extended by the WCET of all exception handlers that can possibly be activated during the execution of the task. If the exception handler inside a node repairs the damage within the time constraints that have been specified at the node interface, then, the fault is corrected; otherwise, the node fails as a unit.

Some of the techniques for implementing fault tolerance, e.g., periodic checkpointing with recovery in case of a detected error [Lee90], which are useful in non real-time systems, are difficult to apply in the context of a hard real-time system because of the unpredictable increase of the WCET in the case of an error. Furthermore, it must be assured that the checkpoint data are still temporally valid at their point of use (see Section 5.4).

6.4   FAULT-TOLERANT UNITS

The purpose of a Fault-Tolerant Unit (FTU) is to mask the failures of a node (see also Section 4.2.3). If a node implements the fail-silent abstraction, then the duplication of nodes is sufficient to tolerate a single node failure. If the node does not implement fail-silence, but can exhibit value errors at the host/network interface CNI, then triple modular redundancy, TMR, must be implemented. We must assume that the behavior of the nodes is replica determinate, and that the nodes do not exhibit babbling idiot timing failures in bus systems.

If no assumptions can be made about the failure behavior of a node, i.e., a node can exhibit Byzantine failures, then four nodes are required to form a fault-tolerant unit. An example of an architecture that makes no assumptions about failure modes of a node is the FTTP architecture developed at the Draper Labs (see Section 13.6.3).

6.4.1   Fail-Silent Nodes

A fail-silent node either produces correct results (in the value and time domain), or does not produce any results at all. In a time-triggered architecture, an FTU that consists of two fail-silent nodes produces either zero, one, or two correct result messages. If it produces no message, it has failed. If it produces one or two messages, it is operational. The receiver must discard redundant result messages. This is simple if the result messages are idempotent, e.g., if they have state semantics (see Section 5.5.4).

Request from Client

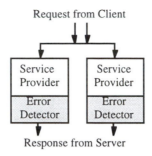

Response from Server

Figure 6.8: Fault-tolerant unit consisting of two fail-silent nodes.

In a bus-based system, an FTU can comprise a *shadow node* in addition to the two active nodes [Kop90a]. The shadow node acts as a *warm standby*: it reads all messages from the bus, and is fully synchronized with the active nodes, but does not produce any output messages as long as it is in the "shadow" state. As soon as one of the active nodes fails, the "shadow" node acquires the output bus slots of the failed node, and thereby becomes an active node. If the failed node is repaired, it reintegrates itself as a shadow node. The advantages of such an FTU with a shadow node are:

(i)   Whenever an active node fails, the redundancy within the FTU is reestablished within a short time interval.

(ii)   During normal operation the shadow node does not consume any bandwidth of the communication system.

(iii) During repair of the failed node, the redundancy within the FTU is maintained.

6.4.2   Triple-Modular Redundancy

If a node can exhibit value failures at the CNI with a probability that cannot be tolerated in the given application domain, then, a fault-tolerant unit must consist of three nodes and a *voter*. The voter detects and masks errors in one step by comparing the three independently computed results, and then selecting the result that has been computed by the majority, i.e., by two out of three in the triple modular redundant (TMR) configuration of Fig 6.9.

Request from Client

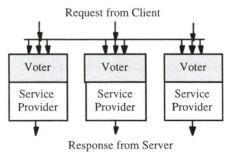

Response from Server

Figure 6.9: Fault tolerant unit consisting of three nodes with voters.

Two different kinds of voting strategies can be distinguished: exact voting and inexact voting.

Exact Voting: In *exact voting,* a bit-by-bit comparison of the data fields in the result messages of the three nodes forming an FTU is performed. If two out of the three available messages have exactly the same bit pattern, then one of the two messages is selected as the output of the triad. The underlying assumption is that correctly operating replica-determinate nodes produce exactly the same results.

Inexact Voting: In *inexact voting,* two messages are assumed to contain the *same* result if the results are within some *application-specific* interval. Inexact voting must be used if the replica determinism of the replicated nodes cannot be guaranteed. The selection of an appropriate interval for an inexact voter is a delicate task: if the interval is too large, erroneous values will be accepted as correct; if the interval is too small, correct values will be rejected as erroneous. Practical experiences with inexact voting have proved to be disappointing [Lal94]. Irrespective of the criterion defined to determine the "sameness" of two results, there seem to be problems [Rus93, p. 132].

6.4.3   Byzantine Resilient Fault-Tolerant Unit

If no assumption can be made about the failure mode of a node, then, four nodes are needed to form a fault-tolerant unit (FTU) that can tolerate a single Byzantine (or *malicious*) fault. These four nodes must execute a Byzantine-resilient agreement protocol to agree on a malicious failure of a node. Theoretical studies [Pea80] have shown that these Byzantine agreement protocols have the following requirements to tolerate the Byzantine failures of k nodes :

(i)   An FTU must consist of at least $3k+1$ nodes.

(ii)   Each node must be connected to all other nodes of the FTU by $k+1$ disjoint communication paths.

(iii) To detect the malicious nodes, $k+1$ rounds of communication must be executed among the nodes. A round of communication requires every node to send a message to all the other nodes.

(iv)   The nodes must be synchronized to with a known precision.

An example of an architecture that tolerates Byzantine failures of the nodes is given in Section 13.6.3.

6.4.4   The Membership Service

The failure of an FTU must be reported in a consistent manner to all operating FTUs with a low latency. This is the task of the *membership service.* A point in real-time when the membership of a node can be established, is called a *membership point* of the node. A small temporal delay between the membership point of a node and the instant when all other nodes of the ensemble are informed in a consistent manner about the membership, is critical for the correct operation of many safety-relevant applications.

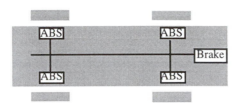

Figure 6.10: Example of an intelligent ABS in a car.

Example: Consider an intelligent ABS (Antiblock System) braking system in a car, where a node of a distributed computer system is placed at each wheel. A distributed algorithm in each of the four computers, one at each wheel, calculates the brake-force distribution to the wheels (Figure 6.10), depending on the position of the brake pedal actuated by the driver. If a wheel computer fails or the communication to a wheel computer is lost, the hydraulic brake-force actuator at this wheel autonomously transits to a defined state, e.g., in which the wheel is free-running. If the other nodes learn about the computer failure at this wheel within a short latency, e.g., a single control loop cycle of about 5 msec, then the brake force can be redistributed to the three functioning wheels, and the car can still be controlled. If, however, the loss of a node is not recognized with such a low latency, then, the brake force distribution to the wheels, based on the assumptions that all four wheel computers are operational, is wrong and the car will go out of control.

ET Architecture: In an ET architecture, messages are only sent when a significant event happens at a node. Silence of a node in an ET architecture therefore means that *either* no significant event has occurred at the node, *or* a fail-silent failure has occurred (the loss of communication or the fail-silent failure of the node). Even if the communication system is assumed to be perfectly reliable, it is not possible to distinguish when there is *no activity at the node* from when a *silent node failure* occurs, in an ET architecture. An additional time-triggered service, e.g., a periodic watchdog service (see Section 10.4.4), must be implemented in an ET architecture to solve the membership problem.

TT Architecture: In a TT architecture the periodic message send times are the membership points of the sender. Let us assume that a failed node remains failed for an interval whose length is greater than the maximum time interval between two membership points. Every receiver knows *a priori* when a message of a sender is supposed to arrive, and interprets the arrival of the message as a life sign at the membership point of the sender [Kop91]. It is then possible to conclude, from the arrival of the expected messages at two consecutive membership points, that the node was alive during the complete interval that is delimited by these two membership points. The membership of the FTUs in a cluster at any point in time can thus be established with a delay of one round of information exchange. Because the delay of one round of information exchange is known *a priori* in a TT architecture, it is possible to derive an *a priori* bound for the temporal accuracy of the membership service.

6.5   REINTEGRATION OF A REPAIRED NODE

The first step following the occurrence of a node failure is a self-test of the node hardware. If this self-test is successful, then, it can be assumed that a transient fault led to the failure of the node, since a transient fault afflicts no permanent damage to the node hardware. The reintegration of the node can be started immediately.

If the self-test shows a permanent node error, or if a transient error occurs repeatedly within a specified time interval, a permanent hardware fault must be assumed. It is then necessary to replace the node hardware. In a fault-tolerant system, it must be possible to replace the hardware while the system is under power.

6.5.1   Finding a Reintegration Point

While a failure can occur at an arbitrary moment outside the control of the system designer, the proper point of reintegration of a repaired node can be planned by the system designer. The key issue during the reintegration of a node in a real-time system is to find a future point in time when the h-state of a node is in synchrony with the node environment. Because real-time data are invalidated by the passage of time, rolling back to a past checkpoint can be futile: it is possible and probable that the progression of time has already invalidated the checkpoint information.

Reintegration is simplified if the h-state that must be reloaded into the reintegrating node has a small size. It was shown in Section 4.6 that the size of the h-state has a relative minimum immediately after the completion of an atomic operation.

In a time-triggered distributed system a component operates periodically with a period called the *component cycle*. Immediately after the completion of a component cycle, all atomic operations in the component are completed and the component should be in a ground state, i.e., all communication channels are flushed, and no task is active (see Figure 4.10). A point in time when a component is in a ground state, is an ideal reintegration point because the size of the h-state is minimal. If the h-state is empty at the ground state, the reintegration of a repaired node is trivial at this moment. In many situations, however, there is no such a point in time during the lifetime of a node, when the h-state is completely empty.

6.5.2   Minimizing the H-State

The points in time when a repaired node can be reintegrated into an operational cluster must be carefully planned during system design. After a reintegration point has been established, the h-state at this selected reintegration point must be analyzed, and minimized to simplify the reintegration procedure.

In a first phase, all system data structures must be investigated to locate any hidden h-state. In particular, all variables that must be initialized must be identified and the state of all semaphores and operating system queues at the reintegration point must be checked. It is good programming practice to output the h-state of the task in a special output message when a task with h-state is detected, and to re-read the h-state of the task when the task is re-activated (see also Figure 4.8). This discerns the h-state, and makes it possible to pack all h-states of the tasks of a node into an *h-state message* particular to this node.

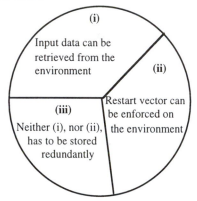

Figure 6.11: Partitioning of the h-State.

In a second phase, the identified h-state must be analyzed and minimized. Figure 6.11 displays a suggested division of the h-state information into three parts:

(i)   This part of an h-state consists of input data that can be retrieved from the instrumentation in the environment. If the instrumentation is state-based, and sends the absolute values of the RT entities (state messages) rather than their relative values (event messages), then, a complete scan of all the sensors in the environment can establish a set of current images in the reintegrating node, and thus resynchronize the node with the external world.

(ii)   This part of the h-state consists of output data that are in the control of the computer, and can be enforced on the environment. We call the set of the output data a *restart vector*. In a number of applications, a restart vector can be defined at development time. Whenever a node must be reintegrated, this restart vector is enforced on the environment to achieve agreement with the outside world. If different process modes require different restart vectors, a set of restart vectors can be defined at development time, one for each mode. For example, when a traffic control system is restarted, it is possible to enforce a restart vector on the traffic lights that sets all cross-road lights first to yellow, and then to red, and finally turns the main street lights to green. This is a relatively simple way to achieve a synchronization between the external world and the computer system. The alternative, which involves the reconstruction of the current state of all traffic lights from some log file that recorded the output commands until the point of failure, would be more complicated.

(iii)   This part of the h-state contains h-state data that do not fall into category (i) or category (ii). This part of the h-state must be recovered from some node-external source: either from an operator, or from some other node that has stored this information redundantly. In some situations, a redesign of the process instrumentation may be considered to transform h-state of category (iii) into h-state of category (i).

In a system with replicated nodes in an FTU, the h-state data that cannot be retrieved directly from the environment must be communicated from one node of the FTU to the other nodes of the FTU by means of an h-state message. In a TT system, sending such an h-state message should be part of the standard component cycle. This "externalization" of the h-state of a node facilitates the validation of the node as well.

6.5.3   Node Restart

The restart of a node after a failure can proceed as follows: once powered up, the node performs a self-test, and verifies the correctness of its i-state by checking the provided signatures in the i-state data structures. If the i-state is erroneous, a copy of the static i-state must be reloaded from stable storage. In a second step, the node scans all instruments, and waits for a cluster cycle to acquire all available current information about its environment. After an analysis of this information, the node decides the *mode* of the controlled object, and selects the restart vector that must be enforced on the environment. Finally, after having retrieved the class (iii) h-state information from an external source, or from the replicated partner node in the FTU, the node starts its task in synchrony with the rest of the cluster.

6.6   DESIGN DIVERSITY

Example: The following quotes are taken from the press report on the failure of the Ariane 5 rocket on June 4, 1996 [Lio96]:

The failure of the Ariane 501 was caused by the complete loss of guidance and attitude information 37 seconds after start of the main engine ignition sequence. This loss of information was due to specification and design errors in the software of the inertial reference system. . . . The problem boils down to a single ADA routine that was supposed to do data conversion during on-ground alignment operations. This alignment software was intentionally left running into the early part of the flight to allow for late countdown stoppages. This software was lifted from Ariane 4, but key things differ between Ariane 4 and Ariane 5. The software raised an exception (that was completely predictable based on the flight path of Ariane 5 versus Ariane 4) and there was no fault-protection mechanism for this exception, so the guidance processor halted. The backup guidance CPU went through exactly the same routine, failing one cycle earlier in the same way. . . . The reason behind this drastic action lies in the culture within the Ariane program of only addressing random hardware failures. From this point of view the exception–(or error)–handing mechanisms are designed for random hardware failure which can quite rationally be handled by a backup system.

Field data on the observed reliability of many large computer systems [Gra93,p.104] indicate that a significant and increasing number of computer system failures is caused by design errors in the software, and not by physical faults of the hardware. While the problems of random physical hardware faults can be solved by applying redundancy, as presented in this chapter, no generally accepted procedure to deal with the problem of software errors has emerged. The techniques that have been developed for handling hardware faults are not directly applicable to the field of software, because there is no physical process that causes the aging of the software.

Software errors are design errors that have their root in the unmanaged complexity of a design. Because many hardware functions of a complex VLSI chip are implemented in microcode that is stored in a ROM, the possibility of a design error in the hardware must be considered in a safety-critical system. The issue of a single design error that is replicated in the software of all nodes of a distributed system warrants further consideration. It is conceivable that an FTU built from nodes based on the same hardware, and using the same system software, exhibits common-mode failures caused by design errors in the software or in the hardware (microprograms).

Three major strategies to attack the problem of unreliable software are discussed in the ARINC document on "Software Considerations in Airborne Systems and Equipment Certification" [ARI92]:

(i)   To improve the understandability of a software system by introducing a clean conceptual structure and simplifying programming paradigms. The techniques of structured programming and object-oriented design fall into this category [Mey88].

(ii)   To apply formal methods in the software development process so that the specification can be expressed in a rigorous form. It is then possible to verify formally–within the limits of today's technology–the consistency between a high-level specification expressed in a formal specification language, and the implementation [Rus93]. The possibilities and limitations of formal methods are discussed in Section 12.2.

(iii)   To design and implement diverse versions of the software analogous to the replication of hardware modules, so that a failure in one version can be detected and masked by the other versions [Vog88].

Over the last few years, an ongoing debate has been attempting to decide which one of these strategies is the most promising, and should be followed widely. In our opinion, these three strategies are not contradictory, but complementary. An understandable and well-structured software system is a prerequisite for the application of any of the other two techniques, i.e., program verification and software diversity. In safety-critical real-time systems, all three strategies should be followed to reduce the number of design errors to a level that is commensurate with the requirement of ultra-high dependability.

6.6.1   Diverse Software Versions

Design diversity is based on the hypothesis that different programmers using different programming languages and different development tools, don't make the same programming errors. This hypothesis has been tested in a number of controlled experiments with the result that it is only partially correct [Avi85]. Design diversity increases the overall reliability of a system. It is, however, not justified to assume that the errors in the diverse software versions are statistically independent [Kni86].

The detailed analysis of field data of large software systems reveals that a significant number of system failures can be traced to flaws in the system specification. To be more effective, the diverse software versions should be based on different specifications. This complicates the design of the voting algorithm. As was already mentioned, practical experience with non-exact voting schemes has not been encouraging.

What place does software diversity have in safety critical real-time systems? The following case study of a fault-tolerant railway signaling system that was installed in a number of train stations to increase the safety and reliability of the train service is a good example of the practical utility of software diversity.

6.6.2   An Example of A Fail-Safe System

The VOTRICS train signaling system that has been developed by Alcatel [Kan95a] is an industrial example of the application of design diversity in a safety-critical real-time environment. The objective of a train signaling system is to collect data about the state of the tracks in train stations, i.e., the current positions and movements of the trains and the positions of the switches, and to set the signals and shift the switches such that the trains can move safely through the station according to the given timetable entered by the operator. The safe operation of the train system is of utmost concern.

The VOTRICS system is partitioned into two independent subsystems. The first subsystem accepts the commands from the station operators, collects the data from the tracks, and calculates the intended position of the switches and signals so that the train can move through the station according to the desired plan. This subsystem uses a TMR architecture to tolerate a single hardware fault.

The second subsystem, called the *safety bag*, monitors the safety of the state of the station. It has access to the real-time database and the intended output commands of the first subsystem. It dynamically evaluates safety predicates that are derived from the traditional "rule book" of the railway authority. In case it cannot dynamically verify the safety of an intended output state, it has the authority to block the outputs to the switching signals, or to even activate an emergency shutdown of the complete station, setting all signals to red and stopping all trains. The safety bag is also implemented on a TMR hardware architecture.

The interesting aspect about this architecture is the substantial independence of the two diverse software versions. The versions are derived from completely different specifications. Subsystem one takes the operational requirements as the starting point for the software specification, while subsystem two takes the established safety rules as its starting point. Common mode specification errors can thus be ruled out. The implementation is also substantially different. Subsystem one is built according to a standard programming paradigm, while subsystem two is based on expert-system technology. If the rule-based expert system does not come up with a positive answer within a prespecified time interval, then, a violation of a safety condition is assumed.

It is thus not necessary to analytically establish a WCET for the expert system (which would be very difficult).

The system has been operational in different railway stations over a number of years. No case has been reported where an unsafe state remained undetected. The independent safety verification by the safety bag also has a positive effect during the commission phase, because failures in subsystem one are immediately detected by subsystem two.

6.6.3 Multilevel System

The technique described above can also be applied to fail-operational applications that are controlled by a two-level computer system (Figure 6.12). The higher-level computer system provides full functionality, and has a high-error detection coverage. If the high-level computer system fails, an independent and differently designed lower-level computer system with reduced functionality takes over. The reduced functionality must be sufficient to guarantee safety.

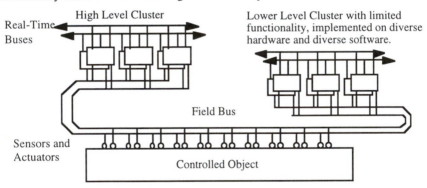

Figure 6.12: Multilevel computer system with diverse software.

Such an architecture has been deployed in the computer system for the space shuttle [Lee90, p.297]. Along with a TMR system that uses identical software, a fourth computer with diverse software is provided in case of a design error that causes the correlated failure of the complete TMR system. Diversity is deployed in a number of existing safety critical real-time systems, as in the Airbus fly by wire system [Tra88], in railway signaling [Kan95a], and in nuclear applications [Vog88].

POINTS TO REMEMBER

- A *failure* is an event that denotes a deviation between the actual service and the specified or intended service, occurring at a particular point in real time.

- To tolerate k failures of a certain type, we need $k+1$ components if the failures are *fail-silent*, $2k+1$ components if the failures are *fail-consistent*, and $3k+1$ components if the failures are *malicious (Byzantine)*.

- The failure rate (permanent failures) of a high quality chip stabilizes in a range between *10–100* FITS (*1* FIT means *1* failure per 10^9 hours, i.e., a MTTF of about *115 000* years).

- An error is a discrepancy between the *intended correct state* and the *current state* of a system. Error detection requires knowledge about the intended correct state.

- The knowledge about the intended correct state can arise from two different sources: either from *a priori* knowledge about the intended properties of the states and behaviors of the computation, or from the comparison of the results of two redundant computational channels.

- Systematic fault tolerance provides the fault-tolerance mechanism at the level of the architecture by using replicated hardware. Application-specific fault tolerance intertwines fault-tolerance functions and application functions, thus increasing the software complexity.

- A fail-silent node must detect all internal failures within a short latency, and must map these failures to a single external failure mode, a fail-silent node failure.

- Knowledge about the regularity in the activation pattern of a computation can be used to detect errors in the temporal domain.

- The cause of an error, and thus indirectly of a failure, is called a *fault*.

- Large systems have many operational states between fully operational and non-operational. As long as a node provides the minimum-service level, it is classified as operational.

- A node that sends messages at the wrong moment is called a *babbling idiot*. A babbling-idiot timing failure is the most serious failure of a node in a system with a shared communication channel, e.g., a bus system.

- In real-time systems exception handling must be used with care. The WCET of a task is extended by the WCET of all exception handlers that can possibly be activated during the execution of the task.

- In *exact voting,* a bit-by-bit comparison of the data fields in the redundant result messages is performed. Exact voting requires replica determinate computational channels.

- In *inexact voting* two messages are assumed to contain the *same* result if the results are within some application-specific interval. Inexact voting must be used if replica determinism of the replicated nodes cannot be guaranteed.

- The practical experiences with inexact voting are disappointing. Whatever criterion is defined to determine the "sameness" of two results, it seems to be wrong.

- Byzantine agreement requires an FTU to contain at least *3k+1* nodes. Each node must be connected to all other nodes of the FTU by $k+1$ disjoint communication paths. To detect the malicious nodes, $k+1$ rounds of communication must be executed among the nodes, and the nodes must be synchronized with a known precision.

- The temporal delay between the membership point of a node and the point where all other nodes of the ensemble are consistently informed about the membership, must be small for the correct operation of many safety-relevant applications.

- Even if the communication system is assumed to be perfectly reliable, it is not possible to distinguish when there is *no activity at the node* from when a *silent node failure* occurs in an ET architecture.

- The key issue during the reintegration of a node in a real-time system is to find a future point in time when the h-state of a node is in synchrony with the node environment.

- A point in time, when a component is in a *ground state,* is an ideal reintegration point, because the size of the h-state is minimal.

- Software errors are design errors that have their root in the unmanaged complexity of a design. Because many hardware functions of a complex VLSI chip are implemented in microcode that is stored in ROM, the possibility of a design error in the hardware must be taken into consideration in a safety-critical system.

- Design diversity increases the overall reliability of a system. It is, however, not justified to assume that the errors in the diverse software versions are statistically independent.

- If, in a multilevel fail-operational computer architecture, the high-level computer system fails, an independent and differently designed lower-level computer system with reduced functionality takes over. This reduced functionality must be sufficient to guarantee the safety.

BIBLIOGRAPHIC NOTES

The Proceedings of the annual Symposium on Fault-Tolerant Computing (FTCS), published by the IEEE, is the world's premier forum for discussing the advances in the field of fault-tolerant computing. A good introduction to the field of fault-tolerant computing is given in the books of Lee and Anderson "Fault Tolerance, Principles and Practice" [Lee90],"Design and Analysis of Fault-Tolerant Digital Systems" by Johnson [Joh89], and "Fault Tolerance in Distributed Systems" by Jalote [Jal94]. The excellent paper "Understanding Fault-Tolerant Distributed Systems" by Cristian [Cri91] is a required reading. "The Design of Predictably Dependable Computing Systems" was the topic of the European ESPRIT Basic Research Project PDCS. Results of this project are published in a book [Ran95] that contains many relevant papers on the topic discussed in this chapter. Suri, Walter and Hugue have put together many of the archival papers on ultra-dependable systems in their tutorial on "Advances in Ultra-Dependable Systems" [Sur95].

REVIEW QUESTIONS AND PROBLEMS

6.1 Give the precise meaning of the terms failure, error, and fault.

6.2 What are typical permanent and transient failure rates of VLSI chips?

6.3 The following fault is observed in the field: before installation, the proper operation of each of a batch of single chip microcontrollers was tested at the usual test points of $-20°$ C, $0°$ C, $+20°$ C, $+40°$ C, $+60°$ C, and at $+80°$ C. During operation, every fifth chip from the batch failed at about $-12°$ C, although it operated correctly at $-20°$ C and at $0°$ C.

How would you classify this fault? How can this fault be detected if this chip is part of large distributed system? What is the probability that a TMR system built out of three such microcontrollers would fail at $-12°$ C?

6.4 Why is a short recovery time from transient faults important?

6.5 What are the basic techniques for error detection? Compare ET systems and TT systems from the point of view of error detection.

6.6 Discuss the topic of *exception handling* in real-time systems.

6.7 Discuss the different types of errors that can be detected by redundant computations.

6.8 What is a membership service? Give a practical example for the need of a membership service. What is the quality parameter of the membership service? How can you implement a membership service in an ET architecture?

6.9 What is the most serious error in a distributed system with a shared communication channel, e.g., a bus? Why?

6.10 Assume a computer system that can control three concurrently operating trains running on a model railway track, containing 10 switches and 15 signals.

Identify the h-state at the reintegration point. Which part of the h-state can be enforced on the environment at the reintegration point? What is the minimal remaining h-state at the reintegration point?

6.11 What is a restart vector? Give an example.

6.12 Fault tolerance can be implemented by two fail-silent components or by TMR. Discuss the advantages and disadvantages of each one of these methods.

6.13 What are the arguments for, and against, using diverse hardware units in a safety-critical real-time application with replicated hardware channels?

6.14 What are the advantages and limits of design diversity? Why is it easier to deploy design diversity in fail-safe applications than in fail-operational applications?

Chapter 7

Real-Time Communication

OVERVIEW

This chapter commences by articulating the requirements of a real-time communication system: low protocol latency with minimal jitter, support for composability, and the need for fast error detection at the receiver. Section 7.2 elaborates on the important topic of flow control, and distinguishes between two different types of flow control, implicit and explicit flow control. The Positive Acknowledgment and Retransmission (PAR) protocol, the most prominent explicit flow-control protocol, is evaluated from the point of view of real-time performance. It is shown that a number of characteristics of the PAR protocol are in conflict with the requirements of real-time systems. In Section 7.3 a communication architecture for a distributed real-time system is presented. This architecture consists of three communication subsystems: a low-cost field bus for interconnecting sensors and actuators, a fault-tolerant real-time network for interconnecting the nodes, and a backbone bus for interconnecting a cluster with other non real-time systems.

In Section 7.4 some fundamental conflicts in the design of real-time protocols are highlighted. For example, the requirement for flexibility is in conflict with many other desirable protocol properties, such as composability, error detection, and replica determinism. These conflicts have lead to the design of many different real-time protocols that try to bridge the gap between these conflicting requirements. Some of these protocols, such as the CAN (Control Area Network), the ARINC 629 and the TTP (Time Triggered Protocol) are discussed in Section 7.5 and compared. Section 7.6 compares the performance of an event-triggered and time-triggered implementation of an alarm monitoring system.

There is an interdependency between the protocol requirements and the layout of the physical protocol layer. The final section is devoted to the physical protocol layer, and a short discussion on transmission codes.

7.1   REAL-TIME COMMUNICATION REQUIREMENTS

The previous chapters discussed the characteristics of hard real-time applications, and presented a set of architectural requirements for communication in a distributed real-time system. This section looks at these requirements that have their root in the necessity for a small and predictable latency of real-time transactions. The first part is a short summary of the material covered in the previous chapters as it relates to the communication system.

7.1.1   Protocol Latency

The *protocol latency* is the time interval between the start of transmission of a message at the communication network interface (CNI) of the sending node, and the delivery of this message across the CNI of the receiving node. To support a consistent behavior of the distributed system as a whole, the message should be *permanent* when delivered across the CNI to the host of a node.

Latency Jitter: A real-time communication protocol should have a predictable and small maximum protocol latency and a minimal jitter. The application programs in the host often rely on this *a priori* known predictable latency. Any variation in the protocol latency, e.g., such as that caused by a jitter that is introduced in handling communication failures by time-redundancy, affects the operation of the application programs adversely.

Simultaneous Delivery in Multicast: The standard communication topology in distributed real-time systems is multicast, not point-to-point. The same image of an RT entity is needed at a number of different nodes, e.g., at the man-machine interface, at a process-model node, and at an alarm-monitoring node. A message should be delivered at all receiver CNIs within a short and known time interval.

7.1.2   Support for Composability

Section 2.2 identified *composability* as the most important property of a real-time system architecture. The communication system plays a central role in establishing composability by the following two means:

Temporal Encapsulation of the Nodes: The communication system should erect a temporal firewall around the operation of a host, forbidding the exchange of control signals across the CNI. Thus, the communication system becomes autonomous and can be implemented and validated independently of the application software in the host. The timing properties of the application software in a temporally encapsulated host can also be validated in isolation.

Fulfilling the Obligations of the Client: A server that is implemented in the host of a node can only guarantee its deadlines if the clients fulfill their obligation: not to overload the server with too many, or uncoordinated, service requests. The communication system should exercise flow control over the requests from the clients, and assist in fulfilling the temporal obligations of the client.

7.1.3 Flexibility

Many real-time communication systems must support different system configurations that change over time. A real-time protocol should be flexible to accommodate these changes without requiring a software modification and retesting of the operational nodes that are not affected by the change. Since the bandwidth of any communication channel is limited, there exists an upper bound on the increase in communication traffic that can be handled within the given time constraints.

Example: A communication system within a car must support different configurations of nodes, depending on customer demand. One customer might demand a car with a sunroof, a computer controlled radio, and automatic seats with memory, while another customer might opt for an air-conditioning system and a sophisticated anti-theft system. All possible combinations of nodes must be supported by the communication system without a need for retesting existing nodes.

Flexibility is also required to service important sporadic messages, such as an "emergency shutdown" message, with minimal delay.

7.1.4 Error Detection

Communication Errors: The communication system must provide predictable and dependable service. Errors that occur during the message transmission must be detected, and should be corrected without increasing the jitter of the protocol latency. If an error cannot be corrected, all the communicating partners, the sender and all the receivers, must be informed about the occurrence of the error with a low latency. In a real-time system, the detection of message loss by the *receiver* of a message is of particular concern.

Example: Consider a node, at a control valve, that receives output commands from another node. In case the communication is interrupted because the wires are cut, the control valve node should enter a safe state autonomously, e.g., it should close the valve. The communication system must inform the control valve node about the loss of communication with a low error detection latency.

In a distributed real-time system, it can happen that external electromagnetic interference (EMI), e.g., a flash of lightning, causes the correlated mutilation of all messages on the communication system. We call such a phenomenon a *blackout*. Blackouts normally last only for a few milliseconds, or for even a shorter period of time. The communication system should detect such a blackout, and continue with its operation as soon as the blackout disappears. Such a service is called *blackout management*.

Detection of Node Errors: The failure of a node must be detected by the communication protocol, and must be reported consistently to all the remaining nodes of the ensemble. In real-time systems, the prompt and consistent detection of node failures at both the receiver and at the sender is important. This is the function of the membership service.

End-to-End   Acknowledgment: In a real-time system, the end-to-end acknowledgment about the success or failure of a communication action can arise from a node that is different from the receiver of an output message. An output message to an actuator in the environment should cause some effect in the environment. This effect is monitored by an independent sensor. The results observed by this sensor ensure that the desired action of the message has actually been achieved. This is an example of an *end-to-end protocol* such as that required at the interface between the computer system and the controlled object.

Example: Figure 7.1 shows an example of an end-to-end acknowledgment of the output message to a control valve by a flow sensor that is connected to a different node.

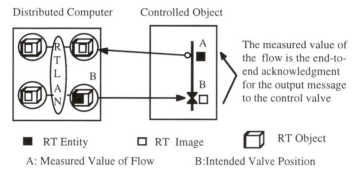

Figure 7.1: End-to-end acknowledgment in real-time systems.

Example: A wrong end-to-end protocol can have serious consequences, as seen in the following quote [Sev81] regarding the Three Mile Island Nuclear Reactor #2 accident on March 28, 1979:

Perhaps the single most important and damaging failure in the relatively long chain of failures during this accident was that of the Pressure Operated Relief Valve (PORV) on the pressurizer. The PORV did not close; yet its monitoring light was signaling green (meaning closed).

In this system, the fundamental design principle "never trust an actuator", was violated. The designers assumed that the acknowledged arrival of a control output signal that commanded the valve to close, implied that the valve *was* closed. Since there was an electromechanical fault in the valve, this implication was not true. A proper end-to-end protocol that mechanically sensed the closed position of the valve would have avoided this catastrophic false information.

7.1.5 Physical Structure

The physical structure of a real-time communication system is determined by technical and economic considerations. The multicast communication requirement suggests a communication structure that supports multicasting at the physical level, e.g., a bus or a ring network. A fully connected point-to-point communication architecture that provides single-hop broadcasting requires N-1 communication ports at each node, in an ensemble of N nodes. For many applications, the high cost of several communication ports at each node, the physical drivers at each node, and the cabling are prohibitive in a point-to-point network.

Bus versus Ring: The decision as to whether the physical network should be based on a bus or a ring structure is less clear. In an automotive environment, where the physical interconnection is realized by twisted pair wires, a bus structure is more attractive than a ring structure because of its simpler interface and better resilience with respect to fail-silent node failures. The simultaneous arrival of a message at all nodes is another advantage of a bus over a ring. On the other hand, if optical fibers form the physical medium, a ring structure is advantageous because the point-to-point connection of fibers is simpler than the construction of a fiber-based bus.

Physical Separation of the Nodes Forming an FTU: In a fault-tolerant system that is based on active redundancy, the nodes (Smallest Replaceable Units–SRUs) that form a Fault-Tolerant Unit (FTU) should be physically separated so that a single physical event cannot cause a common-mode failure of all SRUs.

Example: Consider a car with a steer-by-wire system. The SRUs that form an FTU for this critical function should be at different locations within the car so that a physical damage of a section of the car during an accident will not result in the correlated loss of the safety critical system function of all SRUs.

7.2   FLOW CONTROL

Flow control is concerned with the control of the speed of information flow between a sender and a receiver in such a manner that the receiver can keep up with the sender. In any communication scenario, it is the receiver, rather than the sender, that determines the *maximum* speed of communication. In the following, two types of flow control are distinguished, *explicit flow control* and *implicit flow control*.

7.2.1   Explicit Flow Control

In *explicit flow control,* the receiver sends an explicit acknowledgment message to the sender, informing the sender that the sender's previous message arrived correctly, and that the receiver is now ready to accept the next message. Explicit flow control is based on the sometimes overlooked assumption that the sender is within the sphere of control (SOC) of the receiver, i.e., that the receiver can exert *back pressure* on the sender to control the rate of transmission (*back-pressure flow control*). The most important protocol with explicit flow control is the well-known Positive-Acknowledgment-or-Retransmission (PAR) protocol.

The PAR Protocol: The PAR protocol is an event-triggered one. Given a sender, a receiver, a communication medium, a time-out value, and a retry counter, the basic

PAR protocol operates as follows: whenever a sender is asked by its client to send a new message, the sender initializes a retry counter to zero, starts a local time-out interval, and sends the message to the receiver by way of the communication medium. When the sender receives an acknowledgment message from the receiver within the specified time-out interval, it informs its client of the successful transmission, and duly terminates. If the sender does not receive a positive acknowledgment message from the receiver within the specified time-out interval, the sender checks the retry counter to determine whether the given maximum number of retries has already been exhausted. If so, the sender aborts the communication, and informs its client about the failure. If not, the sender increments the retry counter by one, resends the message, starts the local time-out again, and waits for an acknowledgment message of the receiver. If a new message arrives at the receiver, the receiver checks whether this message has already been received. If not, the receiver sends an acknowledgment message to the sender, and delivers the message to its client. If the receiver has already received the message, it just sends another acknowledgment message back to the sender. Note that the point in time at which the sender's client is informed about the successful transmission, can be significantly different from the point in time at which the receiver's client accepts the delivery of the message.

Many variants of the basic PAR protocol are known, but they all rely on the following principles:

(i)   The client at the sender's site initiates the communication.

(ii)   The receiver has the authority to delay the sender via the bi-directional communication channel.

(iii) A communication error is detected by the sender, and not by the receiver. The receiver is not informed when a communication error has been detected.

(iv)   Time redundancy is used to correct a communication error, thereby increasing the protocol latency in case of errors.

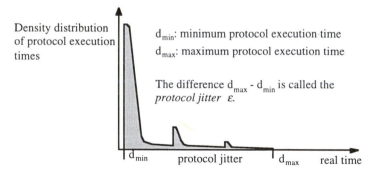

Figure 7.2: Distribution of latencies of a typical PAR protocol.

The protocol latency distribution of a typical PAR protocol with a retry counter of 2 is shown in Figure 7.2. In most cases, the first message transmission is successful. Therefore, immediately after the minimum protocol latency d_{min}, there is a peak in the density distribution of the protocol execution times. After the second attempt, another increase in the probability of success can be seen, and similarly for the third attempt before the transmission efforts are finally abandoned at d_{max}.

Example: Action Delay of PAR. Consider a bus system without global time where a token protocol controls media access to the bus. The token protocol has a maximum token rotation time *TRT* of *10* msec. The time needed to transport the message on the bus is *1* msec. The granularity of the local clock can be neglected. A PAR protocol is implemented at the transport level on top of the medium access protocol. The time-out in the PAR must be set to at least *22* msec, so that the miss of the token in each direction is covered. In the best case (d_{min}), if the sender has the token when the sender's client asks to send a new message, the receiver receives the message after *1* msec. In the worst case (d_{max}), the message transmission takes *55* msec, i.e., when the second retry, occurring after *44* msec, is successful, but the message is delayed for another *10* msec at the sender until the token becomes available. The error detection latency of this PAR protocol is *66* msec, because the sender reports an error to its client after three time-outs, *22* msec each, have elapsed.

The jitter of this PAR protocol is *54* msec. According to Section 5.5.2, the action delay in such a system is $2d_{max} - d_{min}$, i.e., *109* msec. Although in most cases the message will arrive at the receiving node within one token round, i.e., *11* msec, the receiver must hold the message for another *98* msec before it becomes *permanent*. If global time with a granularity of *100* µsec was available, then, the message becomes permanent after $d_{max} + 2g$, i.e., *55.2* msec after its transmission.

7.2.2   Implicit Flow Control

In *implicit flow control*, the sender and receiver agree *a priori*, i.e., at system start up, on the points in time when messages are sent. This requires the availability of a global time-base. The sender commits itself to send a message only at the agreed points in time, and the receiver commits itself to accept all messages sent by the sender, as long as the sender fulfills its obligation. No acknowledgment messages are exchanged during run time. Error detection is the responsibility of the receiver, which knows (by looking at its global clock) when an expected message fails to arrive.

In implicit flow control, fault tolerance can be implemented by active redundancy, i.e., sending k physical copies of every message (if possible by way of different channels). As long as at least one of the k copies arrives, the communication is successful. In implicit flow control, the number of messages that must be delivered by the communication system is always constant. Communication is unidirectional because there is no need for a return channel from the receiver to the sender. Thus, implicit flow control is well-suited to multicast communication.

7.2.3   Thrashing

The often observed phenomenon of the throughput of a system decreasing abruptly with increasing load, is called *thrashing*. Thrashing can be observed in many systems, and is not limited to computer systems; Consider the example of a traffic system in a large city. The throughput of the road system increases with increasing traffic up to a certain critical point. When this critical point is reached, further increase in traffic can lead to a reduction in throughput, or in other words, a "traffic jam".

Many systems can be characterized by a throughput-load dependency as shown in Figure 7.3.

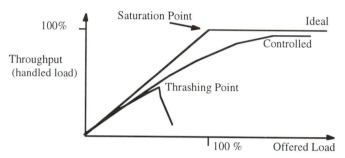

Figure 7.3: Throughput-load characteristic.

An ideal system exhibits the load throughput curve labeled *ideal* in Figure 7.3. The throughput increases with increasing load until the saturation point has been reached. Thereon, the throughput remains constant. A system has a *controlled* load-throughput characteristic if the throughput increases monotonically with the load and reaches the maximum throughput asymptotically. If the throughput increases up to a certain point, the *thrashing point,* and thereafter decreases abruptly, then, we say the system is *thrashing.*

Real-time systems must be free of the thrashing phenomena. If a real-time system contains a mechanism that can cause thrashing, then, it is likely that the system fails in the important *rare-event* scenarios discussed in Section 1.5.

Mechanisms that can Cause Thrashing: Mechanisms that require a more than proportional increase in resources as the load increases, are prone to cause thrashing. Two examples of such mechanisms are:

(i)   The retry mechanism in the PAR protocol: If a communication system slows down because it can barely handle the offered load, a high-level PAR protocol reaches its time-outs, and generates *additional* load.

(ii)   Operating system services: In a dynamic scheduling environment, the time needed to find a feasible schedule increases more than linearly as the offered load reaches the capacity limit. This increase in the amount of scheduling overhead further decreases the computational resources that are available for the application tasks. The same arguments hold for the overhead required for queue management.

The *only* successful technique to avoid thrashing in explicit flow-control schemes is to monitor the resource requirements of the system continuously and to exercise a stringent back-pressure flow control as soon as a decrease in the throughput is observed.

7.2.4   Flow Control in Real-Time Systems

Table 7.1 compares the characteristics of explicit flow control and implicit flow control, and contrasts them with the requirements of hard real-time systems. This comparison suggests that implicit flow control is better suited for real-time systems than explicit flow control.

Characteristic	Explicit Flow Control	Implicit Flow Control	Hard Real-Time System
Control signal	Receiver must be able to control the send events of the sender.	Control signals are generated by the progression of real time at a constant rate.	Receiver cannot fully control the events in the sphere of control of the sender.
Error detection	At the sender	At the receiver	At the receiver
Prone to thrashing	Yes	No	Thrashing must be avoided
Multicast	Difficult	Yes	Multicast required

Table 7.1: Explicit versus implicit flow control.

From the point of view of flow control, the most critical interface in a real-time system is the process interface between the controlled object and the computer system. It cannot be assumed that *all* events occurring in the controlled object are in the sphere of control of the computer system. If, in an event-triggered system, more events occur in the controlled objects than have been anticipated by the designer, then, the computer system may be overloaded by such an "event shower", and thereby miss important deadlines (Figure 7.4).

Example: On August 8, 1993 a prototype of a fly-by-wire fighter plane crashed, because the plane responded too slowly to the pilot's commands [Neu95, p.37].

Computer to Pilot:
"Please fly more slowly, I cannot follow your commands"

Figure 7.4: Explicit flow control in a real-time system.

Example: Consider a monitoring and control system for an electric power grid. There may be more than 100,000 different RT entities and alarms that must be monitored continually. In the case of a rare event, such as a severe thunderstorm when a number of lightning strikes hit the power lines within a short interval of time, many correlated alarms will occur. The computer system cannot exercise explicit flow control over these alarms in case the system enters the thrashing zone.

Interface between Implicit and Explicit Flow Control: It is difficult to design the interface between a producer subsystem that uses implicit flow control and a consumer subsystem that uses explicit flow control. While the subsystem that uses implicit flow control produces information at an *a priori* known rate, the consumer subsystem with explicit flow control can consume information only at the speed determined by its receivers. In order not to lose any information, adequate buffering must be provided at this interface. Determining the proper buffer size is a delicate design issue that is often ignored at the design level, and left to the programmer at the end of the line.

7.3   OSI PROTOCOLS FOR REAL-TIME?

Can a real-time system be built on top of a communication system that conforms to the OSI architecture? This is a relevant question, because many available implementations of communication systems use the OSI reference model [Tan89].

7.3.1   The OSI Reference Model

The purpose of the OSI reference model is to provide a standard conceptual reference architecture so that two computers that are located anywhere in the world can communicate with each other via diverse interconnected computer networks. For this purpose, a seven layer model (Figure 7.5) was introduced. Each layer encapsulates a protocol that is devoted to solve one particular aspect of the communication problem, using the services of the lower layer, and providing more powerful services to the higher layers.

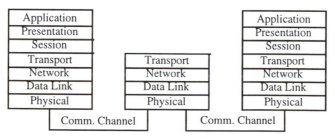

Figure 7.5: The OSI protocol stack.

Although the OSI architecture was originally meant to be a *conceptual reference architecture*, it is often used as an *implementation architecture*, resulting in implementations where a stack of PAR protocols, one in each layer, must be executed before a message is delivered at the application process. These implementations are characterized by high latency jitter and low data efficiency.

The following detailed assumptions are at the base of many OSI conforming protocol implementations:

(i)   The two communicating partners maintain a point-to-point connection.

(ii)   The messages are event-triggered.

(iii)   The communication protocols are of the PAR type with explicit flow control between sender and receiver and retransmission in case of an error.

(iv)   Real-time performance, i.e., latency and latency jitter, is not an issue.

These assumptions do not match up with the requirements of hard real-time systems.

7.3.2   Asynchronous Transfer Mode (ATM) and Real Time

The *Asynchronous Transfer Mode (ATM)* communication technology has been developed to provide real-time communication with low jitter over broadband networks. The information is packed into *ATM cells*, i.e., fixed-sized packets of *53* bytes, consisting of a header of *5* bytes and *48* data bytes. The header contains the control information for the identification and routing of the packet (Figure 7.6). The data bytes can encode any type of data: voice, video, FAX, or computer data.

Cell (53 Bytes)					
Header (5 Bytes)					Information
Generic Flow Control	Channel Identifier	Payload Type Indicator	Cell Loss Priority	Header Checksum	Payload
4 bits	24 bits	2 bits	2 bits	8 bits	48 Bytes

Figure 7.6: Structure of an ATM cell.

On the basic level, an ATM channel carries interleaved periodic ATM cells from different sources. The ATM switches at the ends of a channel performs the multiplexing and demultiplexing of the ATM streams. The application is free to decide which end-to-end protocols to implement on top of the basic ATM service. For example, a higher level ATM protocol can provide forward error correction to increase the reliability of the channel without introducing unpredictable jitter [Kim95]. From the point of view of real-time performance, ATM technology is well-suited to provide basic communication services for wide area real-time systems.

7.3.3   Real-Time Communication Architecture

In many real-time applications, three different types of communication networks are distinguished, the field bus, the real-time network, and the backbone network (Figure 7.7). Two of these networks, the field bus and the real-time network, must provide guaranteed temporal performance.

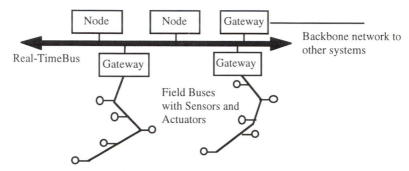

Figure 7.7: Real-time communication architecture.

Field Bus: The purpose of the field bus is to interconnect a node of the distributed computer system to the sensors and actuators in the controlled object. The node often acts as the central field bus controller. Sensors and actuators are often controlled by a local single-chip microcontroller that has a standard UART (Universal Asynchronous Receiver Transmitter) interface. Field bus messages have a short data field, containing state data, typically two bytes in length, and are transmitted periodically with strict real-time requirements for latency and latency jitter. Precise clock synchronization should therefore be provided at the field bus level. On the other hand, fault tolerance is not a major issue at the field bus level, since the reliability bottleneck is in the sensors and actuators. If fault tolerance is needed, redundant sensors that are interconnected by independent field buses to different nodes of the real-time cluster can be provided. The main concern at the field bus level is low cost, both for the controllers and for the cabling. Standard unshielded twisted pair wiring is commonly used to connect the sensors and actuators to the controlling node.

Real-time Network: The real-time network is at the core of the real-time cluster, and must provide the following services to the nodes in the cluster:

(i)   Reliable and temporally predictable message transmission with low latency and minimal latency jitter,

(ii)   Support for fault-tolerance to handle replicated nodes and replicated communication channels,

(iii) Clock synchronization in the range of microseconds, and

(iv)   Membership service with low latency for detecting node failures.

A dependable real-time network must have replicated communication channels. The system must be designed so that a failure in any single unit of the system cannot cause a crash of the total system (*single point of failure*). Special care must be taken to contain the effects of a node with a *babbling idiot failure* that can disrupt the communication between the other correct nodes on the bus. To avoid a central point of control failure, the real-time network should be based on distributed control.

Periodic state messages with implicit flow control are predominantly exchanged on the real-time network.

Backbone Network: The purpose of the backbone network is the exchange of non time-critical information between the real-time cluster and the data-processing systems of an organization. Examples of such information are production schedules, data collected regarding product quality and production times, and standardized production reports.

Table 7.2 compares the service characteristics of the three types of networks.

Service Characteristic	Field Bus	Real-time Network	Backbone Network
Message semantics	state	state	event
Latency/jitter control	yes	yes	no
Typical data field length	1- 6 bytes	6 - 12 bytes	> 100 bytes
Clock synchronization	yes	yes	optional
Fault-tolerance	limited	yes	limited
Membership service	maybe	yes	maybe
Topology	multicast	multicast	point-to-point
Communication control	multi-master	distributed	central or distributed
Flow control	implicit	implicit	explicit
Low cost	very important	important	not very important

Table 7.2: Comparison of field bus, real-time network, and backbone network.

The comparison of the characteristics of the OSI architecture versus the characteristics of a real-time communication architecture suggests that the OSI architecture is suitable for the implementation of the non time-critical backbone network, but is not adequate for the time-critical real-time network and the field bus.

7.4   FUNDAMENTAL CONFLICTS IN PROTOCOL DESIGN

A balanced protocol design tries to reconcile many particular requirements. It is important to understand which requirements are compatible with each other, and which requirements are in fundamental conflict with each other, and cannot be reconciled by any design decisions that are made. This section elaborates on some fundamental conflicts in the design of a real-time protocol that controls the access to a single communication channel, such as a bus.

7.4.1   External Control versus Composability

Consider a distributed real-time system consisting of a set of nodes that communicate with each other. Each node has a host computer with a communication network interface (CNI) that connects the host to this communication network. Composability in the temporal domain requires that:

(i)   The CNI of every node is fully specified in the temporal domain,

(ii) The integration of a set of nodes into the complete system does not lead to any change of the temporal properties of the individual CNIs, and

(iii) The temporal properties of every host can be tested in isolation with respect to the CNI.

If the temporal properties are not contained in the CNI specification, e.g., because the moment when a message must be transmitted is *external and unknown* to the communication system, then it is not possible to achieve composability in the temporal domain. If the temporal properties of the CNI are fully specified, then low-level composability can be achieved. There is, however, always the possibility that the application functions interact in an unpredictable manner that precludes high-level composability.

Example: Consider the call forwarding option of a telephone answering machine. If a number of these machines are connected in a cycle, then a call will be forwarded indefinitely, a situation that cannot be detected at the low-level communication interface.

In an event-triggered system, the temporal control signals originate external to the communication system, in the hosts of the nodes (Section 2.1). It is thus not possible to achieve low-level temporal composability.

Example: If all the nodes can compete at any point in time for a single communication channel on a demand basis, then, it is impossible to avoid the side effects caused by the extra transmission delay resulting from conflicts regarding the access to this single channel, no matter how clever the medium access protocol may be. These extra transmission delays can invalidate the temporal accuracy of the real-time images that are transported in the message (see Section 2.2).

7.4.2 Flexibility versus Error Detection

Another fundamental conflict exists between the requirement for flexibility and the requirement for error detection. Flexibility implies that the behavior of a node is not restricted *a priori*. In an architecture without replication, error detection is only possible if the actual behavior of a node can be compared to some *a priori* knowledge of the expected behavior. If such knowledge is not available, it is not possible to protect the network from a faulty node.

Example: Consider an event-triggered system with no regularity assumptions, where access to a single bus is determined solely by the message priority: if there is no restriction on the rate at which a node may send messages, it is impossible to avoid the monopolization of the network by a single (possibly erroneous) node that sends a continuous sequence of messages of the highest priority.

Example: If a node is not required to send a "heartbeat message" at regular intervals, it is not possible to detect a node failure with a bounded latency.

7.4.3 Sporadic Data versus Periodic Data

A real-time protocol can be effective in either the transmission of periodic data or the transmission of sporadic data, but not with both. The transmission of periodic data (e.g., data exchanges needed to coordinate a set of control loops) must take place with minimal latency jitter. Because the repetitive intervals between the transmissions of periodic data are known *a priori*, conflict-free schedules can be calculated off-line. Sporadic data must be transmitted with minimal delay, on demand, at *a priori* unknown points in time. If an external event requiring the transmission of a sporadic message occurs at the same time as the next point of transmission of the periodic data, then, the protocol must decide to either delay the sporadic data, or to modify the schedules of the periodic data. In either case, the latency jitter increases. It is easy to see that one cannot satisfy both goals simultaneously.

7.4.4   Single Locus of Control versus Fault Tolerance

Any protocol that relies on a single locus of control has a single point of failure. This is evident for a communication protocol that relies on a central master. However, even the access method of token passing relies on a single locus of control at any particular moment, with no consideration of time as the control element. If the station holding the token fails, no further communication is possible until the token loss has been detected by an *additional* time-out mechanism, and the token has been recovered. This takes time, and also interrupts the real-time communication. In some respects, the nontrivial problem of token recovery is related to the problem of switching from a central master to a standby master in a multi-master protocol.

7.4.5   Probabilistic Access versus Replica Determinism

Another fundamental conflict exists between the property of replica determinism (needed if active redundancy is to be implemented) and that of medium access based on probabilistic mechanisms. In systems that rely on a single winner emerging from fine-grained race conditions (e.g., bit arbitration, conflict resolution based on random numbers), it cannot be guaranteed that the access to replicated communication channels is always resolved identically by competing nodes. Without replica determinism, each replica can come to a *different correct* result, thereby leading to inconsistency in the system as a *whole*.

7.5   MEDIA-ACCESS PROTOCOLS

The medium access strategy of a communication protocol specifies which node is allowed to access the single communication channel at a particular point in time, thereby determining many properties of the architecture of a distributed real-time system. In this section, the medium-access strategies of a number of protocols that are proposed for real-time applications, are surveyed. The focus is on event-triggered protocols, since the time-triggered protocols are treated in Chapter 8.

7.5.1   Characteristics of a Communication Channel

A communication channel is characterized by its bandwidth and its propagation delay.

Bandwidth: The bandwidth indicates the number of bits that can traverse a channel in unit time. The bandwidth is determined by the physical characteristics of the channel. For example, in a harsh environment, such as a car, it is not possible to transmit more than 10 kbit/sec over a single-wire channel or 1 Mbit/sec over an unshielded twisted pair because of EMI constraints. In contrast, optical channels can transport gigabits of data per second.

Propagation Delay: The *propagation delay* is the time interval it takes for a bit to travel from one end of the channel to the other end. It is determined by the length of the channel and the transmission speed of the wave (electromagnetic, optical) within the channel. The transmission speed of an electromagnetic wave in vacuum is about *300 000* km/sec, or *1* foot/nsec. Because the transmission speed of a wave in a cable is approximately *2/3* of the transmission speed of light in vacuum, it takes a signal about *5* μsec to travel across a cable of *1* km length.

The term *bit length of a channel* is used to denote the number of bits that can traverse the channel within one propagation delay. For example, if the channel bandwidth is *100* Mbit and the channel is *200* m long, the bitlength of the channel is *100* bits, since the propagation delay of this channel is *1* μsec.

Limit to Protocol Efficiency: In a bus system, the data efficiency of any media access protocol to a single channel is limited by the need to maintain a minimum time interval of one propagation delay between two successive messages. Assume the bit length of a channel to be *bl* bits and the message length to be *m* bits. Then an upper bound for the data efficiency of any media access protocol in a bus system is given by:

$$data\ efficiency < m/(m+bl)$$

Example: Consider a 1km bus with a bandwidth equal to *100* Mbits/sec. The message length that is transmitted over this channel is *100* bits. It follows that the bit length of the channel is *500* bits, and the limit to the data efficiency is *100/(500+100) = 16.6%*.

7.5.2 CSMA/CD–LON

Carrier Sense Multiple Access/Collision Detection Protocols (CSMA/CD) are distributed medium access protocols that do not require any central locus of control. The Ethernet protocol is the classic example of a CSMA/CD protocol.

An example of a protocol from this class that is targeted for real-time systems in building automation is the LON protocol from Echelon [LON90]. The LON Medium-Access Layer is a distributed access-control protocol that relies on a random number generator to reduce the probability of collisions at the start of transmission and during retransmissions as a result of collisions. A node wishing to transmit always accesses the channel after a random delay after the carrier of the previous transmission has disappeared. The size of this randomizing window is a function of the load on the channel and is designed to minimize the probability of a collision under high load. This mechanism thus provides *stochastic* back-pressure flow control.

7.5.3   CSMA/CA–CAN

Carrier Sense Multiple Access Collision Avoidance Protocols (CSMA/CA) are distributed medium-access protocols that avoid the occurrence of collisions, e.g., by bit arbitration. The CAN (Control Area Network) Protocol developed by Bosch is a good example of a CSMA/CA protocol that is targeted for automotive real-time applications [CAN90]. Many European cars use the CAN protocol for in-vehicle data communication.

A CAN message consists of six fields as seen in Figure 7.8. The first field is an *11*-bit arbitration field that also acts as a message identifier. Then there is a *6* bit control field followed by a data field of between *0-64* bits in length. The data in the first three fields are protected by a *16* bit CRC field that ensures a Hamming distance of *6*. The fields after the CRC are used for an immediate acknowledgment message.

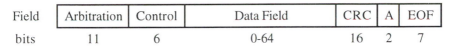

Field	Arbitration	Control	Data Field	CRC	A	EOF
bits	11	6	0-64	16	2	7

Figure 7.8: Data format of a CAN message.

In CAN, the arbitration logic assumes that a recessive and a dominant state on the communication channel exist such that the dominant state can overwrite the recessive state. This is possible if the propagation delay of the channel is smaller than the length of a bitcell. Assume that a '0' is coded into the dominant state and a '1' is coded into the recessive state. Whenever a node intends to send a message, it puts the first bit of the message identifier on the channel. In case of a conflict the node with a '0' in its first identifier bit wins, and the one with a '1' must back off. This arbitration continues for all bits of the identifier. A node with all '0's always wins–this is the bit pattern of the highest priority message. In CAN, the message priority is determined by the message identifier.

7.5.4   Token Bus–Profibus

In a token-bus system, the right to transmit is contained in a special control message, the token. Whoever has the token is allowed to transmit. Two time parameters determine the response of a token-bus system, the token-hold time THT, denoting the longest time a node may hold the token, and the token-rotation time TRT, denoting the longest time for a full rotation of the token. A serious error in any token system is the loss of the token, e.g., if the station that possesses the token fails. In such a situation, the network traffic is disrupted until some other node detects the 'silence' by monitoring a time-out, and generates a new token.

An example of a token bus protocol proposed for real-time systems is the Profibus [Pro92] that is used in German industry for process automation.

7.5.5   Minislotting–ARINC   629

Minislotting is a time-controlled medium access strategy, where the time is partitioned into a sequence of minislots, each longer than the length of the propagation delay of the channel. Every node is assigned a unique number of minislots that must elapse, with silence on the channel, before it is allowed to transmit. A good example of a protocol based on minislotting is the ARINC 629 used by the aircraft industry for real-time communication [ARI91]. The ARINC 629 protocol is used on the Boeing 777 airplane.

ARINC 629 is a "waiting-room protocol" similar to the bakery algorithm of Lamport [Lam74]. In the first phase, the set of processes that wants to transmit a message is admitted to a "distributed waiting room". In the following time interval, called an epoch, all processes that are in the waiting room are allowed to transmit their messages before any new process is allowed to enter the waiting room.

In ARINC 629, the medium access is controlled by three time-out parameters, the synchronization gap SG controlling the entrance to the waiting room, the terminal gap TG controlling the access to the bus, and the transmit interval TI disabling a host from monopolizing the channel. SG and TI are identical for all nodes, whereas TG is the 'personality' timer that is different for each node. The following relations hold between these time-outs: $SG > Max\{TG_i\}$ for all processes i, and $TI > SG$.

The detailed operation of the protocol is explained by looking at two processes P1 and P2 that want to transmit a message. Assume that TG1 of process P1 is shorter than TG2 of process P2. Both processes initially wait for an interval of silence on the channel that is longer than SG, the admit time-out for the waiting room. After they have entered the waiting room, both processes wait for another period of silence corresponding to their individual terminal gaps. Because all TGs are different, the process with the shorter TG, P1 with TG1, starts transmitting if the bus is idle at the moment when its time-out has elapsed (see Figure 7.9). At the start of transmission, P1 sets its time-out TI to block any further sending activity in this epoch by node P1. This protocol mechanism makes it impossible for a single host to monopolize the network.

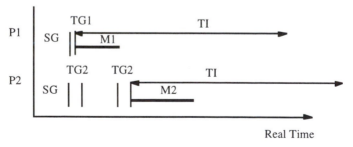

Figure 7.9: Timing diagram of ARINC 629.

As soon as P1 has started transmitting, P2 backs off until P1 has finished. After P1 has finished, P2 waits for TG2 again and starts to send its message if no bus activity is recognized at the point of time-out, as shown in Figure 7.9. All nodes that must send a message in this epoch complete their sending activity before any other node may start a new epoch, because $SG > Max\{TG_i\}$.

Typical values for the time-out parameters on a 2 Mbit/sec channel are: terminal gap (determined by the propagation delay): *4-128* µsec, synchronization gap: longer than the longest terminal gap, transmit interval: *0.5-64* msec. The time-out parameters in the ARINC 629 protocol convey regularity information to the protocol machine that restricts the operation of the host computer of a node. If the protocol operates correctly, a malicious node cannot monopolize the network.

7.5.6   Central Master–FIP

A central master protocol relies on a central master to control the access to the bus. In a case where the central master node fails, another node takes over the role of the central master (multi-master systems). A good example of a central master protocol is the FIP protocol [FIP94].

When a FIP system is configured, a static list containing the names and periods of the messages is generated for the central master (called *the bus arbitrator* in FIP). The master periodically broadcasts the name of a variable from this list on the bus. The node that produces this variable responds with a broadcast of the contents of this variable. All other nodes listen to this broadcast and accept the contents of this variable if needed. The proper operation of all stations attached to the bus is monitored by timers. If free time remains, the nodes can also send sporadic data after being polled by the master.

7.5.7   TDMA–TTP

Time Division Multiple Access (TDMA) is a distributed static medium access strategy where the right to transmit a frame is controlled by the progression of real time. This requires that a (fault-tolerant) global time-base is available at all nodes. In a TDMA-based system, the total channel capacity is statically divided into a number of slots. A unique sending slot is assigned to every node. The sequence of sending slots within an ensemble of nodes is called a *TDMA round*. A node can thus send one frame in every TDMA round. If there are no data to send, an empty frame is transmitted. After the completion of a TDMA round a new TDMA round, possibly with different messages, is started. The sequence of all different TDMA rounds is called a *cluster cycle*. The length of the cluster cycle determines the periodicity of the TDMA system.

An example of a TDMA protocol designed for real-time applications is the Time-Triggered Protocol (TTP) [Kop93a] described in Chapter 8.

7.5.8   Comparison of the Protocols

The characteristics of the protocols that have been surveyed in the previous section are plotted in Figure 7.10. It should be noted, however, that the classification of the design decisions is subjective. Looking at Figure 7.10 it is evident that the protocols CAN and LON on one side, and FIP and TTP on the other side, are positioned in diagonally opposite corners of the design space. The ARINC 629 and the PROFIBUS are at an intermediate position.

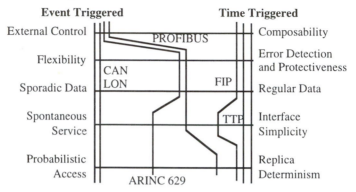

Figure 7.10: Design decisions in the protocols
CAN, LON, ARINC 629, Profibus, and TTP.

There is not, and there will never be, a real-time communication protocol that can satisfy all requirements listed in section 7.1. Figure 7.11 tries to summarize the tradeoffs that must be made in real-time protocol design. On the one side there is the important characteristic of flexibility and immediate response, while on the side there are the issues of composability and error detection.

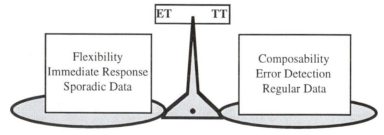

Figure 7.11: Tradeoffs in protocol design.

It is up to the application designer to compare the characteristics of the application requirements with those provided by the protocols to find the most agreeable match.

7.6   PERFORMANCE COMPARISON: ET VERSUS TT

The performance of an ET protocol is superior to that of a TT protocol if the environment requires the exchange of many sporadic messages with unknown request times. In an environment where many periodic messages must be exchanged, such as in control applications, the performance of a TT protocol is better than that of an ET protocol.

The following example tries to give an indication of the efficiency of ET versus TT systems in the transport of alarm messages. An alarm message is difficult to schedule, because it occurs infrequently, but when it occurs it must be serviced within a specified maximum latency.

7.6.1   Problem   Specification

Consider a cluster consisting of ten interface nodes connected to the controlled object, and one alarm monitoring node that processes the alarms and displays them to the operator (Figure 7.12).

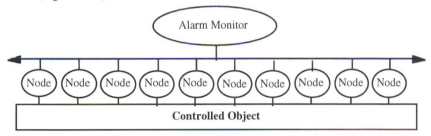

Figure 7.12: Example of an alarm monitoring system.

Each of the ten interface nodes must observe *40* binary alarm signals in the controlled object. Within *100* msec after an alarm signal has changed to "TRUE", the operator must be informed about the occurrence of the alarm.

The communication channel supports a bandwidth of *100* kbits/second.

7.6.2   ET   and   TT   Solutions

We compare two solutions to this problem, both using the same basic protocol, e.g., a CAN protocol. The first implementation is event-triggered, while the second one is time-triggered.

Event-Triggered Implementation: An event-triggered implementation sends an *event* message to the operator *as soon as* an alarm has been recognized. The event message contains the name of the alarm that can be encoded into a CAN message (see Figure 7.7) with a data field of *1* byte. Considering that the overhead of a CAN message is *44* bit, and that an intermessage gap of *4* bits is observed, the total length of an event message that reports an alarm is *56* bits. If a bandwidth of *100* kbits/second is available, about *180* event messages can be transported in the given latency interval of *100*msec. This is less than the *400* alarms that can occur simultaneously in the peak load scenario.

Time-Triggered Implementation: A time-triggered implementation sends a *periodic* state message every *100* msec by every node. This state message is a periodic CAN message with a data field of *40* bits (*5* bytes), one bit for each alarm. Considering the overhead of *44* bits and the intermessage gap of *4* bits, the total state message length is 88 bits. Considering the bandwidth of *100* kbits/second, about *110* state messages can be transported in the given latency interval of *100* msec. Because only *10* periodic state messages are needed to cover the specified peak-load scenario, the TT implementation requires less than *10%* of the available bandwidth to meet the temporal requirements of the specification. The TT implementation provides an error detection capability at the alarm monitor that is not available in the ET implementation.

7.6.3   Comparison of the Solutions

Figure 7.13 compares the performance of the ET implementation versus the TT implementation for different load scenarios. The break-even point between the two implementations is at about *16* alarms per *100* milliseconds, i.e., about 4 % of the peak load. If less than *16* alarms occur within a time interval of *100* msec, then the ET implementation generates less load on the communication system. If more than *16* alarms occur, then the TT implementation is more efficient.

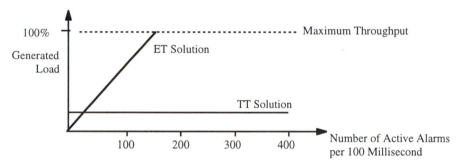

Figure 7.13: Load generated by the ET and TT solution
of the alarm monitoring system.

7.7   THE PHYSICAL LAYER

The physical layer specifies the transmission codes such as the coding of the bit patterns on the physical channel, the transmission medium, the transmission speed, and the physical shape of the bit cells. To some extent, the protocol design is influenced by the decisions made at the physical layer and *vice versa*.

Example: The CAN protocol is based on the assumption that every bit cell stabilizes on the channel such that the priority arbitration can be performed at all nodes. This assumption limits the speed of the network to a bit cell size that is longer than the propagation delay.

7.7.1   Properties of Transmission Codes

The terms *asynchronous* and *synchronous* have different meanings depending on whether they are used in the computer-science community or in the data-communication community. The following section is referring to the meaning of these words as used in the data-communication community.

In *asynchronous* communication, the receiver synchronizes its receiving logic with that of the sender *only at the beginning* of a new message. Since the clocks of the receiver and the sender drift apart during the interval of message reception, the message length is limited in asynchronous communication, e.g., to about *10* bits in a UART (Universal Asynchronous Receiver Transmitter) device that uses a low cost resonator with a drift rate of 10^{-2} sec/sec.

In *synchronous* communication, the receiver resynchronizes its receive logic *during the reception* of a message to the ticks of the sender's clock. This is only possible if the selected data encoding guarantees frequent transitions in the bit stream. A code that supports the resynchronization of the receiver's logic to the clocks of the sender during the transmission is called a *synchronizing code.*

7.7.2   Examples of Transmission Codes

NRZ Code: A simple encoding technique is the NRZ (non-return-to-zero code) where a "1" bit is high and a "0" bit is low (Figure 7.14). If the data stream contains only "1"s or "0"s, this code does not generate any signal transitions on the transmission channel. It is therefore a *non-synchronizing* code because it is impossible for the receiver to retrieve the ticks of the clock of the sender from a monotone transmission signal. An NRZ code can be used in an asynchronous communication environment, but it cannot be used in a synchronous environment without adding "artificial" transitions by inserting additional bits (*bit stuffing*) into the transmission sequence to support the synchronization of the receiver. Bit stuffing makes the length of a message data-dependent, which reduces the data efficiency.

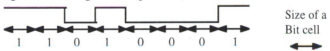

Figure 7.14: Encoding of the bit sequence "1101 0001" in the NRZ code.

Manchester Code: A bitstream encoded by a Manchester code has a synchronization edge in every bit cell of the transmitted signal. The Manchester code encodes a "0" as a high/low bitcell and a "1" as a low/high bitcell as shown in Figure 7.15.

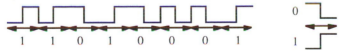

Figure 7.15: Encoding of the bit sequence "1101 0001" in the Manchester Code.

This code is thus ideal from the point of view of resynchronization but it has the disadvantage that the size of a *feature element*, i.e., the smallest geometric element in the transmission sequence, is half a bit cell.

Modified Frequency Modulation (MFM): The MFM code is a code that has a feature size of one bit cell and is also synchronizing [Mie91]. The encoding scheme requires to distinguish between a data point and a clock point. A "0" is encoded by no signal change at a data point, a "1" requires a signal change at a data point. If there are more than two "0"s in sequence, the encoding rules require a signal change at clock points, as shown in Figure 7.16.

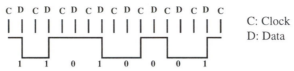

Figure 7.16: Encoding of the bit sequence "1101 0001" in MFM.

7.7.3 Signal Shape

The physical form of the feature element determines the electromagnetic emission (electromagnetic interference, EMI) of a code. An example for the form of a feature element is given in Figure 7.17. In this example, a bitcell is divided into three parts. In the first part, the voltage is increased until it reaches the high level. This high level is maintained during the second part. In the third part, the voltage is decreased again.

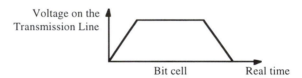

Figure 7.17: Form of a feature element to reduce EMI.

Steep edges of electrical signals must be avoided because steep edges lead to high-frequency Electromagnetic Interference (EMI). The smaller the feature element of a code, the more difficult it becomes to use the code at high transmission rates.

POINTS TO REMEMBER

* *Flow control* is concerned with the control of the speed of the information flow between a sender and a receiver in such a manner that the receiver can keep up with the sender. In any communication scenario, it is the receiver, rather than the sender, that determines the *maximum* speed of communication.

* In *explicit flow control*, the receiver sends an explicit acknowledgment message to the sender, informing the sender that the sender's previous message has arrived correctly, and that the receiver is now ready to accept the next message.

* Explicit flow control requires that the sender is in the sphere of control (SOC) of the receiver, i.e., the receiver can exert *back pressure* on the sender.

* In *implicit flow control*, the sender and receiver agree *a priori*, i.e., at system start up, about the points in time when messages will be sent.

- The communication system can exercise flow control over the requests from the clients, and assist in fulfilling the temporal obligations of the client.

- In a real-time system, the detection of message loss by the *receiver* of a message is of particular concern.

- The end-to-end acknowledgment indicating the success or failure of a communication action does not have to come from the receiver of an output message.

- The multicast communication requirement suggests a communication structure that supports multicasting at the physical level, e.g., a bus or a ring network.

- The *only* successful technique to avoid thrashing in explicit flow-control schemes is to monitor the resource requirements of the system continuously and to exercise a stringent back-pressure flow control as soon as a decrease in the throughput is observed.

- It is difficult to design the interface between a producer subsystem that uses implicit flow control, and a consumer subsystem that uses explicit flow control.

- The assumptions of the OSI reference architecture do not match up with the requirements of hard real-time systems.

- The *Asynchronous Transfer Mode (ATM)* communication technology provides real-time communication with low jitter over broadband networks.

- The purpose of the field bus is to interconnect a node of the distributed computer system to the sensors and actuators in the controlled process. The main concern at the field bus level is low cost, both for the controllers and for the cabling.

- The real-time network must provide reliable and temporally predictable message transmission with small latency and minimal latency jitter, clock synchronization, membership service, and support for fault-tolerance.

- If the temporal properties are not contained in the CNI specification, e.g., because the point in time when a message must be transmitted is *external and unknown* to the communication system, then it is not possible to achieve composability in the temporal domain.

- A fundamental conflict exists between the requirement for flexibility and the requirement for error detection. Flexibility implies that the behavior of a node is not restricted *a priori*. Error detection is only possible if the actual behavior of a node can be compared with some *a priori* known expected behavior.

- In a bus system, the data efficiency of any media access protocol is limited by the need to maintain a minimum time interval of one propagation delay between two successive messages.

Bibliographic Notes

The requirements for distributed safety-critical real-time systems onboard vehicles are analyzed in the SAE report J20056/1 "Class C Application Requirements" [SAE95].

A good overview of the issues in real-time communication systems is contained in the article on "Real-Time Communication" by Verissimo [Ver93]. A communication infrastructure for distributed real-time architecture is described in [Kop95e].

REVIEW QUESTIONS AND PROBLEMS

7.1   Compare the requirements of *real-time* communication systems with those of *non real-time* communication systems. What are the most significant differences?

7.2   What are the special requirements of a communication system for a safety critical application? Why should the SRUs forming an FTU be physically separated?

7.3   Why are end-to-end protocols needed at the interface between the computer system and the controlled object?

7.4   Which subsystem controls the speed of communication if an *explicit* flow control schema is deployed?

7.5   Calculate the latency jitter of a high level PAR protocol that allows three retries, assuming that the lower level protocol used for this implementation has a dmin of *2* msec and a dmax of *20* msec. Calculate the error detection latency at the sender.

7.6   Compare the efficiency of event-triggered and time-triggered communication protocols at low load and at peak load.

7.7   What mechanisms can lead to trashing? How should you react in an event-triggered system if thrashing is observed?

7.8   What are the characteristic of OSI based protocols? How do they match with the requirements of hard real-time systems?

7.9   How is the information organized in an ATM system? Discuss the suitability of ATM systems for the implementation of wide-area real-time systems.

7.10   What are the main differences between a *field bus*, a *real-time network*, and a *backbone network*?

7.11   Discuss the *fundamental conflicts* in the requirements imposed on a real-time protocol.

7.12   Given a bandwidth of *500* Mbits/sec, a channel length of *100* m and a message length of *80* bits, what is the limit of the protocol efficiency that can be achieved at the media access level of a bus system?

7.13   How do the nodes in a CAN system decide which node is allowed to access the bus?

7.14   Explain the role of the three time-outs in the ARINC 629 protocol. Is it possible for a collision to occur on an ARINC 629 bus?

Chapter 8

The Time-Triggered Protocols

OVERVIEW

The Time-Triggered Protocols (TTP) form a new protocol class that has been designed at the Technische Universität Wien to accommodate the specific requirements of fault-tolerant distributed real-time systems. The chapter starts with a statement of the protocol objectives, and explains the rationale that governed the protocol design. There are two different variants of TTP, TTP/C for the implementation of a fault-tolerant intra-cluster communication system, and the low-cost TTP/A version for the implementation of a field bus.

Section 8.2 describes the layers of TTP. Apart from the physical and data link layer, the TTP layers are different from those of the OSI model. The smallest replaceable unit (SRU) layer provides the consistent SRU membership service. The redundancy management layer is responsible for the startup and reconfiguration of a TTP system. The fault-tolerant unit (FTU) layer groups nodes into FTUs, and provides an FTU membership. The most important interface of a TTP system is the node-internal communication-network interface (CNI) that acts as a temporal firewall between the host computer and the communication network. The structure of the CNI is explained in Section 8.3. Section 8.4 outlines the internal logic of TTP/C. The membership service of TTP/C is explained, the novel method for CRC calculation that guarantees the consistency between the protocol state of the sender and the receiver is presented, and the message formats are depicted.

Section 8.5 is devoted to the time-triggered field bus protocol TTP/A. TTP/A is intended for the interconnection of intelligent sensors and actuators to an interface node. The implementation of this low-cost protocol requires only a standard UART channel and a local timer that can be found on almost all single chip microcontrollers.

8.1   INTRODUCTION TO TIME-TRIGGERED PROTOCOLS

The Time-Triggered Protocols (TTP) are designed for the implementing of a time-triggered hard real-time system. There are two versions of the Time-Triggered Protocol, TTP/C [Kop93a] for fault-tolerant hard real-time systems and TTP/A [Kop95c] for low cost applications (e.g., fieldbus applications).

8.1.1   Protocol Objectives

The protocol objectives are in line with the goals established in Chapter 7:

(i)   Message transport with low latency and minimal jitter,

(ii)   Support of composability,

(iii)   Provision of a fault-tolerant membership service,

(vi)   Fault-tolerant clock synchronization,

(v)   Distributed redundancy management,

(vi)   Minimal overhead, both in message length and in the number of messages, and

(vii) Scalability to high data rates, and efficient operation on twisted wires as well as on optical fibers.

TTP provides flexibility as long as the determinism, i.e., the analytical predictability of the timeliness, can be maintained.

8.1.2   Structure of a TTP System

The structure of a TTP system is shown Figure 8.1. A cluster of fault-tolerant units (FTUs), each one consisting of one, two, or more nodes, is interconnected by a communication network.

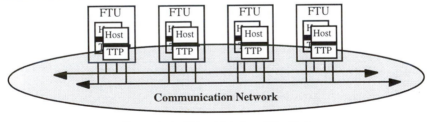

Figure 8.1: Communication-network interface (CNI) in a TTP system.

In TTP, a node is the smallest replaceable unit (SRU) that can be replaced or reconfigured in case of failure. An node consists of two subsystems, the host and the communication controller (Figure 8.2). The Communication-Network Interface (CNI) is the node-internal interface between the communication controller and the host. The CNI is formed by a dual-ported random-access memory (DPRAM), so that the communication controller as well as the host computer can read/write state messages into the CNI. The integrity of the data passed between the host and the communication controller is ensured by a special lock-free synchronization protocol, the Non-Blocking Write (NBW) protocol. The NBW is described in the chapter on operating systems (Section 10.2.2).

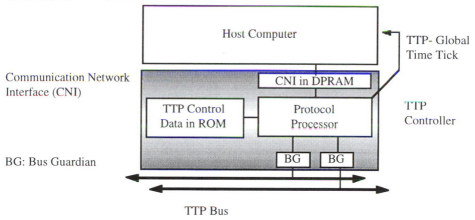

Figure 8.2: Hardware structure of a TTP node.

The communication controller within a node has a local memory to hold the *message descriptor list (MEDL)* that determines at what point in time a node is allowed to send a message, and when it can expect to receive a message from another node. The MEDL has the size of one cluster cycle that is composed of a sequence of TDMA rounds as described in Section 7.5.7. Additionally, a TTP controller contains independent hardware devices, the Bus Guardians (BGs), that monitor the temporal access pattern of the controller to the replicated buses, and terminate the controller operation in case a timing violation in the regular access pattern is detected.

8.1.3   Design Rationale

TTP is a time-division-multiple-access (TDMA) protocol where every node sends a message on the shared communication channel during a predetermined statically assigned time slot. The regularity of the TDMA system is used to optimize the TTP protocol.

Composability: The operation of the TTP communication controller is autonomous, and is controlled by the MEDL inside the controller and the fault-tolerant global time. The CNI between the TTP controller and the host computer is fully specified in the value and temporal domain, thus supporting the composability of an architecture (see Section 2.2). An error (software or hardware) in any one of the hosts cannot interfere with the proper operation of the communication system because no control signal crosses the CNI (impossibility of control error propagation), and the MEDLs are inaccessible to the hosts.

Best Use of *A Priori* Knowledge: In a time-triggered architecture, the information about the behavior of the system, e.g., which node must send what message at a particular point in time of a sparse time-base, is known at design time to all nodes of the ensemble. TTP tries to make best use of this *a priori* information.

Example: A receiver can detect a missing message immediately after the *a priori* known receive time has elapsed.

Naming: The message and sender name need not be part of a message because they can be retrieved from the MEDL using the point in time of message transmission as an index. The data element names that are used in the host software to identify a given RT entity can differ in different hosts.

Acknowledgment Scheme: The acknowledgment scheme of TTP takes advantage of the broadcast facility of the communication medium. It is known *a priori* that every correct member of the ensemble hears every message transmitted by a correct sender. As soon as one receiver has acknowledged a message from a sender, it can be concluded that the message has been sent correctly and that all correct receivers have received it. To make the acknowledgment scheme fault-tolerant, redundancy is introduced. This line of reasoning is valid as long as the probability of successive asymmetric communication failures is negligible.

Fail Silence in the Temporal Domain: TTP is based on the assumption that the nodes support the fail-silent abstraction in the temporal domain, i.e., a node either delivers a message at the correct moment or not at all. This helps to enforce error confinement at the system level. The fail-silent behavior of an node in the time domain is realized by the independent bus guardian at each channel. A membership service is provided to detect the failure of a node consistently with a small latency.

Fail Silence in the Value Domain: The TTP controller provides fail silence in the temporal domain. Designing fail silence in the value domain is in the responsibility of the host. The host software must ensure by space and/or time redundancy (see Section 14.1.1) that all the internal failures of a host are detected before a non-detectable erroneous output message is transmitted. Value failures introduced at the communication level are detected by the CRC mechanism provided by TTP.

Design Tradeoffs: In TTP, the design tradeoff between processing requirements at the nodes and bandwidth requirements of the channel is tilted towards optimal usage of the available channel bandwidth, even at the expense of increased processing load at the communication controllers. Considering the advances of the VLSI technology, we feel that the inherent bandwidth limitations of the channels in the envisioned application domain of automotive electronics are much more severe than the limitations in the processing and storage capabilities of the communication controllers [Kop94].

8.1.4   Protocol Variants

Two variants of the Time-Triggered Protocol are available, the full version TTP/C and the scaled-down version TTP/A. The communication-network interface has a compatible structure for both protocol versions.

TTP/C: The TTP/C protocol is the full version of the protocol that provides all services needed for the implementation of a fault-tolerant distributed real-time system. TTP/C supports FTUs that comprise replicated communication channels and different replication strategies, e.g., replicated fail-silent nodes or TMR nodes (see Section 6.4.2). TTP/C requires a specially designed communication controller that contains hardware mechanisms for the implementation of the protocol functions.

TTP/A: The TTP/A protocol is a scaled-down version that is intended for non fault-tolerant field bus applications. TTP/A requires only a standard UART hardware port and a local real-time clock, both of which are available on most low-cost microcontrollers. The protocol logic can be implemented in the software of a microcontroller.

Table 8.1 compares the services provided by TTP/A and TTP/C.

Service	TTP/A	TTP/C
Clock Synchronization.	Central Multimaster	Distributed, Fault-Tolerant
Mode Switches	yes	yes
Communication Error Detection	Parity	16/24 bit CRC
Membership Service	simple	full
External Clock Synchronization	yes	yes
Time-Redundant Transmission	yes	yes
Duplex Nodes	no	yes
Duplex Channels	no	yes
Redundancy Management	no	yes
Shadow Node (see Section 6.4.1)	no	yes

Table 8.1: Services of TTP/A and TTP/C.

8.2   OVERVIEW OF THE TTP/C PROTOCOL LAYERS

The protocol mechanisms are organized into a set of conceptual layers, as shown in Figure 8.3. The interface between the redundancy management layer and the FTU layer is called the *Basic Communication-Network Interface (CNI)*. The interface between the FTU Layer and the Host Layer is called the *FTU Communication-Network Interface.*

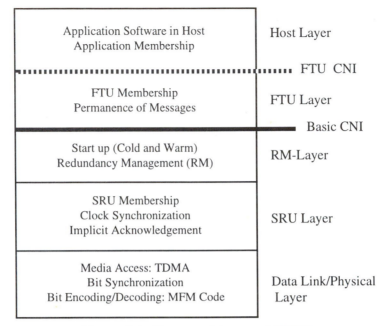

Figure 8.3: Conceptual layers of TTP/C.

8.2.1 Data Link/Physical Layer

The data-link/physical layer provides the means to exchange frames between the nodes. The data-link/physical layer must provide media-access control, bit synchronization and bit encoding/decoding. The access scheme to the channel is time-division-multiple access (TDMA), and is controlled by the data stored in the message descriptor list (MEDL) of the TTP controller. Bit synchronization and bit encoding/decoding uses the Modified Frequency Modulation (MFM) code. On a twisted-wire pair, the physical layer can be that of a CAN network, because the requirements on the physical layer of a TTP system are less demanding than those of a CAN system (TTP does not require bit arbitration).

8.2.2 SRU Layer

The SRU layer stores the data fields of the received frames into the memory area of the CNI DPRAM according to the control data contained in the MEDL. The SRU layer establishes the node membership. An implicit acknowledgment scheme uses the node membership to acknowledge the messages. Byzantine-resilient clock synchronization by the fault-tolerant average algorithm (see Section 3.4.3) is performed at the SRU layer. The SRU layer provides an immediate and deferred mode change service to the higher layers. An immediate mode change is executed immediately after a permitted mode change request. The execution of the deferred mode-change service is delayed until the beginning of the next cluster cycle.

8.2.3   Redundancy Management Layer (RM Layer)

The redundancy management layer *(RM Layer)* provides the mechanisms for the cold start of a TTP/C cluster. The RM layer uses the mode-change service that is part of the SRU layer during startup. The reintegration of a repaired node is also performed in the RM layer. A further function of the RM layer is the dynamic redundancy management, i.e., the replacement of a failed node by a shadow node. For this purpose a node reconfiguration field is provided in the CNI. If the host decides to reconfigure to a new node role, then the name of the requested node role is written into this reconfiguration field. The TTP controller checks whether the requested new node role is permitted. If so, it performs a node role change to the new node role, and reinitializes the bus guardian to protect the bus access in the new role.

Example: Consider the TMR configuration of Fig. 8.4. Assume that a shadow node is provided to replace any one of the three active nodes in case an active node fails. If the FTU layer of the shadow node detects the failure of an active node, the FTU layer requests a reconfiguration to the role of the failed node and takes its empty TDMA slot. After the reconfiguration, the TMR triad again contains three active nodes.

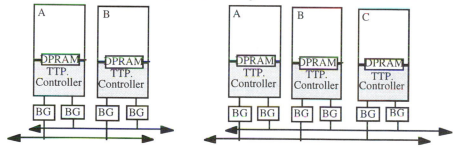

Figure 8.4 Different FTU configurations in TTP/C.

8.2.4   FTU Layer

The FTU layer groups two or more nodes into FTUs. The FTU layer must ensure that data are only visible in the FTU CNI after they have become *permanent.* (see Section 5.5.1). Depending on the chosen strategy, differing FTU configurations (Figure 8.4) can be supported by different FTU layers.

Some examples of different FTU layers are:

(i)   Two fail-silent nodes can be grouped into an FTU that provides the specified service as long as one of the two fail-silent nodes is operating. Fail silence in the value domain has to be ensured by the host. To improve the error-detection coverage in the value domain, the FTU layer supports the *High-Error-Detection-Coverage (HEDC) mode* (see Section 14.1.2).

(ii)   Three nodes can be grouped into a TMR (Triple Modular Redundancy) FTU. A TMR FTU can tolerate a single value failure in any of its nodes. The synchronization of the three nodes of a TMR FTU is realized by the lower layers.

(iii) It is possible to form FTUs of software subsystems executing on different nodes.

Each of these different FTU layers has a different FTU membership service, and a different structure of the FTU CNI. The FTU membership service is provided by the FTU layer. The FTU layer can be implemented in the host computer or in the TTP/C controller.

A basic TTP/C controller, which is implemented in hardware, does not contain an FTU layer but provides the basic CNI interface to the software in the host computer. It is, in this case up to the software of the host computer to implement the FTU layer.

8.3   THE BASIC CNI

The CNI is the most important interface within a time-triggered architecture, because it is the only interface of the communication system that is visible to the software of the host computer. It thus constitutes the programming interface of a TTP network. Every effort has been made to make the CNI simple to understand and easy to program. The CNIs for the TTP/A protocol and for the TTP/C protocol are upward compatible.

Status Registers	Control Registers
Global Internal Time	Watchdog
SRU-Time (part of C State)	Timeout Register
MEDL (part of C State)	Mode Change Request
Membership (part of C State)	Reconfiguration Request
Status Information	External Rate Correction

Figure 8.5: Status and control registers at the CNI.

8.3.1   Structure of the CNI

The basic CNI is a data-sharing interface between the RM layer and the FTU layer. The design of the CNI as a data sharing interface is reflected by its structure–it consists primarily of data fields.

(i) The *Status/Control Area* contains system information. It provides a facility for the TTP controller and the host CPU to communicate with each other via dedicated data fields.

(ii) The *Message Area* contains the messages sent or received by the node, and includes a control byte for each message.

There is a single control line from the TTP controller to the host that signals the tick of the global clock.

8.3.2   Status/Control Area

The status/control area of the CNI is a memory area of the DPRAM containing the control and status information that is shared between the TTP controller and the host CPU. The memory layout of the registers of the status/control is shown in Figure 8.5.

Status Registers Updated by the TTP Controller: The two-byte global internal time register contains the current global time of the cluster, established by the mutual internal synchronization of the TTP controllers.

The next three status fields contain the current h-state of the protocol, the *controller state* (*C-state*). The C-state consists of the SRU time, the MEDL position, and the node membership vector. The SRU time contains the current global time in SRU slot granularity. This time stays constant during a complete SRU slot and is increased at the beginning of the next SRU slot. The MEDL position denotes the current operating mode of the cluster and the current position in the message descriptor list MEDL. The node membership field contains the current node membership vector. The node membership vector comprises as many bits as there are nodes in a cluster. Each node is assigned to a specified bit position of the membership vector. When this bit is set to "TRUE" the node was operating during its last sending slot, if this bit is set to "FALSE", this node was not operating. The membership is adjusted at the end of each SRU slot after all messages from the sending node must have arrived and the cyclic-redundancy check (CRC) fields of the messages have been analyzed. The protocol does only operate correctly if all members of the ensemble have the same C-state. This is why C-state agreement between sender and receiver is continually enforced by the protocol (see also Section 8.4.2).

The final field of the status area contains diverse status information and diagnosis information regarding the operation of the protocol that can be evaluated by the host.

Control Registers Written by the Host: The first control register, the watchdog field, must be updated periodically by the host CPU. The controller checks this field periodically to determine if the host CPU is alive. If the host CPU fails to update the watchdog field within the specified interval, then the controller assumes a failure of the host and stops sending messages on the network.

The time-out register provides the host with the possibility of requesting a temporal control signal (a time interrupt) at a specific future point of the global time. This register can be used to synchronize an activity of the host with the global time in the cluster. The host CPU writes a future time point into this register. When the value of the global time reaches this value, the TTP controller raises the interrupt.

The mode-change register can be used to request a mode change to a new schedule in all nodes of a cluster (see also Section 11.4.2). This mode-change request is transmitted to all other nodes at the next predetermined sending point of this node. TTP distinguishes between two types of mode changes, an *immediate* mode change and a *deferred* mode change. As the name implies, an immediate mode change is executed immediately by all nodes. A deferred mode change is delayed until the start of the next cluster cycle. A mode change is a very powerful–and therefore dangerous–mechanism that brings data dependency into the temporal control structure. In safety critical systems mode changes should be used with great care. The controller internal data structure MEDL of the communication controller in each node contains a static lock that can be turned on before system start up so that a given set of (or all) mode changes originating from the host of the node is disabled.

The reconfiguration-request register is used by the host to request a role change of the node. If a host detects that an important node has failed then the host can request a role change to perform the function of the failed node. This mechanism is provided to avoid spare exhaustion in a fault-tolerant system that has to operate over long mission times. To avoid erroneous role changes, the role-change mechanism is protected by special permission fields in the MEDL.

The external rate-correction field is provided for external clock synchronization. A time gateway can request a bounded common-mode drift of all nodes in a cluster to achieve synchronism with an external time source, such as a GPS time receiver (see Section 3.5).

8.3.3   Message Area

The application specific structure of the Message Area is determined by the MEDL of the TTP controller. Besides the data contained in the messages, a message entry also carries a status byte (Figure 8.6) that informs of potential error conditions.

Figure 8.6: Entry in the message area of the CNI.

8.3.4   Consistent Data Transfer

The consistency of single-word data transfers across the CNI is guaranteed by the hardware arbitration of the DPRAM. The consistency of a multi-word data transfer is realized at the CNI as follows:

Controller to Host: The data transfer from the TTP controller to the host CPU is under the control of the current MEDL. It consists of copying one message from the receive buffer of the TTP controller into the message area of the CNI at an *a priori* known time. Along with the message data, the status byte containing status information about the message reception must be set by the TTP controller. The status byte and the data field of a message are written to the CNI before the end of each SRU slot.

If the host CPU derives its read-access intervals from the global time base, then, access conflicts between the controller and the host can be avoided by making use of this *a priori* information. If the host CPU accesses the CNI at arbitrary points in time, the non-blocking write protocol NBW is provided to assure data integrity (see Section 10.2.1). This non-blocking protocol enables the host CPU to detect any write operation of the TTP controller that occurs while a message is read by the host.

In this case, the read operation of the host must be repeated. The TTP controller is never delayed while accessing the CNI.

Host to Controller: The host is aware of the current time and knows *a priori* when the TTP controller reads from the CNI. The host operating system must synchronize its output action such that it does not write into the CNI when the TTP controller performs a read operation. The NBW protocol provides an error-detection mechanism for data transfer from the host to the TTP controller.

8.4   INTERNAL OPERATION OF TTP/C

8.4.1   The Message Descriptor List (MEDL)

The MEDL is the static data structure within each TTP controller that controls when a message must be sent on or received from the communication channels and contains the position of the data in the CNI (Figure 8.7). During protocol operation, the MEDL serves as a dispatching table for the TTP controller. The length of MEDL is determined by the length of the cluster cycle, i.e., the sequence of TDMA rounds after which the operation of the cluster repeats itself.

SRU-Time	Address	D	L	I	A

(Attributes: D L I A)

Figure 8.7: Format of the MEDL.

MEDL Entry: An entry in the MEDL comprises three fields: a time field, an address field, and an attribute field (Figure 8.7). The time field contains the point in global time (with SRU granularity) when the message specified in the address field must be communicated. The address field points to the CNI memory cells where the data items must be stored to or retrieved from. The attribute field comprises four subfields:

(i)   a direction subfield (D) that specifies if the message is an input message or an output message,

(ii)   a length subfield (L), denoting the length of the message that must be communicated,

(iii) an initialization subfield (I) that specifies whether the message is an initialization message or a normal message, and

(iv)   an additional parameter subfield (A) that contains additional protective information concerning mode changes and node role changes.

The host can only execute mode changes that are permitted by the attribute field of the MEDL. In a safety-critical system, all mode changes requested by a host can be blocked by the MEDL.

The physical layout of the MEDL depends on the particular TTP controller implementation. Every node must have its *personal* MEDL–only one node can send a message on a channel at a particular time–and the set of all MEDLs of a cluster must be consistent. The MEDLs are generated automatically by a software development tool, the *cluster compiler* [Kop95a]. The cluster compiler takes as input a generic *application description* of a cluster, stored in a data base. This application description contains all attributes of the messages and modes of the cluster. The output of the cluster compiler is a set of MEDLs, one for each TTP controller, in a format prescribed by the particular TTP controller implementation.

Name Mapping: TTP provides a flexible naming scheme so that the same data element can be named differently in communicating hosts. Of course, it is possible and advisable to use the same name for the same RT entity in all nodes of a cluster, but the name-space design does not *require* such a uniform name structure. Flexible naming is of great advantage if legacy software is integrated into a cluster. The system integrator just knows about the function of the software, the meaning and address of the input and output data at the CNI, but may not have any idea about the internal structure or naming within the legacy code.

Name mapping is performed under the control of the MEDL in each controller. A TTP message does not carry a name on the physical channel. The first level of name mapping of the point in time of message tansmission to the appropriate memory position in the CNI is under control of the local MEDL of each node (Figure 8.8). The *a priori* known point in time of sending and receiving is sufficient to uniquely identify each message at the end points of the communication. Because real-time messages are normally very short–only a few bytes of data–the elimination of the name field reduces the message size and increases the data efficiency of the protocol significantly.

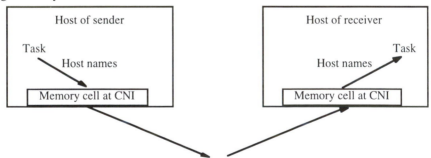

Name mapping to/from the global points in time determined by the contents of the MEDL

Figure 8.8: Naming in TTP.

A second level of name translation is possible between the CNI memory location and the name used in the software of the host.

Example: Consider an elevator system in a multi-story building where every floor has its local floor-controller node to control the door of the elevator and the displays at the door. Since the name mapping between the global network data and the local node data is performed under the control of the MEDL in the communication controller, the host software in each one of the floor-controller nodes can be identical.

8.4.2   Frame Format

During normal operation, a node transmits two frames during an SRU slot, one on each one of the replicated channels. A TTP/C frameconsists of three fields (Figure 8.9), a four-bit header, the variable-length data field of up to sixteen bytes, and a two (or a three) byte CRC field.

Frame Format:
Header	Data Bytes (up to 16)	16 bit CRC

HeaderFormat:
I/N Message	Mode bit 1	Mode bit 2	Mode bit 3

Figure 8.9: TTP frame format.

First Bit of the Header: The first bit of the header informs whether the message is an initialization (I) message or a normal (N) message. I-messages are used to initialize the system. They carry the C-state of the sender in the data field and make it possible for a new node to get the current C-state of the protocol when joining the ensemble.

Mode Bits: The three mode bits can be used to request a mode change in all nodes of the cluster. One out of seven application-specific successor modes to any given mode can be selected. The mode change mechanism can be restricted or disabled by setting parameters in the MEDL.

Data Field: The data field contains up to sixteen data bytes from the CNI at the sending node.

CRC Field: The CRC field contains the CRC check bits for communication error detection, as explained above.

8.4.3   CRC   Calculation

The CRC of an I-message is calculated over the concatenation of the header and the data bytes.

N-messages are used during normal system operation, and carry the host data in the data field. To enforce agreement of the controller states (C-state–see Figure 8.3) among the ensemble without having to include the C-state in each message, TTP uses an innovative technique of CRC calculation for N-Messages (Figure 8.10). The CRC at the sender is calculated over the message contents concatenated with the sender's C-state. The CRC check at the receiver is calculated over the received message contents concatenated with the receiver's C-state. If the result of the CRC check at the receiver is negative, then, either the message has been corrupted during transmission or there is a disagreement between the C-states of the sender and receiver. In both cases, the message must be discarded.

CRC Calculation at Sender:

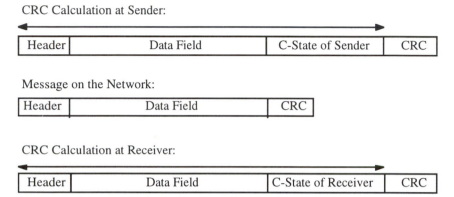

Figure 8.10: Calculation of the CRC of normal messages.

8.4.4 The Membership Service

The SRU layer of TTP provides a timely node membership service. The number of bits in the membership field of the C-state (Figure 8.9) corresponds to the maximum number of nodes in a cluster. Every node-send slot is a membership point for the sending node. If one out of the redundant messages of the sending node is correctly received by a receiving node, the receiving node considers the sending node operational at this membership point. The node is considered operational until its following membership point in the next TDMA cycle (see Section 6.4.4). If a node fails within this interval, the failure is only be recognized at the coming membership point. The delay of the membership information is at most one TDMA cycle. Therefore, the join protocol must wait until at least one TDMA cycle after a failure. If none of the expected messages arrives with a correct CRC, then, a receiver considers the sending node as failed at this membership point and clears the membership bit of this node at the end of the current SRU slot.

If a particular node did not receive any correct message from a sending node–e.g., because the incoming link of the receiver has failed–it assumes that this sending node has crashed, and it eliminates the sending node from its membership vector at the end of the SRU slot. If, however, all other nodes received at least one of these messages they come to a different conclusion about the membership. From this moment onward, two cliques have formed that cannot communicate with each other because they contain a different C-state. TTP contains a mechanism that makes sure that in such a conflict situation the majority view wins, i.e., that the node with the failed input port, which is in the minority, is eliminated from the membership. Before sending a message, a node counts its negative CRC-check results during the last TDMA round. If more than half of the messages received have been discarded because of a failed CRC check, the node assumes that its C-state differs from the majority, terminates its operation and thus leaves the membership. This mechanism avoids clique formation among the nodes of the ensemble. Agreement on membership is thus tantamount to an indirect acknowledgment of message reception by the majority.

8.4.5   Clock Synchronization

TTP provides the fault-tolerant internal synchronization of the local clocks to generate a global time-base of known precision. Because every receiving node knows *a priori* the expected time of arrival of each message, the deviation between the *a priori* specified arrival time and the observed arrival time is an indication of the clock difference between the sender's clock and the receiver's clock.

It is not necessary to exchange explicit synchronization messages or to carry the value of the send time in the message, thus extending the message length. Continuous clock synchronization is performed without any overhead in message length or message number by periodically applying a fault-tolerant clock synchronization algorithm, e.g., the FTA algorithm (see Section 3.4.3), preferably with hardware support [Kop87].

8.5   TTP/A FOR FIELD BUS APPLICATIONS

The TTP/A protocol is a scaled down version of the time-triggered protocol. TTP/A is intended for low-cost field bus applications. It is a multi-master protocol, not a distributed protocol. The node that interfaces a TTP/A fieldbus to a cluster is the natural master of a TTP/A network (see Figure 7.7 of Chapter 7).

TTP/A can be implemented on standard UARTs (Universal Asynchronous Receiver Transmitter) that are available on most low-cost eight-bit microcontrollers. A standard UART message consists of a start bit, 8 data bits (one-byte user data), a parity bit, and a stop bit, i.e., 11 bits in total.

8.5.1   Principles of Operation

TTP/A is based on one-byte state messages. Most of these messages are data messages, while only one special message, the *fireworks message*, is a control message. Every protocol event occurs either at a predefined point of time (e.g., sending a message) or must happen in a predefined time window (e.g., receipt of a message).

Round: In TTP/A all communication activities are organized into rounds (Figure 8.11). A round is the transmission of a sequence of one-byte messages that is specified *a priori* in the MEDL. A round starts with a special control byte, the Fireworks byte, that is transmitted by the active master. The Fireworks byte serves two purposes:

(i)   It is the global synchronization event for the start of a new round, and

(ii)   It contains the name of the active MEDL for this round.

The Fireworks byte is followed by a sequence of data bytes from the individual nodes as specified in the active MEDL. A round terminates when the end of the active MEDL is reached. Every round is independent of the previous round.

To be able to differentiate between a Fireworks byte and a data byte, the Fireworks byte has characteristic features in the value domain and in the time domain: the Fireworks byte has an odd parity while all data bytes have even parity. The intermessage gap between the Fireworks byte and the first data byte is significantly longer than the intermessage gap between the succeeding data bytes. These characteristic features make it possible for all nodes to recognize a new Fireworks byte, even if some faults have disturbed the communication during the previous round. The characteristic features of the Fireworks byte simplify the reintegration of repaired nodes--a repaired node monitors the network until a correct Fireworks byte is detected.

Because the sequence of messages is determined *a priori* by the definition of the active MEDL, it is not necessary to carry the identifier of a message as part of the message. All eight data bits of a message are true data bits. This improves the data efficiency of the protocol, particularly for the short one byte messages that are typical for field bus applications.

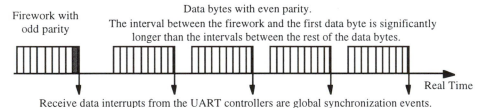

Receive data interrupts from the UART controllers are global synchronization events.

Figure 8.11: Structure of a TTP/A round.

Modes: From the point of view of protocol operation, every round is independent of the previous round. In many applications, the termination of a round causes the initiation of an identical next round by the active master. We call a sequence of identical rounds controlled by the same MEDL a mode. With the start of every new round a mode change can be initiated by the active master by transmitting the name of the new MEDL in the Fireworks byte.

Time-outs: The progression of the protocol through the active MEDL is controlled by a set of time-outs. The start of these time-outs is initially synchronized with the reception of the Fireworks byte and can be resynchronized with the reception of every new correct data message at every node. The "Receive Data Interrupt" (RDI) of the UART controller is considered a global synchronization event. The time-out values can be derived analytically from the parameters of the TTP/A controller [Kop95c].

To provide high error detection coverage, the occurrence of this global event RDI is monitored at every node. In case a node fails or a message is lost, a local time-out continues the protocol operation. In case the master does not send a new Fireworks byte within a specified time–the multi-master time-out–a backup node takes up the role of the active master.

8.5.2 Error Detection and Error Handling

The Fireworks Protocol TTP/A takes advantage of all error detection mechanisms of a UART controller to detect value errors, and provides a number of mechanisms to detect errors in the time domain with a short error detection latency. Note that in systems that support the fail silent abstraction, the error detection in the time domain is the primary error detection mechanism.

Error Detection in the Time Domain: The temporal control scheme of TTP/A is restrictive. After a new round has been initiated by the master, the temporal sequence of all correct send and receive events is specified in detail in the active MEDL and monitored by all nodes. If a "receive data interrupt" (RDI) is observed outside the specified window, a control error has occurred and the corresponding error flag is raised.

If an expected message is not received within the specified window, the old version of the data is not modified and an error is reported to the host through the control byte. The very short error detection latency of TTP/A makes it possible to initiate fail-safe actions with minimal delay. A missing data message does not corrupt the control scheme. If a control error is detected by a node–a message is received outside the expected window–then the present round at this node is terminated immediately and the node-local protocol is reinitialized to wait for a new Fireworks byte by the master. If the master does not send such a Fireworks byte within a specified multimaster time-out, then, a backup master takes control of the network.

Error Detection in the Value Domain: The error detection in the value domain relies on the facilities of the particular UART controller and on data redundancy provided and checked by the application software in the host. The TTP/A protocol requires that the controller supports odd and even parity. The Fireworks byte has odd parity, while all data bytes have even parity. Besides the parity check, many UART controllers provide mechanisms to detect various other kinds of reception errors, such as noise errors detected by oversampling, and framing errors. Whenever a data error is detected by a receiver, the old version of the state variable is not modified, and the data error is reported to the host through the status byte of the CNI.

8.5.3 Response Time of a TTP/A System

The time-out values of a TTP/A system depend on the bandwidth of the field bus, the drift of the resonators in the nodes, the interrupt response time of the node OS, the granularity of the clock of the node, and the time it takes for the host in the node to process the protocol logic. If these parameters are known, the time-out values of a TTP/A system can be calculated analytically [Kop95c].

Table 8.2 gives an example of an estimate of the TDMA round duration of a TTP/A system consisting of ten nodes, each one transmitting one data byte of 8 bits in each round. The data efficiency is the relation between the user data (measured in number of bits) transmitted during one round in relation to the total number of bitcells transmitted on the channel.

Parameter	Value
Bandwidth of the network	10 kbits/second
Drift rate of the resonators	10^{-4} sec/sec
Processing of protocol logic by the host	50 μsec
Interrupt response time in host OS	5 μsec
Granularity of the local clock	4 μsec
TDMA duration in system with 10 nodes	13 msec
Data efficiency	>60 %

Table 8.2: Data efficiency of TTP/A.

The installation of a field bus introduces an additional delay into the observations. If the observation of an analog value by the field bus node is temporally coordinated with the TTP/A schedule, then this additional delay is about 1.3 msec in the above example. The observation of an event can be delayed by a complete TDMA round, implying a delay of 13 msec in the above example. These delays can be reduced by the installation of a field bus with a wider bandwidth, e.g., 48 kbit/sec or 100 kbit/sec.

POINTS TO REMEMBER

- TTP is a time-division-multiple-access (TDMA) protocol where every node is allowed to send a message in a predetermined statically assigned time slot on a shared communication channel.

- In TTP, the operation of the communication system is autonomous, and independent of the software in the host. Even a malicious host cannot interfere with the proper operation of the protocol.

- The regularity of a TDMA system is used to optimize the TTP protocol. The message and sender name are not be part of a message because the identity of a message can be uniquely retrieved from the *a priori* known point in time of message transmission.

- TTP/C is the full version of the time-triggered protocol that provides all services needed for the implementation of a fault-tolerant distributed system.

- TTP/A is a scaled-down version of the time-triggered protocol that is intended for non fault-tolerant low-cost field bus applications.

- A node of a TTP system consists of two subsystems, the communication controller and the host.

- The communication-network interface (CNI) is the node-internal interface between the communication system and the host. It is the most important interface within a time-triggered architecture because it is the only interface that is visible to the software of the host computer, and thus constitutes the programming interface of a TTP network.

- The CNI contains state messages. It is a data-sharing interface that can be implemented in a dual-ported memory (DPRAM).

- The Message Descriptor List (MEDL) is the static data structure within each TTP controller that controls when a message must be sent on, or received from, the communication channels.

- In TTP the same data element can be named differently in the communicating hosts. On the network, the name of the data element is mapped into the *a priori* known point of time of message transmission.

- The consistency of the data transfer across the CNI is controlled by the non-blocking-write protocol (NBW).

- The node membership vector contains as many bits as there are nodes in a cluster. Each node is assigned to a specified bit position of the membership vector. When this bit is set to "TRUE" the node is operating at the current SRU time, if this bit is set to "FALSE", this node is not operating.

- The h-state of a TTP controller (C-state) consists of the SRU time, the node membership vector and the current position in the message descriptor list.

- To enforce agreement on the C-state of all nodes of an ensemble, TTP calculates the CRC at the sender over the message contents concatenated with the C-state of the sender. The CRC at the receiver is calculated over the received message contents concatenated with the C-state of the receiver. If the result of the CRC check at the receiver is negative then either the message was corrupted during transmission, or there is a disagreement between the C-states of the sender and receiver. In both cases the message is discarded.

- If more than half of the messages received were discarded because of a failed CRC check, the node assumes that its C-state differs from the majority, terminates its operation and thus leaves the membership. This mechanism avoids clique formation among the nodes of the ensemble.

- A TTP/C frame consists of three fields, a one-byte header, up to sixteen bytes of data, and a two byte CRC field.

- In TTP/A the communication is organized into rounds that start with a special control byte, the Fireworks byte, that is transmitted by the active master. The Fireworks byte contains the name of the active MEDL.

- The Fireworks byte has characteristic features in the value domain and in the time domain that differentiate the Fireworks byte from the data bytes within a TTP/A round.

BIBLIOGRAPHIC NOTES

The insights gained during more than ten years of research on fault-tolerant real-time systems in the context of the MARS project [Kop89] formed the basis for the development of the time-triggered protocols. The first publication of the protocol occurred in 1993 at the FTCS conference [Kop93a]. The TTP/A protocol was first published at the annual congress of the Society of Automotive Engineers (SAE) in 1995 [Kop95c].

REVIEW QUESTIONS AND PROBLEMS

8.1   What services are provided by the TTP/C protocol?

8.2   How is the regularity inherent in the TDMA access strategy used to increase the data efficiency of the protocol and to improve the robustness of the protocol?

8.3   Explain the programming interface of a TTP controller? What are the contents of the status area and the control area of the CNI? What are the contents of the status byte of each message.

8.4   How is the consistency of the data transfer across the CNI enforced by the protocol?

8.5   Why is the control data structure that controls the protocol operation stored in the TTP controller and not in the host?

8.6   What mechanism helps to ensure the fail-silence of a TTP controller in the temporal domain?

8.7   What system must implement the fail-silence in the value domain?

8.8   What are the differences between the TTP/C protocol and the TTP/A protocol?

8.9   What is the controller state (C-state) of a TTP/C controller? How is the agreement of the C-state enforced within an ensemble?

8.10   Explain the operation of the membership service of the TTP/C protocol. How is the situation that a node does not receive a message from its immediate predecessor resolved? (In this scenario the node does not know if its incoming link is faulty or the predecessor has not sent a correct message).

8.11   Explain the clock synchronization of the TTP/C protocol.

8.12   Sketch the contents of the Message Descriptor List (MEDL) that controls the protocol operation.

8.13   What is the difference between an immediate mode change and a delayed mode change?

8.14   What is the frame format of a TTP/C frame on the network? What are the contents of the header byte?

8.15   Explain the principle of operation of the TTP/A protocol. Describe the concept of a "round".

8.16   How can one distinguish between a Fireworks byte and a data byte in the TTP/A protocol?

8.17 Estimate the average and worst-case response time of a TTP/C system with 5 FTUs, each one consisting of two nodes that exchange messages with 6 data bytes on a channel with a bandwidth of 1 Mbit/sec. Assume that the interframe gap is 8 bits.

8.18 Calculate the data efficiency of a TTP/A system that consists of 8 nodes where each node sends periodically a two byte message (user data). Assume that the intermessage gap between the Fireworks byte and the first data byte is 4 bitcells, and the intermessage gap between two successive data bytes is two bitcells. The gap between the end of one round and the start of the next round is 6 bitcells. What is the data efficiency of a functionally equivalent CAN system with a two byte data field (see Section 7.5.3)? Assume that the intermessage gap in the CAN system is 4 bitcells.

Chapter 9

Input/Output

OVERVIEW

This chapter covers the input/output between a node and the controlled object. It starts with a discussion on the dual role of time at the I/O interface: time can act as a control signal causing the immediate activation of a computational activity, and time can be treated as data that records the occurrence of an external event on the time line. If time is treated as data, then the temporal control structure within the computer is not affected by the occurrence of the external event. In many situations, the I/O interface can be simplified by treating time as data and not as a control signal. Section 9.2 introduces the notions of *raw data, measured data,* and *agreed data.* It then continues with a discussion about the different types of agreement, syntactic agreement and semantic agreement.

The differences between sampling, polling, and interrupts are the topic of Section 9.3. From the functional point of view, sampling and polling are identical. However, from the robustness point of view, sampling is superior to polling. Section 9.4 is devoted to a discussion of interrupts. An interrupt is a powerful, and therefore potentially dangerous, mechanism that interferes with the temporal control structure within a node.

Sensors and actuators are the topic of Section 9.5. The concept of the intelligent instrumentation that hides the concrete world interface and interacts with the computer by a standard, more abstract message interface is elaborated. The notion of fault-tolerant actuators and fault tolerant sensors is introduced. Some hints concerning the physical installation of the I/O system are given in Section 9.6.

A node can interact with its environment by two subsystems: the communication subsystem and the input/output subsystem (instrumentation interface). The implementation of a field bus (see Section 7.3.3) extends the scope of the communication system and pushes the "real" I/O issues to the field bus nodes that interact directly with the sensors and actuators in the (remote) environment. At the expense of an additional delay, a field bus simplifies the I/O interface of a node, both from the logical and the installation point of view.

9.1   THE DUAL ROLE OF TIME

Every I/O signal has two dimensions, the value dimension and the temporal dimension. The value dimension relates to the value of the I/O signal. The temporal dimension relates to the moment when the value was recorded from the environment or released to the environment. In the context of hardware design, the value dimension is concerned with the contents of a register and the temporal dimension is concerned with the *trigger signal,* i.e., the control signal that determines when the contents of an I/O register are transferred to another subsystem.

An event that happens in the environment of a real-time computer can be looked upon from two different perspectives:

(i)   It defines the point in time of a value change of an RT entity. The precise knowledge of this point in time is an important input for the *later* analysis of the consequences of the event (*time as data*).

(ii)   It may demand *immediate* action by the computer system to react as soon as possible to this event (*time as control*).

It is important to distinguish between these two different roles of time. In the majority of situations, it is sufficient to treat time as data and only in the minority of cases an immediate action of a computer system is required (time as control).

Example: Consider a computer system that must measure the time interval between "start" and "finish" during a downhill skiing competition. In this application it is sufficient to treat time as data and to record the precise time of occurrence of the start event and finish event. The messages that contain these two time points are transported to a central computer that later calculates the difference. The situation of a train-control system that recognizes a red alarm signal, meaning the train should stop immediately, is different. Here, an immediate action is required as a consequence of the event occurrence. The occurrence of the event must initiate a control action without delay.

9.1.1   Time as Data

The implementation of *time as data* is simple if a global time-base of known precision is available in the distributed system. The observing field bus node must include the timestamp of the event into the observation message. We call a message that contains the timestamp of an event, a *timed message.* The timed message can be sent at a preplanned point in time and does not require any dynamic data-dependent modification of the temporal control structure. Alternatively, if a field bus communication protocol with a known constant delay is used, the time of message arrival, corrected by this known delay, can be used to derive the send time of the message.

The same technique of timed messages can be used on the output side. If an output signal must be invoked on the environment at a precise point in time, the granularity of which is much finer than the static periods or the jitter of the output messages, then, a timed output message can be sent to the node controlling the actuator. This node interprets the time in the message and acts on the environment precisely at the intended moment.

In a TT system that exchanges messages at *a priori* known points in time, with a fixed period between messages, the representation of time in a timed message can take advantage of this *a priori* information. The time value can be coded in fractions of the period of the message, thus increasing the data efficiency. For example, if an observation message is exchanged every 10 msec, then a 7 bit time representation of time relative to the start of the period will identify the event with a granularity of better than 100 μsec. Such a 7-bit representation of time, along with the additional bit to denote the event occurrence, can be packed into a single byte.

9.1.2   Time as Control

Time as control is much more difficult to implement than time as data, because it may require a dynamic data-dependent modification of the temporal control structure (see Section 4.4). It is prudent to scrutinize the application requirements carefully to identify those cases where such a dynamic scheduling of the tasks is absolutely necessary. The issue of dynamic task scheduling will be discussed in Chapter 11.

If an event requires immediate action, the worst-case delay of the message transmission is a critical parameter. In an event-triggered protocol, such as CAN, the message priorities are used to resolve access conflicts to the common bus that result from nearly simultaneous events. The worst-case delay of a particular message can be calculated by taking the peak-load activation pattern of the message system into account [Tin95]. In a time-triggered protocol such as TTP, the mode change mechanism is provided to implement a data dependent change of the control structure. This mechanism guarantees that a mode change request will be honored within a worst-case delay of a basic TDMA round.

Example: The prompt reaction to an emergency shutdown request requires time to act as control. Assume that the emergency message is the highest priority message. In a CAN system the worst-case delay of the highest priority message is bounded by the transmission duration of the longest message, because a message transmission cannot be preempted. In a TTP system, the worst-case delay for a mode change is bounded by the duration of a TDMA round.

9.2   AGREEMENT PROTOCOLS

Sensors and actuators have failure rates that are considerably higher than those of single-chip microcomputers. No critical output action should rely on the input from a single sensor. It is necessary to observe the controlled object by a number of different sensors and to relate these observations to detect erroneous sensor values, to observe the effects of actuators, and to get an *agreed* image of the state of the controlled object. In a distributed system, agreement always requires an information exchange among the agreeing partners. The number of rounds of such an information exchange that are needed depends on the type of agreement and the assumptions about the possible sensor failures.

9.2.1   Raw Data, Measured Data, and Agreed Data

In Section 1.2.1, the concepts of raw data, measured data, and agreed data have been introduced: *raw data* are produced at the digital hardware interface of the physical sensor. *Measured data*, presented in standard engineering units, are derived from one or a sequence of raw data samples by the process of signal conditioning. Measured data that are judged to be a correct image of the RT entity, e.g., after the comparison with other measured data elements that have been derived by diverse techniques, are called *agreed data*. Agreed data form the inputs to control actions. In a safety critical system, where no single point of failure is allowed to exist, an agreed data element may not originate from a *single* sensor. The challenge in the development of a safety critical input system is the selection and placement of the redundant sensors, and the design of the agreement algorithms. We distinguish between two types of agreement, *syntactic agreement* and *semantic agreement*.

9.2.2   Syntactic Agreement

Assume that a single RT entity is measured by two independent sensors. When the two observations are transformed from the domain of analog values to the domain of discrete values, a slight difference between the two raw values caused by a measurement and digitalization error is unavoidable. These different raw data values will cause different measured values. A digitalization error also occurs in the time domain when the time of occurrence of an event in the controlled object is mapped into the discrete time of the computer. Even in the fault-free case, these different measured values must be reconciled in some way to present an agreed view of the RT entity to the, possibly replicated, control tasks. In syntactic agreement, the agreement algorithm computes the agreed value without considering the context of the measured values. For example, the agreement algorithm always takes the average of a set of measured data values.

If one of the sensor readings can be erroneous, then the assumed failure model of the failed sensor determines how many measured data values are needed to detect the erroneous sensor [Mar90]. In the worst case, when the sensor can behave in a Byzantine fashion, up to four raw data values may be needed to tolerate such a malicious sensor fault (see Section 6.4). Syntactic agreement without any restrictions of the failure modes of a sensor is the most costly form of agreement among a set of sensor values. In case a more restrictive failure mode of a sensor can be assumed, e.g., a fail-silent failure, then the number of rounds and the amount of information that must be exchanged to achieve syntactic agreement can be considerably reduced [Pol95a].

9.2.3   Semantic   Agreement

If the meanings of the different measured values are related to each other by a process model that is based on *a priori* knowledge about the physical characteristics of the controlled object, then we speak of *semantic agreement*. In semantic agreement it is not necessary to duplicate or triplicate every sensor. Different RT-entities are observed by different sensors. These sensor readings are related to each other to find a set of plausible agreed values and to locate implausible values that indicate a sensor failure. Such an erroneous sensor value must be replaced by a calculated estimate of the most probable value at the given point in time, based on the inherent semantic redundancy in the set of measurements.

Example: A number of laws of nature govern a chemical process: the conservation of mass, the conservation of energy, and some known maximum speed of the chemical reaction. If the input and output entities are measured by individual sensors, these fundamental laws of nature can be applied to check the plausibility of the measured data set. In case one sensor reading deviates significantly from all other sensors, a sensor failure is assumed and the failed value is replaced by an estimate of the correct value at this moment, to be able to proceed with the control of the chemical process.

Semantic agreement requires a fundamental understanding of the applied process technology. It is common that an interdisciplinary team composed of process technologists, measurement specialists and computer engineers cooperates to find the RT entities that can be measured with good precision at reasonable cost. Typically, for every output value, about three to seven input values must be observed, not only to be able to diagnose erroneous measured data elements, but also to check the proper operation of the actuators. The proper operation of every actuator must be monitored by an independent sensor that observes the intended effect of the actuator (see Section 7.1.4).

In engineering practice, semantic agreement of measured data values is more important than the syntactic agreement. As a result of the agreement phase, an agreed (and consistent) set of digital input values is produced. These agreed values, defined in the value domain and in the time domain, are then used by all (replicated) tasks to achieve a replica-determinate behavior of the control system.

9.3   SAMPLING AND POLLING

In *sampling,* the state of an RT entity is periodically interrogated by the computer system at points in time called the *sampling points.* The temporal control always remains within the computer system. The constant time interval between two consecutive sampling points is called the *sampling interval.*

9.3.1   Sampling of Analog Values

The most recent current value of an analog RT entity is observed at a moment determined by the computer system (Figure 9.1).

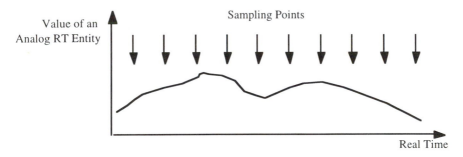

Figure 9.1: Sampling of an analog value.

In a TT architecture, the sampling points can be coordinated *a priori* with the transmission schedule to generate *phase-aligned transactions* (see Section 5.4.1). In a phase-aligned transaction, all processing and communication activities of a transaction follow each other without any unnecessary latency within the transaction. Such a phase-aligned transaction provides the shortest possible response time of a transaction (Figure 9.2).

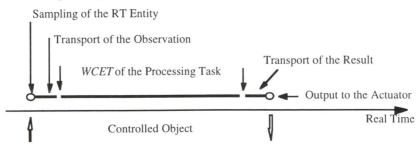

Figure 9.2: Sequence of communication and processing steps in a phase-aligned transaction.

9.3.2   Sampling of Digital Values

When sampling a digital value, the current state and the temporal position of the *most recent state change* are often of interest. While the current state is observed at the sampling point, the temporal position of the most recent state change can only be inferred by comparing the current observation with the most recent observation. The precision of this time measurement is limited by the duration of the sampling interval.

If the state of the RT entity changes more than once within a single sampling interval, some state changes will evade the observation. Figure 9.3 shows the sequence of values taken by an RT-entity and the values as seen by the observer without a memory element at the RT entity (Figure 9.3(a)). The small peak in the middle does not appear in the observations because it occurs just between two sampling points.

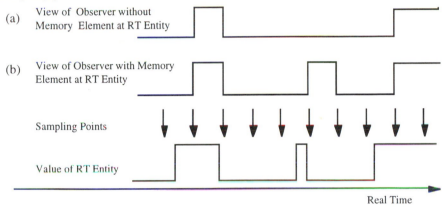

Figure 9.3: Sampling of RT entity, (a) without a memory element and (b) with a memory element at the observer.

If every event in the RT entity is significant, then a memory element (Figure 9.4) must be implemented at the RT entity that stores any state change until the next sampling point (Figure 9.3 (b)). The memory element can be reset after it has been read.

Figure 9.4: Sensor with memory element at sensor.

In the example of Section 4.4.2, describing the time-triggered solution to the lift control problem, the memory element in the lift call button stores a call request until the computer samples the call button.

Even with a memory element at the observer it is possible for some state changes to evade the observation. The small additional peak in the value sequence of the RT entity of Figure 9.5 does not show up in the observed values.

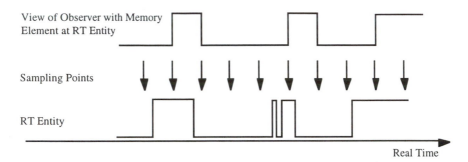

Figure 9.5: Short-lived states evade the observation.

A sampling system acts as a low-pass filter and cuts off all high frequency parts of the signal. From the point of view of system specification, a sampling system can be seen as protecting a node from more events in the environment than are stated in the system specification.

9.3.3 Polling

The difference between polling and sampling is in the position of the memory element. While in sampling systems the memory element is at the sensor and thus outside the sphere of control of the computer, in polling systems the memory element resides inside the computer system as shown in Figure 9.6.

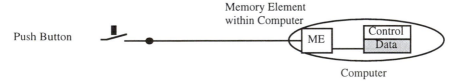

Figure 9.6: Polling system.

From a functional point of view, there is no difference between sampling and polling as long as no faults occur. Under fault conditions, the sampling system is more robust than the polling system for the following two reasons:

(i)   A transient disturbance that occurs on the transmission line between the sensor and the computer will only affect a sampling system if the fault overlaps the sampling point. If in the above mentioned lift-call button example in Section 4.4.2, the sampling period is 100 msec and the sampling action takes 100 μsec, the probability that the fault will interfere with the operation of the sampling system is about 0.1%. In a polling system, every single fault will be stored in the memory element at the computer and thus manifest itself as an error in the data. The memory element in the polling system acts as an "integrator" of all faults.

(ii)   In case of a node shutdown and restart, the contents of all RAM like memory in the sphere of control of the computer are lost. The external memory element in a sampling system survives the computer reset and can be read after the restart of the computer.

9.4   INTERRUPTS

The interrupt mechanisms empower a device outside the sphere of control of the computer to govern the temporal control pattern inside the computer. This is a powerful and potentially dangerous mechanism that must be used with great care. When a state change in the memory element of Figure 9.7 takes place and the corresponding interrupt is enabled, then, a hardware mechanism forces a control transfer to an interrupt service routine to service the recognized event. Because an enabled interrupt can occur at any point of the logical control flow, an interrupt is even more dangerous than the often forbidden *GOTO* statement.

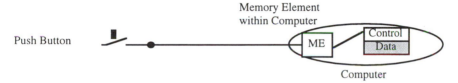

Figure 9.7: The interrupt mechanism.

From the fault-tolerance point of view, an interrupt mechanism is even less robust than the already denounced polling mechanism. Every transient error on the transmission line will interfere with the temporal control scheme within the computer. It will generate an additional unplanned processing load for the detection of a faulty sporadic interrupt, making it more difficult to meet the specified deadlines.

9.4.1   When Are Interrupts Needed?

Interrupts are needed when an external event requires such a short reaction time from the computer that it is not possible to implement this reaction time efficiently with sampling, i.e., when the event occurrence must influence the temporal control inside the computer ("time as control"). When sampling analog values, an interrupt does not lead to any response time improvement if the transaction is phase aligned.

In Section 4.4.4 the concept of a trigger task was introduced to sample external RT entities. A trigger task extends the response time of an RT transaction by at most one period of the trigger task, even if the rest of the transaction is phase aligned. This additional delay caused by the trigger task can be reduced by increasing the trigger task frequency at the expense of an increased overhead. [Pol95b] has analyzed this increase in the overhead for the periodic execution of a trigger task as the required response time approaches the WCET of the trigger task. As a rule of thumb, if the required response time is less than ten times the WCET of the trigger task, then the implementation of an interrupt should be considered for performance reasons.

Example: Consider the application depicted in Figure 9.8. The level of water in a water reservoir is controlled by a computer system. The water level is measured by a digital sensor. If the water rises above the high-level mark, the sensor produces a rising edge to the state "high". If the water falls below the high-level mark, the sensor produces a falling edge to the state "low". Whenever the water level exceeds the high-level mark, an overflow valve must be opened by the computer to start generating electric power.

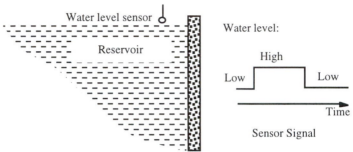

Figure 9.8: Computer system controlling the water level in a reservoir.

If the water-level sensor is connected to an interrupt line of the computer, then an interrupt will be generated whenever a wave covers the sensor. Since there are big waves, and superimposed small waves, and so on, it is difficult to derive the maximum interrupt frequency. The system will be more robust if the sensor is attached to a digital input line, and is sampled by a periodic trigger task. If, over a specified interval of time, the number of sensor readings that indicate "high" is larger than the number of sensor readings that indicate "low", the valve will be opened.

9.4.2   Monitoring the Occurrence of an Interrupt

In an interrupt driven system, a transient error on the interrupt line may upset the temporal control pattern of the complete node and may cause the violation of important deadlines. Therefore, the time interval between the occurrence of any two interrupts must be continuously monitored, and compared to the minimum duration between interrupting events that must be contained in the specification.

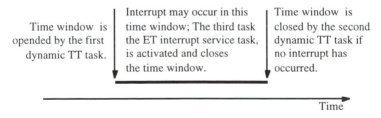

Figure 9.9: Time window of an interrupt.

There are three tasks in the computer associated with every monitored interrupt [Pol96a] (Figure 9.9). The first and second one are dynamically planned TT tasks that determine the interrupt window. The first one enables the interrupt line and thus opens the time window during which an interrupt is allowed to occur. The third task is the interrupt service task that is activated by the interrupt. Whenever the interrupt has occurred the interrupt service task closes the time window by disabling the interrupt line. It then deactivates the scheduled future activation of the second task. In case the third task was not activated before the start of the second task, the second task, a dynamic TT task scheduled at the end of the time window, closes the time window by disabling the interrupt line. The second task then generates an error flag to inform the application of the missing interrupt.

The two time-triggered tasks are needed for error detection. The first task detects a sporadic interrupt that should not have occurred. The second task detects a missing interrupt that should have occurred. These different errors require different types of error handling. The more we know about the regularity of the controlled object, the smaller we can make the time window in which an interrupt may occur. This leads to better error-detection coverage.

Example: The engine controller example of Section 1.7.2 has such a stringent requirement regarding the point of fuel injection relative to the position of the piston in the cylinder that the implementation must use an interrupt for measuring the position. The position of the piston and the rotational speed of the crankshaft are measured by a number of sensors that generate rising edges whenever a defined section of the crankshaft passes the position of the sensor. Since the speed and the maximum angular acceleration (or deceleration) of the engine is known, the next correct interrupt must arrive within a small dynamically defined time window from the previous interrupt. The interrupt logic is only enabled during this short window, and disabled at all other times to reduce the impact of sporadic interrupts on the temporal control pattern within the host software.

9.5   SENSORS AND ACTUATORS

A set of *transducers* (sensor and actuators) is located in the controlled object to measure the selected RT entities, or to accept RT images from the controlling computer. These transducers deliver/accept different types of input/output signals.

9.5.1   Analog Input/Output

Many RT entities are observed by sensors that produce analog values in the standard 4-20 mA range (4 mA meaning 0% of the value, and 20 mA meaning 100% of the value). If a measured value is encoded in the 4-20 mA range, then, it is possible to distinguish between a broken wire, where no current flows (0 mA), and a measured value of 0% (4 mA).

Without special precautions, the accuracy of any analog control signal is limited by the electrical noise level, even in favorable situations, to about 0.1%. Analog-to-digital (AD) converters with a resolution of more than 10 bits require a carefully controlled physical environment that is not available in typical industrial applications. A 16-bit word length is thus more than sufficient to encode the value of an RT entity measured by an analog sensor. This is one reason why 16-bit wide computer architectures are common in the field of industrial control.

The time interval between the occurrence of a value in the RT entity and the presentation of this value by the sensor at the sensor/computer interface is determined by the transfer function of the particular sensor. The step response of a sensor (see Figure 1.4), denoting the lag and the rise time of the sensor, gives an approximation of this transfer function. When reasoning about the temporal accuracy of a sensor/actuator signal, the parameters of the transfer functions of the sensors and the actuators must be considered (Figure 9.10). They reduce the available time interval between the occurrence of a value at the RT entity, and the use of this value for an output action by the computer. Transducers with short response times increase the length of the temporal accuracy interval that is available to the computer system.

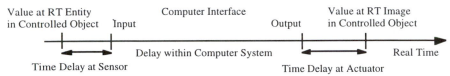

Figure 9.10: Time delay of a complete I/O transaction.

9.5.2   Digital Input/Output

A digital I/O signal transits between the two states TRUE and FALSE. In many applications, the length of the time interval between two state changes is of semantic significance. In other applications, the moment when the transition occurs is important.

If the input signal originates from a simple mechanical switch, the new stable state is not reached immediately but only after a number of random oscillations (Figure 9.11), called the *contact bounce,* caused by the mechanical vibrations of the switch contacts. This contact bounce must be eliminated either by an analog low-pass filter or, more often, within the computer system by software tasks, e.g., debouncing routines. Due to the low price of a microcontroller, it is cheaper to debounce a signal by software techniques than by hardware mechanisms (e.g., a low pass filter).

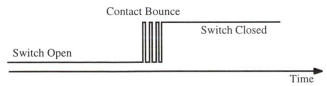

Figure 9.11: Contact bounce of a mechanical switch.

A number of sensor devices generate a sequence of pulse inputs, where each pulse carries information about the occurrence of an event. For example, distance measurements are often made by a wheel rolling along the object that must be measured. Every rotation of the wheel generates a defined number of pulses that can be converted to the distance traveled. The frequency of the pulses is an indication of the speed. If the wheel travels past a defined *calibration point*, an additional digital input is signaled to the computer to set the pulse counter to a defined value. It is good practice to convert the relative event values to absolute state values as soon as possible.

Time Encoded Signals: Many output devices are controlled by pulse sequences of well-specified shape (pulse width modulation–PWM). For example, a control signal for a stepping motor must adhere precisely to the temporal shape prescribed by the motor hardware supplier. A number of microcontrollers designed for I/O provide special hardware support for generating these digital pulse shapes.

9.5.3 Fault-Tolerant Actuators

An actuator must transduce the electrical signal generated at the output interface of the computer into some action in the controlled object (e.g., opening of a valve). The actuators form the last element in the chain between sensing the values of an RT-entity and realizing the intended effect in the environment. In a fault-tolerant system, the actuators must also be fault-tolerant to avoid a single point of failure. Figure 9.12 shows an example where the intended action in the environment is the positioning of a mechanical lever. At the end of the lever there may be any mechanical device that acts on the controlled object, e.g., there may be a piston of a control valve mounted at the point of action.

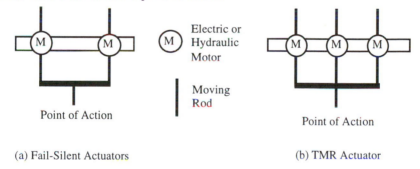

(a) Fail-Silent Actuators   (b) TMR Actuator

Figure 9.12: Fault-tolerant actuators.

In a replica-determinate architecture, the correct replicated channels produce identical results in the value and in the time domains. We differentiate between the cases where the architecture supports the fail-silent property (Figure 9.12(a)), i.e., all failed channels are silent, and where the fail-silence property is not supported (Figure 9.12(b)), i.e., a failed channel can show an arbitrary behavior in the value domain.

Fail-Silent Actuator: In a fail-silent architecture, all subsystems must support the fail-silence property. A fail-silent actuator will either produce the intended (correct) output action or no result at all. In case a fail-silent actuator fails to produce an output action, it may not hinder the activity of the replicated fail-silent actuator. The fail-silent actuator of Figure 9.12(a) consists of two motors where each one has enough power to move the point of action. Each motor is connected to one of the two replica-determinate output channels of the computer system. If one motor fails at any location, the other motor is still capable to move the point of action to the desired position.

Triple Modular Redundant Actuator: The Triple-Modular Redundant (TMR) actuator (Figure 9.12 (b)) consists of three motors, each one connected to one of the three replica-determinate output channels of the fault-tolerant computer. The force of any two motors must be strong enough ʊ override the force of the third motor, however, any single motor may not be strong enough to override the other two. The TMR actuator can be viewed as a "mechanical" voter that will place the point of action into a position that is determined by the majority of the three channels, outvoting the disagreeing channel.

9.5.4   Intelligent Instrumentation

There is an increasing tendency to encapsulate a sensor/actuator and the associated microcontroller into a single physical housing to provide a standard abstract message interface to the outside world that produces *measured values* at the field bus (Figure 9.13). Such a unit is called an *intelligent instrument.*

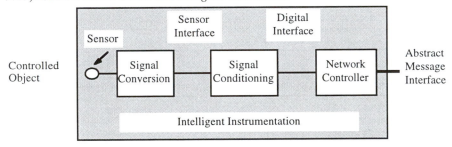

Figure 9.13: Intelligent instrumentation.

The intelligent instrument hides the concrete sensor interface. Its single chip microcontroller provides the required control signals to the sensor/actuator, performs signal conditioning, signal smoothing and local error detection, and presents/takes a meaningful RT image in standard measuring units to/from the field bus message interface. Intelligent instruments simplify the connection of the plant equipment to the computer.

Example: An acceleration sensor, micromachined into silicon, mounted with the appropriate microcontroller and network interface into a single package, forms an intelligent sensor.

To make the measured value fault-tolerant, a number of independent sensors can be packed into a single intelligent instrument. Inside the intelligent instrument an agreement protocol is executed to arrive at an agreed sensor value, even if one of the sensors has failed. This approach assumes that independent measurements can be taken in close spatial vicinity.

The integration of a field bus node with an actuator produces an intelligent actuator device.

Example: An actuator of an airbag in an automobile must ignite an explosive charge to release the gas of a high-pressure container into the airbag at the appropriate moment. A small explosive charge, placed directly on the silicon of a microcontroller, can be ignited on-chip. The package is mounted at the proper mechanical position to open the critical valve. The microcontroller including the explosive charge forms an intelligent actuator.

Because many different field bus designs are available today, and no generally accepted industry wide field bus standard has emerged, the sensor manufacturer must cope with the dilemma to provide a different intelligent instrument network interface for every different field bus. One solution, proposed by the emerging IEEE Standard P1451 on Transducer to Microprocessor Interface [Woo96], is the definition of a standard digital interface between the intelligent sensor and the network controller (Figure 9.4)

9.6   PHYSICAL INSTALLATION

It is beyond the scope of this book to cover all the issues that must be considered in the physical installation of a sensor based real-time control system. These complex topics are covered in books on computer hardware installation. However, a few critical issues are highlighted.

Power Supply: Many computer failures are caused by power failures. According to [Gra94, p.108], there are on average about 2.3 power outage events per year with an average duration of 54 minutes in North America. These numbers do not include sags, i.e., outages of less than a second, and surges, i.e., over voltages that can damage the sensitive electronic equipment. The provision of a reliable and clean power source is thus of crucial importance for the proper operation of any computer system.

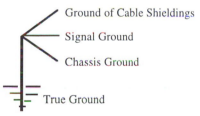

Figure 9.14: Tree-like structure of a grounding system.

Grounding: The design of a proper grounding system in an industrial plant is a major task that requires considerable experience. Many transient computer hardware failures are caused by deficient grounding systems. It is important to connect all units in a tree-like manner (Figure 9.14) to a high quality true ground point. Loops in the ground circuitry must be avoided because they pick up electromagnetic disturbances.

Electric Isolation: In many applications, complete electric isolation of the computer terminals from the signals in the plant is needed. Such isolation can be achieved by optocouplers for digital signals or signal transformers for analog signals.

POINTS TO REMEMBER

- The implementation of a field bus extends the scope of the communication system and pushes the "real" I/O issues to the field bus nodes.

- The value dimension of an I/O signal relates to the value of the signal. The temporal dimension relates to the moment when the value was recorded from the environment, or released to the environment.

- In the majority of situations, it is sufficient to treat time as data, and only in the minority of cases an immediate action of a computer system is required (time as control).

- If time can be treated a *data*, a timed message can be introduced which can be sent at a preplanned point in time. A timed message does not require any dynamic data-dependent modification of the temporal control structure.

- *Time as control* may require a dynamic data-dependent modification of the temporal control structure.

- A data element that is measured at the I/O interface of a sensor, is called a *raw data* element. A raw data element that is calibrated and converted to standard technical units is called a *measured data* element. A measured data element that is consistent with other measured data elements (from different sensors) is called an *agreed data* element.

- In syntactic agreement, the agreement algorithm computes the agreed data without considering the context of the measured data. Syntactic agreement without any restrictions of the failure modes of a sensor is the most costly form of agreement among a set of sensor values.

- In semantic agreement, different RT-entities are observed by different sensors and these sensor readings are related to each other to find a set of plausible agreed values, and to locate implausible values that indicate a sensor failure. It is not necessary to duplicate or triplicate every sensor.

- In *sampling and polling,* the state of an RT entity is periodically interrogated by the computer system at points in time that are in the sphere of control of the computer system.

- From the functional point of view, sampling and polling are the same. From the fault-tolerance point of view, sampling is more robust than polling.

- The interrupt mechanisms empower a device outside the sphere of control of the computer to govern the temporal control pattern inside the computer. This is a powerful and potentially dangerous mechanism that must be used with great care.

- Interrupts are needed when an external event requires such a short reaction time from the computer that it is not possible to implement this reaction time efficiently with sampling.

- The time interval between the occurrence of any two interrupts must be continuously monitored and compared with the specified minimum duration between interrupting events.

- When reasoning about the temporal accuracy of a sensor/actuator signal, the parameters of the transfer functions of the sensors and the actuators must be considered because they reduce the available time interval between the occurrence of a value at the RT entity and the use of this value for an output action by the computer.

- In a fault-tolerant system, the actuators must also be fault-tolerant to avoid a single point of failure.

- A fail-silent actuator will either produce the intended (correct) output action or no result at all. In case a fail-silent actuator fails to produce an output action, it may not hinder the activity of the replicated fail-silent actuator.

- There is a tendency to encapsulate a sensor/actuator and the associated microcontroller into a single physical housing to provide a standard abstract message interface to the outside world that produces *measured values* at the field bus (*intelligent instrument.*).

- Many real-time computer systems fail because of a deficient physical installation (power supply, grounding, electric isolation of sensor signals).

BIBLIOGRAPHIC NOTES

The generic problems that must be considered in the design of an I/O system are covered in basic books on computer hardware architecture, such as the book by Patterson and Hennessy [Pat90]. More specific advice is contained in special electronics publications, such as [Ban86] and, more importantly, in the documentation of computer system vendors or the chip suppliers. This topic is receiving relatively little coverage in the computer science literature. The presented technique for monitoring the interrupt occurrence has been published by Poledna [Pol95b], and is used in the design of computer controlled engine management.

REVIEW QUESTIONS AND PROBLEMS

9.1   Compare the advantages and disadvantages of connecting a sensor directly to a node of a distributed system versus the introduction of a field bus.

9.2   Explain the difference between "time as data" and "time as control"?

9.3   Assume that a single event is transmitted in a one-byte state message with a period of 50 msec. What is the finest temporal resolution of the time of event occurrence that can be encoded in this one-byte message?

9.4   Why is it important that a field bus protocol provides a known constant transmission latency?

9.5   Discuss the worst-case response time to an emergency event recorded in a field bus node in an event-triggered and in a time-triggered communication system.

9.6   What is the difference between *raw data*, *measured data*, and *agreed data?*

9.7   What is the difference between *syntactic agreement* and *semantic agreement?*

9.8   What is the differences between *sampling* and *polling?*

9.9   What is a *phase-aligned transaction?*

9.10   Why is an interrupt potentially dangerous and when is it needed?

9.11   What can be the consequence of a sporadic erroneous interrupt?

9.12   How can we protect the computer system from the occurrence of sporadic erroneous interrupts?

9.13   What are accuracy limits of an analog control signal in typical industrial applications?

9.14   Estimate the order of magnitude of the rise time of the step response function of some typical sensors, e.g., a temperature sensor, a pressure sensor, and a position sensor.

9.15   Sketch a software routine for a field bus node that will eliminate the contact bounce.

9.16   What are the characteristics of *fail-silent* actuators and *TMR* actuators?

9.17   What are the advantages of an *intelligent instrument?*

9.18   Give an example of a fault-tolerant sensor.

9.19   Estimate the MTTF of the power system in your neighborhood.

Chapter 10

Real-Time Operating Systems

OVERVIEW

This chapter covers the essential services that must be provided by a real-time operating system. It focuses on the real-time aspects of operating systems. It is assumed that the reader is already familiar with general operating system concepts. A real-time operating system must provide a predictable service to the application tasks such that the temporal properties of the complete software in a node can be statically analyzed. Many dynamic mechanisms, such as dynamic task creation or virtual memory management, which are standard in workstation operating systems, interfere with this predictability requirement of real-time systems.

The chapter starts with a section on task management. The state transition diagrams of time-triggered and event-triggered tasks, with and without internal blocking, are presented. The application program interface of the different task models is discussed. The simpler the application program interface, the easier it is to write portable application software. Section 10.2 covers the topic of interprocess communication. It is argued that the classic interprocess coordination primitives, such as semaphore operations, are too expensive for many embedded applications and simpler alternatives must be found.

Section 10.3 is devoted to time management. A real-time operating system must provide a clock synchronization service and a number of additional time services that are discussed in this section. Error detection is the topic of Section 10.4. Error detection in the time domain is of particular importance if an architecture is based on the fail-silent assumption.

The final section presents a case study of the real-time operating system ERCOS (Embedded Real-time Control Operating System). ERCOS is an industrial real-time operating system used in embedded automotive applications. It provides many of the services that are discussed in this chapter.

A real-time operating system must provide predictable service to the application tasks executing within the host. The worst-case administrative overhead (*WCAO*) of every operating system service must be known *a priori*, so that the temporal properties of the behavior of the complete host can be determined analytically.

To make such an analytic analysis of the WCAO feasible, a hard real-time operating system must be very careful in supporting the dynamic services that are common in standard operating systems: dynamic task creation at run time, virtual memory management, and dynamic queue management.

There are a number of standard workstation operating systems, e.g., UNIX-based systems, that provide extensions to improve the temporal performance, e.g., the capability to lock tasks in main memory, to implement user supplied real-time scheduling algorithms and others. An example of such a system is real-time UNIX [Fur89]. As long as these systems do not support the analytical analysis of their temporal behavior under all specified load and fault conditions, they can only be applied in a soft real-time environment, where a failure to miss a deadline is not catastrophic. If the temporal performance of an operating system cannot be guaranteed *a priori*, the operating system lacks one of the most important requirements of a hard real-time system.

10.1 TASK MANAGEMENT

Task management is concerned with the provision of the dynamic environment within a host for the initialization, execution, and termination of application tasks.

10.1.1   TT Systems

In an entirely time-triggered system, the temporal control structure of all tasks is established *a priori* by off-line support tools. This temporal control structure is encoded in a *Task-Descriptor List (TADL)* that contains the cyclic schedule for all activities of the node (Figure 10.1). This schedule considers the required precedence and mutual exclusion relationships among the tasks such that an explicit coordination of the tasks by the operating system at run time is not necessary.

Time	Action	WCET
10	Start T1	12
17	Send M5	
22	Stop T1	
38	Start T3	20
47	Send M3	

Figure 10.1: Task descriptor list in a TT operating system.

The dispatcher is activated by the synchronized clock tick. It looks at the TADL, and then performs the action that has been planned for this instant. If a task is started, the operating system informs the task of its activation time, which is synchronized within the cluster. After task termination, the operating system copies the results of the task to the CNI.

A task of a TT system with non- preemptive S-tasks (see Section 4.2.1) is in one of the two states: inactive or active (Figure 10.2)

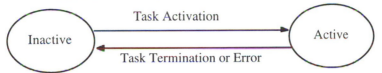

Figure 10.2: State diagram of a non-preemptive S-Tasks.

In a preemptive S-task, two sub-states of the active state can be distinguished, ready or running, depending on whether the task is in possession of the CPU or not (Figure 10.3).

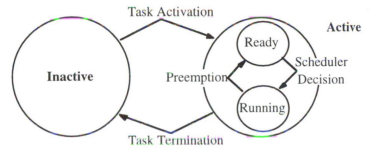

Figure 10.3: State diagram of preemptive S-tasks.

The Application Program Interface (API): The application program interface (API) of an S-task in a TT system consists of three data structures and two operating system calls. The data structures are the input data structure, the output data structure, and the h-state data structure (see Section 4.6) of the task. A stateless S-task does not have an h-state data structure at its API. The system calls are TERMINATE TASK and ERROR. The TERMINATE TASK system call is executed whenever the task has reached its normal termination point. In the case of an error that cannot be handled within the application task, the task terminates its operation with the ERROR system call.

10.1.2   ET Systems with S-Tasks

In an entirely event-triggered system, the sequence of task executions is determined dynamically by the evolving application scenario. Whenever a significant event happens, a task is released to the active (ready) state, and the dynamic scheduler is invoked. It is up to the scheduler to decide at run-time which one of the ready tasks is selected for the next service by the CPU. Different dynamic algorithms to solve the scheduling problem are discussed in the following chapter. The *WCET* (Worst-Case Execution Time) of the scheduler contributes to the *WCAO* (Worst-Case Administrative Overhead) of the operating system.

The significant events that cause the activation of a task are:

(i)   an event from the node's environment, i.e., the arrival of a message or an interrupt from the controlled object, or

(ii)   a significant event inside the host, i.e., the termination of a task or some other condition within a currently executing task, or

(iii)   the progression of the clock to a specified point in time. This time point can be specified either statically or dynamically.

Non-preemptive S-tasks: An ET operating system that supports non-preemptive S-tasks will take a new scheduling decision after the currently running task has terminated. This simplifies the task management in the operating system but severely restricts its responsiveness. If a significant event arrives immediately after the longest task has been scheduled, this event will not be considered until this longest task has completed.

Preemptive S-tasks: In a RT operating system that supports task preemption, each occurrence of a significant event can potentially activate a new task and cause an immediate interruption of the currently executing task to invoke a new decision by the scheduler. Depending on the outcome of the dynamic scheduling algorithm, the new task will be selected for execution or the interrupted task will be continued (Figure 10.3). Data conflicts between concurrently executing S-tasks can be avoided if the operating system copies all input data required by this task from the global data area and the communication-network interface (CNI) into a private data area of the task at the time of task activation.

The Application Program Interface (API): The API of an operating system that supports event-triggered S-tasks requires more system calls than an operating system that only supports time-triggered tasks. Along with the data structures and the already introduced system calls of a TT system, the operating system must provide system calls to ACTIVATE a new task, either immediately or at some future point in time. Another system call is needed to DEACTIVATE an already activated task.

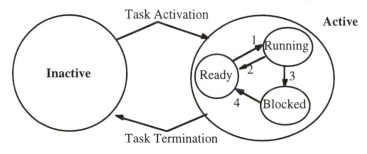

1 Scheduler Decision   3 Task executes WAIT-FOR-EVENT
2 Task Preemption   4 Blocking Event occurs

Figure 10.4: State diagram of a preemptive C-tasks with blocking.

10.1.3   ET Systems with C-Tasks

The state transition diagram of an ET system with C-tasks has three sub-states of the active state, as shown in Figure 10.4.

In addition to the *ready* and *running* state, a C-task can be in the *blocked* state waiting for an event outside the C-task to occur. Such an event can be a *time-event*, meaning that the real-time clock has advanced to a specified point, or any other occurrence that has been specified in the wait statement. An example of a blocked state is the suspension of the task execution to wait for an input event message.

The WCET of a C-task cannot be determined independently of the other tasks in the node. It can depend on the occurrence of an event in the node environment, as seen from the example of waiting for an input message. The timing analysis is not a local issue of a single task anymore; it becomes a global system issue. In the general case it is impossible to give an upper bound for the WCET.

The Application Program Interface (API): The application program interface of C-tasks is more complex than that of S-tasks. In addition to the three data structures already introduced, i.e., the input data structure, the output data structure, and the h-state data structure, the global data structures that are accessed at the blocking point must be defined. System calls must be provided that specify a WAIT-FOR-EVENT and a SIGNAL-EVENT occurrence. After the execution of the WAIT-FOR-EVENT the task enters the blocked state. The event occurrence releases the task from the blocked state. It must be monitored by a time-out task to avoid permanent blocking. The time-out task must be *deactivated* in case the awaited event occurs within the time-out period, otherwise the blocked task must be *killed*.

10.1.4   Software Portability

The complexity of the API determines the portability of the application software. A pure TT system provides the simples API that completely separates the issues of logical control and temporal control. Whenever this task model is used, a high portability of the application software is ensured. The larger number and variety of system calls in an ET system increases the coupling between application tasks and operating system, and diminishes the portability of the application software.

Combined TT and ET Tasks: In some applications, there is a need for a combination of TT tasks and ET tasks. If possible, an attempt should be made to limit the number of ET tasks to situations where they are absolutely needed and to restrict the implementation to the simpler S-task model. As shown in the following section, there are a number of possibilities to optimize the resources required for the coordination of TT tasks off-line, both regarding memory usage and processing overhead. Such an optimization is only possible if *a priori* knowledge about the time of task activation is available.

10.2 INTERPROCESS COMMUNICATION

Interprocess communication is needed to exchange information among concurrently executing tasks so progress towards the common goal can be achieved. There are possible types of information exchange: the direct exchange of messages among the involved tasks and the indirect exchange of information via a common region of data.

Messages: If interprocess communication is based on messages, a choice must be made between event-message semantics and state-message semantics (see Section 2.1.3). In many real-time systems the sender and receiver tasks are periodic with differing periods. In these systems the *one-to-one synchronization requirement* of event messages is not satisfied. Because state messages support the information exchange among tasks of differing periods, state-message semantics matches better the needs of real-time applications. The operating system must implement the atomicity property of a state message: a process is allowed to see only a complete version of a state message. The intermediate states that occur during a state message update must be hidden by the operating system.

Common Region of Data: The indirect exchange of information by a common region of data is related to the state message mechanism. The main difference is the missing atomicity property of common memory. Common memory is thus a low-level concept of data sharing, leaving it up to the application tasks to implement data consistency.

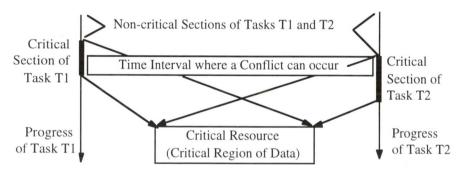

Figure 10.5: Critical task sections and critical data regions.

10.2.1   Semaphore Operations

Data inconsistency can arise if two tasks access a common region of data during overlapping critical sections, and at least one of the tasks is a writing task (Figure 10.5).

The "classic" mechanism to avoid data inconsistency is to enforce mutual exclusive execution of the critical task sections by a WAIT operation on a semaphore variable that protects the resource. Whenever one task is in its critical section, the other task must wait in a queue until the critical section is freed (*explicit synchronization*).

The implementation of a semaphore-initialize operation is expensive, both regarding memory requirements and operating system processing overhead. If a process runs into a blocked semaphore, a context switch must be made. The process is put into a queue and is delayed until the other process finishes its critical section. Then, the process is dequeued and another context switch is made to reestablish the original context. If the critical region is very small (this is the case in many real-time applications), then, the processing time for the semaphore operations can take *hundreds* of times longer than the actual reading or writing of the common data.

TT Systems: In a TT system, the static schedules of the tasks can be coordinated off-line in a way that two tasks with critical sections that access the same region of data will never overlap. It is then possible to maintain data consistency without the use of semaphores (*implicit synchronization*).

ET Systems: In an ET system, the overhead for the semaphore operations can be reduced if every task gets a private copy of the global data at the time of task activation and the operating system updates the global data after task termination, i.e., the number of accesses to the global data is bounded by two for every task activation.

10.2.2   The Non-Blocking Write (NBW) Protocol

The implementation of the atomicity property of state messages that are exchanged between the host computer and the communication controller at the Communication Network Interface (CNI) requires special consideration. The CNI forms the interface between two autonomous subsystems residing in different spheres of control. The communication subsystem delivers new data at the CNI at its autonomous rate. It is thus not possible for the host to delay the communication system, i.e., to exercise *back-pressure* flow control.

If the software in the host is time-triggered, and synchronized with the global time of the communication system, then, the task schedule in the host can be designed off-line to avoid any write/read conflict at the CNI. If, however, the host software is event-triggered, then a lock-free synchronization protocol must be implemented at the CNI that never blocks the writer, i.e., the communication system. The non-blocking write (NBW) protocol is an example of such a lock-free protocol [Kop93c].

The NBW protocol can be used to implement the atomicity property of messages at the CNI of a time-triggered communication system. Let us analyze the operation of the NBW for the data transfer across the CNI in the direction from the communication system to the host computer. At this interface, there is one writer, the communication system, and many readers, the tasks of the host. A reader does not destroy the information written by a writer, but a writer can interfere with the operation of the reader. In the NBW protocol, the writer is never blocked. It will thus write a new version of the message into the DPRAM of the CNI whenever a new message arrives. If a reader reads the message while the writer is writing a new version, the retrieved message will contain inconsistent information and must be discarded. If the reader is able to detect the interference, then the reader can retry the read operation until it retrieves a consistent version of the message. It must be shown that the number of retries performed by the reader is bounded.

The protocol requires a concurrency control field, CCF, for every message written. Atomic access to the CCF must be guaranteed by the hardware. The concurrency control field is initialized to zero and incremented by the writer before the start of the write operation. It is again incremented after the completion of the write operation. The reader starts by reading the CCF at the start of the read operation. If the CCF is odd, then the reader retries immediately because a write operation is in progress. At the end of the read operation the reader checks whether the CCF has been changed by the writer during the read operation. If so, it retries the read operation again until it can read an uncorrupted version of the data structure.

Initialization: CCF := 0

Writer:

start: CCF_old := CCF;
   CCF := CCF_old + 1;
   CCF := CCF_old + 2;

Reader:

start: CCF_begin := CCF;
   If CCF_begin = *odd*
   then goto *start*;
   <read data structure>
   CCF_end := CCF;
   If CCF_end ≠ CCF_begin
   then goto *start*;

Figure 10.6: The non-blocking write (NBW) protocol.

It can be shown that an upper bound for the number of read retries exists if the time between write operations is significantly longer than the duration of a write or read operation. The worst-case extension of the execution time of a typical real-time task caused by the retries of the reader is about a few percent of the worst-case execution time (WCET) of the task [Kop93c].

Non-locking synchronization has been implemented recently in other real-time systems, e.g., in a multimedia system [And95]. It has been shown that systems with non-locking synchronization achieve better performance than systems that lock the data.

10.3   TIME MANAGEMENT

In many real-time applications, the majority of tasks will be time-triggered, either at *a priori* known points in time or at dynamically established points in time. The operating system must provide flexible time management services to simplify the application software.

10.3.1   Clock Synchronization

Clock synchronization is an essential service in a distributed real-time system. If this service is not part of the communication system, it must be provided by the operating system. The precision of the clock synchronization that is implemented at the operating system level is significantly better than the precision that is achievable at the application level. The subject of clock synchronization has been covered extensively in Chapter 3.

10.3.2   Provision of Time Services

Real-time applications require the following time services which must be provided by a real-time operating system:

(i)   The static (off-line) specification of a potentially infinite sequence of events at absolute time-points that reappear with a given constant period. This service is required for the static time-triggered activation of a task.

(ii)   The dynamic (on-line) specification of a sequence of events with a given constant period. This service is required for the dynamic time-triggered activation of tasks.

(iii)   The specification of a future point in time within a specified temporal distance from "now". This service is required for the specification of time-outs.

(iv)   The time stamping of events immediately after their occurrence.

(v)   The output of a message (or a control signal) at a precisely defined point in time in the future, either relative to "now" or at an absolute future time point.

(vi)   A time conversion service that converts International Atomic Time (TAI) to the "wall clock time" and *vice versa*. This is the Gregorian calendar function.

10.3.3   Support for Time Stamping

There are a number of single chip microcomputers that support time stamping and the precise output of a timed message (functions (iv) and (v) from above) by hardware mechanisms. For example, the MOTOROLA 68332 microcontroller has an on-chip Time-Processing Unit (TPU) for the generation of precise time-stamps. The TPU can be (micro)programmed to execute a sequence of time-triggered actions autonomously, e.g., the generation of a signal with a specified pulse form.

10.4 ERROR DETECTION

A real-time operating system must support error detection in the temporal domain and error detection in the value domain by generic methods. Some of these generic methods are described in this section.

10.4.1   Monitoring Task Execution Times

A tight upper bound on the worst-case execution time (WCET) of a real-time task must be established during software development (see Section 4.5). This WCET must be monitored by the operating system at run time to detect transient or permanent hardware errors. In case a task does not terminate its operation within the

WCET, the execution of the task is terminated by the operating system. It is up to the application to specify which action should be taken in case of an error. There are essentially two options: termination of the operation of the node or continuation with the next task after setting an error flag in the global data area of the node to inform subsequent tasks of the occurrence of the error.

10.4.2   Monitoring Interrupts

An erroneous external interrupt has the potential to disrupt the temporal control structure of the real-time software within the node. At design time, the minimum interarrival periods of interrupts must be known to be able to estimate the peak load that must be handled by the software system. At run time, this minimum interarrival period must be enforced by the operating system by disabling the interrupt line to reduce the probability of erroneous sporadic interrupts (see Section 9.4.2).

10.4.3   Double Execution of Tasks

The fault-injection experiments in the context of the PDCS (Predictably Dependable Computing Systems) project have shown that the double execution of tasks and the subsequent comparison of the results is a very effective method for the detection of transient hardware faults that cause undetected errors in the value domain (see Section 12.4.2). The operating system can provide the execution environment for the double execution of application tasks without demanding any changes to the application task *per se*. It is thus possible to decide at the time of system configuration which tasks should be executed twice, and for which tasks it is sufficient to rely on a single execution (see also Section 14.1.2).

10.4.4   Watchdogs

A fail-silent node will produce correct results or no results at all. The failure of a fail-silent node can only be detected in the temporal domain. A standard technique is the provision of a watchdog signal (*heart-beat*) that must be periodically produced by the operating system of the node. If the node has access to the global time, the watchdog signal should be produced periodically at known absolute points in time. An outside observer can detect the failure of the node as soon as the watchdog signal disappears.

A more sophisticated error detection mechanism that also covers part of the value domain is the periodic execution of a challenge-response protocol by a node. An outside error detector provides an input pattern to the node and expects a defined response pattern within a specified time interval. The calculation of this response pattern should involve as many functional units of the node as possible. If the calculated response pattern deviates from the *a priori* known correct result, an error of the node is detected.

10.5 A CASE STUDY: ERCOS

In the following sections the structure and the services of a modern operating system for embedded applications are highlighted. As already mentioned in Chapter 1, the high production volume of embedded systems demands reliable system solutions that minimize the hardware resource requirements. Many design decisions in ERCOS (Embedded Real-Time Control Operating System) [Pol96a], an operating system for embedded real-time applications in the automotive industry, have been influenced by this quest for optimum performance and utmost reliability.

ERCOS is used for the implementation of embedded systems, such as engine control or transmission control, in vehicles. A typical state-of-the-art engine controller has a memory consisting of 256 kbyte ROM and 32 kbyte RAM. It interfaces to about 80 external sensors and actuators, and is connected to the other system by a real-time communication network, such as a CAN bus (see Section 7.5.3). The software is organized into about 100 concurrently executing tasks. The most demanding task, the injection control, must be precise within a few microseconds.

10.5.1   Task Model

The basic task model of ERCOS consists of S-tasks. A set of S-tasks that follow one another in sequence forms a *schedule sequence*. A schedule sequence is built off-line during the static analysis of the application software. Each schedule sequence is assigned a given priority level, and is treated as a single *unit of scheduling* by the operating system. Whenever the activation event of a schedule sequence occurs, the whole schedule sequence is executed. The grouping of tasks into schedule sequences reduces the number of scheduling units that must be managed at run-time by the operating system, thus reducing memory requirements and processing load.

10.5.2   Scheduling

ERCOS supports static and dynamic scheduling of schedule sequences. The time-triggered static schedules are developed off-line such that the required dependency relations, such as mutual exclusion and precedence between the tasks, are integrated into the off-line schedules and no explicit synchronization is needed.

Dynamic scheduling decisions are based on the priorities of ready schedule sequences. Two different scheduling strategies, *cooperative scheduling* and *preemptive scheduling*, are distinguished. Cooperative scheduling is non-preemptive at the task level. A context switch may only take place between the tasks of a schedule sequence. This simplifies the maintenance of data consistency, since a complete critical section is encapsulated in a single task.

Preemptive scheduling allows the context switch at (almost) any point in time. It is required for the realization of short response times and minimal jitter. The disadvantage of preemptive scheduling is the higher dynamic overhead for context switching and data consistency assurance. To guarantee mutually exclusive access to resources, and to avoid blocking, ERCOS uses a variant of the priority ceiling protocol [Sha90] (discussed in Section 11.3.3). A process that accesses a shared resource elevates its priority to the priority ceiling of the resource until it releases the resource again. It is thus not possible to preempt a task that holds a needed resource.

10.5.3   Interprocess Communication

Interprocess communication in ERCOS is realized by state messages. During task activation, the input messages are copied to the private input data structure of the task. After completion of the task, the output data structure is copied back into the global data area. To improve the performance of the interprocess communication, a number of optimizations are performed off-line:

(i)   The in-line expansion of *send* and *receive* operations makes it possible to implement send and receive operations as simple assignment statements.

(ii)   If a static analysis of the source code precludes the possibility of access conflicts to the data, no copy of a message must be made.

(iii)   Batching of message send and receive operations of a schedule sequence: the *a priori* knowledge of the execution order of tasks within a schedule sequence can be used to reduce the number of message copies in a schedule sequence.

10.5.4   Error Detection

ERCOS provides many mechanisms for run-time error detection, such as:

(i)   A deadline checking service is provided by the operating system to detect late system responses, and to make it possible for an exception handler to react to such a failure.

(ii)   The occurrence of interrupts originating from the controlled object is continuously monitored. After each interrupt occurrence, the interrupt line is disabled for the duration of the minimum interarrival period.

(iii)   The actual number of active instances of a task is monitored by the operating system at run time and compared with the permitted maximum number of concurrently active instances of a task that has been determined off-line.

(iv)   A watchdog process generates a life-sign message with a known period so that an outside observer is continuously informed of the proper operation of a node.

10.5.5   Off-line Software Tools

An extensive off-line software development tool (OLT) supports the design and implementation of application code for the ERCOS run-time system. The OLT performs a static source code analysis of the application code and generates the necessary interface code to link the application to the run-time kernel. An overview on the OLT's functionality is given in the following:

(i)   Support for object-based software construction and software reuse:
    The OLT provides the functions to structure the application software according to the ERCOS real-time object model. This object model supports

autonomously active objects and concurrent activity within and between objects. To support the reuse of software in widely varying contexts, the OLT generates the necessary code to ensure data consistency in the presence of preemptive scheduling. Object interfaces are checked for consistency, completeness and conformance to visibility rules.

(ii)   Automatic operating system configuration:

The ERCOS kernel configured and generated automatically by the OLT for each individual application. All the necessary RAM and ROM data structures are reserved by the OLT based on the static source code analysis. This avoids the effort for dynamic memory handling and ensures that only a minimal amount of memory is configured.

(iii)   Optimization of operating system functions:

Based on the static analysis of the source code, the OLT selects optimized implementations for operating system functions. For example, the static source code analyzer detects the situations where concurrency conflicts cannot arise during execution. In typical applications, it reduces the number of message copy operations and the required memory amount for message copies by an order of magnitude [Pol96c]. To guarantee mutual exclusive access to resources, the OLT decides which implementation is most efficient in a given context. If it is known by static analysis that no resource conflict can arise, then, the OLT decides that no actions have to be taken at run-time to ensure mutual exclusive access.

POINTS TO REMEMBER

- The worst-case administrative overhead (WCAO) of every operating system call of a real-time operating system must be known *a priori*, so that the temporal properties of the behavior of the complete host can be determined analytically.

- The *a priori* designed task schedule of a TT system must consider the required precedence and mutual exclusion relationships between the tasks such that an explicit coordination of the tasks by the operating system at run time is not necessary.

- The simplest application program interface (API) is the API of a time-triggered S-task.

- The coupling between the application program and the operating system increases with the number and variety of the operating system calls.

- The determination of the worst case execution time (WCET) of a C-task is not a local issue of the C-task, but a system issue.

- Explicit synchronization of tasks by semaphore operations can be very costly if the protected region of data is small. Implicit synchronization by properly designed static schedules is orders of magnitudes cheaper.

- Data exchanges at the CNI should be protected by non-blocking protocols because it can be difficult to exercise back-pressure flow control on the sender.

- The precision of the clock synchronization that is implemented at the operating system level is significantly better than the precision that is achievable at the application level.

- A real-time operating system must support error detection in the temporal domain and in the value domain.

- The ERCOS operating system uses the *a priori* information about the application to improve the efficiency and to increase the robustness of the software.

BIBLIOGRAPHIC NOTES

Many of the standard textbooks on operating systems, such as "Distributed Operating Systems" by Tanenbaum [Tan95], "Distributed Operating Systems" by Goscinski [Gos91], or "Operating Systems" by Stallings [Stal95] contain sections on real-time operating systems. The most recent research contributions on real-time operating systems can be found in the annual Proceedings of the IEEE Real-Time System Symposium. The ERCOS operating system was presented at the SAE World Congress in Detroit [Pol96a] and the Real-Time System Symposium in Washington in 1996 [Pol96c].

REVIEW QUESTIONS AND PROBLEMS

10.1   Why is it not recommended to use standard workstation operating systems for hard real-time applications?

10.2   Explain the task management of a time-triggered system versus that of an event-triggered operating system.

10.3   Compare the determination of the WCET of an S-tasks with that of a C-task, considering the WCAO of the operating system.

10.4   Consider a real-time system consisting of 100 concurrent tasks, running on 5 different priority levels. How large is the worst-case number of active task control blocks if the tasks are (a) S-tasks, and (b) C-tasks.

10.5   Identify all system calls that have to be provided at the API of an event-triggered operating system that supports preemptive C-tasks.

10.6   Discuss the interdependence between software portability and API complexity.

10.7   What is the difference between interprocess communication based on state messages and interprocess communication based on common memory?

10.8   A critical region of data can be protected either by properly designed static schedules or by semaphore operations. Compare these two alternatives from the point of view of performance.

10.9   What are the difficulties in implementing back-pressure flow control at the communication network interface?

10.10   How is data integrity at the reader achieved in the NBW protocol?

10.11   Estimate the worst-case delay of a reader when using the NBW protocol. What are the critical parameters?

10.12   List the time services that are required by a real-time application.

10.13   Identify some methods that can be implemented in the operating system for detecting errors in the temporal domain.

10.14   How can the operating system support the detection of transient errors in the value domain?

10.15   Estimate an upper bound for the number of instruction that must be executed to implement a semaphore operation WAIT (including the necessary queue management).

Chapter 11

Real-Time Scheduling

OVERVIEW

Many thousands of research papers have been written about how to schedule a set of tasks in a system with a limited amount of resources such that all tasks will meet their deadlines. This chapter tries to summarize some important results that are relevant to the designer of real-time systems. The chapter starts by introducing the notion of a schedulability test to determine whether a given task set is schedulable or not. It distinguishes between a sufficient, an exact, and a necessary schedulability test. A scheduling algorithm is *effective* if it will find a schedule whenever there is a solution. The adversary argument shows that in the general case it is not possible to design an effective on-line scheduling algorithm.

Section 11.3 covers the topic of dynamic scheduling. It starts with looking at the problem of scheduling a set of independent tasks by the rate-monotonic algorithm. Next, the problem of scheduling a set of dependent tasks is investigated. After the kernelized monitor, the priority-ceiling protocol is discussed and a schedulability test for the priority ceiling protocol is presented. Finally, the scheduling problem in distributed systems is touched.

The final section elaborates on static scheduling. The concept of the schedule period is introduced and an example of a simple search tree that covers a schedule period is given. A heuristic algorithm has to examine the search tree to find a feasible schedule. If it finds one, the solution can be considered a constructive schedulability test. The flexibility of static schedules can be increased by introducing a periodic server task to service sporadic requests. Finally, the topic of mode changes to adapt the temporal control structure even further is discussed.

11.1 THE SCHEDULING PROBLEM

A hard real-time system must execute a set of concurrent real-time tasks in such a way that all time-critical tasks meet their specified deadlines. Every task needs computational and data resources to proceed. The scheduling problem is concerned with the allocation of these resources to satisfy all timing requirements.

11.1.1   Classification of Scheduling Algorithms

The following diagram presents a taxonomy of real-time scheduling algorithms [Chen87].

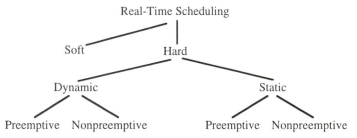

Figure 11.1: Taxonomy of real-time scheduling algorithms.

Dynamic versus Static Scheduling: A scheduler is called *dynamic* (or *on-line*) if it makes its scheduling decisions at run time, selecting one out of the current set of *ready* tasks (see Section 10.1). Dynamic schedulers are flexible and adapt to an evolving task scenario. They consider only the *current* task requests. The run-time effort involved in finding a schedule can be substantial.

A scheduler is called static (or pre-run-time) if it makes its scheduling decisions at compile time. It generates a dispatching table for the run-time dispatcher off line. For this purpose it needs complete prior knowledge about the task-set characteristics, e.g., maximum execution times, precedence constraints, mutual exclusion constraints, and deadlines. The dispatching table contains all information the dispatcher needs at run time to decide at every point of a discrete time-base which task is to be scheduled next. The run-time overhead of the dispatcher is small.

Preemptive versus Nonpreemptive Scheduling: In preemptive scheduling, the currently executing task may be preempted, i.e., interrupted, if a more urgent task requests service.

In nonpreemptive scheduling, the currently executing task will not be interrupted until it decides on its own to release the allocated resources–normally after completion. The shortest guaranteed responsiveness in single processor systems based on nonpreemptive scheduling is the sum of the longest and the shortest task execution time. Nonpreemptive scheduling is reasonable in a task scenario where many short tasks (compared to the time it takes for a context switch) must be executed.

Centralized versus Distributed Scheduling: In a dynamic distributed real-time system, it is possible to make all scheduling decisions at one central site or to devise cooperative distributed algorithms for the solution of the scheduling problem. The central scheduler in a distributed system is a critical point of failure. Because it requires up-to-date information on the load situations in all nodes, it can also contribute to a communication bottleneck.

11.1.2   Schedulability   Test

A test that determines whether a set of ready tasks can be scheduled such that each task meets its deadline is called a *schedulability test*. We distinguish between *exact*, *necessary* and *sufficient* schedulability tests (Figure 11.2).

A scheduler is called *optimal* if it will always find a schedule provided an *exact* schedulability test indicates the existence of such a schedule. Garey and Johnson [Gar75] have shown that in nearly all cases of task dependency, even if there is only one common resource, the complexity of an exact schedulability test algorithm belongs to the class of NP-complete problems and is thus computationally intractable. *Sufficient schedulability test* algorithms can be simpler at the expense of giving a negative result for some task sets that are in fact schedulable. A task set is definitely not schedulable if a *necessary schedulability* test gives a negative result. If a necessary schedulability test gives a positive result, there is still a probability that the task set may not be schedulable.

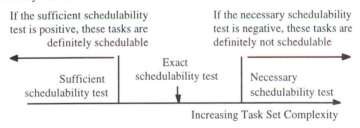

Figure 11.2: Necessary and sufficient schedulability test.

11.2 THE ADVERSARY ARGUMENT

The *task request time* is the point in time when a request for a task execution is made. Based on the request times, it is useful to distinguish between two different task types: *periodic* and *sporadic* tasks. This distinction is important from the point of view of schedulability.

If we start with an initial request, all future request times of a periodic task are known *a priori* by adding multiples of the known period to the initial request time. Let us assume that there is a task set $\{T_i\}$ of periodic tasks with periods p_i, deadline interval d_i and execution time c_i. The deadline interval is the difference between the deadline of a task and the task request time, i.e., the time when a task becomes ready for execution. We call the difference $d_i - c_i$ the *laxity* l_i of a task. It is sufficient to examine schedules of length of the least common multiples of the periods of these tasks, the *schedule period*, to determine schedulability. A necessary schedulability test for a set of periodic tasks states that the sum of the utilization factors:

$$\mu = \sum_i c_i/p_i \le n,$$

must be less or equal to n, where n is the number of available processors. This is evident because the utilization factor of task T_i, $\mu_{i,}$ denotes the percentage of time the task T_i requires service from a processor.

The request times of *sporadic* tasks are not known *a priori*. To be schedulable, there must be a minimum interval between any two request times of sporadic tasks. Otherwise, the necessary schedulability test introduced above will fail. If there is no constraint on the request times of task activations, the task is called an *aperiodic* task.

Let us assume that a real-time computer system contains a dynamic scheduler with full knowledge of the past but without any knowledge about future request times of tasks. It determines which task is to be scheduled next on the basis of the current requests. In such a scenario an exact schedulability test is impossible, because we do not have enough information about future request times. Schedulability of the current task set may depend on when a sporadic task will request service in the future. We therefore need a new definition of optimality of a dynamic scheduler. A dynamic on-line scheduler is called *optimal*, if it can find a schedule whenever a clairvoyant scheduler, i.e., a scheduler with complete knowledge of the future request times, can find a schedule.

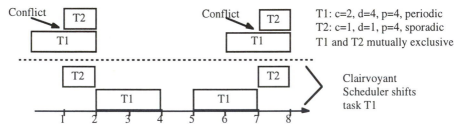

Figure 11.3: The adversary argument.

The *adversary argument* [Mok83,p.41] states that, in general, it is not possible to construct an optimal totally on-line dynamic scheduler if there are mutual exclusion constraints between a periodic and a sporadic task. The proof of the adversary argument is relatively simple.

Consider two mutually exclusive tasks, task *T1* is periodic and the other task *T2* is sporadic, with the parameters given in Figure 11.3. The necessary schedulability test introduced above is satisfied, because

$$\mu = 2/4 + 1/4 = 3/4 \leq 1.$$

Whenever the periodic task is executing, the adversary requests service for the sporadic task. Due to the mutual exclusion constraint, the sporadic task must wait until the periodic task is finished. Since the sporadic task has a laxity of 0, it will miss its deadline.

The clairvoyant scheduler knows all the future request times of the sporadic task and at first schedules the sporadic task, and thereafter the periodic task in the gap between two sporadic task activations (Figure 11.3).

The adversary argument demonstrates how valuable information on the future behavior of tasks is for solving the scheduling problem. If the on-line scheduler does not have any further knowledge about the request times of the sporadic task, the scheduling problem is not solvable, although the processor capacity is more than sufficient for the given task scenario. The design of predictable hard real-time systems is simplified if regularity assumptions about the future scheduling requests can be made. This is the case in cyclic systems that restrain the points in time at which external requests are recognized by the computing system.

11.3 DYNAMIC SCHEDULING

After the occurrence of a significant event, a dynamic scheduling algorithm determines on line which task out of the ready task set must be serviced next. The algorithms differ in the assumptions about the complexity of the task model and the future task behavior.

11.3.1   Scheduling Independent Tasks

The classic algorithm for scheduling a set of periodic independent hard real-time tasks in a system with a single CPU, the *rate monotonic algorithm*, was published in 1973 by [Liu73].

Rate Monotonic Algorithm: The rate monotonic algorithm is a dynamic preemptive algorithm based on static task priorities. It makes the following assumptions about the task set:

(i)   The requests for all tasks of the task set $\{T_i\}$ for which hard deadlines exist, are periodic.

(ii)   All tasks are independent of each other. There exists no precedence constraints or mutual exclusion constraints between any pair of tasks.

(iii) The deadline interval of every task T_i is equal to its period p_i.

(iv)   The required maximum computation time of each task c_i is known *a priori* and is constant.

(v)   The time required for context switching can be ignored.

(vi)   The sum of the utilization factors μ of the n tasks is given by

$$\mu = \sum_i c_i/p_i \le n(2^{1/n} - 1).$$

The term $n(2^{1/n} - 1)$ approaches $ln\ 2$, i.e., about 0.7, as n goes to infinity.

The rate monotonic algorithm assigns static priorities based on the task periods. The task with the shortest period gets the highest static priority, and the task with the longest period gets the lowest static priority. At run time, the dispatcher selects the task request with the highest static priority.

If all the assumptions are satisfied, the rate monotonic algorithm guarantees that all tasks will meet their deadline. The algorithm is optimal for single processor systems. The proof of this algorithm is based on the analysis of the behavior of the task set at the *critical instant*. A critical instant of a task is the moment at which the request of this task will have the longest response time. For the task system as a whole, the critical instant occurs when requests for all tasks are made simultaneously. Starting with the highest priority task, we can show that all tasks will meet their deadlines, even in the case of the critical instant. In a second phase of the proof it must be shown that any scenario can be handled if the critical instant scenario can be handled For the details of the proof refer to [Liu73].

It is also shown that assumption (vi) above can be relaxed in case the task periods are multiples of the period of the highest priority task. In this case the utilization factor μ of the n tasks,

$$\mu = \sum_i c_i/p_i \le 1,$$

can approach the theoretical maximum of unity in a single processor system.

In recent years, the rate monotonic theory has been extended to handle a set of tasks where the deadline interval can be different from the period [Bur96].

Earliest-Deadline-First (EDF) Algorithm: This algorithm is an optimal dynamic preemptive algorithm in single processor systems which is based on dynamic priorities. The assumptions (i) to (v) of the rate monotonic algorithm must hold. The processor utilization μ can go up to 1, even when the task periods are not multiples of the smallest period. After any significant event, the task with the earliest deadline is assigned the highest dynamic priority. The dispatcher operates in the same way as the dispatcher for the rate monotonic algorithm.

Least-Laxity (LL) Algorithm: In single processor systems, the least laxity algorithm is another optimal algorithm. It makes the same assumptions as the EDF algorithm. At any scheduling decision point the task with the shortest laxity l, i.e., the difference between the deadline interval d and the computation time c

$$d - c = l$$

is assigned the highest dynamic priority.

In multiprocessor systems, neither the earliest-deadline-first nor the least-laxity algorithm is optimal, although the least-laxity algorithm can handle task scenarios which the earliest-deadline-first algorithm cannot handle.

11.3.2   Scheduling Dependent Tasks

From a practical point of view, results on how to the schedule tasks with precedence and mutual exclusion constraints are much more important than the analysis of the independent task model. Normally, the concurrently executing tasks must exchange information and access common data resources to cooperate in the achievement of the overall system objective. The observation of given precedence and mutual exclusion constraints is thus rather the norm than the exception in distributed real-time systems.

The general problem of deciding whether it is possible to schedule a set of processes that use semaphores only to enforce mutual exclusion is an NP complete problem. It is prohibitively expensive to look for an optimal schedule for a set of dependent tasks. The computational resources required for solving the dynamic scheduling problem compete with those needed for executing the real-time tasks. The more resources are spent on scheduling, the fewer resources remain available to perform the actual work.

There are three possible ways out of this dilemma:

(i)   Providing extra resources such that simpler sufficient schedulability tests and algorithms can be applied.

(ii)   Dividing the scheduling problem into two parts such that one part can be solved off-line at compile time and only the second (simpler) part must be solved at run time.

(iii)   Introducing restricting assumptions concerning the regularity of the task set.

The second and third alternatives point towards a more static solution of the scheduling problem.

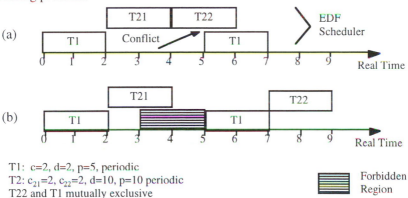

T1: c=2, d=2, p=5, periodic
T2: c_{21}=2, c_{22}=2, d=10, p=10 periodic
T22 and T1 mutually exclusive

Figure 11.4: Scheduling dependent tasks
(a) without, (b) with forbidden regions.

The Kernelized Monitor: Let us assume a set of short critical sections such that the longest critical section of this set is smaller than a given duration q. The kernelized monitor algorithm [Mok83,p.57] allocates the processor time in uninterruptible quanta of this duration q, assuming that all critical sections can be started and completed within this single uninterruptible time quantum. The only difference between this new scheduling problem and the rate monotonic scheduling problem is that a process may be interrupted only after it has been given an integral number of time quanta q. This little difference is already sufficient to cause problems.

Example: Let us assume two tasks, $T1$ and $T2$ with the parameters given in Figure 11.4. The second part of $T2$, $T22$ is mutually exclusive to $T1$. Assume that the preemption time quantum has a length of two units. Then, the EDF scheduler will schedule the tasks according to Figure 11.4 (a). At time 4 the only task that is in the ready set is $T22$, so the EDF scheduler schedules $T22$ which cannot be preempted by $T1$ within the next two time units. At time 5 a conflict occurs. $T22$ has not finished yet, but $T1$ that is strictly periodic and mutually exclusive to $T22$, must be executed immediately because it has a latency of zero. A wiser scheduling algorithm could solve this problem by designing the schedule depicted in Figure 11.4 (b). The critical section of the second task, Task $T22$, is not allowed to start during the two timeslots before the second execution of $T1$. This second schedule meets all deadlines and respects all mutual exclusion constraints.

The region that must be reserved to guarantee that the future request by $T1$ can be serviced on-time is called a *forbidden region*. During compile time, all forbidden regions must be determined and passed to the dispatcher so that the dispatcher will not schedule any unwanted critical sections in the forbidden region.

11.3.3   The Priority Ceiling Protocol

The priority ceiling protocol [Sha90] is used to schedule a set of periodic tasks that have exclusive access to common resources protected by semaphores. These common resources, e.g., common data structures, can be utilized to realize an interprocess communication.

If a set of 3 tasks $T1,T2$, and $T3$ ($T1$ has the highest priority and $T3$ has the lowest priority), is scheduled with the rate-monotonic algorithm, and $T1$ and $T3$ require exclusive access to a common resource protected by the semaphore S, it can happen that the low priority task $T3$ has exclusive access to the common resource when the service of the high priority task $T1$ is requested. $T1$ must wait until $T3$ finishes its critical section and releases the semaphore S. If during this time interval $T2$ requests service, this service will be granted and $T2$, the medium priority task, effectively delays $T3$ and consequently $T1$, the high priority task. This phenomenon is called *priority inversion*.

It has been proposed to elevate the priority of the low priority task $T3$ during its blocking critical section to the high priority of the blocked task $T1$, and thereby eliminate the possibility that the medium priority task $T2$ interferes during the critical section of the low priority task. This is the basic idea of the *priority inheritance protocol*. However, an analysis shows that this protocol can lead to chained blocking and deadlocks. To solve these problems, the *priority ceiling protocol* was developed by [Sha90].

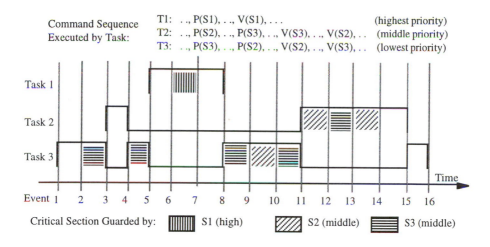

Figure 11.5: The priority ceiling protocol (example taken from [Sha90]).

Event	Action
1	T3 begins execution.
2	T3 locks S3.
3	T2 is started and preempts T3.
4	T2 becomes blocked when trying to access S2 since the priority of T2 is not higher than the priority ceiling of the locked S3. T3 resumes the execution of its critical section at the inherited priority of T2.
5	T1 is initiated and preempts T3.
6	T1 locks the semaphore S1. The priority of T1 is higher than the priority ceiling of all locked semaphores.
7	T1 unlocks semaphore S1.
8	T1 finishes its execution. T3 contintues with the inherited priority of T2.
9	T3 locks semaphore S2.
10	T3 unlocks S2.
11	T3 unlocks S3 and returns to its lowest priority. At this point T2 can lock S2.
12	T2 locks S3.
13	T2 unlocks S3.
14	T2 unlocks S2.
15	T2 completes. T3 resumes its operation.
16	T3 completes.

The *priority ceiling* of a semaphore is defined as the priority of the highest priority task that may lock this semaphore. A task T is allowed to enter a critical section only if its assigned priority is higher than the priority ceilings of all semaphores currently locked by tasks other than T. Task T runs at its assigned priority unless it is in a critical section and blocks higher priority tasks. In this case it inherits the highest priority of the tasks it blocks. When it exits the critical section it resumes the priority it had at the point of entry into the critical section.

The example of Figure 11.5, taken from [Sha90], illustrates the operation of the priority ceiling protocol. A system of *3* tasks, *T1* (highest priority), *T2* (middle priority) and *T3* (lowest priority) compete for three critical regions protected by the three semaphores *S1*, *S2* and *S3*.

Schedulability Test for the Priority Ceiling Protocol: The following sufficient schedulability test for the priority ceiling protocol has been given by [Sha90]. Assume a set of periodic tasks, $\{T_i\}$ with periods p_i and computation times c_i. We denote the worst-case blocking time of a task t_i by lower priority tasks by B_i. The set of n periodic tasks $\{T_i\}$ can be scheduled, if the following set of inequalities holds:

$$\forall\ i,\ 1 \le i \le n:$$
$$(c_1/p_1 + c_2/p_2 + .. + c_i/p_i + B_i/p_i) \le i(2^{1/i} - 1)$$

In these inequalities the effect of preemptions by higher priority tasks is considered in the first i terms (in analogy to the rate monotonic algorithm), whereas the worst case blocking time due to all lower priority tasks is represented in the term B_i/p_i. The blocking term B_i/p_i, which can become very significant if a task with a short period (i.e., small p_i) is blocked for a significant fraction of its time, effectively reduces the CPU utilization of the task system. In case this first sufficient schedulability test fails, more complex sufficient tests can be found in [Sha90]. The priority ceiling protocol is a good example of a predictable, but *non-deterministic* scheduling protocol.

11.3.4   Dynamic Scheduling in Distributed Systems

It is difficult to guarantee tight deadlines by dynamic scheduling techniques in a single processor multi-tasking system if mutual exclusion and precedence constraints among the tasks must be considered. The situation is more complex in a distributed system, where non-preemptive access to the communication medium must be controlled. At present, work is ongoing to extend the rate-monotonic theory to distributed systems. Tindell [Tin95] analyzes distributed systems that use the CAN bus as the communication channel and establishes analytical upper bounds to the communication delays that are encountered by a set of periodic messages. These results are then integrated with the results of the node-local task scheduling to arrive at the worst-case execution time of distributed real-time transactions. One difficult problem is the control of transaction jitter.

The problem of investigating the real-time temporal performance in a best-effort distributed system is a current research topic [Mos94]. The critical issue in the evaluation of the timeliness of a distributed best-effort architecture by probabilistic models concerns the assumptions on the input distribution. Rare event occurrences in the environment, e.g., a lightning stroke into an electric power grid, will cause a highly correlated input load on the system (e.g., an alarm shower) that is very difficult to model adequately. Even an extended observation of a real-life system is not conclusive, because these rare events, by definition, cannot be observed frequently.

This section has only presented a coarse overview of recent results in the field of dynamic scheduling. For a more detailed discussion, the reader is referred to an excellent survey by [Ram96].

11.4 STATIC SCHEDULING

In static or pre-runtime scheduling, a feasible schedule of a set of tasks is calculated off line. The schedule must guarantee all deadlines, considering the resource, precedence, and synchronization requirements of all tasks. The construction of such a schedule can be considered as a constructive sufficient schedulability test. The precedence relations between the tasks executing in the different nodes can be depicted in the form of a *precedence graph* (Figure 11.6).

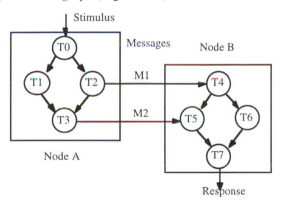

Figure 11.6: Example of a precedence graph of a distributed task set [Foh94].

11.4.1   Static Scheduling Viewed as a Search

Static scheduling is based on strong regularity assumptions about the points in time when future service requests will be honored. Although the occurrence of external events that demand service is not under the control of the computer system, the recurring points in time when these events will be serviced can be established *a priori* by selecting an appropriate sampling rate for each class of events (see also Section 9.3). During system design, it must be ascertained that the sum of the maximum delay times until a request is recognized by the system plus the maximum transaction response time is smaller than the specified service deadline.

The Role of Time: A static schedule is a periodic time-triggered schedule. The timeline is partitioned into a sequence of basic granules, the *basic cycle time*. There is only one interrupt in the system: a periodic clock interrupt denoting the start of a new basic granule. In a distributed system, this clock interrupt must be globally synchronized to a precision that is much better than the duration of a basic granule. Every transaction is periodic, its period being a multiple of the basic granule. The least common multiple of all transaction periods is the *schedule period*. At compile time, the scheduling decision for every point of the schedule period must be determined and stored in a dispatcher table for the operating system. At run time, the preplanned decision is executed by the dispatcher after every clock interrupt.

Static scheduling can be applied to a single processor, to a multiple-processor, or to a distributed system. In addition to preplanning the resource usage in all nodes, the access to the communication medium must also be preplanned in distributed systems. It is known that finding an optimal schedule in a distributed system is in almost all realistic scenarios an NP-complete problem, i.e., computationally intractable. But even a non-optimal solution is sufficient if it meets all deadlines.

The Search Tree: The solution to the scheduling problem can be seen as finding a path, a feasible schedule, in a *search tree* by applying a search strategy. An example of a simple search tree for the precedence graph of Figure 11.6 is shown in Figure 11.7. Every level of the search tree corresponds to one unit of time. The depth of the search tree corresponds to the period of the schedule. The search starts with an empty schedule at the root node of this tree. The outward edges of a node point to the possible alternatives that exist at this point of the search. A path from the root node to a particular node at level *n* records the sequence of scheduling decisions that have been made up to time-point *n*. Each path to a leaf node describes a complete schedule. It is the goal of the search to find a complete schedule that observes all precedence and mutual exclusion constraints, and which completes before the deadline. From Figure 11.7, it can be seen that the right branch of the search tree will lead to a shorter overall execution time than the left branches.

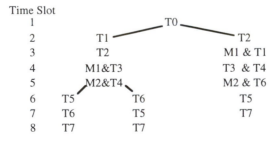

Time Slot			
1		T0	
2	T1		T2
3	T2		M1 & T1
4	M1&T3		T3 & T4
5	M2&T4		M2 & T6
6	T5	T6	T5
7	T6	T5	T7
8	T7	T7	

Figure 11.7: A search tree for the precedence graph of figure 11.6.

A Heuristic Function Guiding the Search: To improve the efficiency of the search, it is necessary to guide the search by some heuristic function. Such a heuristic function can be composed of two terms, the actual cost of the path encountered until the present node in the search tree, i.e., the present point in the schedule, and the estimated cost until a goal node. Fohler [Foh94] proposes a heuristic function that estimates the time needed to complete the precedence graph, called TUR (time until response). A lower bound of the TUR can be derived by summing up the maximum execution times of all tasks and message exchanges between the current task and the last task in the precedence graph, assuming true parallelism constrained by the competition for CPU resources of tasks that reside at the same node. If this necessary TUR is not short enough to complete the precedence graph on time, all the branches from the current node can be pruned and the search must backtrack.

11.4.2   Increasing the Flexibility in Static Schedules

One of the weaknesses of static scheduling is the assumption of strictly periodic tasks. Although the majority of tasks in hard real-time applications is periodic, there are also sporadic requests for service that have hard deadline requirements. An example of such a request is an emergency stop of a machine. Hopefully it will never be requested–the mean time between emergency stops can be very long. However, if an emergency stop is requested, it must be serviced within a small specified time interval.

The following three methods increase the flexibility of static scheduling:

(i)   The transformation of sporadic requests into periodic requests,

(ii)   The introduction of a sporadic server task, and

(iii) The execution of mode changes.

Transformation of a Sporadic Request to a Periodic Request: While the future request times of a periodic task are known *a priori*, only the minimum interarrival time of a sporadic task is known in advance. The actual points in time when a sporadic task must be serviced are not known ahead of the request event. This limited information makes it difficult to schedule a sporadic request before run time. The most demanding sporadic requests are those that have a short response time, i.e., the corresponding service task has a low latency.

It is possible to find solutions to the scheduling problem if an independent sporadic task has a laxity l. One such solution, proposed by Mok [Mok83,p.44], is the replacement of a sporadic task T by a pseudo-periodic task T' as seen in Table 11.1.

Parameter	sporadic task	new pseudo-periodic task
Computation time c	c	$c'=c$
Deadline interval d	d	$d'=c$
Period p	p	$p'=Min(l\text{-}1, p)$

Table 11.1: Parameters of the pseudo-periodic task.

This transformation guarantees that the sporadic task will always meet its deadline if the pseudo-periodic task can be scheduled. The pseudo-periodic task can be scheduled statically. A sporadic task with a short latency will continuously demand a substantial fraction of the processing resources to guarantee its deadline, although it might request service very infrequently.

Sporadic Server Task: To reduce the large resource requirements of a pseudo-periodic task with a long interarrival time (period) but a short latency, Sprunt et al. [Spr89] have proposed the introduction of a periodic server task for the service of sporadic requests. Whenever a sporadic request arrives during the period of the server task, it will be serviced with the high priority of the server task. The service of a sporadic request exhausts the execution time of the server. The execution time will be replenished after the period of the server. Thus, the server task preserves its execution time until it is needed by a sporadic request. The sporadic server task is scheduled dynamically in response to the sporadic request event.

Mode Changes: During the operation of most real-time applications a number of different operating modes can be distinguished. Consider the example of a flight control system in an airplane. When a plane is taxiing on the ground a different set of services is required than when the plane is flying. Better resource utilization can be realized if only those tasks that are needed in a particular operating mode must be scheduled. If the system leaves one operating mode and enters another, a corresponding change of schedules must take place.

During system design, one must identify all possible operating and emergency modes. For each mode, a static schedule that will meet all deadlines is calculated off line. Mode changes are analyzed and the appropriate mode change schedules are developed. Whenever a mode change is requested at run time the applicable mode change schedule will be activated immediately. The topic of mode changes is an area of active research, see, e.g., [Foh92].

We conclude this chapter with a comment by Xu and Parnas [Xu91, p.134]

For satisfying timing constraints in hard real-time systems, predictability of the systems behavior is the most important concern; pre-run-time scheduling is often the only practical means of providing predictability in a complex system.

POINTS TO REMEMBER

*   A scheduler is called *dynamic* (or *on-line*) if it makes its scheduling decisions at run time, selecting one out of the current set of *ready* tasks. A scheduler is called static (or pre-run-time) if it makes its scheduling decisions at compile time. It generates a dispatching table for the run-time dispatcher off line.

*   In preemptive scheduling the currently executing task may be preempted, i.e., interrupted, if a more urgent task requests service. In nonpreemptive scheduling, the currently executing task will not be interrupted until it decides on its own to release the allocated resources--normally after completion.

*   A test that determines whether a set of ready tasks can be scheduled so that each task meets its deadline is called a *schedulability test*. We distinguish between *exact*, *necessary* and *sufficient* schedulability tests. In nearly all cases of task

dependency, even if there is only one common resource, the complexity of an exact schedulability test algorithm belongs to the class of NP-complete problems, and is thus computationally intractable.

- The moment when a request for a task execution is made is called the *task request time*. Starting with an initial request, all future request times of a periodic task are known *a priori* by adding multiples of the known period to the initial request time.

- While the future request times of a periodic task are known *a priori*, only the minimum interarrival time of a *sporadic* task is known in advance. The actual points in time when a sporadic task must be serviced are not known ahead of the request event.

- If there is no constraint on the request times of task activations, the task is called an *aperiodic* task.

- The *adversary argument* states that, in general, it is not possible to construct an optimal totally on-line dynamic scheduler if there are mutual exclusion constraints between a periodic and a sporadic task. The adversary argument accentuates the value of *a priori* information about the behavior in the future.

- The rate monotonic algorithm is a dynamic preemptive scheduling algorithm based on static task priorities. It assumes a set of periodic and independent tasks with deadlines equal to their periods.

- The Earliest-Deadline-First (EDF) algorithm is a dynamic preemptive scheduling algorithm based on dynamic task priorities. The task with the earliest deadline is assigned the highest dynamic priority.

- The Least-Laxity (LL) algorithm is a dynamic preemptive scheduling algorithm based on dynamic task priorities. The task with the shortest laxity is assigned the highest dynamic priority.

- During compile time, all *forbidden regions* must be determined, and passed to the dispatcher so that the dispatcher will not schedule any unwanted critical sections in the forbidden region.

- The priority ceiling protocol is used to schedule a set of periodic tasks that have exclusive access to common resources protected by semaphores.

- The *priority ceiling* of a semaphore is defined as the priority of the highest priority task that may lock this semaphore.

- According to the priority ceiling protocol, a task T is allowed to enter a critical section only if its assigned priority is higher than the priority ceilings of all semaphores currently locked by tasks other than T. Task T runs at its assigned priority unless it is in a critical section and blocks higher priority tasks. In this case, it inherits the highest priority of the tasks it blocks. When it exits the critical section, it resumes the priority it had at the point of entry into the critical section.

- The priority ceiling protocol is a good example of a predictable, but *non-deterministic* scheduling protocol.

- The critical issue in best-effort scheduling concerns the assumptions about the input distribution. Rare event occurrences in the environment will cause a highly correlated input load on the system that is difficult to model adequately. Even an extended observation of a real-life system is not conclusive, because these rare events, by definition, cannot be observed frequently.

- In static or pre-run-time scheduling, a feasible schedule of a set of tasks that guarantees all deadlines, considering the resource, precedence, and synchronization requirements of all tasks, is calculated off line. The construction of such a schedule can be considered as a constructive sufficient schedulability test.

- A static schedule is a periodic time-triggered schedule that is repeated after the schedule period. The timeline is partitioned into a sequence of basic granules, the *basic cycle time*. There is only one interrupt in the system: a periodic clock interrupt denoting the start of a new basic granule.

- One of the weaknesses of static scheduling is the assumption of strictly periodic tasks. Although the majority of tasks in hard real-time applications is periodic, there are also sporadic requests for service that have hard deadline requirements.

- The following three techniques increase the flexibility in static scheduling: the transformation of a sporadic task to a pseudo-periodic task, the introduction of periodic server tasks, and mode changes.

BIBLIOGRAPHIC NOTES

Scheduling is one of the best researched topics in the field of real-time computing. Starting with the seminal works of Serlin [Ser72] in 1972 and of Liu and Layland [Liu73] in 1973 on scheduling of independent tasks, hundreds of papers on scheduling have been published each year. In 1975 Garey and Johnson published their important paper "Complexity Results for Multiprocessor Scheduling under Resource Constraints" [Gar75] that contains fundamental results about the complexity of the scheduling problem. Mok presented the adversary argument and the kernelized monitor as part of his PhD work [Mok83, Mok84]. The problem of scheduling real-time tasks in multiprocessor systems has been analyzed by [Ram89]. A major step forward was the development of the priority ceiling protocol for scheduling dependent tasks [Sha90]. The development of static schedules has been investigated by Fohler in his PhD thesis [Foh94, Foh95]. The literature contains a number of good survey papers on scheduling, such as the recent contributions by Burns and Wellings [Bur96] and Ramamritham [Ram96].

REVIEW QUESTIONS AND PROBLEMS

11.1   Give a taxonomy of scheduling algorithms.

11.2   Develop some necessary schedulability tests for scheduling a set of tasks on a single processor system.

11.3   What are the differences between *periodic* tasks, *sporadic* tasks, and *aperiodic* tasks?

11.4   Given the following set of independent periodic tasks, where the deadline interval is equal to the period: {T1(5,8); T2(2,9); T3(4,13)}; (notation: task name(CPU time, period)).

(a) Calculate the laxities of these tasks.

(b) Determine, using a necessary schedulability test, if this task set is schedulable on a single processor system.

(c) Schedule this task set on a two processor system with the LL algorithm.

11.5   Given the following set of independent periodic tasks, where the deadline interval is equal to the period: {T1(5,8); T2(1,9); T3(1,5)}; (notation: task name(CPU time, period)).

(a) Why is this task set not schedulable with the rate monotonic algorithm on a single processor system?

(b) Schedule this task set on a single processor system with the EDF algorithm.

11.6   Why is it not possible to design, in general, an optimal dynamic scheduler?

11.7   What is a *forbidden* region, and why is it needed?

11.8   Assume that the task set of Figure 11.5 is executed without the priority ceiling protocol. At what moment will a deadlock occur? Can this deadlock be resolved by *priority inheritance*?

11.9   Given the task set of Figure 11.5, determine the point where the priority ceiling protocol prevents a task from entering a critical section.

11.10   Discuss the schedulability test of the priority ceiling protocol. What is the effect of blocking on the processor utilization?

11.11   What are the problems with dynamic scheduling in distributed systems?

11.12   Discuss the issue of temporal performance in best-effort distributed system.

11.13   What is the role of time in static scheduling?

11.14   How can the flexibility in static scheduling be increased?

Chapter 12

Validation

OVERVIEW

Validation deals with the question "Is this system fit for its purpose?". Before a safety critical system can be put into operation, convincing evidence must be gathered from independent sources to ensure that the system is trustworthy. Combining this evidence to support the conclusion "yes, this system is safe to deploy" is a subjective process, which must be supported by judicious arguments taking the results of rational analysis and experimental observations into consideration wherever possible.

This chapter starts with a discussion of what constitutes a convincing safety case. It is argued that the properties of the architecture have a decisive influence on the structure of the safety case. Section 12.2 investigates the state of the art of formal methods and their contribution to the validation of ultradependable real-time systems. The use of a semi-formal notation during requirements capture and in the documentation increases the accuracy and helps to avoid the ambiguity of natural language. Fully automatic verification environments that cover the complete system from the high-level specification to the hardware are beyond the current state of the art.

Section 12.3 is devoted to the topic of testing real-time systems. The challenge in testing real-time systems is to find a layout that does not influence the temporal behavior of the system. After presenting some techniques that lead to a testable design, the question of test data selection is raised. Finally, we pose the question: "What do we know about the dependability if the system has been operating correctly during the testing phase?".

Section 12.4 focuses on dependability analysis. After an explanation of the terms *hazard* and *risk*, the techniques of Fault-Tree Analysis and Failure-Mode-And-Effect Analysis are outlined.

12.1 BUILDING A CONVINCING SAFETY CASE

A *safety case* is a combination of a sound set of arguments supported by analytical and experimental evidence concerning the safety of a given design. The safety case must convince an independent certification authority that the system under consideration is safe to deploy. What exactly constitutes a proper safety case of a safety-critical computer system is a subject of intense debate.

12.1.1   Outline of the Safety Case

The safety case must argue why it is extremely unlikely that a single fault will cause a catastrophic failure. The arguments that are included in the safety case will have a major influence on design decisions at later stages of the project. Hence, the outline of the safety case should be planned during the early stages of a project.

Computer systems can fail for external and internal reasons. External reasons are related to the operational environment (e.g., mechanical stress, external electromagnetic fields, temperature), and to the system specification. The two main internal reasons for failure are:

(i)   The computer hardware fails because of a random physical fault. Section 6.4 presented a number of techniques how to detect and handle random hardware faults by redundancy. The effectiveness of these fault-tolerance mechanisms must be demonstrated as part of the safety case, e.g., by fault injection (Section 12.4).

(ii)   The design, which consists of the software and hardware, contains residual design faults. The elimination of the design faults and the validation that a design (software and hardware) is *fit for purpose* is one of the great challenges of the scientific and engineering community. No single validation technology can provide the required evidence that a computer system will meet the ultra-high dependability requirement (Section 1.4.2).

A safety case will therefore combine the evidence from independent sources to convince the certification authority that the system is safe to deploy. A disciplined software-development process with inspections and design reviews reduces the number of design faults that are introduced into the software during initial development [Fag86]. Experimental evidence from testing, which in itself is infeasible to demonstrate the safety of the software in the ultra-dependable region, must be combined with structural arguments about the partitioning of the system in autonomous error-containment regions. The credibility can be further augmented by presenting results from formal analysis of critical properties and the experienced dependability of previous generations of similar systems. Experimental data about field-failure rates of critical components form the input to reliability models of the architecture to demonstrate that the system will mask random component failures with the required high probability. Finally, *diverse* mechanisms play an important role in reducing the probability of common-mode design failures.

12.1.2   Properties of the Architecture

It is a common requirement of a safety critical application that no single fault, which is capable of causing a catastrophic failure, may exist in the whole system. This implies that for a *fail-safe application* every critical error of the computer must be detected within such a short latency that the application can be forced into the safe state *before* the consequences of the error affect the system behavior. In a *fail-operational application,* a safe system service must be provided even *after* a single fault in any one of the components has occurred.

Error-Containment Regions: At the architectural level, it must be demonstrated that *every* single fault can only affect a defined error-containment region and will be detected at the boundaries of this error-containment region. The partitioning of the system into independent error-containment regions is thus of grave concern.

Experience has shown that there are a number of sensitive points in a design that can lead to a common-mode failure of all nodes within a distributed system:

(i)   A single source of time, such as a central clock.

(ii) A babbling node that disrupts the communication among the correct nodes in a bus system.

(iii) A single fault in the power supply or in the grounding system.

(iv) A single design error that is replicated when the same hardware or system software is used in all nodes.

Example: Assume an architecture as depicted in Figure 12.1, where four nodes are connected by a replicated bus. If the communication controller implements an event-triggered protocol, then a single faulty host can corrupt the communication among all correct nodes by sending high-priority event messages on both buses at arbitrary points in time. If the communication controller implements the ARINC 629 protocol (Section 7.5.5), then the protocol has enough information to detect such a misbehavior of the host. However, if the ARINC 629 controller is itself faulty and generates babbling messages, then the communication among the correct nodes will still be disrupted. If the communication controller implements the TTP protocol, then the independent Bus Guardian (Figure 8.2) will detect a babbling fault of the controller, and prevent disruption of the communication.

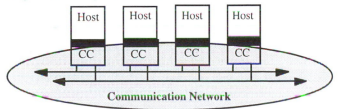

Communication Network Interface within a Node

CC   Communication Controller

Figure 12.1: Real-time communication system.

Composability: Composability is another important architectural property, and helps in designing a convincing safety case (see also Section 2.4.3). Assume that the nodes of a distributed system can be partitioned into two groups: one group of nodes that is involved in the implementation of safety critical functions, and another group of nodes that is not involved (Figure 2.7). If it can be shown, at the architectural level, that no error in any one of the not-involved nodes can affect the proper operation of the nodes that implement the safety critical function, then, it is possible to exclude the not-involved nodes from further consideration during the safety case analysis.

12.2 FORMAL METHODS

By the term *formal methods,* we mean the use of mathematical and logical techniques to express, investigate, and analyze the specification, design, documentation, and behavior of computer hardware and software. In highly ambitious projects, formal methods are applied to *prove formally* that a piece of software implements the specification correctly.

12.2.1   Formal Methods in the Real World

Any formal investigation of a real-world phenomenon requires the following steps to be taken:

(i)   Conceptual model building: Building a conceptual model of a real-world application has been discussed in detail in Section 4.1. This important *informal* first step leads to a reduced natural language representation of the real-world phenomenon that is the subject of investigation. All assumptions, omissions, or misconceptions that are introduced in this first step will remain in the model, and limit the validity of the conclusions derived from the model (see also Section 4.1.1 on assumption coverage).

(ii)   Model formalization: In this second step, the natural language representation of the problem is transformed, and expressed in a formal specification language with precise syntax and semantics. Different degrees of rigor can be distinguished, as discussed in the following section.

(iii) Analysis of the formal model: In the third step, the problem is formally analyzed. In computer systems the analysis methods are based on discrete mathematics and logic. In other engineering disciplines, the analysis methods are based on different branches of mathematics, e.g., the use of differential equations to analyze a control problem.

(iv)   Interpretation of the results: In the final step, the results of the analysis must be interpreted and applied to the real-world.

Only step (iii) out of these four steps can be mechanized. Steps (i), (ii), and (iv) will always require human involvement and human intuition, and are thus as fallible as any other human activity.

An *ideal and complete* verification environment takes the specification, expressed in a formally defined specification language, and the implementation, written in a formally defined implementation language, as inputs, and establishes mechanically the *consistency* between specification and implementation. In a second step it must be ensured that all assumptions and architectural mechanisms of the target machine (e.g., the properties and timing of the instruction set of the hardware) are consistent with the model of computation that is defined by the implementation language. Finally, the correctness of the verification environment itself must be established. Such an ideal and complete verification environment has yet to be built.

12.2.2   Classification of Formal Methods

Rushby [Rus93] classifies the use of formal methods in computer science according to the increasing rigor into the following three levels:

(i)   *Use of concepts and notation from discrete mathematics.* At this level, the sometimes ambiguous natural language statements about requirements and specification of a system are replaced by the symbols and conventions from discrete mathematics and logic, e.g., set theory, relations, and functions. The reasoning about the completeness and consistency of the specification follows a semi-formal manual style, as it is performed in many branches of mathematics.

(ii) *Use of formalized specification languages with some mechanical support tools.* At this level, a formal specification language with a fixed syntax is introduced that allows the mechanical analysis of some properties of the problems expressed in the specification language. At level (ii), it is not possible to generate complete proofs mechanically.

(iii) *Use of fully formalized specification languages with comprehensive support environments, including mechanized theorem proving or proof checking.* At this level, a precisely defined specification language with a direct interpretation in logic is supplied, and a set of support tools is provided to allow the mechanical analysis of specifications expressed in the formal specification language.

12.2.3   Benefits from the Application of Formal Methods

Level (i) Methods: The compact mathematical notation introduced at this level forces the designer to clearly state the requirements and assumptions without the ambiguity of natural language. Since familiarity with the basic notions of set theory and logic is part of an engineering education, the disciplined use of level (i) methods will improve the communication within a project team and within an engineering organization, and enrich the quality of documentation. Parnas [Par90,Par92] advocates the use of the semiformal notation at this level to improve the quality of documentation of real-time software. Since most of the serious faults are introduced early in the lifecycle, the benefits of the level (i) methods at the early phases of requirements capture and architecture design are most pronounced. Rushby [Rus93, p.39] sees the following benefits from using level (i) methods early in the lifecycle:

(i)   The need for effective and precise communication between the software engineer and the engineers from other disciplines is greatest at an early stage, when the interdependencies between the mechanical control system and the computer system are specified.

(ii)   The familiar concepts of discrete mathematics (e.g., set, relation) provide a repertoire of mental building blocks that are precise, yet abstract. The use of a precise notation at the early stages of the project helps to avoid ambiguities and misunderstandings.

(iii) Some simple mechanical analysis of the specification can lead to the detection of inconsistencies and of omission faults, e.g., that symbols have not been defined or variables have not been initialized.

(iv)   The reviews at the early stages of the lifecycle are more effective if the requirements are expressed in a precise notation than if ambiguous natural language is used.

(v)   The difficulty to express vague ideas and immature concepts in a semiformal notation helps to reveal problem domains that need further investigation.

Level (ii) Methods: Level (ii) methods are a mixed blessing. They introduce a rigid formalism that is cumbersome to use, without offering the benefit of mechanical proof generation. Many of the specification languages that focus on the formal reasoning about the temporal properties of real-time programs (see, e.g., the different mathematically based methods for the design of real-time systems presented in the book [Mat96]) are based at this level. Level (ii) formal methods are an important intermediate step on the way to provide a fully automated verification environment. They are interesting from the point of view of research.

Level (iii) Methods: The full benefits of formal methods are only realized at this level. However, the available systems for verification are not complete in the sense that they cover the entire system from the high level specification to the hardware architecture. They introduce an intermediate level of abstraction that is above the functionality of the hardware. Nevertheless, the use of such a system [Rus93a] for the rigorous analysis of some critical functions of a distributed real-time system, e.g., the correctness of the clock synchronization, can uncover subtle design faults and lead to valuable insights.

To summarize, we quote Rushby [Rus93, p.87]:

Formal methods can provide important evidence for consideration in certification, but they can no more "prove" that an artifact of significant logical complexity is fit for its purpose than a finite-element calculation can "prove" that a wing span will do its job. Certification must consider multiple sources of evidence, and ultimately rests on informed engineering judgment and experience.

12.3 TESTING

During *testing,* a computer system is exercised with valued inputs with the goal of determining whether the system provides all specified functions, and whether *all* residual design errors have been removed. The latter goal cannot be fully achieved by testing. In real-time systems, the functional as well as temporal behavior of the system must be tested. In this section, we focus on the peculiarities of testing distributed real-time systems.

12.3.1   The Probe Effect

Observability of the outputs of the subsystem under test and *controllability* of the test inputs are at the core of any testing activity. In non-real time systems, the observability and controllability are provided by test- and debug monitors that halt the program flow at a testpoint and give the tester the opportunity to monitor and change program variables. In real-time systems, such a procedure is not suitable for the following two reasons:

(i)   The temporal delay introduced at the testpoint modifies the temporal behavior of the system in such a manner that existing errors can be hidden, and new errors can be introduced.

(ii)   In a distributed system, there are many *loci* of control. The halting of one control path introduces a temporal distortion in the coordinated control flow that can lead to new errors.

The modification of the behavior of the object under test by the introduction of a test probe is called the *probe effect*. The challenge in testing distributed real-time system lies in designing a test environment that is free of the probe effect [Sch93].

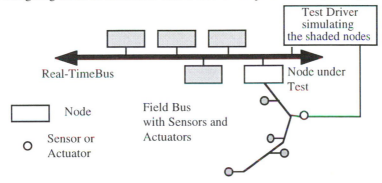

Figure 12.2: Test driver in a distributed system.

Distributed systems that contain a broadcast communication channel (bus) have the advantage that all messages on the real-time bus can be observed by a non-intrusive test monitor. If the sensors and actuators are connected by a field bus, then the I/O information of a node can also be monitored without the probe effect. The observability of the input/output messages of a node is thus given.

In distributed systems, controllability can be achieved by a test driver that generates the messages of the node environment on the real-time bus and on the field bus for the node under test (Figure 12.2). If the system is time-triggered, then, any scenario that has been observed in the environment can be reproduced by the test driver deterministically on the sparse time-base.

12.3.2   Design for Testability

By *design for testability*, we mean the design of a system structure and the provision of mechanisms that facilitate the testing of the system [Wil83]. The following techniques improve the testability:

(i)   Partitioning the system into composable subsystems so that each subsystem can be tested in isolation, and no unintended side-effects will occur during system integration. This topic has been discussed extensively throughout this text, particularly in Sections 2.4 and 7.4.1.

(ii)   Establishment of a static temporal control structure so that the temporal control structure is independent of the input data. It is then possible to test the temporal control structure in isolation.

(iii)   Reducing the size of the input space by introducing a sparse time-base of proper granularity. The granularity of this time-base should be small enough to accommodate the application at hand but should not be any smaller. The smaller the granularity of the sparse time-base, the larger the potential input space. The *test coverage*, i.e., the fraction of the total input space that is tested, can be increased by decreasing the input space or by increasing the number of test cases.

(iv)   Output of the h-state of a node in an h-state message at the point in time when the node is in the ground state. This measure improves the observability of the internal state of the node.

(v)   Provision of replica determinism in the software, which guarantees that the same outputs will be produced if the same input messages are applied to a node.

Because of their deterministic properties, time-triggered systems are easier to test than event-triggered systems.

12.3.3   Test Data Selection

During the test phase, only a tiny fraction of the potential input space of a software system can be exercised. The challenge for the tester is to find an effective and representative set of test-data that will uncover a high percentage of the unknown faults. In the literature on testing [The95], many test data selection criteria have been proposed. In this section, we focus on three test data selection criteria that are unique to real-time systems.

Peak Load: A hard real-time system must provide the specified timely service under all conditions covered by the load- and fault-hypothesis, i.e., also under peak load. Rare-event scenarios often generate peak-load activity. The peak-load scenario puts extreme stress on the software and should be tested extensively. The behavior of the system in above-peak load situations must also be tested. If peak load activity is handled correctly, the normal load case will take care of itself.

Worst-Case Execution Time (WCET): To determine the WCET of a task experimentally, the task source code can be analyzed to generate a test data set that is biased towards the worst-case execution time.

Fault-Tolerance Mechanisms: Testing the correctness of the fault-tolerance mechanism is difficult, because faults are not part of the *normal* input domain. Mechanisms must be provided that can activate the faults during the test phase. For example, software- or hardware-implemented fault injection can be used to test the correctness of the fault-tolerance mechanisms (see the following section).

12.3.4   What can be Inferred from "Perfect Working"?

Is it possible to accept a software-intensive control system for a safety critical application on the basis of evidence gathered during the testing phase? Section 1.4.2 states that safety critical systems must meet the ultra-high dependability requirement of less than one critical failure in 10^9 hours, i.e., an MTTF of about 100 000 years of operation. In [Lit95, p.479] Littlewood and Strigini raise the question: "How long must a single system operate without a failure to be able to conclude that the stated reliability objective has been reached?". Referring to arguments from Bayesian statistics, they conclude that if no prior belief is brought to the problem, then a failure-free operation in the same order of magnitude as the MTTF is needed to infer that the system meets the ultra-high dependability requirements. Butler and Finelly [But93] reach a similar conclusion about the infeasibility of quantifying the reliability of life critical real-time software by statistical methods.

If 100 000 identical systems are observed in the field, then the necessary operational hours accumulate within a single year. The wide deployment of computers in safety-critical mass products (e.g., automobiles) offers the prospect that a statistical data base that can be used for the certification of future critical systems can be built. For example, an automotive company might install a new real-time network in hundred thousands of cars in a non safety-critical applications to observe the system during billions of operating hours before installing the system in a safety-critical application. If every single failure is scrutinized, it is possible to get a sufficient statistical base for reasoning about the probability of a critical failure in a fault-tolerant system.

12.4 FAULT INJECTION

Fault injection is the intentional activation of faults by hardware or software means to be able to observe the system operation under fault conditions. During a fault-injection experiment, the target system is exposed to two types of inputs: the injected faults and the input data. The faults can be seen as *another type of input* that activate the fault-management mechanisms.

12.4.1   Why Fault Injection?

Careful testing and debugging of the fault-management mechanisms are necessary because a notable number of system failures is caused by errors in the fault-management mechanisms. A fault in a system manifests itself either as an *error* (see Section 6.1.2) or as an incorrect *trigger* (see Section 1.5.5).

Fault injection serves two purposes during the evaluation of a dependable system:

(i)   Testing and Debugging: During normal operation, faults are *rare events* that occur only infrequently. Because a fault-tolerance mechanism requires the occurrence of a fault for its activation, it is very cumbersome to test and debug the operation of the fault-tolerance mechanisms without artificial fault injection.

(ii)   Dependability Forecasting: This is used to get experimental data about the likely dependability of a fault-tolerant system. For this second purpose, the types and distribution of the expected faults in the envisioned operational environment must be known. Only then is it possible to carry out a realistic physical simulation of this environment in the laboratory.

Table 12.1 compares these two different purposes of fault injection.

	Testing and Debugging	Dependability Forecasting
Injected faults	Faults derived from the specified fault hypothesis.	Faults expected in the operational environment.
Input data	Selected input data to activate the injected faults.	Input data taken from the operational environment.
Results	Information about the operation and effectiveness of the fault-tolerance mechanisms.	Information about the envisioned dependability of the fault-tolerant system.

Table 12.1: Fault injection for testing and debugging versus dependability forecasting [Avr92].

It is possible to inject faults at the physical level of the hardware (*physical fault injection*) or into the state of the computation (*software implemented fault-injection*).

12.4.2   Physical Fault Injection

During physical fault-injection the target hardware is subjected to adverse physical phenomena that interfere with the correct operation of the computer hardware. In the following section, we describe a set of hardware fault-injections experiments that have been carried out on the MARS (Maintainable Real-time System) architecture in the context of the ESPRIT Basic Research Project *Predictably Dependable Computing Systems (PDCS)* [Kar95].

The objective of the MARS fault-injection experiments was to determine the *error-detection coverage* of the MARS nodes experimentally. Two replica-determinate nodes receive identical inputs and should produce the same result. One of the nodes is subjected to fault-injections (the *FI-node*), the other node serves as a reference node (a *golden node*). As long as the consequences of the faults are detected within the FI-node, and the FI-node turns itself off, or the FI-node produces a detectably incorrect result message at the correct point in time, the error has been classified as detected. If the FI-node produces a result message different from the result message of the golden node without any error indication, a fail-silence violation has been observed.

Fault Injection Technique	Heavy-ion	Pin-level	EMI
Controllability, space	low	high	low
Controllability, time	none	high/medium	low
Flexibility	low	medium	high
Reproducibility	medium	high	low
Physical reachability	high	medium	medium
Timing measurement	medium	high	low

Table 12.2: Characteristics of different physical fault-injection techniques.

Injected Faults: Three different fault-injection techniques were chosen at three different sites. At Chalmers University in Goeteborg, the CPU chip was bombarded with α particles until the system failed. At LAAS in Toulouse, the system was subjected to pin-level fault-injection, forcing an equi-potential line on the board into a defined state at a precise moment of time. At the Technische Universität Wien, the whole board was subjected to Electromagnetic Interference (EMI) radiation according to the IEC standard IEC 801-4.

The potential interference of electromagnetic radiation with the operation of an embedded computer system is a serious issue. Since such an interference is infrequent and sensitive to specific geometry parameters between the emitter and the device under consideration, the interference is difficult to reproduce. Statistics from the aviation industry suggest that EMI is a hazard that cannot be neglected.

Example: To reduce the risk of EMI with the operation of the electronic equipment onboard an aircraft, the operation of electronic equipment during critical flight maneuvers is restricted [Per96]. For the same reason, patients with a heart pacemaker are not recommended to pass by a metal detector at an airport.

Table 12.2 gives a comparison of the characteristics of the diverse fault-injection techniques.

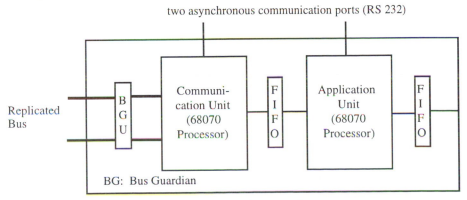

Figure 12.3: The hardware under test.

The Hardware under Test: Figure 12.3 gives an overview of the hardware under test. The hardware consisted of two major subsystems, a communication-control unit implementing the time-triggered communication protocol, and an application unit (host) for implementing the application. The Bus Guardian (BG) protected the bus from babbling nodes. A more detailed description of the hardware can be found in [Rei95].

The replica-determinate MARS operating system described in [Rei95] was implemented on the application unit and the communication unit. The application software consisted of a control program that implemented a typical cyclic real-time application. The following error detection mechanisms were implemented in the node under test:

(i)   Hardware: standard mechanisms onboard the 68070 CPU such as: illegal instruction, illegal address; special mechanisms such as: bus guardian, FIFO overflow, and power supply monitor.

(ii) System Software: compiler generated run-time assertions, timing checks to check the WCET of the real-time tasks.

(iii) Application Software: double execution, triple execution (two dynamic, one static test in-between), end-to-end CRC.

Most of the error-detection mechanisms could be deactivated to learn about the effectiveness of each mechanism by comparing test runs with and without a particular mechanism. A more detailed description of the error-detection mechanisms can be found in [Rei95].

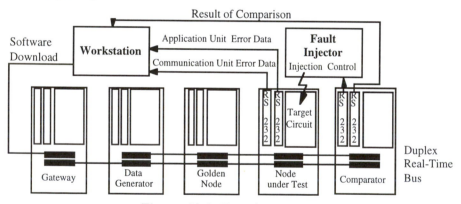

Figure 12.4: Experiment setup.

Experiment Setup: Figure 12.4 shows the experiment setup. A sequence of input messages was produced by a data generator node. These input messages were received by the two nodes, the *node under test* and the *golden node*. The result messages of these two nodes were compared by the comparator node. The nodes were connected to a gateway that downloaded the core-images from a workstation. The results of the experiments were transmitted to the workstation for later analysis.

Results: Many different test runs, each one consisting of 2000 to 10000 experiments, were carried out with differing combinations of error detection techniques enabled. The results of the experiments can be summarized as follows:

(i)   With all error detection mechanisms enabled, no fail-silence violation was observed in any of the experiments.

(ii)   The end-to-end error detection mechanisms and the double execution of tasks were needed in experiments with every one of the three fault-injection methods if error-detection coverage of > 99 % must be achieved.

(iii)   In the experiment that used heavy-ion radiation, a triple execution was needed to eliminate all coverage violations. The triple execution consisted of a test-run with known outputs between the two replicated executions of the application task. This test run was not needed in the EMI experiments and the pin-level fault injection.

(iv)   The bus guardian unit was needed in all three experiments if a coverage of > 99% must be achieved. It eliminated the most critical failure of a node, the *babbling idiots*.

A more detailed discussion of the results can be found in [Kar95].

12.4.3   Software-Implemented Fault Injection

In *software-implemented fault injection*, errors are seeded into the memory of the computer by software techniques. These seeded errors mimic the effects of hardware faults or design faults in the software. The errors can be seeded either randomly or according to some preset strategy to activate specific fault-management tasks. A distinction is made between an injection of faults in the *i-state* or in the *h-state* (see Section 4.2.2). While an error in the h-state corresponds to a data error, an error in the i-state can mimic a control error as well as a data error.

Software implemented fault injection has a number of potential advantages over physical fault injection:

(i)   Predictability: The space (memory cell) where and the moment when a fault is injected is fixed by the fault-injection program. It is possible to reproduce every injected fault in the value domain and in the temporal domain.

(ii)   Reachability: It is possible to reach the inner registers of large VLSI chips. Pin-level fault injection is limited to the external pins of a chip.

(iii)   Less Effort than Physical Fault Injection: The experiments can be carried out with software tools without any need to modify the hardware.

A number of software fault-injection environments are discussed in the literature, e.g., FIAT [Seg88], FERRARI [Kan95], and DOCTOR [Ros93]. One of the key issues is whether software implemented fault-injection leads to results that are comparable to physical fault injections.

Fuchs [Fuc96] conducted an extensive set of experiments to answer this question experimentally by comparing the characteristics of software implemented fault-injection versus physical fault injection. He performed software-implemented fault-injection on the experimental setup described in Section 12.3.2 and came to the following conclusions:

(i)   The results from software fault-injection experiments with the bit-flip fault model (the fault changes a single bit) in the *h-state* indicate that error-detection coverage is similar to that of the hardware fault-injection experiments.

(ii) The application software error detection is higher for the software-implemented fault injection than for the three physical fault-injection experiments. Most of the faults injected by pin-level fault injection and EMI fault injection are detected by the hardware and the system software, and do not propagate to the application level.

(iii) If the application level error detection mechanisms are turned off, software fault injection generates a higher number of coverage violations than EMI or pin level fault injections for the single execution configuration.

In summary, Fuchs [Fuc96] concluded from his experiments that software-implemented fault-injection with the simple bit-flip model is capable to produce a similar error set as the physical techniques of EMI and pin level fault injection. However, heavy-ion radiation is more stressful and requires a more malicious fault model than the single bit-flip model.

12.5 DEPENDABILITY ANALYSIS

A safety-critical system must be carefully analyzed before it is put into operation to reduce the probability that an *accident* will occur. For example, the probability of a catastrophic failure must be less than 10^{-9}/hour in many applications in the transportation sectors (see Section 1.4.2). The *damage* is a pecuniary measure for the loss in an accident, e.g., death, illness, injury, loss of property, or environmental harm. Undesirable conditions that have the potential to cause or contribute to an accident are called *hazards*. A hazard is thus a state that can lead to an accident, given certain environmental conditions. Hazards have a *severity* and a *probability*. The severity is related to the worst potential damage that can result from the accident associated with the hazard. The severity of hazards is often classified in a severity class. The product of hazard severity and hazard probability is called *risk*. The goal of dependability analysis and safety engineering is to identify hazards, and to propose measures that eliminate or at least reduce the hazard or reduce the probability of a hazard turning into a catastrophe, i.e., to minimize the risk [Lev95]. According to the IEC Standard 604 for programmable medical equipment [IEC96], a risk originating from a particular hazard should be reduced to a level which is "as low as reasonably practical (ALARP)". This is a rather imprecise statement that must be interpreted with good engineering judgment. An example of a risk minimization technique is the implementation of an independent safety monitor that detects a hazardous state of the controlled object and forces the controlled object into a safe state (see the example of Section 6.6.2).

12.5.1   Fault Tree Analysis

A fault tree provides graphical insight into the possible combinations of component failures that can lead to a particular system failure. Fault-tree analysis is an accepted methodology to identify hazards and to increase the safety of complex systems.

The fault-tree analysis begins at the system level with the identification of the undesirable failure event (the *top event* of the fault tree). It then investigates the subsystem failure conditions that can lead to this top event and proceeds down the tree until the analysis stops at a basic failure, usually a component failure mode (events in ellipses). The parts of a fault-tree that are still undeveloped are identified by the diamond symbol. The failure conditions can be connected by the AND or the OR symbol. AND connectors typically model redundancy or safety mechanisms.

Example: Figure 12.5 depicts the fault tree of an electric iron. The undesirable top event occurs if the user of the electric iron receives an electric shock. Two conditions must be satisfied for this event to happen: the metal parts of the iron must be under high voltage (hazardous state) and the user must be in direct or indirect contact with the metal parts, i.e., the user either touches the metal directly or touches a wet piece of cloth that conducts the electricity. The metal parts of the iron will be under high voltage if the insulation of a wire that touches the metal inside the iron is defect and the ground-current monitor that is supposed to detect the hazardous state (the metal parts are under high voltage) is defect.

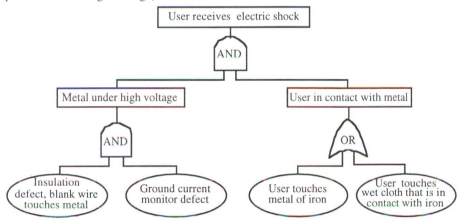

Figure 12.5: Fault tree for an electric iron.

Fault trees can be formally analyzed with mathematical techniques. Given the probability of basic component failures, the probability of the top event of a static fault-tree can be calculated by standard combinatorial approaches.

Warm and cold spares, shared pools of resources, and sequence dependencies in which the order of the failure occurrence determines the state of the system, require more elaborate modeling techniques. A fault tree that cannot by analyzed by combinatorial approaches is called a *dynamic fault tree* [Pul96]. A dynamic fault tree is transformed into a Markov chain that can be solved by numerical techniques. There are many excellent computer programs available that assist the design engineer in evaluating the reliability and safety of a given design, e.g., UltraSAN [Cou91], or SHARPE [Sah95].

12.5.2   Failure Mode and Effect Analysis (FMEA)

Failure Mode and Effect Analysis (FMEA) is a technique for systematically analyzing the effects of possible failure modes of components within a system to detect weak spots of the design, and to prevent system failures from occurring. The original FMEA requires a team of experienced engineers to identify all possible failure modes of each component and to investigate the consequences of every failure on the service of the system at the system/user interface. The failure modes are entered into a standardized work-sheet as sketched in Figure 12.6.

Component	Failure Mode	Failure Effect	Probability	Criticality

Figure 12.6 Worksheet for an FMEA.

A number of software tools have been developed to support the FMEA. The first efforts attempted to reduce the bookkeeping burden by introducing customized spreadsheet programs. Recent efforts have been directed towards assisting the reasoning process [Bel92] and to provide a system wide FMEA simulation [Mon96].

The FMEA is complementary to the Fault-Tree Analysis discussed in the previous section. While the Fault-Tree Analysis starts from the undesirable top event, and proceeds down to the component failures that are the cause of this system failure, the FMEA starts with the components and investigates the effects of the component failure on the system functions.

12.5.3   Software Reliability Growth

Since it is impossible to determine the reliability of a software-intensive product in the ultra-high dependability region quantitatively by analyzing the product *per se* (by testing or formal analysis of the software), evidence regarding the anticipated reliability of the product is gathered from another source: the software development process. It is assumed that a disciplined and structured development process with semi-formal reviews and inspections of the intermediate documents (requirements specification, architecture design, detailed design, program code, and test plan) reduces the probability that design errors are introduced into the product during its development. The ARINC RTCA/DO-178 B [ARI92] document "Software Considerations in Airborne Systems and Equipment Certification", and the emerging IEC Standard IEC-1508 part 5 [IEC95] on software in safety related systems follow this route.

In a disciplined development process, every error that is detected at a later stage of development (e.g., during integration testing) is recorded and analyzed to determine in which earlier phase the error was made and what caused the error. This data (e.g., the MTTF between system failures) is gathered during the later phases of the development cycle and during the operation of the software to predict the reliability growth of the software as the system is debugged. Elaborate models for the prediction of the reliability growth of software have been published [Lit95].

In ultra-high dependability applications, reliability-growth models are of little help. The system must be reliable to a degree that the number of error-data points available is insufficient to support a statistical analysis.

POINTS TO REMEMBER

- A *safety case* is a combination of a sound set of arguments supported by analytical and experimental evidence concerning the safety of a given design.

- A safety case will combine the evidence from independent sources to convince the certification authority that the system is safe to deploy. Examples of sources of evidence are: disciplined development process, results from inspection and testing, formal verification of critical properties, experience with similar systems, diverse designs.

- The term *formal methods* we denotes the use of mathematical and logical techniques to express, investigate, and analyze the specification, design, documentation, and behavior of computer hardware and software.

- The important *informal* first step in applying formal methods concerns constructing a conceptual model of the application. This model serves as the basis for the formal model. All assumptions, omissions or misconceptions that are introduced in this first step will remain in the model and limit the validity of the conclusions derived from the model

- The compact mathematical notation resulting from the use of discrete mathematics at the early phases of a project forces the user and designer to clearly state the requirements and assumptions without the ambiguity of natural language. This will improve the communication within an engineering organization, lead to more precise requirements statement, and enrich the quality of documentation.

- The modification of the behavior of the object under test by introducing of a test probe is called the *probe effect*. The challenge in testing distributed real-time systems lies in designing of a test environment that is free of the probe effect.

- *Fault injection* is the intentional activation of faults by hardware or software means to be able to observe the system operation under fault conditions. During a fault-injection experiment the target system is exposed to two types of inputs: the injected faults and the input data.

- Software-implemented fault-injection with the simple bit-flip model is capable to produce a similar error set as the physical techniques of EMI and pin level fault injection.

- A *hazard* is an undesirable condition that has the potential to cause or contribute to an accident.

- A hazard has a severity, denoting the worst-case damage of a potential accident, and a probability. The product of hazard severity and hazard probability is called *risk*.

- A fault tree provides graphical insight into the possible combinations of component failures that can lead to a particular system failure.

- Failure Mode and Effect Analysis (FMEA) is a technique for systematically analyzing the effects of possible failure modes of components within a system to detect weak spots of the design and to prevent system failures from occurring.

- Because it is impossible to determine the reliability of a software-intensive product in the ultra-high dependability region quantitatively by analyzing the product *per se* (by testing or formal analysis of the software), evidence about the anticipated reliability of the product is gathered from another source: the software development process.

BIBLIOGRAPHIC NOTES

The research report "Formal Methods and the Certification of Critical Systems" [Rus93] by John Rushby is a seminal work on the role of formal methods in the certification of safety-critical systems. Methodologies for the specification and verification of assertions about real-time in higher-level programming languages have been proposed by a number of authors. Haase [Haa81] extends Dijkstra's guarded commands to reason about time. Jahanian and Mok introduce a formal logic (Real-Time Logic, RTL) [Jah86] to analyze the timing properties of real-time systems. Mathai presents a number of different formal methodologies in the book "Real-Time Systems, Specification, Verification and Analysis" [Mat96].

In the book "Predictably Dependable Computing Systems" [Ran95] the issues of the design and validation of ultradependable systems are investigated. The book contains many references to the up-to-date literature in this field. An good treatment of the topic of testing is given by Howden [How87]. The recent PhD thesis by Fuchs on "Software-Implemented Fault Injection" gives an overview and literature survey of this field. The book by Leveson "Safeware: System Safety and Computers" [Lev95] discusses the prominent role of software in safety critical computer systems. Babaoglu [Bab87] investigates the probability that a fault-tolerant system delivers a correct output depending on diverse replication strategies. Recent advances on the topics of fault-tree analysis and FMEA are documented in the annual Reliability and Maintainability Symposium [RMS96]. A good overview of the tools and techniques on reliability estimation is contained in [Gei91].

REVIEW QUESTIONS AND PROBLEMS

12.1   What is a "safety case"?

12.2   What properties of the architecture support the design of a "safety case"?

12.3   List some causes for common-mode failures in a distributed system.

12.4   Discuss the different steps that must be taken to investigate a real-world phenomenon by a formal method. Which one of these steps can be formalized, which cannot?

12.5   In Section 12.2.2, three different levels of formal methods have been introduced. Explain each one of these levels and discuss the costs and benefits of applying formal methods at each one of these levels.

12.6   What is the "probe effect"?

12.7   How can the "testability" of a design be improved?

12.8   What is the role of testing during the certification of a ultra-dependable system?

12.9   Which are the purposes of fault-injection experiments?

12.10   Compare the characteristics of hardware and software fault-injection methods.

12.11   Explain the notions of "risk" and "hazard".

12.12   Design a fault-tree for the brake system of an automobile.

Chapter 13

System Design

OVERVIEW

This chapter on system design starts with a philosophical discussion on design in general. In computer system design, the most important goal is controlling the complexity of the solution by introducing structure. This introduction of structure restricts the design phase and has a negative impact on the performance of the system. In the context of real-time systems, these performance penalties must be carefully evaluated.

The architecture design phase starts with analyzing the requirements. There are two opposing views on how to proceed in this phase: (i) to complete an unbiased and consistent capture of all requirements before starting the "real" design work, or (ii) to learn about the requirements by starting a rapid prototype implementation of key system functions at an early stage. In any case, the designer must get a deep insight into all the different aspects of the problem domain before she/he can design the application architecture. The crucial step is the development of the system structure, the clustering of the functions into nearly decomposable subsystems of high internal cohesion with simple external interfaces. In distributed systems, a complete node forms such a subsystem of defined functionality. The node interfaces define the boundaries of the error-containment regions.

Design is an iterative process. As more is learned about the problem domain, with different design alternatives being explored, there is the need to start all over again more often than once. At the end of the design phase the alternate solutions must be evaluated and compared. Section 13.4 contains checklists that can assist the designer in evaluating a design. After the architecture design is completed and frozen, the detailed design and implementation of the node software can be performed by a number of teams in parallel.

13.1 THE DESIGN PROBLEM

Design is an inherently creative activity. There is a common core to design activities in many diverse fields: building design, product design, and computer system design are all closely related. The designer must find a solution that accommodates a variety of seemingly conflicting goals to solve an often ill-specified design problem. At the end, what differentiates a good design from a bad design is often liable to subjective judgment.

Example: Consider the design of an automobile. An automobile is a complex mass product that is composed of a number of sophisticated subsystems (e.g., engine, transmission, chassis, etc.). Each of these subsystems itself contains hundreds of different components that must meet given constraints: functionality, efficiency, geometrical form, weight, dependability, and minimal cost. All these components must cooperate, and interact smoothly, to provide the transportation service and the *look and feel* that the customer expects from the system "car".

13.1.1   Complexity

The phenomenal improvement in the price/performance ratio of computer hardware over the past twenty years has led to a situation where the software costs and not the hardware costs are limiting the application of computers in many domains. Software costs are directly related to the complexity of designing, implementing, and testing a large software system. The main effort of computer software design must be directed towards controlling this complexity by conceptual integrity.

System complexity increases more than linearly with the number of elements and the intensity of the interactions among elements, i.e., with the system size (see Section 2.3.2 and Chapter 4). The most successful approach to cope with the complexity of large systems is the introduction of system structure: the definition of subsystems with high inner connectivity in contrast to weak interactions among these subsystems across small and stable interfaces [Cou85].

Two kinds of structuring of a computer system can be distinguished to reduce the system complexity: *horizontal* versus *vertical* structuring.

(i)   **Horizontal Structuring**: Horizontal structuring (or *layering*) is related to the process of stepwise abstraction, of defining successive hierarchically-ordered new layers that are reduced representations of the system. Many software-engineering techniques (e.g., structured programming, virtual machines) propose one or another form of horizontal structuring.

(ii)   **Vertical Structuring:** Vertical structuring is related to the process of *partitioning* a large system into a number of *nearly* independent subsystems with well-specified interfaces among these subsystems so that these subsystems can be validated in isolation of each other. In distributed real-time systems *clusters* and *nodes* are the tangible units of partitioning.

While in a central computer system, layering is the only effective technique to combat complexity, the designer of a distributed computer system can take advantage of both techniques. A large application can first be partitioned into nearly decomposable subsystems of high inner connectivity and low external connectivity. These subsystems will be mapped into clusters and nodes of the distributed system. In a second step, each subsystem can be structured internally according to the layering technique.

The major advantage of *partitioning* over *layering* is that the abstractions of partitioned systems also hold in case of failures (see Section 6.3). While in a layered system, it is very difficult to define clean error-containment regions, the partitions (nodes and clusters) of a distributed system can be considered units of failures where small and observable interfaces (the message interfaces) around these error-containment regions facilitate the error detection and error containment.

13.1.2   Grand Design versus Incremental Development

In the feasibility analysis, the organizational goals and the economic constraints of an envisioned computer solution are outlined. If the evaluation at the end of the feasibility phase results in a "go ahead" decision, then a project team is formed to start the requirements analysis and the architecture design phase. There are two opposing empirical views how to proceed in these first life cycle phases when designing a large system:

(i)   A disciplined sequential approach, where every life-cycle phase is thoroughly completed and validated before the next one is started (*Grand Design*), and

(ii)   A rapid-prototyping approach, where the implementation of a key part of the solution is started before the requirements analysis has been completed (*Rapid Prototyping*).

Grand Design: The rationale for the *grand design* is that a detailed and unbiased specification of the complete problem (the "What?") must be available before a particular solution (the "How?") is designed. The difficulty with grand design is that there are no clear "stopping rules". The analysis and understanding of a large problem is never complete and there are always good arguments for asking more questions concerning the requirements before starting with the "real" design work. The paraphrase "paralysis by analysis" has been coined to point to this danger.

Rapid Prototyping: The rationale for the *rapid prototyping* approach is that, by investigating a particular solution at an early stage, a lot is learned about the problem space. The difficulties met during the search for a concrete solution guide the designer in asking the right questions about the requirements. The dilemma of rapid prototyping is that ad hoc implementations are developed with great expense that do not address all important aspects of the design problem. It is often necessary to completely discard these first prototypes and to start all over

A Compromise: Both sides have valid arguments that suggest the following compromise: In the architecture design phase a small number of key designers should try to get a good understanding of the architecture properties, leaving detailed issues that affect only the internals of a subsystem open. Chapter 4 distinguished between the *relevant properties* and the *irrelevant details* at the level of the system architecture. If it is not clear how to solve a particular problem, then a preliminary prototype of the most difficult part should be investigated with the explicit intent of discarding the solution if the looked-for insight has been gained.

13.1.3   Legacy   Systems

Nowadays there are only few large projects that can start on the "green lawn" with complete freedom in the design of the architecture and the selection of software and hardware. Most projects are extensions or redesigns of already existing systems, the *legacy systems*. Furthermore, there is a strong tendency in industry to use "COTS" (Commercial Off The Shelf) components to reduce the development time and the cost. The integration of these "legacy systems" into a newly designed application is an issue of major concern and difficulty.

In Section 4.3, we introduced the concept of a "resource controller" to connect partitioned subsystems that use a differing syntactic structure and a differing coding scheme for the presentation of the information. The integration of legacy systems into a new architecture can be facilitated if wide use is made of these resource controllers. Wherever possible, the interfaces between the legacy systems and the new architecture should be free of control signals to eliminate the possibility of control-error propagation from the legacy system into the new architecture.

13.1.4   Design Problems are Wicked

Some years ago, Peters [Pet79] in a paper about software design argued that software design belongs to the set of "wicked" problems. Wicked problems are described by the following characteristics:

(i)   A wicked problem cannot be stated in a definite way, abstracted from its environment. Whenever one tries to isolate a wicked problem from its surroundings, the problem loses its peculiarity. Every wicked problem is somehow unique, and cannot be treated in the abstract.

(ii)   Wicked problems cannot be specified without having a solution in mind. The distinction between specification ("what?") and implementation ("how?) is not as easy as is often proclaimed.

(iii)   Solutions to wicked problems have no stopping rule: for any given solution, there is always a better solution. There are always good arguments to learn more about the requirements to produce a better design.

(iv)   Solutions to wicked problems cannot be right or wrong; they can only be "better" or "worse".

(v)   There is no definite test for the solution to a wicked problem: Whenever a test is "successfully" passed, it is still possible that the solution will fail in some other way.

13.2 REQUIREMENTS ANALYSIS

Design is a creative holistic human activity that cannot be reduced to following a set of rules out of a design rule book. Design is an art, supplemented by scientific principles. It is therefore in vain to try to establish a complete set of design rules and to develop a fully automated design environment. Design tools can assist a designer in handling and representing the design information and can help in the analysis of design problems. They can, however, never replace the designer.

At the start of the requirements phase the designer must

(i)   Obtain a good insight and a deep understanding of the many aspects of the application domain: functional, temporal, dependability, and, above all, the economic constraints. Most often, economic constraints drive a project to a much larger extent than realized by the designers. The understanding comes from learning, experience, and from exploring the design space by analyzing existing solutions and working on prototypical solutions.

(ii) Select a computer system architecture that matches the requirements of the application domain. An appropriate architecture restricts the design space, and leads the designer to ask the right questions, and to find elegant solutions to the given design problems. The early selection of a computer system architecture is contrary to the often proclaimed separation of the "what?" from the "how?"–a separation that is unrealistic to maintain during the design of a large real-time system. The analysis of the temporal behavior of a system is always closely related to the implementation, the "how?", and cannot be postponed to a later design phase.

(iii) Develop a set of project standards. This issue is discussed in the following section.

13.2.1   Developing Project Standards

The communication between the client and the designers, as well as within a design team, is facilitated if all concerned parties agree to a common technical language. A set of project standards defines such a common set of concepts. The following list of topics is intended to serve as a check list for the most important project standards.

Information Representation: Distributed systems provide the opportunity to hide peculiar data representations within a node–a resource controller as introduced in Section 4.3.1–and to expose at the architecture level a unified representation of the information. Standards for these representations must be established at the project start. Examples of topics that need standardization are: categories for information classification, technical measurement units, and data structures that are visible at the message interfaces.

Naming: "Name space design is architecture design"–this sentence underscores the importance of establishing a set of generic rules for the formation of names for all data elements that are going to be used in the project.

Message Interfaces: The structure of the abstract message interfaces introduced in Section 4.3.1 should be unified within a project. Standard protocols must be defined that govern the exchange of information across these interfaces.

Documentation: A consistent and well-structured project documentation, including a project glossary that contains all project-related terms, is a prerequisite for smooth communication within a project. It is important that a disciplined version control of the documentation is performed, and that the consistency between the documentation and the code is maintained.

Software Development Tools: The software tools that will be used within a project should be selected and frozen before the project starts. Although many tools, such as compilers, proclaim to adhere to industry standards, full compatibility among different tools or different versions of the same tool should never be assumed.

Change Control: A disciplined procedure for change control is part of any standard project management system, and should be included in the initial project standards.

13.2.2   Essential System Functions

The focus of the requirements phase is to get a good understanding and a concise documentation of the essential system functions that provide the economic justification of the project. There is always the temptation to get side-tracked by irrelevant details about representational issues that obscure the picture of the whole. Often, it is easier to work on a well-specified detailed side problem than to keep focus on the critical system issues. It requires an experienced designer to decide between a *side problem* and a *critical system issue*.

An Approach: Starting from the given control objectives, it is practical to work backwards from the identified control outputs of the computer system to the key control algorithms and further to the required sensor inputs. In this way, the data transformation tasks and the relevant RT entities can be identified. The dynamics of the RT entities determine the temporal characteristics of the essential RT transactions, such as the sampling periods and the response times.

In the next step, the end-to-end protocols for monitoring the effects of the outputs can be sketched. Additional sensor inputs will result from this analysis. Further sensor inputs will be needed to discover alarm conditions within the process, and to detect any single sensor error by correlating the readings of the sensors with a process model to arrive at *agreed* data values (see Section 9.2).

After the RT-entities have been identified, it is necessary to investigate the attributes of the RT-entities, such as their value domain, their maximum rate of change, and the temporal accuracy intervals of the observations. The list of RT entities establishes a first version of the RT database. This is an important input to the subsequent design phase.

The other input to the design phase comes from an analysis of the data-transformation requirements, most importantly from the control algorithms. The structure of the control algorithms, their estimated execution time, their h-state between activations (if any), and the source of the control signals to activate the control algorithm must be studied.

Acceptance Test: Every requirement must be accompanied by an acceptance criterion that allows to measure, at the end of the project, whether the requirement has been met. If it is not possible to define a distinct acceptance test for a requirement, then the requirement cannot be very important: it can never be decided whether the implementation is meeting this requirement or not. Assuming that the original problem statement formulated during the feasibility study is the best one or even the right one, is definitely not wise [Rec91]. A critical designer will always be suspicious of postulated requirements that cannot be substantiated by a rational chain of arguments that, at the end, leads to a measurable contribution of the stated requirement to the economic success of the project.

13.2.3   Exploring the Constraints

In every project, there is an ongoing conflict between *what is desired* and *what can be done* within the given technical and economic constraints. A good understanding and documentation of these technical and economic constraints reduce the design space and help to avoid exploring unrealistic design alternatives.

Minimum Performance Criterion: The minimum performance criteria establish the borderline between what constitutes *success* and what constitutes *failure* during the operation of a system (see Section 6.3.1). The minimum system performance must be maintained under all fault and load conditions specified in the load and fault hypothesis (Section 1.5.3). A precise specification of the minimum performance, both in the value domain and in the temporal domain, is necessary for the design of a fault-tolerant system architecture that does not demand excessive resources. Of course, one must try to go way beyond the minimal performance under *normal* operating conditions. But the constraints on system performance under *adverse* conditions must be well-defined in the requirements document.

Dependability Constraints: The dependability constraints of the application are often design drivers. These constraints can concern any one of the measures of dependability introduced in Section 1.4: reliability, safety, availability, maintainability, and security. A precise specification of the minimal dependability requirements helps to reduce the design space, and guides the designer in finding acceptable technical solutions.

Cost Constraints: As already mentioned, the economic constraints are most often of overriding concern. A good understanding of the economies of an application domain is absolutely essential to arrive at proper system solutions. One is sometimes perplexed at the naiveté of the so-called system architects that propose a new architecture solution for an application domain that has not been clearly defined.

Example: In the automotive industry 95% of the cost is in production and marketing and only 5% is in the design of a product. Therefore, every effort must be made to reduce the production cost, even if this entails a more expensive and rigorous system design phase. For example, the manufacturing cost of a complete node of a distributed system should be in the order of $ 10. To achieve this cost level, a single chip microcomputer implementation with all memory and I/O circuitry on chip is the only technical alternative. This cost constraint excludes design alternatives that cannot be implemented on a single chip within the envisioned time span of the project.

13.3 DECOMPOSITION OF A SYSTEM INTO SUBSYSTEMS

After the essential requirements have been captured and documented, the most crucial phase of the life cycle, the design of the system structure, is reached. *Complex systems will evolve from simple systems much more rapidly if there are stable intermediate forms than if there are not* [Sim81]. Stable intermediate forms are encapsulated by small and stable interfaces that restrict the interactions among the subsystems. In the context of distributed real-time systems, a node with autonomous temporal control can be considered a stable intermediate form. The specification of the interface between the nodes and the communication system, the CNI, is thus of critical importance.

In general, introducing structure restricts the design space and may have a negative impact on the performance of a system. The more rigid and stable the structure, the more notable the observed reduction in performance will be. The key issue is to find the *most appropriate* structure where the performance penalties are outweighed by the other desirable properties of the structure, such as composability, understandability, and the ease of implementing fault-tolerance.

	RT E1	RT E2	RT E3	DT T1	DT T2	
RT Entity 1	-	P	D	I		P: Physical Proximity
RT Entity 2	P	-	P	I		D: Physical Distance
RT Entity 3	D	P	-	O	I	I: Input
Data Transformation Task 1	I	I	O	-		O: Output
Data Transformation Task 2			I		-	

Figure 13.1: Example of a simple interaction matrix.

13.3.1   Identification of the Subsystems

The list of RT entities forming the RT database, and the list of data-transformation tasks that have been collected during the requirements phase, form the starting point for the formation of subsystems. It is often helpful to construct an interaction matrix (Figure 13.1) that visualizes the interactions between the design elements.

In the rows and columns of the interaction matrix are the RT entities and data transformation tasks. The elements of the matrix inform of relations between these entities. These could be relations regarding the physical proximity, the temporal cohesion, or the input/output.

The analysis of the interaction matrix, enhanced by the engineering insight in the application domain, will lead to clustering of RT entities and data transformation functions, suggesting a first version of a cluster and node structure. This first version of a cluster structure will lead to some intercluster interfaces that must be scrutinized with respect to their temporal cohesion and data complexity. The same analysis must be done for the message interfaces at the CNIs of the nodes. The world interfaces of the nodes, i.e., the I/O interfaces of the nodes to the controlled object are of lesser concern at this phase of the analysis. These interfaces are to become local interfaces of the nodes with no global visibility. It is a good rule to trade local complexity for global simplicity.

The well-established design principle "form follows function" should not be violated. The allocation of functions to nodes must be guided by the desire to build functional units (nodes) with a high inner connectivity and small external interfaces. It can be expected that there will be misfits, that some requirements cannot be accommodated in any sensible way. It is good practice to challenge these clashing requirements and to reexamine their economic utility. Extreme requirements should never drive a design process, and determine an architecture [Rec91,p.46]..

13.3.2   The Communication Network Interface

The communication network interface (CNI) between a node and the intracluster communication system is the most important interface of a distributed architecture (see also Section 2.1.3). The CNI determines the complexity at the cluster level. It also acts as an error-detection interface that defines the error-containment regions within a cluster. Any error that is not detected at the CNI has the potential to cause a total system failure.

If the CNI is designed as a data-sharing interface without any control signals, then there is no possibility of control error propagation across the CNI. If a control signal is allowed to cross the CNI, an important concern is the peak load activation--the normal load will take care of itself. Ask yourself the questions: What are the mechanisms that detect any control-error propagation across the CNI, what is the worst thing that other nodes could do across the CNI, which mechanisms will detect and stop such behavior? [Rec91, p.89] It is a wise decision to design the CNI in such a way that it is insensitive to unknown or uncontrollable external influences from the controlled object. It is up to the nodes to maintain control over these external influences and to force them into a disciplined behavioral pattern at the CNI.

What is the right degree of flexibility at the CNI? This is a difficult question to answer. On the one hand, one should build and maintain options as long as possible during the design and implementation of complex systems–they may be needed at some future point in time. [Rec91,p.93] On the other hand, flexibility is not free–it has a dear price. It reduces the predictability and limits the error-detection capability. The key issue is to find the right level of controlled flexibility–to provide flexibility as long as the price for the flexibility can be justified. For example, the provision of extra data-fields at the CNI will impact the performance but will not have any other adverse side effect. If the performance at the CNI is not a bottleneck, then the price paid for this added flexibility is negligible.

Development of the Message Schedules: If the communication system within a cluster is time-triggered, then the CNI is a data-sharing interface that hides the communication behind the memory abstraction as outlined in Section 8.2. The design of the static message schedules, i.e., the MEDL for the communication controllers, must be performed during the architecture design phase. This can proceed according to the following steps:

(i)   Allocation of the Tasks: Based on the results of the clustering analysis and the constraints of the application (e.g., input/output requirements), and the available characteristics of the computational tasks (estimated WCET, required images of RT-entities, temporal accuracy requirements), the allocation of tasks to computational nodes can be performed.

(ii) Forming of Messages: The allocation of the tasks to the nodes establishes the communication requirements among the nodes. Data elements can be grouped into messages for internode communication.

(iii) Scheduling of the Messages: The dispatcher table (MEDL) for the communication controller of each node must be constructed for each operational mode. Care must be taken that the constraints on the mode changes are observed.

It is well known that the allocation/scheduling problem belongs to the class of NP complete problems. The search for a good solution can be guided by sensible heuristics as discussed in Chapter 11.

13.3.3   Result of the Architecture Design Phase

At the end of the architecture design phase, a document that describes the computer system architecture must be produced. This document must contain at least the following information:

(i)   The decomposition of the system problem into clusters, and the function of each cluster. The identification of orthogonal operating modes of the whole cluster.

(ii) A specification of the data semantics and timing at the intercluster interfaces. These intercluster interfaces will be implemented later by gateway nodes that often must interact with *legacy* systems. A legacy system is an already existing operational hardware/software system that is difficult to modify.

(iii) For each cluster, a decomposition of the cluster into nodes, a description of the functions of each node, and a high-level specification of the input/output interfaces of each node to the controlled object. A detailed specification of these node-local interfaces is not required at the architectural level.

(iv) A precise specification of all messages exchanged among the nodes, including the message formats and timing. All details of the CNIs must be fixed at the end of the architecture design phase.

(v) A description of the data transformations performed in each node, a listing of the output data, the input data and the data transformation algorithms.

(vi) An analysis of the dependability requirements and a suggestion of how these requirements are addressed at the cluster level, i.e., the formation of fault-tolerant units (FTUs) and the replication of messages.

At the end of the architecture design phase, the CNIs of all nodes of a cluster should be frozen for the given version, such that the detailed design and implementation of the nodes can proceed in isolation. In a time-triggered architecture the exact contents of the message descriptor lists (MEDL) that control the intracluster communication should be available at the end of the architecture design phase.

The design of a large system is never a linear sequence of activities. During the design process, the designer learns more about the application, which forces the designer to go back to challenge previously made decisions and to iterate. Alternative designs must be developed and compared.

13.4 TEST OF A DECOMPOSITION

We do not know how to measure the quality of a design on an absolute scale. The best we can hope to achieve is to establish a set of guidelines and checklists that facilitate the comparison of two design alternatives relative to each other. It is good practice to develop a project-specific checklist for the comparison of design alternatives at the beginning of a project. The guidelines and checklists presented in this section can serve as a starting point for such a project-specific checklist.

13.4.1   Functional Coherence

A node of a distributed system should implement a self contained function with high internal coherence and low external interface complexity. If the node is a gateway or an interface node, i.e., it processes input/output signals from its environment, only the abstract message interface to the cluster and not the concrete world interface to the environment (see Section 4.3.1) is of concern. The following list of questions is intended to help determine the functional coherence and the interface complexity of a node:

(i) Does the node implement a self-contained function?

(ii) Is the h-state at the ground state defined?

(iii) Is it sufficient to provide a single level of error recovery after any failure, i.e., a restart of the complete node? A need for a multi-level error recovery is always an indication of a weak functional coherence.

(iv)   Are there any control signals crossing the message interface or is it a strict data-sharing interface? A strict data-sharing interface is simpler and should therefore be preferred.

(v)   How many different data elements are passed across the message interface? What are the timing requirements?

(vi)   Are there any phase-sensitive data elements passed across the message interface?

13.4.2   Testability

Since a node implements a single function, it must be possible to test the node in isolation. The following questions should help to evaluate the testability of a node:

(i)   Are the temporal as well as the value properties of the message interface precisely specified such that they can be simulated in a test environment?

(ii)   Is it possible to observe all input/output messages and the h-state of a node without the probe effect?

(iii)   Is it possible to set the h-state of a node from the outside to reduce the number of test sequences?

(iv)   Is the node software replica deterministic, so that the same input cases will always lead to the same results?

(v)   What is the procedure to test the fault-tolerance mechanisms of the node?

(vi)   Is it possible to implement an effective built-in self test into the node?

13.4.3   Dependability

The following checklist of questions refers to the dependability of a design:

(i)   What is the effect of the worst malicious failure of the node to the rest of the cluster? How is it detected? How does this failure affect the minimum performance criterion?

(ii)   How is the rest of the cluster protected from an erroneous mode-change request from a faulty node?

(iii)   In case the communication system fails completely, what is the local control strategy of a node to maintain a safe state?

(iv)   How long does it take the other nodes of the cluster to detect a node failure? A short error-detection latency simplifies the error handling drastically.

(v)   What is the error-detection coverage of the node regarding value failures and timing failures?

(vi)   How long does it take to restart a node after a crash failure? Focus on the fast recovery from a single failure. The zero failure case takes care of itself and the two or more failure case is expensive and unlikely to succeed. How complex is the recovery?

(vii)   Are the normal operating functions and the safety functions implemented in different nodes, such that they are in different error-containment regions?

(viii) How stable is the message interface with respect to anticipated change requirements? What is the probability and impact of changes on the rest of the cluster?

13.4.4   Physical Characteristics

There are many possibilities to introduce common-mode failures by a careless physical installation. The following list of questions should help to check for these:

(i)   Are mechanical interfaces of the replaceable units specified, and do these mechanical boundaries of replaceable units coincide with the diagnostic boundaries?

(ii)   Are the two SRUs of an FTU mounted at different physical locations, such that a common mode external fault (e.g., water, EMI, mechanical damage in case of an accident) will not destroy both SRUs?

(iii)   Do different nodes of an FTU have different power sources to reduce the possibility of common mode failures induced by the power supply? Is there a possibility of a common mode failure via the grounding system (e.g., lightning stroke)? Are the SRUs of an FTU electrically isolated?

(iv)   What are the cabling requirements? What are the consequences of transient faults caused by EMI interference via the cabling or by bad contacts?

(v)   What are the environmental conditions (temperature, shock) of the node? Are they in agreement with the component specifications?

13.5 DETAILED DESIGN AND IMPLEMENTATION

At the end of the architectural design phase, the message interfaces among the nodes within a cluster are established and stable. The design effort can now be broken down into a set of loosely-related concurrent activities, each one focusing on the design, implementation, and testing of an individual node.

13.5.1   Definition of the I/O Interfaces

The world interface between a node and its environment (e.g., the controlled object) has not been investigated in detail during the architectural design phase. It is up to the detailed design of a node to specify and implement this interface. In some cases, such as the design of the concrete man-machine interface for the operator, this can be a major activity. The protocols to control the field bus nodes and the software for the field bus nodes are part of this detailed design phase.

13.5.2   Task Development

In this phase, the task structure within a node is designed and the programs that implement the specified functions must be developed. If at all possible, only the S-task model should be used (Section 4.2.1). Every S-task starts by reading the input data items and terminates with the production of the output data items. The h-state of every S-task must be identified and stored in a single data structure. The sum of the h-states of all tasks at predetermined points in time form the ground state of the node (Section 4.6.2). The ground state of a node should be sent to the cluster via a periodic output message for the following two reasons:

(i)   To be able to monitor from the outside, without inducing the probe effect, whether the ground state of a node is correct, and

(ii)   To offer the ground state to a replicated node that has to reintegrate itself into an operational cluster periodically.

13.5.3   Task Scheduling

In this phase, the *temporal control structure* within a node is developed. The temporal control structure determines at what point in time a particular task must be executed and at what point in time a message has to be sent to some other node. When designing a time-triggered architecture, care must be taken that the periodic schedule contains a ground state where all tasks are inactive and no message is in transit, i.e., all channels are flushed. This is the ideal point for reintegrating joining nodes.

13.6 REAL-TIME ARCHITECTURE PROJECTS

Many of the current real-time systems are based on stripped-down versions of time-sharing operating systems. Although fast mechanisms for context switching and interrupt processing are provided, and some user control over the scheduling strategy is possible, these systems are still based on the following questionable assumptions [Stan91]:

(i)   Hardly any knowledge about the run-time environment, i.e., the controlled object, is assumed to be available *a priori*. Therefore, it is not possible to optimize the run-time system with respect to minimal resource requirements and robustness. This is in contrast to modern real-time operating systems for embedded applications, such as ERCOS (see Section 10.5).

(ii)   The task model is based on C-tasks with arbitrary blocking points within a task and unspecified blocking times. It is thus impossible to predict the worst-case execution time (WCET) of tasks.

(iii) One attempts to minimize the *average* response time and maximize the throughput. No effort is made to limit the *maximum* response time, the most important metric for real-time systems.

(iv)   The issue of replica determinism is not addressed, because fault tolerance is considered an application concern.

Over the past few years, a number of real-time system research projects have challenged these basic assumptions and developed solutions that are in better agreement with the requirements of real-time systems. In the following sections, overviews of three of these research projects, SPRING, MAFT, and FTPP are presented. The fourth project, MARS, that has been developed at the Technische Universität Wien, is covered in Chapter 14.

13.6.1   SPRING

A *SPRING system* [Sta91] is a physically distributed real-time system composed of a network of multiprocessor nodes. Each node contains system processors, application processors, a network controller, and an I/O subsystem to interconnect to the controlled object. The system processors execute the scheduling algorithms, handle the high-priority interrupts and support the operating system services. The I/O subsystem handles the slow I/O devices and the process input/output (sensors and actuators). The application processors execute the application tasks.

The software is organized into the SPRING operating system (*the SPRING kernel*) and the application tasks. The operating system performs the task management, scheduling, memory management, and intertask communication. All operating system calls have a bounded WCET (worst-case execution time). An application task consists of the reentrant code, local data, global data, a stack, a task descriptor, and a task control block. Each task requires *all* resources before it starts, and it releases the resources upon completion, thus avoiding any unpredictable blocking during task execution. An application task is characterized by its

(i)   WCET which may be a function that depends on various execution time parameters, such as the input data or current state information,

(ii)   Type and importance level (critical, essential or unessential),

(iii)   Time parameters, such as deadline and period,

(iv)   cCommunication and precedence graph,

(v)   Resource requirements, such as memory and I/O ports, and

(vi)   Administrative data, e.g., the location of the task copy in memory.

The SPRING scheduler categorizes the application tasks by their importance and their effect on the environment. For the purpose of scheduling, three task classes are formed: critical tasks, essential tasks, and unessential tasks. Critical tasks must meet their deadlines to avoid a system failure. If an essential task does not meet its deadline, the performance of the system is degraded. The execution of unessential tasks (they do not have hard deadlines) can be delayed if there is an overload scenario.

The goal of the SPRING scheduling algorithm is to dynamically guarantee the deadlines of newly arriving tasks in the context of the current load. Scheduling is performed at four levels:

(i)   At the lowest level, a dispatcher for each application processor takes the next ready task from the prearranged scheduling queue.

(ii)   At level two, a local scheduler for each node determines if a newly arriving task can be accepted and guaranteed locally, considering the current load at the node. If accepted, the local scheduler rearranges the scheduling queue.

(iii)   At level three, a distributed scheduler tries to redistribute the load among the nodes.

(iv) At the fourth level, a meta-scheduler monitors the system and adapts various parameters to improve the adaptability and flexibility of the SPRING system.

Fault tolerance is not a focus of the SPRING project. A more detailed description of the SPRING project can be found in [Sta91].

13.6.2   MAFT

The Multicomputer Architecture for Fault Tolerance (MAFT) is a distributed computer architecture designed to combine ultrahigh reliability with high performance in a real-time environment. It consists of a set of nodes connected by a broadcast bus network. Each node contains two processors, an *operations controller* and an *applications processor*. The operations controller handles the majority of the system's executive functions, such as intranode communication, clock synchronization, error detection, task scheduling, and system reconfiguration. The application processors are thus free to execute the application tasks.

In MAFT, a frame-based synchronization is achieved by the periodic exchange of system state messages such that every node is informed about the state of the clocks at the other nodes. A fault-tolerant internal synchronization algorithm is used to calculate a correction term for each local clock. (The accuracy of the internal clock synchronization depends on the parameters discussed in Section 3.4.3.)

Each operations controller stores a copy of all shared data values in its own data memory and handles the management and voting on the application values in a manner that is transparent to the application processor. Different voting algorithms can be selected if an *approximate* voting strategy is demanded. Byzantine agreement and converging voting algorithms are applied to maintain agreement even in case a node behaves maliciously faulty. Every operations controller monitors the message traffic to detect any error in a node, as revealed by its output messages. The errors are reported to all other nodes in error messages such that every node can maintain a local *penalty count* for all nodes. Byzantine agreement on these penalty counts is maintained.

In MAFT, the application software is organized into non-preemptable tasks. A task must be executed without interruption on a single application processor. Each task has several attributes: iteration frequency, priority, desired redundancy, and intertask dependencies. The allocation of tasks to nodes is determined by the reconfiguration process. This allocation is static for any given set of operating nodes and changes only if the set of operating nodes changes. In MAFT, task schedules are cyclic. The smallest schedule period is called an *atomic period*. In the current implementation, 1024 atomic periods form the *master period*, the longest iteration period. The scheduler selects a task with the highest relative priority from the ready set. The scheduler is fully replicated, and selects tasks for every node in the system. The selections for the own node are executed locally, the selections for the other nodes are monitored to acquire information about the "health" of the other nodes.

A more detailed description of the MAFT project can be found in [Kie88].

13.6.3   FTPP

The Fault-Tolerant Parallel Processor (FTPP) is a high-reliability high-throughput real-time computer designed at Draper Labs [Har88] that can tolerate Byzantine failures. The building blocks of the architecture are processing elements and network elements. Processing elements and network elements are interconnected in a hierarchical manner as shown in Figure 13.2. The interconnection structure observes the Byzantine protocol requirements as outlined in Section 6.4.3. A network element with the four associated processing elements forms a *primary fault-containment region*. The primary fault-containment regions communicate with each other by dedicated point-to-point communication links to exchange synchronization information and interprocess messages. A processing element is connected to its network element by a single dedicated communication channel. A processing element including its communication channel forms a *secondary fault-containment region*.

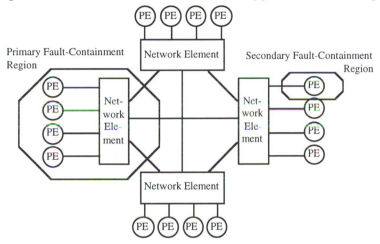

Figure 13.2: 16 Processing element cluster of FTPP [Har88].

A Byzantine resilient FTU (in FTPP an FTU is called a *computational group*) must comprise processing elements from disjoint network elements. Since not all functions in a system are safety-critical, and since they must tolerate Byzantine failures, FTUs of different replication degree can be formed to increase the throughput. If a processing element fails, another processing element from the same primary fault-containment region can be used as a replacement.

FTPP does not provide global time, but performs a *functional* synchronization of the application tasks. The redundant processing elements that form an FTU synchronize each other by exchanging messages at recurring interaction points of the application. Because Byzantine agreement (see Section 6.4.3) has to be performed at these interaction points, a faulty processing element can be detected. A processing element that deviates from the majority beyond an *a priori* defined time bound is considered faulty by the majority, and is excluded from the ensemble.

A more detailed description of the FTPP can be found in [Har88].

POINTS TO REMEMBER

- Design is a creative holistic human activity that cannot be reduced to following a set of rules out of a design rule book. Design is an art, supplemented by scientific principles.

- In every project, there is an ongoing conflict between *what is desired* and *what can be done* within the given technical and economic constraints. A good understanding and documentation of these technical and economic constraints reduces the design space, and helps to avoid exploring unrealistic design alternatives.

- Two kinds of structuring of a computer system can be distinguished to reduce the system complexity: *horizontal* versus *vertical* structuring. Horizontal structuring (or *layering*) is related to the process of stepwise abstraction. Vertical structuring is related to the process of *partitioning* a large system into a number of nearly independent subsystems.

- The analysis and understanding of a large problem is never complete and there are always good arguments for asking more questions concerning the requirements before starting with the "real" design work.

- Often it is easier to work on a well-specified detailed side problem than to keep focus on the critical system issues. It requires an experienced designer to decide *what is a side problem* and *what is a critical system issue*.

- Every requirement must entail an acceptance criterion that allows to measure, at the end of the project, whether the requirement has been met. If it is not possible to define a distinct acceptance test for a requirement, then the requirement cannot be very important: it can never be decided whether the implementation is meeting this requirement or not.

- The minimum performance criteria establish a borderline between what constitutes *success* and what constitutes *failure*. A precise specification of the minimum performance, both in the value domain and in the temporal domain, is necessary for the design of a fault-tolerant system architecture that does not demand excessive resources.

- The dependability constraints of the application are often design drivers. A precise specification of the minimal dependability requirements helps to reduce the design space, and guides the designer in finding acceptable technical solutions.

- In the context of distributed real-time systems, a node with an autonomous temporal control can be considered *a stable intermediate form*. The specification of the interface between the nodes and the communication system, the CNI, is thus of critical importance.

- The introduction of structure restricts the design space, and may have a negative impact on the performance of a system. The key issue is to find the *most appropriate* structure where the performance penalties are outweighed by the other desirable properties of the structure.

- The allocation of functions to nodes must be guided by the desire to build functional units (nodes) with a high inner connectivity and small external interfaces. It can be expected that there will be misfits, that some requirements cannot be accommodated in any sensible way. It is good practice to challenge these clashing requirements and to reexamine their economic utility. Extreme requirements should never drive a design process, and determine an architecture.

- The CNI determines the complexity at the cluster level, and acts as an error detection interface that defines the error-containment regions within a cluster. Any error that is not detected at the CNI has the potential to cause a total system failure.

BIBLIOGRAPHIC NOTES

Many books have been written about design, most of them emanating from the field of architecture design. The work of the Roman architect Vitruvius [Vit60], written B.C., contains design guidelines that are still valid today. "Design Methods, Seeds of Human Futures" by Jones [Jon78] takes an interdisciplinary look at design that makes an enjoyable reading for a computer scientist. More recently, the excellent book "Systems Architecting, Creating and Building Complex Systems" by Rechtin [Rec91] presents many empirically observed design guidelines that have been an important input in writing this chapter.

Space does not permit to cover all interesting real-time system-architecture projects in this chapter. The interested reader is advised to look at the following additional projects: the two famous "historical" projects, the SIFT project [Wen78] at SRI and the FTMP project at MIT Draper Laboratory [Hop78], the *Autonomous Decentralized Computer Control System* [Iha82, Iha84] developed by Hitachi in Japan, the ARTS project at CMU [Tok89], and the Real-Time Mach Project at CMU [Tok90], the ERICA project at Philips Eindhoven [Dri90], the HARTS project at the University of Michigan [Shi91, Shi95], the ESPRIT project DELTA 4 [Pow91] and the Maruti-II project at the University of Maryland [Sak95].

REVIEW QUESTIONS AND PROBLEMS

13.1   What is the difference between *layering* and *partitioning*? Which one of these structuring techniques supports the design of error-containment regions?

13.2   Discuss the advantages and disadvantages of *grand design* versus *incremental development*.

13.3   Which are the characteristics of a "wicked" problem?

13.4   Make a list of the project standards that should be available at the begin of a project.

13.5   Discuss the different types of constraints that restrict a design. Why is it important to explore these constraints before starting a design project?

13.6   What is the *minimum performance criterion,* and why is it important in the design of fault-tolerant systems?

13.7   Discuss the advantages and disadvantages of introducing *structure* into a design.

13.8   Discuss the most important interfaces in a distributed real-time system architecture.

13.9   Which are the results of the architecture design phase?

13.10   Establish a checklist for evaluation in design from the point of view of *functional coherence, testability, dependability,* and *physical installation.*

13.11   Compare the fundamental design decisions in the three real-time architecture projects SPRING, MAFT, and FTPP.

13.12   Sketch the interaction matrix for the seven nodes of the rolling mill problem (Figure 1.9).

Chapter 14

The Time-Triggered Architecture

OVERVIEW

In the final chapter, the different concepts that have been developed in the previous thirteen chapters are brought together into a coherent time-triggered architecture (TTA). This architecture is being implemented at the Technische Universität Wien with industrial support, taking advantage of the lessons learned during the more than fifteen years of research on dependable distributed real-time systems.

The chapter starts with a short description of the MARS (MAintainable Real-time System) project. It then gives an overview of the time-triggered architecture (TTA) and emphasizes the essential role of the real-time database in this architecture. The building blocks of a TTA prototype implementation are described. The only non-standard hardware unit is the TTP/C communication controller. The TTP/C controller implements all functions of the TTP/C protocol and interfaces to the host via a dual-ported memory. The TTP controller contains independent bus guardians to protect the bus against "babbling idiot" failures of the nodes.

Section 14.3 is devoted to the software support tools that are being implemented and planned for the development of software in the TTA. The time-triggered operating system that has been developed for MARS has been ported to the TTA host, and adapted to the Communication Network Interface of the TTP controller. The generation of the message descriptor lists for the TTP controller is supported by a "cluster compiler". The fault-tolerance strategy of the TTA is covered in Section 14.4. TTA supports the implementation of replicated communication channels and fault-tolerant units consisting of replicated fail-silent nodes, TMR nodes, and other FTU organizations.

Finally. Section 14.5 speculates on the implementation of TTA systems that are dispersed over a wide geographical area.

14.1 LESSONS LEARNED FROM THE MARS PROJECT

The time-triggered architecture evolved out of the many years of university research centered on the topic of distributed fault-tolerant real-time systems, and carried out in the context of the MARS project.

14.1.1   The MARS Project

Project Goals: The goal of the MARS project was the design and implementation of a distributed fault-tolerant architecture for hard real-time applications from the point of view of maintainability in hardware and software. The project, which started in 1979, took the vision that within twenty years it would be possible to build compact nodes of a distributed real-time system on a single chip. This chip should be so inexpensive that the system architect would be free to use as many chips as necessary to implement the given application requirements within a clean functional structure that would not be unnecessarily complicated by multiplexing diverse functions on a single hardware node. A hardware node is considered a *unit of failure* with a single external failure mode: fail-silence. Fault-tolerance can be implemented by replicating the replica-deterministic nodes.

The MARS Architecture: The MARS architecture decomposes a real-time system into clusters, fault-tolerant units, nodes and tasks as outlined in Section 4.2. It is based on the assumption that the nodes exhibit a fail-silent behavior, i.e., they produce either correct results, detectably incorrect results at the correct point in time, or no results at all. Nodes can be grouped into FTUs. As long as any one node of an FTU is operational, the FTU delivers a correct service to its clients.

It was recognized at an early stage of the project that only time-triggered architectures offer the predictability required by hard real-time applications. A distributed time-triggered architecture requires a fault-tolerant global time-base. For distributed clock synchronization, a special VLSI chip, the clock synchronization unit CSU [Kop87] was designed and built around 1986 to support the fault-tolerant clock synchronization within MARS. This chip was used in the subsequent implementations of the MARS hardware.

In 1989, a number of European University and Research Laboratories formed the ESPRIT project, Predictably Dependable Computer Systems (PDCS) [Ran95]. Within PDCS a new prototype implementation of MARS was funded, and extensive fault-injection experiments on this prototype were carried out at three different sites, at LAAS in Toulouse, France, at Chalmers University in Gothenburg, Sweden, and at the Technical University of Vienna, Austria. These fault-injection experiments led to a number of new insights that were instrumental for the design of the Time-Triggered Architecture (TTA).

Building Fail-Silent Nodes: A number of techniques are known for building a fail-silent node that will tolerate any single hardware fault. One common technique is the duplication of the hardware of every module (e.g., in the STRATUS system [Web91]), and to compare the results of both modules by a self-checking checker (*pair and spare* technique, [Joh89, p. 67]). If the results of the two modules differ, then an error has been detected. The two modules operate in tight synchronization driven by single fault-tolerant clock. One problem with this approach is that a single fault that hits both computational channels at the same time can lead to correlated errors. Experiments conducted by Kanekawa [Kan96] show that phase-locked tightly synchronized modules have a non-negligible probability of correlated errors.

14.1.2 The High Error Detection Coverage Mode (HEDC)

The MARS implementation uses a different approach to achieve fail-silence. Every critical computation is calculated twice on a standard commercial-off-the-shelf (COTS) microprocessor and the results of these computations are compared. Each one of the nodes has its own clock that is not tightly synchronized with the other clock so that the probability of a single fault causing correlated errors in both nodes is reduced. Additional error detection mechanisms have been implemented in the PDCS prototype of the MARS architecture, as described in [Rei95].

The duplicate execution of application tasks is supported by the operating system by providing a special execution mode, the *High-Error-Detection-Coverage (HEDC)* mode, that is transparent to the application software. The High-Error-Detection-Coverage (HEDC) mode provides two extra mechanisms to increase the error-detection coverage with respect to transient faults:

(i) The time-redundant execution of application tasks at the sender.

(ii) The calculation of an end-to-end CRC by the application task at the sending host to protect the complete path of the message between the sender task and the receiver task.

Time Redundant Task Execution: In safety-critical applications, the designer can request the host operating system to repeat the execution of each task at different times, to calculate an application level end-to-end CRC after each execution and to compare these signatures. This service can be provided by the operating system in the host without any modification of the application software. If the CRCs of the two task executions are not identical, then, one of the task executions has been corrupted by a transient fault. In this situation, it cannot be determined which one of the executions is incorrect. Therefore, both results are considered suspect, and none of the messages is sent. Since in a fault-tolerant configuration, there is a replicated node providing the identical service, no service interruption is seen by the client of this FTU.

End-to-End CRC: The end-to-end CRC is calculated in addition to the 16 bit communication CRC. In a safety-critical application, the messages are thus protected by two CRC fields, one at the communication level, and one at the end-to-end (application) level. To avoid the possibility that a syntactically correct but semantically incorrect message is selected by the operating system (this failure mode was observed in the fault-injection experiments discussed Section 12.4.2), the expected send time and a unique message key are concatenated with the message before the end-to-end CRC is calculated (Figure 14.1) for each message at the application level. This mechanism makes sure that a transient error corrupting a message between the point in time when a message has been generated by the application software at the sending node, and the point in time when a message is used by the application software at the receiving node is detectable.

End-to-end CRC Calculation of an HEDC messages:

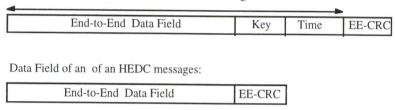

Data Field of an of an HEDC messages:

Figure 14.1: End-to-end CRC of HEDC messages.

14.2   THE TIME-TRIGGERED ARCHITECTURE

The Time-Triggered Architecture is an architecture for distributed real-time systems in safety critical applications, such as computer controlled brakes, computer controlled suspension, or computer assisted steering in an automobile. A TTA-node consists of two subsystems, the communication controller and the host computer, as depicted in Figure 8.2. The Communication Network Interface between these two subsystem is a strict data-sharing interface as explained in Section 8.2.

The following problems must be addressed in any fault-tolerant distributed real-time system that is based on a bus architecture. In the TTA, they are solved at the level of the communication systems:

(i)   Fault-tolerant clock synchronization.

(ii)   Timely membership service.

(iii) Reconfiguration management.

(iv)   Provision of fail-silence in the temporal domain.

In this section the architectural principles and a concrete prototype implementation of the time-triggered architecture are presented. This implementation tries to use commercial-off-the-shelf (COTS) components wherever possible.

14.2.1   Economy of Concepts

The time-triggered architecture is based on the principle of "economy of concepts", i.e., a small number of orthogonal concepts are used over again to simplify the understanding of a design. Examples of these recurring concepts are:

(i)   The introduction of stable interfaces, free of control signals, to partition a system into nearly decomposable subsystems that act as error containment regions. The precise specification of all interfaces in the value domain and the temporal domain makes it possible to test every design unit in isolation, and to avoid unintended interactions during system integration (composability).

(ii)   The unification of the input/output interface to the controlled object and the communication interface to other nodes in a cluster into a single interface type, the CNI. The CNI provides temporally accurate state messages for the exchange of information so that a periodic sender and receiver do not have to proceed at the same rate.

(iii) The separation of the temporal control structure from the logical control structure so that the temporal control structure can be validated in isolation.

(iv)   The separation of the fault-tolerance mechanisms from the functions of the application software so that no unintended interactions between these functions can take place.

(v)   The recursive application of these concepts to build large real-time systems.

The time-triggered architecture decomposes a real-time system in the same manner as the MARS architecture: into clusters, FTUs, nodes, and tasks. There are two types of nodes in the architecture, a fail-silent *TTA-node* and a *fieldbus node*. The TTA-nodes are interconnected by a single or replicated real-time bus using the TTP/C protocol. TTA-nodes can be replicated to form different types of FTUs (see Section 8.2.4). The fieldbus node can be any single-chip microcontroller with a UART interface and a timer supporting the TTP/A protocol.

The three-level communication architecture (Section.7.3.2) uses the following protocols

(i)   Field bus: the TTP/A protocol described in Section 8.4 is used to connect the sensors and actuators of the controlled object to a TTA-node.

(ii)   Real-time bus: the TTP/C protocol described in Section 8.3 connects the TTA-nodes of a cluster. The communication controller of a TTA-node provides clock synchronization, membership service, and redundancy management.

(iii) Backbone bus: The TCP/IP protocol on a standard 10 Mbit Ethernet realizes the non-time-critical connection of a cluster to other data processing systems within an organization.

14.2.2   The Real-Time Database

Conceptually, the distributed real-time database, formed by the temporally accurate images of all relevant RT entities, is at the core of the time-triggered architecture. The real-time database is autonomously and periodically updated by the nodes of the cluster that observe the environment or produce RT images. The real-time data base contains a temporally valid "snapshot" of the current state of the cluster and the cluster environment. Ideally, the elements of the real-time database should be *parametric* (see Section 5.4.2). The real-time database forms a stable data-sharing interface between the nodes that is free of any temporal control signals. The data structures that control the updating of the real-time database are in the TTP communication controller, physically and logically separated by the CNI from the host software. These data structures are designed during the architecture design phase of a cluster. A change in the host software cannot affect the communication pattern that updates the real-time database.

Two different types of TTA-nodes are distinguished:

(i)   *Active TTA-nodes*: An active TTA-node produces RT-images for the RT database and therefore needs a time-slot on the RT bus. The set of active nodes form the membership of the cluster.

(ii)   *Passive TTA-nodes*: A passive TTA-node reads from the RT database but does not produce any information for the RT database. It needs no time slot on the bus and is not part of the membership. A good example of a passive TTA-node is a node that monitors the operation of the real-time system. Passive nodes do not contribute to the software complexity at the system level.

A multi-cluster TTA system will contain an RT database in each cluster. All clusters have access to the synchronized external time. A cluster gateway connects the RT database of one cluster to that of another cluster and implements the relative views of the two clusters. In most cases, only a subset of the RT database will be needed in both clusters.

Growth of a TTA architecture is easy since there is no central element in the architecture. Nodes can be expanded into gateway nodes by implementing a second CNI interface in the node. The CNI interface to the original cluster is not affected by this node-local change (see Section 2.3). Understanding a large TTA system can be decomposed into understanding each cluster. Every cluster views all other clusters as its "natural environment", not being able to distinguish a controlled-object cluster from a computational cluster. This architectural characteristic is of value during software development and testing, because a test simulator will have exactly the same interface, both in the value and time domain, as will the controlled object have later-on.

14.2.3   The Hardware Building Blocks

We have implemented a prototype of a TTA system by using the following four hardware building blocks:

(i)   The TTP controller is built on a specially designed printed circuit board that corresponds mechanically, electrically and logically to the Greensprings IP Interface Standard [Gre93].

(ii)   Any commercially available motherboard that supports the Greensprings IP Interface Standard an be used as a host.

(iii) Any commercially available microcomputer with a standard UART interface can be programmed to act as a field bus node.

(iv)   Any commercially available Ethernet interface board that supports the Greensprings IP Interface Standard can be used as a gateway to a standard Ethernet.

TTP Controller: The TTP Controller is a specially designed IP interface card. A block diagram of the controller is shown in Figure 14.2. The TTP controller uses the Motorola 68332 CPU as a protocol processor. The Motorola 68332 CPU contains a powerful Time-Processing Unit (TPU) on chip that is used for the clock synchronization and for measuring the exact arrival time of messages.

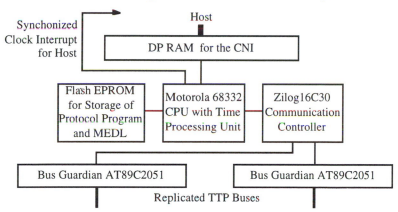

Figure 14.2: Hardware block diagram of the TTP controller.

By changing the software in the Flash EPROM, a TTP/A controller can be implemented which supports four TTP/A channels to sensor/actuator buses. (A VLSI chip that implements the TTP/C protocol is under development in the ESPRIT OMI project TTA (Time-Triggered Architecture) that started in December 1996).

TTA-Nodes: Any commercially available IP compatible motherboard can be used as a host in the TTA. A number of different processors are available on motherboards with IP interface slots. A typical TTA node will have a motherboard with two interface slots for two IP compatible interfaces. These two interface slots can be used for different interface cards, resulting in different TTA-nodes (Figure 14.3).

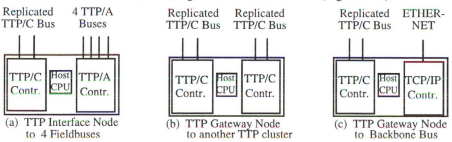

Figure 14.3: Different types of TTA nodes.

The TTP/A and the TTP/C controller of a TTA-node use the same hardware, but different protocol software. Both controllers have the same CNI as outlined in Section 8.2. The software of the host sees the controlled object and the network through identical data-sharing interfaces, thereby simplifying the operating system at the host.

Fieldbus Nodes: The TTP/A fieldbus protocol can be implemented in software in any inexpensive field bus node built around any standard microcontroller that contains a UART interface and a timer. The fieldbus nodes provide the analog and digital input/output lines that are used to interface to the sensors and actuators in the controlled object. The fieldbus nodes execute the local I/O functions, perform the conversion from raw sensor data to measured or even agreed data and send the data on the TTP/A bus to the TTA-node. As mentioned in Section 7.3.3, fault-tolerance is not an issue at the field bus level because the reliability bottleneck is in the sensor/actuator.

14.3 SOFTWARE SUPPORT

Designing software for a time-triggered architecture is substantially different from designing software for a conventional real-time computer system. The worst-case execution time (WCET) of the tasks and the worst-case administrative overhead (WCAO) of the operating system must be carefully controlled at design time. The static schedules must be developed off-line. The software-design phase requires more attention than in an event-triggered architecture.

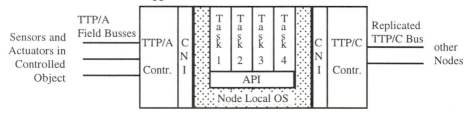

Figure 14.4: Node-local operating system in a TTA gateway.

14.3.1   Operating System

In the time-triggered architecture, the communication system autonomously controls the exchange of information among the nodes, and provides the distributed services for node coordination, such as clock synchronization, membership, and redundancy management. The node-local operating system must support the following functions (Figure 14.4):

(i)   control the execution of the application tasks within a node via the application-program interface (API), and

(ii)   service the information transfer across the external node interfaces. If a TTA-node accesses the controlled object exclusively via the field bus, then, there are two instances of the data sharing CNI interface to service: one to the controlled object, and the other to the cluster.

In principle, any operating system that has a handler for the CNI interface can be used in a TTA-node. If fault-tolerance is implemented by active redundancy, then the host OS must provide a replicate-determinate service.

Time-Triggered Operating System: A replica-determinate TT operating system was designed and implemented for the MARS architecture and is available for the TTA-nodes. This operating system has a data-independent temporal control structure that is established and tested at compile time. In the design phase the cluster compiler, described below, coordinates this static temporal control structure with the arrival and departure times of the messages at the CNI to eliminate all access conflicts by implicit synchronization. The MARS TT operating system supports the double and triple (if required) execution of tasks and the end-to-end signatures specified in the HEDC mode of operation. The API of a time-triggered OS has been discussed in Section 10.1.

Event-Triggered Operating System: It is possible to execute any ET operating system in the host, provided it has a handler for the CNI interface. The concurrency control flags at the CNI can be used to maintain the integrity of the data exchanged across the CNI between the autonomously operating protocol tasks and the node tasks in the host. For example, the ERCOS OS that has been presented in Section 10.5 has been ported to the TTA. The implementation of replica determinism within an event-triggered OS is an interesting research issue that is currently being investigated.

Interrupts: If the controlled object requires an immediate reaction from the computer system (time as control–see Section 9.2.2) within a time interval of less than 1 msec, then the interrupt mechanism must be used within the node-local operating system. The issues that must be considered when the control is delegated outside a node have been discussed in Chapter 9. In systems with interrupts, the implementation of replica determinism is difficult.

14.3.2   The Cluster Compiler

In the MARS implementation, the Message Descriptor Lists have to be configured manually. This is a tedious and error-prone task. For TTA, a MEDL generation tool-- called the *cluster compiler*-- has been developed. The cluster compiler requires the following inputs:

(i)   the data elements that must be exchanged between the nodes,

(ii)   the update period and the temporal accuracy requirements of the data elements,

(iii)   the sender and receiver nodes of the information exchanges, and

(iv)   the redundancy strategy to implement fault-tolerance.

This input is entered into a design database. The input must be produced either by hand or by some other high-level design tool. The benchmark problem of an automotive real-time system that has been defined by the SAE provides these input data as part of the benchmark specification [SAE95].

The cluster compiler generates the message schedules and tries to make the real-time images *parametric* by selecting appropriate update frequencies. At the end it produces the MEDL for each node [Kop95a].

14.3.3   Testing

The interfaces of a TTA-node are fully defined in the temporal domain and in the value domain. A test simulator can simulate the external interfaces of a TTA-node, both to the controlled objects and to the RT network. Every TTA-node can be tested in isolation against this environment simulator and a complete TTP control system can be tested before it is connected to the actual controlled equipment. Since the simulator does not require any modification of the software in the tested node, the probe effect is avoided and the system integration does not change the temporal behavior at the CNI of a TTA-node.

14.4 FAULT TOLERANCE

One design goal of the TTA is the generic support of fault-tolerant operation without any modification of the application software. This approach avoids any increase in the complexity of the application software which is caused by introducing fault-tolerance.

14.4.1   Fault-Tolerant Units

As explained in Section 6.4, a set of replica-determinate nodes can be grouped into a fault-tolerant unit (FTU) that will mask a failure of a node of the FTU without any effect on the external service provided by this FTU. The TTA supports the formation of FTUs and performs the redundancy management within the TTP controller such that the CNI to the host computer is not affected by the replication of nodes and communication channels.

A necessary precondition for the implementation of active redundancy is the replica-determinate behavior of the host software. The TTA provides replica determinism at the CNI of a node, but it is up to the host software to guarantee replica determinism within the complete node. If a time-triggered operating system is used, and the application software in the host is organized into S-tasks (see Section 4.2.1), then, the replica determinism of the node software is given.

14.4.2   Redundant Sensors

If the sensors need to be replicated to achieve fault-tolerance, then two separate field buses must be installed (Figure 14.5). Each one of those field buses is controlled by one of the TTA-nodes in the FTU. The other node is passive and listens to the field bus traffic to capture the sensor data.

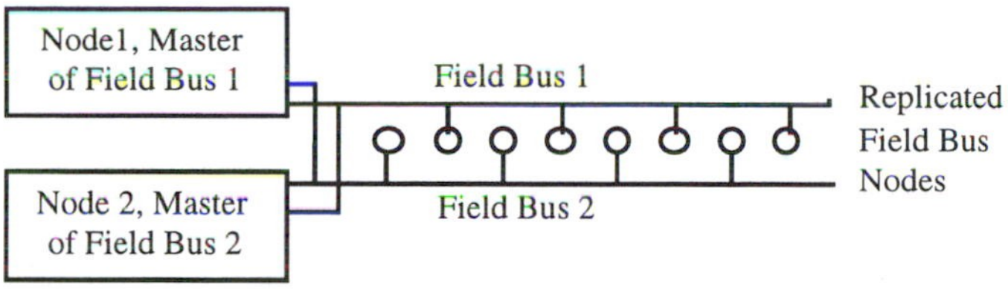

Figure 14.5: FTU configuration with replicated field buses.

An agreement protocol is executed in the controller of the TTA-node to reconcile the values received from the replicated sensors. Then, a single agreed value from each redundant sensor set is presented to the host software at the CNI.

14.5 WIDE-AREA REAL-TIME SYSTEMS

The Time-Triggered Architecture presented above supports real-time applications that are located at a single site. There are, however, a number of real-time applications that cover a wide geographical area, e.g., an electric-power distribution system covering a large geographical region or an air-traffic control system across an entire continent. In this section, it is speculated that the emerging ATM technology can be used to build the wide-area communication system for the TTA.

14.5.1 The Emergence of ATM Technology

The Asynchronous Transfer Mode (ATM) technology, briefly introduced in Section 7.3.2, is developed with the following objectives in mind [Vet95]:

(i) It must be cost-effective and scalable.

(ii) It must support applications requiring high bandwidth and low latency.

(iii) It must support multicast operation efficiently.

(iv) It should provide interoperability with existing local- and wide-area networks, using existing standards and protocols wherever possible.

There are speculations that most of the world's voice and data traffic will be transmitted by the ATM technology within the next decades [McK94], thus providing the reliable low-cost wide-area communication services of the future.

The ATM technology supports the construction of a *virtual private network* on top of an ATM network [Fot95]. A *virtual connection* with defined traffic attributes (bandwidth, delay) between any two endpoints can be established. This connection is then managed, and further multiplexed by the end users to meet their data communication needs.

14.5.2 An ATM Gateway

To interconnect TTA systems located at dispersed geographical sites, virtual private ATM connections with constant guaranteed bandwidth and minimal delay and jitter must be set up between the sites. The endpoints of these ATM connections are gateway nodes of the local TTA systems. Figure 14.6 depicts the possible architecture of such an ATM connection between local gateway FTUs.

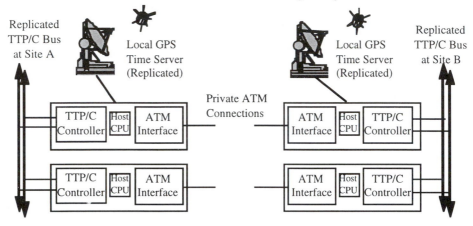

Figure 14.6: Connection of geographically dispersed TTA sites.

Since the ATM traffic will be relayed via a number of ATM switches, which leads to an accumulation of the jitter, it is proposed to perform the external clock synchronization between the dispersed sites outside of the ATM network. The global time is retrieved from a replicated local GPS receiver at each site. The accuracy of the GPS time is better than 1 μsec anywhere on earth. The Time-Triggered Protocol as outlined in Section 8.3 has to be modified to account for the unavoidable delay in a wide-area network. From the point of view of the local TTP network, the communication network interface (CNI) to the wide area ATM network is the same as that to another local node.

POINTS TO REMEMBER

*   The time-triggered architecture is based on the vision that a node can be built on an inexpensive single chip. The system architect is then free to use as many nodes as necessary to implement the given application requirements within a clean functional structure.

*   In the TTA a hardware node is considered a *unit of failure* with a single external failure mode: fail-silence.

*   The TTA is based on a small number of orthogonal concepts that are used over again to simplify the understanding of a design.

*   The distributed real-time database, formed by the temporally accurate images of all relevant RT entities, is at the core of the time-triggered architecture. The real-time database contains a temporally valid "snapshot" of the current state of the cluster and the cluster environment.

- In the time-triggered architecture the communication system controls autonomously the exchange of information among the nodes and provides the distributed services for node coordination, such as clock synchronization, membership, and redundancy management.

- The cluster compiler generates the message schedules and tries to make the real-time images *parametric* by selecting appropriate update frequencies. At the end it produces the MEDL for each node

- It is proposed to build wide-area time-triggered real-time systems by making use of the emerging ATM technology.

BIBLIOGRAPHIC NOTES

The Time-Triggered Architecture evolved out of the MAintainable Real-Time System project (MARS). MARS was started in 1979 at the Technical University of Berlin. The first MARS report MA 82/2 "The Architecture of MARS" was published at the Technical University of Berlin in April 1982. A condensed version of the report was presented at the 15th Fault-Tolerant Computing Symposium at Ann Arbor, Mich., in 1985 [Kop85]. At the time, three important open research issues were identified: (i) how to implement a precise fault-tolerant internal clock synchronization, (ii) how to design a real-time communication protocol for the communication among the nodes, and (iii) how to guarantee the fail-silent property of the nodes. A VLSI chip for the MARS clock synchronization was subsequently designed and implemented [Kop87]. This chip was used in the subsequent implementations of the MARS architecture [Kop89]. The time-triggered protocol TTP for the communication among the nodes of MARS was published at the FTCS 23 in Toulouse [Kop93]. The experimental validation of the fail-silent property was one important result of the ESPRIT Basic Research project PDCS [Kar95]. The PDCS books contains the first overview of the Time-Triggered Architecture [Kop95b], which is now developed with generous support from the European automotive industry, and the European Commission via the Brite Euram project "X-by-Wire", the ESPRIT OMI project "TTA", Time-Triggered Architecture, and the ESPRIT LTR project "DEVA", Design for Validation.

List of Abbreviations

Note: This annex contains a list of frequently used abbreviations. At the end of each entry the section of the book that introduces or discusses the term is mentioned in the parenthesis. Most of the terms expanded in this annex are contained in the glossary (Annex 2).

ALARP	As Low As Reasonably Practical (12.5)
API	Application Program Interface (10.1)
ATM	Asynchronous Transfer Mode (7.3.2)
BG	Bus Guardian (8.2.1)
C-State	Controller State (8.2.2)
C-Task	Complex Task (4.2.1)
CAN	Control Area Network (7.5.3)
CCF	Concurrency Control Field (10.2.2)
CNI	Communication Network Interface (2.1.3)
COTS	Commercial off the shelve
CRC	Cyclic Redundancy Check (6.2.1)
CSU	Clock Synchronization Unit (14.1.1)
EDF	Earliest-Deadline-First (11.3.1)
EMI	Electro-Magnetic Interference (7.6.3)
ET	Event-Triggered
FI	Fault Injection (12.4.2)
FTA	Fault-Tolerant Average (3.4.3)
FTU	Fault-Tolerant Unit (6.4)

H-State	History State: (4.2.2)
I-State	Initialization State (4.2.2)
I/O	Input/Output
LL	Least-Laxity (11.3.1)
MARS	Maintainable Real-Time System (14.1.1)
MEDL	Message Descriptor List (8.3.1)
MMI	Man-Machine Interface (4.3.1)
NBW	Non-Blocking Write (10.2.2)
OLT	Off-line Software Development Tool (10.5.5)
PAR	Positive-Acknowledgment-or-Retransmission (7.2.1)
RT	Real-Time
SOC	Sphere of Control (5.1.1)
SRU	Smallest Replaceable Unit (1.4.3)
TADL	Task Descriptor List (10.1.1)
TAI	International Atomic Time (3.1.4)
TDMA	Time-Division Multiple Access (7.5.7)
TMR	Triple-Modular Redundancy (6.4.2)
TPU	Time-Processing Unit (14.2.3)
TT	Time Triggered
TTA	Time-Triggered Architecture (14.2)
TTP	Time-Triggered Protocol (8.1)
TUR	Time Unit Response (11.4.1)
UART	Universal Asynchronous Receiver Transmitter (8.4)
UTC	Universal Time Coordinated (3.1.4)
WCAO	Worst-Case Administrative Overhead (4.4.3)
WCCOM	Worst-Case Communication Delay (5.4.1)
WCET	Worst-Case Execution Time(4.5)

Glossary

Note: All terms that are defined in this glossary are put in *italics*. At the end of each entry the section of the book that introduces or discusses the term is mentioned in the parenthesis.

Absolute Timestamp: An *absolute timestamp* of an *event e* is the *timestamp* of this *event* that is generated by the *reference clock* (3.1.2).

Abstract Message Interface: The *abstract message interface* is the message *interface* between an *interface node* and the other *nodes* of a *computational cluster* (4.3.1).

Accuracy Interval: The maximum permitted time interval between the *point of observation* of a *real-time entity* and the *point of use* of the corresponding *real-time image* (1.2.1).

Accuracy of a Clock: The *accuracy* of a clock denotes the maximum offset of a given clock from the external time reference during the time interval of interest (3.1.3).

Action: An *action* is the execution of a program or a communication protocol (4.1.2).

Action Delay: The *action delay* is the maximum time interval between the start of sending of a message and the point in time when this message becomes *permanent* at the receiver (5.5.1).

Actuator: A *transducer* that accepts data and *trigger* information from an *interface node* and realizes an intended effect in the *controlled object* (9.5).

Agreed Data: An *agreed data element* is a *measured data element* that has been checked for plausibility and related to other measured data , e.g., by the use of model of the *controlled object*. An agreed data element has been judged to be a correct image of the corresponding real-time entity (➔*raw data, measured data*) (9.3.1).

Agreement Protocol: An *agreement protocol* is a protocol that is executed among a set of *nodes* of a distributed system to come to a common (agreed) view about the state of the world, both in the value domain and in the time domain (e.g., state of a *RT entity*, state of the *membership*) (3.3.1).

Alarm Monitoring: *Alarm monitoring* refers to the continuous observation of the *RT entities* to detect an abnormal behavior of the *controlled object* (1.2.1).

Alarm Shower: An *alarm shower* is a correlated set of alarms that is caused by a single *primary event* (1.2.1).

Aperiodic Task: An *aperiodic task* is a *task* where neither the *task request times* are known nor the minimum time interval between successive requests for execution (➔*periodic task*, ➔*sporadic task*) (11.2).

Application Program Interface (API): The *application program interface* is the data and control *interface* between an application program and the operating system (10.1).

Application Specific Fault Tolerance: Fault tolerance mechanisms that are introduced within the application code (➔*systematic fault tolerance*) (6.1.4).

A Priori Knowledge: Knowledge about the future behavior of a system that is available ahead of time (1.5.5).

ARINC 629 Protocol: A medium access protocol that controls access to a single communication channel by a set nodes. It is based on a set of carefully selected time-outs (7.5.5).

Assumption Coverage: *Assumption coverage* is the probability that assumptions that are made in the model building process hold in reality. The *assumption coverage* limits the probability that conclusions derived from a model will be valid in the real world (4.1.1).

Asynchronous Transfer Mode (ATM): The *Asynchronous Transfer Mode (ATM)* is an asynchronous communication technology for communication over broadband networks where the information is organized into constant length cells (48 data bytes, 5 header bytes) (7.3.2).

Atomic Action: An *atomic action* is an action that has the all-or-nothing property. It either completes and delivers the intended result or does not have any effect on its environment (4.6.2).

Atomic Data Structure: An atomic data structure is a data structure that has to be interpreted as a whole (5.2.1)

Availability: *Availability* is a measure of the correct service delivery regarding the alternation of correct and incorrect service, measured by the fraction of time that the system is ready to provide the service (1.4.1).

Babbling Idiot: A *node* of a distributed computer system that sends messages outside the specified time interval is called a *babbling idiot* (6.3.3).

Back-Pressure Flow Control: In *back-pressure flow control* the receiver of a sequence of messages exerts back pressure on the sender so that the sender will not outpace the receiver (7.2.1).

Backbone Network: The *backbone network* is a non real-time communication network for the exchange of non time-critical information between the *RT cluster* and the data-processing systems of an organization (7.3.3).

Bandwidth: The maximum number of bits that can be transmitted across a channel in one second (7.5.1)

Benign Failure: A *failure* is *benign* if the worst-case failure costs are of the same order of magnitude as the loss of the normal utility of the system (6.1.1).

Best Effort: A *real-time system* is a *best-effort* system if it is not possible to establish the temporal properties by analytical methods, even if the *load- and fault hypothesis* holds (➔guaranteed timeliness) (1.5.3).

Bit-length of a Channel: The *bit length of a channel* denotes the number of bits that can traverse the channel within one *propagation delay* (7.5.1).

Bus Guardian: The independent hardware unit of a *TTP controller* that ensures *fail silence* in the temporal domain (8.1.2).

Byzantine Error: A *Byzantine error* occurs if a set of receivers receive different (conflicting) values about a *RT entity* at some point in time. Some or all of these values are incorrect (synonym: malicious error) (3.4.1).

Calibration Point: A point in the domain of an *event* sensor where the full state of the *RT entity* is known for calibration purposes (9.5.2).

Causal Order: A *causal order* among a set of *events* is an order that reflects the cause-effect relationships between the *events* (3.1.1).

Clock: A *clock* is a device for time measurement that contains a counter and a physical oscillation mechanism that periodically generates an *event* to increase the counter (3.1.2).

Cluster: A *cluster* is a subsystem of a real-time system. Examples of clusters are the *real-time computer system*, the operator, or the *controlled object* (1.1).

Cluster Cycle: A *cluster cycle* of a *time-triggered system* is the sequence of *TDMA rounds* after which the operation of the *cluster* is repeated. The *cluster cycle* determines the length of the *MEDL* (8.3.1).

Communication Controller: A *communication controller* is that part of a *node* that controls the communication within a distributed system (4.2.2).

Communication Network Interface (CNI): The *interface* between the *communication controller* and the *host computer* within a *node* of a distributed system (2.1.3).

Complex Task (C-task): A *complex task (C-task)* is a *task* that contains a blocking synchronization statement (e.g., a semaphore operation *wait*) within the *task* body (4.2.1).

Composability: An architecture is *composable* regarding a specified property if the system integration will not invalidate this property, provided it has been established at the subsystem level (2.2).

Computational Cluster: A subsystem of a real-time system that consists of a single *node* or a set of *nodes* interconnected by a *real-time communication network* (1.1).

Concrete World Interface: The *concrete world interface* is the physical I/O *interface* between an *interface node* and an external device in the *cluster* environment (4.3.1).

Concurrency Control Field (CCF): The *concurrency control field (CCF)* is a single-word data field that is used in the *NBW protocol* (10.2.2).

Consistent Failure: A *consistent failure* occurs if all users see the same erroneous result in a multi-user system (6.1.1).

Contact Bounce: The random oscillation of a mechanical contact immediately after closing (9.5.2).

Control Area Network (CAN): The *control area network (CAN)* is a low-cost *event-triggered* communication network that is based on the carrier-sense multiple-access collision-avoidance technology (7.5.3).

Controlled Object: The *controlled object* is the industrial plant, the process, or the device that is to be controlled by the *real-time computer system* (1.1).

Controller State (C-State): The *controller state* of a *TTP/C controller* consists of the time, the mode, and the *membership* (8.2.2).

Convergence Function: The *convergence function* denotes the maximum *offset* within an ensemble of *clocks* immediately after resynchronization (3.4.1).

Critical Failure: A failure is *critical* if the cost of the failure can be orders of magnitude higher than the utility of the system during normal operation (synonym: *malign* failure) (➔*safety*) (6.1.1).

Cyclic Redundancy Check (CRC) Field: An extra field in a message for the purpose of detection of value errors (6.2.1).

Data Encoding Technique: The *data encoding technique* defines the way in which the logical bits are translated into physical signals on the transmission medium (7.7).

Deadline: A *deadline* is the point in time when a result should/must be produced (➔*soft deadline, firm deadline, and hard deadline*) (1.1).

Deadline Interval: The *deadline interval* is the interval between the *task request time* and the *deadline* (11.2).

Delay Compensation Term: The *delay compensation term* contains the minimum delay of a synchronization message containing a time value of a clock. The delay is measured between the event of reading the clock at the sender and the timestamping of the arrival of this message at the receiver (3.4.3).

Drift: The *drift* of a physical *clock k* between *microtick i* and *microtick i+1* is the frequency ratio between this *clock k* and the *reference clock* at the time of *microtick i*. (3.1.2).

Drift Rate: The *drift-rate* of a clock is $|drift - 1|$ (3.1.2)

Drift Offset: The *drift offset* denotes the maximum deviation between any two good *clocks* if they are free running during the resynchronization interval (3.1.4).

Duration: A *duration* is a section of the timeline (3.1.1).

Dynamic Scheduler: A *dynamic scheduler* is a *scheduler* that decides at run time after the occurrence of a significant *event* which *task* is to be executed next (11.1.1).

Earliest-Deadline-First (EDF) Algorithm: An optimal dynamic preemptive scheduling algorithm for scheduling a set of independent periodic *tasks* (11.3.1).

Electro-Magnetic Interference (EMI): The disturbance of an electronic system by unintentional electromagnetic radiation (7.6.3).

Embedded System: A *real-time computer system* that is embedded in a well specified larger system, consisting in addition to the embedded computer system of a mechanical subsystem and, often, a man-machine *interface* (➔ *intelligent product)* (1.6.1).

End-to-End Protocol: An *end-to-end protocol* is a protocol between the users residing at the end points of a communication channel (7.1.4).

Environment of a Computational Cluster: The *environment* of a given *computational cluster* is the set of all *clusters* that interact with this *clusters*, either directly or indirectly (1.1).

Error: An *error* is that part of the state of a system that deviates from the specification (6.1.2).

Error-Containment Coverage: Probability that an *error* that occurs in an *error-containment region* is detected at one of the *interfaces* of this region (2.4.1)

Error-Containment Region: A subsystem of a computer system that is encapsulated by error-detection *interfaces* such that the there is a high probability (the *error containment coverage*) that the consequences of an *error* that occurs within this subsystem will not propagate outside this subsystem without being detected (2.4.1, 12.1.2).

Error Masking: A mechanism that prevents an *error* from causing a *failure* at a higher level by making immediate use of the provided redundancy (e.g., error correcting codes, replicated *idempotent messages*) (4.2.3).

Event: An *event* is a happening at a cut of the time-line. Every change of state is an *event* (3.1.1).

Event Message: A message is an *event message* if every new version of the message is queued at the receiver and consumed on reading (➔ *state message*) (2.1.3).

Event-Triggered (ET) Observation: An *observation* is *event-triggered* if the *point of observation* is determined by the occurrence of an *event* other than a *tick* of a *clock*.

Event-Triggered (ET) System: A *real-time computer system* is *event-triggered* (ET) if all communication and processing activities are triggered by an *event* other than a clock *tick* (1.5.5).

Exact Voter: A *voter that* considers two messages the same if they contain the exactly same sequence of bits (➔ inexact voter) (6.4.2).

Execution Time: The *execution time* is the time it takes to execute an *action*. The *worst-case execution time* is called *WCET* (4.1.2).

Explicit Flow Control: In *explicit flow control* the receiver sends an explicit acknowledgment message to the sender, informing the sender that the previously sent message has correctly arrived and that the receiver is now ready to accept the next message (➔*flow control,* ➔*implicit flow control*) (7.2.1).

Explicit Synchronization: The dynamic synchronization of *tasks* by synchronization statements, such as "WAIT-FOR-EVENT" (➔*implicit synchronization*) (10.2.1).

External Clock Synchronization: The process of synchronization of a *clock* with the *reference clock* (3.1.3).

Fail-Operational System: A *fail-operational system* is a *real-time system* where a safe state cannot be reached immediately after the occurrence of a *failure.* An example of a fail-operational system is a flight-control system without mechanical or hydraulic back-up onboard an airplane (1.5.2).

Fail-Safe System: A *fail-safe system* is a *real-time system* where a safe state can be identified and quickly reached after the occurrence of a *failure* (1.5.2).

Fail-Silence: A subsystem is *fail-silent* if it either produces correct results or no results at all, i.e., it is quiet in case it cannot deliver the correct service (6.1.1).

Fail-Silent Actuator: A *fail-silent actuator* is an actuator that either performs the specified output action or is silent. If it is silent it may not hinder replicated actuators (9.5.3).

Failure: A *failure* is an *event* that denotes a deviation of the actual service from the specified or intended service (6.1.1).

Fault: A *fault* is the cause of an *error* (6.1.3).

Fault Hypothesis: The *fault hypothesis* identifies the assumptions that relate to the type and frequency of faults that the computer system is supposed to handle (4.1.1).

Fault-Tolerant Average Algorithm (FTA): A particular distributed clock synchronization algorithm that handles *Byzantine* failures of *clocks* (3.4.3).

Fault-Tolerant Unit (FTU): A unit consisting of a number of *replica determinate nodes* that provides the specified service even if some of its *nodes* fail (6.4).

Feature Element: The *feature element* is the smallest geometric element in a transmission sequence (7.6.2).

Field Bus: A *field bus* is low cost bus for the interconnection of the sensor and actuator *nodes* in the *controlled object* to a *node* of the distributed computer system.

FIP Protocol: The *FIP protocol* is a *field-bus* protocol that is based on a central master station (7.5.6).

Firm Deadline: A *deadline* for a result is *firm* if the result has no utility after the deadline has passed (1.1).

FIT: A *FIT* is a unit for expressing the failure rate. 1 FIT is 1 $failure/10^{-9}$ hours. (1.4.1).

Flow Control: *Flow control* assures that the speed of the information flow between a sender and a receiver is such that the receiver can keep up with the sender (➔*explicit flow control,* ➔*implicit flow control*) (7.2).

Forbidden Region: A time interval during which it is not allowed to schedule a *task* that may conflict with another critical *task* (11.3.2).

Gateway: A *node* of a distributed real-time system that is a member of two *clusters* and implements the relative views of these two interacting *clusters* (2.1.4).

Global Time: The *global time* is an abstract notion that is approximated by a properly selected subset *of the microticks* of each synchronized local clock of an ensemble. The selected *microticks* of a local *clock* are called the *ticks* of the *global time.* (3.2.1).

Granularity of a Clock: The *granularity* of a *clock* is the nominal number of *microticks* of the *reference clock* between two *microticks* of the *clock* (3.1.2).

Ground State: The *ground state* of a *node* of a distributed system at a given level of abstraction is a state where no *task* is active and where all communication channels are flushed, i.e., there are no messages in transit (4.6.2).

Guaranteed Timeliness: A *real-time system* is a *guaranteed timeliness* system if it is possible to reason about the adequacy of the design without reference to probabilistic arguments, provided the assumptions about the *load- and fault hypothesis* hold (➔*best effort*) (1.5.3).

h-State: The *h-state* is the dynamic data structure of a *task* or *node* that is changed as the computation progresses. The *h-state* must reside in read/write memory (4.6.1).

Hamming Distance: The *Hamming distance* is one plus the maximum number of bit errors in a codeword that can be detected by syntactic means (6.2.1).

Hard Deadline: A *deadline* for a result is *hard* if a catastrophe can occur in case the deadline is missed (1.1).

Hard Real-Time Computer System: A *real-time computer system* that must meet at least one *hard deadline* (Synonym: *safety-critical real-time computer system.*) (1.1).

Hazard: A *hazard* is an undesirable condition that has the potential to cause or contribute to an accident (12.4).

Heartbeat: ➔*lifesign*

Hidden Channel: A communication channel outside the given *computational cluster* (5.5.1).

Host Computer: The *host computer* (or *host*) is the computer within a *node* that executes the application software (4.2.2).

i-State: The *i-state* is the static data structure of a *node* that comprises the reentrant program code and the initialization data of the *node*. The *i-state* can be stored in a Read-Only Memory (4.2.2).

Idempotency: *Idempotency* is a relation between a set of replicated messages arriving at the same receiver. A set of replicated messages is *idempotent* if the effect of receiving more than one copy of a message is the same as receiving only a single copy (5.5.4).

Implicit Flow Control: In *implicit flow control*, the sender and receiver agree *a priori,* i.e., at system start up, about the points in time when messages will be sent. The sender commits itself to send only messages at the agreed points in time, and the receiver commits itself to accept all messages sent by the sender, as long as the sender fulfills its obligation (➔*explicit flow control,* ➔*flow control)* (7.2.2).

Implicit Synchronization: The static synchronization of *tasks* by *a priori* temporal control of the *task* activation (➔*explicit synchronization*) (10.2.1).

Inexact Voter: A *voter* that considers two messages the "same" if both of them conform to some application specific "sameness" criterion (➔*exact voter)* ((6.4.2).

Instant: An *instant* is a cut of the timeline (3.1.1).

Instrumentation Interface: The *instrumentation interface* is the *interface* between the *real-time computer system* and the *controlled object* (1.1).

Intelligent Actuator: An *intelligent actuator* consists of an actuator and a processing unit, both mounted together in a single housing (9.5.4).

Intelligent Product: An *intelligent product* is a self-contained system that consists of a mechanical subsystem, a user *interface,* and a controlling embedded *real-time computer system* (➔*embedded system)* (1.6.1).

Intelligent Sensor: An *intelligent sensor* consists of a sensor and a processing unit such that *measured data* is produced at the output *interface.* If the *intelligent sensor* is fault-tolerant, *agreed data* is produced at the output *interface* (9.5.4).

Interface: An *interface* is a common boundary between two subsystems (4.3).

Interface Node: A *node* with an instrumentation *interface* to the *controlled object.* An *interface node* is a *gateway* (1.1, 2.1.4).

Internal Clock Synchronization: The process of mutual synchronization of an ensemble of *clocks* in order to establish a *global time* with a bounded *precision* (3.1.3).

International Atomic Time (TAI): An international time standard, where the second is defined as 9 192 631 770 periods of oscillation of a specified transition of the Cesium atom 133 (3.1.4).

Irrevocable action: An action that cannot be undone, e.g., drilling a hole, activation of the firing mechanism of a firearm (5.5.1).

Jitter: The *jitter* is the difference between the maximum and the minimum duration of an *action* (processing action, communication action) (4.1.2).

Laxity: The *laxity* of a *task* is the difference between the *deadline interval* minus the *execution time* (the *WCET)* of the *task* (11.2).

Least-Laxity (LL) Algorithm: An optimal dynamic preemptive *scheduling* algorithm for scheduling a set of independent periodic *tasks* (11.3.1).

Life Sign: A *life sign* is a periodic signal generated by a computer. The life sign is monitored by a *watchdog* . A lifesign is sometimes called a *heartbeat* (10.4.4)

Load Hypothesis: The *load hypothesis* specifies the peak load that the computer system is supposed to handle (4.1.1).

Logical Control: *Logical control* is concerned with the control flow *within* a *task*. The *logical control* is determined by the given program structure and the particular input data to achieve the desired data transformation (➔*temporal control*) (4.4.1).

LON Network: The *LON network* is a low cost *event*-triggered communication network that is based on the carrier-sense multiple-access collision-detection technology (7.5.3).

Low-Pass Filter: A *low-pass filter* is a filter, either analog or digital, which passes all frequencies below a specified value and attenuates all frequencies above that value (9.5.2).

Maintainability: The *Maintainability M(d)* is the probability that the system is restored within a time interval *d* after a failure (1.4.3).

Major Decision Point: A *major decision* point is a decision point in an algorithm that provides a choice between a set of significantly different courses of action (5.6.1).

Malign Failure: ➔*critical failure* (1.4.2).

Man-Machine Interface: The *man-machine interface* is the *interface* between the *real-time computer system* and the operator (1.1).

Measured Data: A *measured data element* is a *raw data element* that has been preprocessed and converted to standard technical units. A sensor that delivers *measured data* is called an *intelligent sensor* (➔*raw data, agreed data*) (9.3.1).

Media-Access Protocol: A *media-access* protocol is a protocol that defines the method used to assign the single communication channel (bus) to one of the nodes requesting the right to transmit a message (7.5).

Membership Service: A *membership service* is a service in a distributed system that generates consistent information about the operational state (operating or failed) of all *nodes* at agreed points in time (membership points). The length and the jitter of the interval between a membership point and the moment when the consistent membership information is available at the other *nodes* are quality of service parameters of the membership service (5.3.2).

Message Descriptor List (MEDL): The *Message Descriptor List (MEDL)* is the static data structure within each *TTP controller* that determines when a message must be sent on, or received from, the communication channels (8.3.1).

Microtick: A *microtick* of a physical clock is a periodic *event* generated by this *clock* (➔*tick*) (3.1.2).

Minimum Performance Criteria: The *minimum performance criteria* establish a borderline between what constitutes *success* and what constitutes *failure* during the operation of a system (13.2.3).

Minimum Time Between Events (*mint*): The *minimum time between events* (*mint*) is the minimal interval between two *events* of the same type (9.4.2).

Mode: A *mode* is a set of related states of a *real-time system*. For example, an airplane can be in taxiing *mode* or in flying *mode*. In the temporal domain different *modes* are mutually exclusive (6.5.3).

Node: A *node* is a self-contained computer that performs a well-defined function within the distributed computer system. A *node* consists at least of a *host computer* (or *host*) (including the system- and application software) and a *communication controller* (4.2.2).

Non-Blocking Write Protocol (NBW): The *non-blocking write protocol* (*NBW*) is a synchronization protocol between a single writer and many readers that achieves data consistency without blocking the writer (10.2.2).

Observation: An *observation* of a *real-time entity* is an atomic triple consisting of the name of the *real-time entity*, the point in time of the *observation*, and the value of the *real-time entity* (5.2).

Offset: The *offset* between two *events* denotes the time difference between these *events* 3.1.3).

Parametric RT Image: A RT image is *parametric* or *phase insensitive* if the *RT image* remains *temporally accurate* until it is updated by a more recent version (5.4.2).

Periodic Task: A *periodic task* is a *task* that has a constant time interval between successive *task* request times (➔*aperiodic task*, ➔*sporadic task*) (11.2).

Permanence: *Permanence* is a relation between a given message and all messages that have been sent to the same receiver before this given message has been sent. A particular message becomes *permanent* at a given *node* at the moment when it is known that all messages have arrived (or will never arrive) that have been sent to this *node* before the send time of the particular message (5.5.1).

Phase Sensitive RT Image: A RT image is *phase sensitive* if the RT image becomes temporally inaccurate before it is updated by a more recent version (5.4.2).

Phase-Aligned Transaction: A *phase-aligned transaction* is a *real-time transaction* where the constituting processing and communication *actions* are tightly synchronized (5.4.1).

Point of Observation: The moment when a *real-time entity* is observed (1.2.1).

Polling: In *polling*, the state of a *RT entity* is periodically interrogated by the computer system at points in time that are in the *sphere of control* of the computer system. If a memory element is required to store the effect of an *event*, the memory element is inside the *sphere of control* of the computer system (➔*sampling*) (9.3).

Positive-Acknowledgment-or-Retransmission (PAR) protocol: The *Positive-Acknowledgment-or-Retransmission (PAR) protocol* is an *event*-triggered protocol where a message sent by the sender must be positively acknowledged by the receiver (7.2.1).

Precision: The *precision* of an ensemble of clocks denotes the maximum *offset* of respective ticks of any two clocks of the ensemble over the period of interest. The *precision* is expressed in the number of *ticks* of the *reference clock* (3.1.3).

Primary Event: A *primary event* is the cause of an *alarm shower* (1.2.1).

Priority Ceiling Protocol: A *scheduling* algorithm for *scheduling* a set of dependent periodic *tasks* (11.3.3).

Priority Inversion: *Priority inversion* refers to a situation, where a high priority task is directly or indirectly blocked by a low priority task that has exclusive access to a resource (11.3.3).

Process: The execution of a program (synonym to ➔*action*) (see also ➔*task*) (10.2.1).

Process Lag: The delay between applying a step function to an input of a *controlled object* and the start of response of the *controlled object* (1.3.1).

Propagation Delay The *propagation delay* of a communication channel denotes the time interval it takes for a single bit to traverse the channel (7.5.1).

Protocol: A *protocol* is a set of rules that governs the communication among partners (1.7.1).

Rare Event: A *rare event* is a seldom occurring event that is of critical importance. In a number of applications the predictable performance of a *real-time computer system* in *rare event* situations is of overriding concern (1.2.1).

Rate-Monotonic Algorithm: A dynamic preemptive *scheduling* algorithm for *scheduling* a set of independent periodic *tasks* (11.3.1).

Raw Data: A *raw data element* is an analog or digital data element as it is delivered by an unintelligent sensor (➔*measured data, agreed data*) (9.3.1).

Real-Time (RT) Entity: A *real-time (RT) entity* is a state variable, either in the *environment* of the *computational cluster,* or in the *computational cluster* itself, that is relevant for the given purpose. Examples of *RT entities* are: the temperature of a vessel, the position of a switch, the setpoint selected by an operator, or the intended valve position calculated by the computer (1.2.1, 5.1).

Real-Time (RT) Image: A *real-time (RT) image* is a current picture of a *real-time entity* (1.2.1, 5.3.1).

Real-Time Communication Network: A real-time communication system within a *cluster* that provides all services needed for the timely and dependable transmission of data between the *nodes* (7.3.3).

Real-Time Computer System: A *real-time computer system* is a computer system, in which the correctness of the system behavior depends not only on the logical results of the computations, but also on the physical time when these results are produced. A real-time computer system can consist of one or more *computational clusters* (1.1).

Real-Time Data Base: The *real-time data base* is formed by the set of all *temporally accurate real-time images* (1.2.1).

Real-Time Object: A *real-time (RT) object* is a container inside a computer for a *RT entity* or a *RT image*. A *clock* with a granularity that is in agreement with the dynamics of the *RT object* is associated with every RT object (5.3.2).

Real-Time Transaction: A *real-time (RT) transaction* is a sequence of communication and computational *actions* between a stimulus from the environment and a response to the environment of a *computational cluster* (1.7.3).

Reasonableness Condition: The *reasonableness condition* of clock synchronization states that the *granularity* of the *global time* must be larger than the *precision* of the ensemble of *clocks* (3.2.1).

Reference Clock: The *reference clock* is an ideal *clock* that ticks always in perfect agreement with the international standard of time (3.1.2).

Reliability: The *reliability R(t)* of a system is the probability that a system will provide the specified service until time *t*, given that the system was operational at $t = t_o$. (1.4.1).

Replica Determinism: *Replica Determinism* is a desired relation between replicated *RT objects*. A set of replicated *RT objects* is *replica determinate* if all objects of this set have the same visible external *h-state* and produce the same output messages at points in time that are at most an interval of *d* time units apart (5.6).

Resource Adequacy: A *real-time computer system* is *resource adequate* if there are enough computing resources available to handle the specified *peak load* and the *faults* specified in the *fault hypothesis*. Guaranteed response systems must be based on *resource adequacy* (➔*guaranteed timeliness*) (1.4.5).

Resource Controller: A *resource controller* is a computational unit that controls a resource, hides the *concrete world interface* of the resource, and presents a standard *abstract message interface* to the clients of the resource (4.3.10).

Rise Time: The *rise time* is the time required for the output of a system to rise to a specific percentage of its final equilibrium value as a result of step change on the input (1.3.1).

Risk: *Risk* is the product of *hazard* severity and *hazard* probability. The severity of a *hazard* is the worst-case damage of a potential accident related to the *hazard*. (12.4).

Safety: *Safety* is *reliability* regarding *critical failure* modes (1.4.2).

Safety Case: A *safety case* is a combination of a sound set of arguments supported by analytical and experimental evidence substantiating the *safety* of a given system (12.1).

Safety Critical Real-Time Computer System: Synonym to *hard real-time computer system* (1.1).

Sampling: In *sampling,* the state of a RT entity is periodically interrogated by the computer system at points in time that are in the *sphere of control* of the computer system. If a memory element is required to store the effect of an *event*, the memory element is outside the *sphere of control* of the computer system (➔*polling*) (9.3).

Schedulability Test: A *schedulability test* determines whether there exists a schedule such that all *tasks* of a given set will meet their deadlines (11.1.2).

Scheduler: A software module, normally in the operating system, that decides which *task* will be executed at a particular point in time (11.1).

Semantic Agreement: An agreement is called *semantic agreement* if the meanings of the different *measured values* are related to each other by a process model that is based on *a priori* knowledge about the physical characteristics of the *controlled object* (9.2.3).

Setpoint: A *setpoint* is an intended value for the position of an actuator or the intended value of a *real-time entity* (1.2.2).

Shadow Node: A *shadow node* is a *node* of a *Fault-Tolerant Unit* that receives input messages but does not produce output messages as long as the redundant nodes of the FTU are operational (6.4.1).

Signal Conditioning: *Signal conditioning* refers to all processing steps that are required to generate a *measured data element* from a *raw data element*. (1.2.1).

Smallest Replaceable Unit (SRU): A *smallest replaceable unit* is a subsystem that is considered atomic from the point of view of a repair action (1.4.3).

Soft Deadline: A *deadline* for a result is *soft* if the result has utility even after the *deadline* has passed (1.1).

Soft Real-Time Computer System: A *real-time computer system* that is not concerned with any *hard deadline* (1.1).

Sphere of Control (SOC): The *sphere of control* of a subsystem is the set of *RT entities* the values of which are established within this subsystem (5.1.1).

Sporadic Task: A *sporadic task* is a *task* where the *task* request times are not known but where it is known that a minimum time interval exists between successive requests for execution (➔*periodic task*, ➔*aperiodic task*) (11.2).

State Estimation: *State estimation* is the technique of building a model of a *RT entity* inside a *RT object* to compute the probable state of a *RT entity* at a selected future point in time, and to update the related *RT image* accordingly (5.4.3).

State Message: A message is a *state message* if a new version of the message replaces the previous version, and the message is not consumed on reading (➔*event message*) (2.1.3).

Synchronization Condition: The *synchronization condition* is a necessary condition for the synchronization of clocks. It relates the *convergence function*, the *drift offset* and the *precision* (3.4.1).

Syntactic Agreement: An agreement is called *syntactic agreement* if the agreement algorithm computes the *agreed value* without considering the semantics of the *measured values* (9.3.2).

Systematic Fault Tolerance: Fault tolerance mechanisms that are introduced at the architecture level, transparent to the application code (➔*application specific fault tolerance*) (6.1.4).

Task Descriptor List (TADL): The *task* descriptor list (TADL) is a static data structure in a time-triggered operating systems that contains the points in time when the *tasks* have to be dispatched (10.1.1).

Task Request Time: The *task request time* is the point in time when a *task* becomes ready for execution (11.2).

Task: A *task* is the execution of a sequential program (➔*simple task,* ➔*complex task)* (4.2.1).

TDMA Round: A *TDMA round* is a complete transmission round in a *TDMA* system (7.5.7).

Temporal Accuracy: A *real-time image* is *temporally accurate* if the time interval between the moment "now" and point in time when the current value of the real-time image was the value of the corresponding *RT entity* is smaller than an application specific bound (5.4).

Temporal Control: *Temporal control* is concerned with the determination of the points in time when a *task* must be activated or when a *task* must be blocked because some conditions outside the *task* are not satisfied at a particular moment (➔*logical control)* (4.4.1).

Temporal Order: The *temporal order* of a set of *events* is the order of *events* as they occurred on the time line (3.1.1).

Thrashing: The phenomenon that a system's throughput decreases abruptly with increasing load is called *thrashing* (7.2.3).

Tick: A *tick* (synonym: macrotick) of a synchronized clock is a specially selected *microtick* of this clock. The *offset* between any two respective ticks of an ensemble of synchronized *clocks* must always be less than the *precision* of the ensemble (➔*microtick, reasonableness condition)* (3.2.1).

Time Stamp: A *timestamp* of an *event* with respect to a given clock is the state of the clock at the point of time of occurrence of the *event* (3.1.2).

Time-Division Multiple Access (TDMA): *Time-Division Multiple Access* is a time-triggered communication technology where the time axis is statically partitioned into slots. Each slot is statically assigned to a *node*. A *node* is only allowed to send a message during its slot (7.5.7).

Time-Triggered (TT) Observation: An *observation* is *time-triggered* if the *point of observation* is *triggered* by a *tick* of the *global time* (4.4.2).

Time-Triggered Protocol (TTP): A communication protocol where the point in time of message transmission is derived from the progression of the global time (8.1).

Time-Triggered System: A *real-time system* is *time-triggered (TT)* if all communication and processing activities are initiated at predetermined points in time at an *a priori* designated tick of a clock.

Timed Message: A *timed message* is a message that contains the timestamp of an *event* (e.g., point of observation) in the data field of the message (9.1.1).

Timing Failure: A *timing failure* occurs when a value is presented at the system-user *interface* outside the specified interval of real-time. Timing failures can only exist if the system specification contains information about the expected temporal behavior of the system (6.1.1).

Token Bus: A bus based communication system where the right to transmit is contained in a token that is passed among the communicating partners (7.5.4).

Transducer: A device converting energy from one domain into another. The device can either be a *sensor* or an *actuator* (9.5)

Transient Error: A *transient error* is an error that exists only for a short period of time after which it disappears (6.1.2).

Transient Fault: A *transient fault* is a fault that exists only for a short period of time after which it disappears (6.1.3).

Trigger: A *trigger* is an *event* that causes the start of some action (1.5.5).

Trigger Task: A *trigger task* is a time-triggered *task* that evaluates a condition on a set of temporally accurate real-time variables and generates a *trigger* for an application *task* (4.4.4).

Triple-Modular Redundancy (TMR): A fault-tolerant system configuration where a *fault-tolerant unit (FTU)* consists of three synchronized *nodes*. A value failure of one *node* can be masked by the majority (→*voting*) (6.4.2).

Universal Asynchronous Receiver Transmitter (UART): A standardized low cost communication controller for the transmission/reception of asynchronous bytes, encoding a single byte into a 10 bit or 11 bit mark/space format (one start bit, eight data bits, one optional parity bit, and one stop bit) (8.4).

Universal Time Coordinated (UTC): An international time standard that is based on astronomical phenomena (→*International Atomic Time*) (3.1.4).

Value Failure: A *value failure* occurs if an incorrect value is presented at the system-user *interface* (6.1.1).

Voter: A *voter* is a unit that detects and masks errors by accepting a number of independently computed input messages and delivers an output message that is based on the analysis of the inputs (→*exact voting*, →*inexact voting*) (6.4.2).

Watchdog: A *watchdog* is an independent external device that monitors the operation of a computer. The computer must send a periodic signal (*life sign*) to the *watchdog*. If this life sign fails to arrive at the *watchdog* within the specified time interval, the *watchdog* assumes that the computer has failed and takes some action (e.g., the *watchdog* forces the *controlled object* into the safe state) (1.5.2, 10.4.4).

Worst-Case Administrative Overhead (WCAO): The *worst-case execution time* of the administrative services provided by an operating system (4.4.3).

Worst-Case Communication Delay (WCCOM): The *worst-case communication delay* is the maximum duration it may take to complete a communication action under the stated *load- and fault hypothesis* (5.4.1).

Worst-Case Execution Time (WCET): The *worst-case execution time (WCET)* is the maximum duration it may take to complete an *action* under the stated *load- and fault hypothesis*, quantified over all possible input data (4.5).

References

[Agn91]   Agne, R. (1991). *Global Cyclic Scheduling: A Method to Guarantee the Timing Behavior of Distributed Real-Time Systems.* Real-Time Systems. Vol. 3 (1). (pp. 45-66).

[Ahu90]   Ahuja, M., Kshemkalyani, A. D., & Carlson, T. (1990). *A Basic Unit of Computation in a Distributed System.* 10th IEEE Distributed Computer Systems Conference. IEEE Press. (pp. 12-19).

[And95]   Anderson, J., Ramamurthy, S., & Jeffay, K. (1995). *Real-Time Computing with Lock-Free Shared Objects.* Proc. Real-Time Systems Symposium. Pisa, Italy. IEEE Press. (pp. 28-37).

[ARI91]   ARINC (1991). *Multi-Transmitter Data Bus ARINC 629--Part 1: Technical Description.* Aeronautical Radio Inc., Annapolis, Maryland 21401.

[ARI92]   ARINC (1992). *Software Considerations in Airborne Systems and Equipment Certification.* Document RTCA/DO-178B. ARINC, Annapolis, Maryland 21401.

[Avi78]   Avizienis, A. (1978). *Fault-Tolerance, The Survival Attribute of Digital Systems.* Proc. of the IEEE. Vol. 66 (10). (pp. 1109-1125).

[Avi85]   Avizienis, A. (1985). *The N-version Approach to Fault-Tolerant Systems.* IEEE Trans. on Software Engineering. Vol. 11 (12). (pp. 1491-1501).

[Avi96]   Avizienis, A. (1996). *Systematic Design of Fault-Tolerant Computers.* Safecomp 96. Vienna, Austria. Springer Verlag. (pp. 3-20).

[Avr92]   Aversky, D., Arlat, J., Crouzet, Y., & Laprie, J. C. (1992). *Fault Injection for the Formal Testing of Fault Tolerance.* Proc. of the 22nd Fault-Tolerant Computing Symposium. IEEE Press. (pp. 345-354).

[Bab87]   Babaoglu, O. (1987). *On the Reliability of Consensus-Based Fault-Tolerant Distributed Computing Systems.* ACM Trans. on Computer Systems. Vol. 5 (3). (pp. 394-416).

[Ban86]   Bannister, B. R., & Whitehead, D. G. (1986). *Transducers and Interfacing, Principles and Techniques.* VanNostrand Reinhold. Berkshire, U.K.

[Bel92]   Bell, D., Cox, L., Jackson, S, & Schaefer, P. (1992). *Using Causal Reasoning for Automated Failure Mode and Effect Analysis.* Proc. Annual Reliability and Maintability Symposium. IEEE Press. (pp. 343-353).

[Ber85]   Berry, G., & Cosserat, L. (1985). *The Synchronous Programming Language ESTEREL and its Mathematical Semantics.* Proc. of the Seminar on Concurrency (LNCS 197). Springer-Verlag.

[Bou95]   Bourgonjon, R. H. (1995). *The Evolution of Embedded Software in Consumer Products* In: B. Randell (Ed.), *The Future of Software.* The University of Newcastle upon Tyne. (pp. I.3-I.35).

[Bou96]   Boussinot, F., & Simone, R. (1996). *The SL Synchronous Language.* IEEE Trans. on Software Engineering. Vol. 22 (4). (pp. 256-266).

[Bri89]   Brilliant, S., Knight, J., & Leveson, N. (1989). *The Consistent Comparison Problem in N-Version Software.* IEEE Trans. on Software Engineering. Vol. 15 (11). (pp. 1481-1485).

[Bur89]   Burns, A., & Wellings, A. J. (1989). *Real-Time Systems and Their Programming Languages.* Addison Wesley.

[Bur96]   Burns, A., & Welling, A. (1996). *Advanced Fixed Priority Scheduling* In: J. Mathai (Ed.), *Real-Time Systems.* Prentice Hall. London. (pp. 32-65).

[But93]   Butler, R. W., & Finelli, G. B. (1993). *The Infeasibility of Quantifiying the Reliablility of Life-Critical Real-Time Software.* IEEE Trans. on Software Engineering. Vol. 19 (1). (pp. 3-12).

[CAN90]   CAN (1990). *Controller Area Network CAN, an In-Vehicle Serial Communication Protocol* In: *SAE Handbook 1992.* SAE Press. (pp. 20.341-20.355).

[Che87]   Cheng, S. C. (1987). *Scheduling Algorithms for Hard Real-Time Systems--A Brief Survey* In: J. A. Stankovic (Ed.), *Hard Real-Time Systems.* IEEE Press. Los Angeles.

[Cou85]   Courtois, P.-J. (1985). *On Time and Space Decomposition of Complex Structures.* Comm. ACM. Vol. 28 (6). (pp. 590-603).

[Cou91]   Couvillion, J. A., Freire, R., Johnson, R., Obdal II, W. D., Qureshi, M. A., Rai, M., Sanders, W. H., & Tvedt, J. E. (1991). *Performability Modeling with UltraSAN.* IEEE Software. Vol.: 8 (5). (pp. 69-80).

[Cri89]   Cristian, F. (1989). *Probabilistic Clock Synchronization.* Distributed Computing. Vol. 3 (Springer Verlag). (pp. 146-185).

[Cri91]   Cristian, F. (1991). *Understanding Fault-Tolerant Distributed Systems.* Comm. ACM. Vol. 34 (2). (pp. 57-78).

[Dav79]   Davies, C. T. (1979). *Data Processing Integrity* In: B. Randell & T. Anderson (Ed.), *Computing Systems Reliability.* Cambridge University Press. (pp. 288-354).

[Dri90]   Driel, C. L., Follon, R. J. B., Kohler, A. A. C., Osch, R. P. M., & Spanjers, J. M. (1990). *The Error-Resistant Interactively Consistent Architecture (ERICA).* Proc. FTCS 20. IEEE Press. (pp. 474-480).

[Ebe94]   Ebert, R. E. (1994). *User Interface Design.* Prentice Hall, Inc. Englewood Cliffs, NJ.

[Fag86]   Fagan, M. E. (1986). *Advances in Software Inspections.* IEEE Trans. on Software Engineering. Vol. SE-12 (7). (pp. 744-751).

[FIP94]   FIP (1994). *The FIP Protocol* In: World FIP Europe, 3 Rue de Salpetiere, 5400 Nancy, France.

[Foh94]   Fohler, G. (1994). *Flexibility in Statically Scheduled Hard Real-Time Systems*. PhD Thesis, Technical University of Vienna.

[Foh95]   Fohler, G. (1995). *Joint Scheduling of Distributed Complex Periodic and Hard Aperiodic Tasks in Statically Scheduled Systems*. IEEE Real-Time Systems Symposium. Pisa, Italy. IEEE Press. (pp. 152-161).

[Fot95]   Fotedar, S., Gerla, M., Crocetti, P., & Fratta, L. (1995). *ATM Virtual Private Networks*. Comm. ACM. Vol. 38 (2). (pp. 101-108).

[Fuc96]   Fuchs, E. (1996). *Software Implemented Fault Injection*. PhD Thesis, Technical University of Vienna/182, A 1040 Vienna, Treitlstrasse 3.

[Fur89]   Furth, B., Parker, J., & Grostick, D. (1989). *Performance of Real/IX--A Fully Preemptive Real-Time UNIX*. Operating System Review. Vol.: 23 (4).

[Gar75]   Garey, M. R., & Johnson, D. S. (1975). *Complexity Results for Multiprocessor Scheduling under Resource Constraints*. SIAM Journal of Computing. Vol. 4 (4). (pp. 397-411).

[Geb88]   Gebman, J., McIver, D., & Schulman, H. (1988). *Maintenance Data on the Fire-Control Radar*. Proc. of the AIAA Avionics Conference. San Jose, Cal.

[Gei91]   Geist, R., & Trivedi, K. (1991). *Reliability Estimation of Fault-Tolerant Systems: Tools and Techniques*. Computer. Vol. 23 (7). (pp. 52-61).

[Gos91]   Goscinski, A. (1991). *Distributed Operating Systems*. Addison-Wesley. Sydney, Australia.

[Gra94]   Gray, J., & Reuter, A. (1993). *Transaction Processing: Concepts and Techniques*. Morgan Kaufmann. San Francisco, California.

[Gre93]   Greenspring (1993). *Industry Pack Logic Interface Specification* Greenspring Computers, 1204 O'Brien Dirve, Menlo Park, CA, 94025.

[Haa81]   Haase, V. (1981). *Real-Time Behavious of Programs*. IEEE Trans. on Software Engineering. Vol. SE-7 (5). (pp. 451-509).

[Hal92]   Halbwachs, N. (1992). *Synchronous Programming of Reactive Systems*. Kluwer Academic Press.

[Har88]   Harper, R. E., Lala, J. H., & Deyst, J. J. (1988). *Fault-Tolerant Parallel Processor Architecture Overview*. Proc. FTCS 18. IEEE Press. (pp. 252-257).

[Hea95]   Healy, C. A., Whalley, D. B., & Harmon, M. G. (1995). *Efficient Microarchitecture Modeling and Path Analysis for Real-Time Software*. Proc. 16th RTSS. Pisa Italy. IEEE Press. (pp. 288-297).

[Hix93]   Hix, D., & Hartson, H.R. (1993). *Developing User Interfaces: Ensuring Usability through Product and Process*. John Wiley and Sons, Inc. New York, N.Y.

[Hop78]   Hopkins, A. L., Smith, T. B., & Lala, J. H. (1978). *FTMP: A Highly Reliable Fault-Tolerant Multiprocessor for Aircraft Control*. Proc. IEEE. Vol. 66 (10). (pp. 1221-1239).

[How87]   Howden, B. (1987). *A Functional Approach to Program Testing and Analysis*. McGraw-Hill. New York.

[IEC95]   IEC 1508 (1995). *International Electrotechnical Commission (IEC) Standard 1508*

[IEC96]   IEC 601-1-4, (1996). *Medical Electrical Equipment, General Requirements for Safety, Collateral Standard: Programmable Electrical Medical Systems.* International Electrotechnical Commission.

[IFA95]   IFAC (1995). *Proceedings of the Distributed Computing Systems Workshop.* International Federation of Automatic Control (IFAC).

[Iha82]   Ihara, H., & Mori, K. (1982). *Highly Reliable Loop Computer Network System Based on Autonomous Decentralization Concept.* Proc. 12th Fault-Tolerant Computing Symposium. IEEE Press. (pp. 187-194).

[Iha84]   Ihara, H., & Mori, K. (1984). *Autonomous Decentralized Computer Control Systems.* IEEE Computer. Vol. (August 1984). (pp. 57-66).

[Jah86]   Jahainan, F., & Mok, A. K. (1986). *Safety Analysis of Timing Properties in Real-Time Systems.* IEEE Trans. on Software Engineering. Vol. 12 (9). (pp. 890-904).

[Jal94]   Jalote, P. (1994). *Fault Tolerance in Distributed Systems.* Prentice Hall. Englewood Cliffs, N.J.

[Joh89]   Johnson, B. (1989). *Design and Analysis of Fault-Tolerant Digital Systems.* Addison Wesley. Reading, Mass. USA.

[Joh92]   Johnson, S. C., & Butler, R. W. (1992). *Design for Validation.* IEEE Aerospace and Electronic Systems Magazine. Vol. 7 (1). (pp. 38-43).

[Jon78]   Jones, J., C. (1978). *Design Methods, Seeds of Human Futures.* John Wiley. London.

[Kan95a]   Kantz, H., & Koza, C. (1995). *The ELECTRA Railway Signalling-System: Field Experience with an Actively Replicated System with Diversity.* Proc. FTCS 25. Los Angeles. IEEE Press. (pp. 453-458).

[Kan95]   Kanawati, G. A., Kanawati, N. N., & Abraham, J. A. (1995). *FERRARI: A Flexible Software-based Fault and Error Injection System.* IEEE Trans. Computers. Vol. 44 (2). (pp. 248-260).

[Kan96]   Kanekawa, N., Nohmi, M., Satoh, Y., & Satoh, H. (1996). *Self-Checking and Fail-Safe LSIs by Intra-Chip Redundancy.* Proc. FTCS 26. Sendai, Japan. (pp. 426-430).

[Kar95]   Karlsson, J., Folkesson, P., Arlat, J., Crouzet, Y., & Leber, G. (1995). *Integration and Comparison of Three Physical Fault Injection Techniques.* In: B. Randell, J. L. Laprie, H. Kopetz, & B. Littlewood (Ed.), *Predictably Dependable Computing Systems.* Springer Verlag. Heidelberg. (pp. 309-327).

[Kav92]   Kavi, K. M. (Ed.). (1992). *Real-Time Systems.* IEEE Press.

[Kie88]   Kiekhafer, R. M., Walter, C. J., Finn, A. M., & Thambidurai, P. M. (1988). *The MAFT Architecture for Distributed Fault Tolerance.* IEEE Trans. on Computers. Vol.: 37 (4). (pp. 398-405).

[Kim94]   Kim, K. H., & Kopetz, H. (1994). *A Real-Time Object Model RTO.k and an Experimental Investigation of its Potential.* Proc. COMPSAC 94 Taipei. IEEE Press.

[Kim95]   Kim, B. G., & Wang, P. (1995). *ATM Networks: Goals and Challenges.* Communication of the ACM. Vol. 38 (2). (pp. 39-44).

[Kli86]   Kligerman, E., & Stoyenko, A. D. (1986). *Real-Time Euclid: A Language for Reliable Real-Time Systems.* IEEE Trans. on Software Engineering. Vol. 12 (9). (pp. 941-949).

[Kni86]   Knight, J. C., & Leveson, N. G. (1986). *An Experimental Evaluation of the Assumption of Independence in Multiversion Programming.* IEEE Trans. Software Engineering. Vol. SE-12 (1). (pp. 96-109).

[Kop82]   Kopetz, H. (1982). *The Failure-Fault Model.* Proc. FTCS 12. IEEE Press. (pp. 14-17).

[Kop85]   Kopetz, H., & Merker, W. (1985). *The Architecture of MARS.* Proc. 15th IEEE Int. Symp. on Fault-Tolerant Computing (FTCS-15). Ann Arbor, Mich. (pp. 274-279). This is a condensed version of the Research Report No. MA 82/2 *The Architecture of MARS* that appeared in April 1992 at the Technical University of Berlin.

[Kop87]   Kopetz, H., & Ochsenreiter, W. (1987). *Clock Synchronisation in Distributed Real-Time Systems.* IEEE Trans. Computers. Vol. 36 (8). (pp. 933-940).

[Kop89]   Kopetz, H., Damm, A., Koza, C., Mulazzani, M., Schwabl, W., Senft, C., & Zainlinger, R. (1989). *Distributed Fault-Tolerant Real-Time Systems: The MARS Approach.* IEEE Micro. Vol. 9 (1). (pp. 25-40).

[Kop90a]   Kopetz, H., Kantz, H., Grünsteidl, G., Puschner, P., & Reisinger, J. (1990). *Tolerating Transient Faults in MARS.* Proc. 20th Int. Symp. on Fault-Tolerant Computing (FTCS-20). Newcastle upon Tyne, UK. (pp. 466-473).

[Kop90b]   Kopetz, H., & Kim, K. (1990). *Temporal Uncertainties in Interactions among Real-Time Objects.* Proc. 9th Symposium on Reliable Distributed Systems. Huntsville, AL, USA. IEEE Computer Society Press. (pp. 165-174).

[Kop91]   Kopetz, H., Grünsteidl, G., & Reisinger, J. (1991). *Fault-Tolerant Membership Service in a Synchronous Distributed Real-Time System* In: A. Avizienis & J. C. Laprie (Ed.), *Dependable Computing for Critical Applications.* Springer-Verlag. (pp. 411-429).

[Kop92]   Kopetz, H. (1992). *Sparse Time versus Dense Time in Distributed Real-Time Systems.* Proc. 14th Int. Conf. on Distributed Computing Systems. Yokohama, Japan. IEEE Press. (pp. 460-467).

[Kop93a]   Kopetz, H., & Gruensteidl, G. (1993). *TTP - A Time-Triggered Protocol for Fault-Tolerant Real-Time Systems.* Proc. 23rd IEEE International Symposium on Fault-Tolerant Computing (FTCS-23). Toulouse, France. IEEE Press. (pp. 524-532), appeared also in a revised version in IEEE Computer. Vol. 24 (1). (pp. 22-66).

[Kop93b]   Kopetz, H. (1993). *Should Responsive Systems be Event-Triggered or Time-Triggered?* IEICE Trans. on Information and Systems Japan (Special Issue on Responsive Computer Systems). Vol. E76-D(11). (pp.1325-1332).

[Kop93c]   Kopetz, H., & Reisinger, J. (1993). *The Non-Blocking Write Protocol NBW: A Solution to a Real-Time Synchronisation Problem.* Proc. 14th Real-Time Systems Symposium. Raleigh-Durham, North Carolina.

[Kop94]   Kopetz, H. (1994). *A Solution to an Automotive Control System System Benchmark.* Proc. 15th IEEE Real-Time Systems Symposium. Puerto Rico. IEEE Press. (pp. 154-158).

[Kop95a]   Kopetz, H., Nossal, R., (1995). *The Cluster Compiler--A Tool for the Design of Time-Triggered Real-Time Systems.* Proc. of ACM SIGPLAN Workshop on Languages, Compilers and Tools for Real-Time Systems, La Jolla, California, June 1995.

[Kop95b]   Kopetz, H. (1995). *The Time-Triggered Approach to Real-Time System Design* In: B. Randell, J. L. Laprie, H. Kopetz, & B. Littlewood (Ed.), *Predictably Dependable Computing Systems.* Springer Verlag. Heidelberg. (pp. 53-66).

[Kop95c]   Kopetz, H. (1995). *TTP/A -- A Time-Triggered Protocol of Body Electronics Using Standard UARTS.* Proc. SAE World Congress. Society of Automotive Engineers, SAE Technical Paper 950039. (pp. 1-9).

[Kop95d]   Kopetz, H., Hexel, R., Krueger, A., Millinger, D., & Schedl, A. (1995). *A Synchronization Strategy for a Time-Triggered Multicluster Real-Time System.* Proc., 14th Symp. on Reliable Distributed Systems. Bad Neuenahr, Germany. IEEE Press. (pp. 154-161).

[Kop95e]   Kopetz (1995). *A Communication Infrastracture for a Fault-Tolerant Real-Time System.* Control Engineering Practice-- A Journal of IFAC. Vol. 3 (8). (pp. 1139-1146).

[Kop96]   Kopetz, H. (1996). *A Node as a Real-Time Object.* Proc. of the IEEE Workshop on Object Oriented Real-Time Systems. Laguna Beach, Cal. IEEE Press. (pp. 2-8).

[Lal94]   Lala, J. H., & Harper, R. E. (1994). *Architectural Principles for Safety-Critical Real-Time Applications.* Proc. of the IEEE. Vol. 82 (1). (pp. 25-40).

[Lam74]   Lamport, L. (1974). *A New Solution of Dijkstra's Concurrent Programming Problem.* Comm. ACM. Vol. 8 (7). (pp. 453-455).

[Lam78]   Lamport, L. (1978). *Time, Clocks, and the Ordering of Events.* Comm. ACM. Vol. 21 (7). (pp. 558-565).

[Lam84]   Lamport, L. (1984). *Using Time instead of Time-Outs for Fault-Tolerant Distributed Systems.* ACM Trans. on Programming Languages and Systems. Vol. 6 . (pp. 254-280).

[Lam85]   Lamport, L., & Melliar-Smith, P. M. (1985). *Synchronizing Clocks in the Presence of Faults.* Journal Ass. Comp. Mach. Vol. 21. (pp. 52-78).

[Lap92]   Laprie, J. C. (Ed.). (1992). *Dependability: Basic Concepts and Terminology - in English, French, German, German and Japanese.* Springer-Verlag. Vienna, Austria.

[Lap95]   Laprie, J. C., Arlat, J., Beounes, C., & Kanoun, K. (1995). *Definition and Analysis of Hardware and Software Fault-Tolerant Architectures* In: B. Randell, J. C. Laprie, H. Kopetz, & B. Littlewood (Ed.), *Predictably Dependable Computing Systems.* Springer Verlag. Heidelberg. (pp. 103-122).

[Law92]   Lawson, H. W. (1992). *Cyclone - An Approach to the Engineering of Resource Adequate Cyclic Real-Time Systems.* Real-Time Sytems. Vol. 4 (1). (pp. 55-84).

[Lee90]   Lee, P., A., & Anderson, T., (1990). *Fault Tolerance: Principles and Practice.* Springer Verlag. Vienna.

[LeL90]   LeLann, G. (1990). *Critical Issues for the Development of Distributed Real-Time Computing Systems.* Proc. of the Second IEEE Workshop on Future Trends in Distributed Computing. IEEE Press. (pp. 96-105).

[Lev95]   Leveson, N. G. (1995). *Safeware: System Safety and Computers.* Addison Wesley Company. Reading, Mass.

[Li95]   Li, Y. T. S., Malik, S., & Wolfe, A. (1995). *Efficient Microarchitecture Modeling and Path Analysis for Real-Time Software.* Proc. of the 16th RTSS. Pisa, Italy. IEEE Press. (pp. 298-307).

[Lim94]   Lim, S. S. (1994). *An Accurate Worst-Case Timing Analysis for RISC Processors.* Real-Time Systems Symposium RTSS 94. San Juan, Puerto Rico. IEEE Computer Society. (pp. 97-108).

[Lin96]   Lin, K. J., & Herkert, A. (1996). *Jitter Control in Time-Triggered Systems.* Hawaii Conf. on System Science. (pp. 451-459).

[Lio96]   Lions, J. L. (1996). *Ariane 5--Flight 501 Failure.* www.esrin.esa.it./ htdocs/tidc/Press/Press96/ariane5rep.html.

[Lit95]   Littlewood, B., & Strigini, L. (1995). *Validation of Ultradependability for Software Based Systems* In: B. Randell, J. L. Laprie, H. Kopetz, & B. Littlewood (Ed.), *Predictably Dependable Computing Systems.* Springer Verlag. Heidelberg. (pp. 473-493).

[Liu73]   Liu, C. L., & Layland, J. W. (1973). *Scheduling Algorithms for Multiprogramming in a Hard-Real-Time Environment.* Journal of the ACM. Vol. 20 (1). (pp. 46-61).

[Loc92]   Locke, C. D. (1992). *Software Architectures for Hard Real-Time Applications: Cyclic Executives versus Fixed Priority Executives.* Real-Time Systems. Vol. 4 (1).

[LON90]   LON (1990). *LON Protocol Overview* In: Echelon Systems Corporation, 727 University Avenue, Los Gatos, California.

[Lun84]   Lundelius, L., & Lynch, N. (1984). *An Upper and Lower Bound for Clock Synchronization.* Information and Control. Vol. 62 . (pp. 199-204).

[Mal94]   Malek, M. (1994). *Responsive Computing.* Kluwer Academic Press.

[Mar90]   Marzullo, K. (1990). *Tolerating Failures of Continuous Valued Sensors.* ACM Trans. on Computer Systems. Vol.: 8 (4). (pp. 284-304).

[Mat96]   Mathai, J. (Ed.). (1996). *Real-Time Systems.* Prentice Hall. London.

[McK94]   McKinney, R., & Gordon, T. (1994). *ATM for Narrowband Services.* Comm. Magazine. Vol. 32 (4). (pp. 64-72).

[Mey88]   Meyer, B. (1988). *Object-Oriented Software Construction.* Prentice Hall.

[Mie91]   Miesterfeld, F., & R., H. (1991). *Survey of vehicle multiplexing encoding techniques* In: M. Scarlett (Ed.), *Automotive Technology International '92'.* Sterling Publications International. London. (pp. 253-265).

[Mil91]   Mills, D. L. (1991). *Internet Time Synchronization: The Network Time Protocol.* IEEE Trans. on Comm. Vol. 39 (10). (pp. 1482-1493).

[Mok83]   Mok, A. (1983). *Fundamental Design Problems of Distributed Systems for the Hard Real-Time Environment.* PhD, Massachusetts Institute of Technology.

[Mok84]   Mok, A. K. (1984). *The Design of Real-Time Programming Systems based on Process Models.* Proc. of the IEEE Real-Time Systems Symposium. (pp. 125-134).

[Mon96]   Montgomery, T.A., Pugh, R. D., Leedham, S. T., & Twitchett, S. R. (1996). *FMEA Automation for the Complete Design Process.* Annual Reliability and Maintainability Symposium. Las Vegas, Nevada. IEEE Press. (pp. 30-36).

[Mos94]   Moser, L. E., & Melliar-Smith, P. M. (1994). *Probabilistic Bounds on Message Delivery for the Totem Single-Ring Protocol.* Proc. of the Real-Time System Symposium. San Juan, Puerto Rico. IEEE Press. (pp. 238-248).

[Mul95]   Mullender, S. (1995). *Distributed Systems, 2nd ed.* Addison Wesley. Reading, Mass, USA.

[Neu95]   Neumann, P. G. (1995). *Computer Related Risks.* Addison Wesley--ACM Press. Reading, Mass.

[Neu96]   Neumann, P. G. (1996). *Risks to the Public in Computers and Related Systems.* Software Engineering Notes. Vol.: 21 (5). (p. 18).

[Ols91]   Olson, A., & Shin, K. G. (1991). *Probabilistic Clock Synchronization in Large Distributed Systems.* Proc. of the 11th IEEE Distributed Computing Conference. Arlington, Texas. IEEE Press. (pp. 290-297).

[Par90]   Parnas, D. L., van Schouwen, A. J., & Shu Po Kwan (1990). *Evaluation of Safety-Critical Software.* Comm. of the ACM. Vol. 33 (6). (pp. 636-648).

[Par92]   Parnas, D. L., & Madey, J. (1992). *Documentation of Real-Time Requirements* In: K. M. Kavi (Ed.), *Real-Time Systems.* IEEE Press. (pp. 48-59).

[Pat90]   Patterson, D. A., & Hennessy, J. L. (1990). *Computer Architecture, A Quantitative Approach.* Morgan Kaufmann. San Mateo, Cal.

[Pea80]   Pease, M., Shostak, R., & Lamport, L. (1980). *Reaching Agreement in the Presence of Faults.* Journal of the ACM. Vol. 27 (2). (pp. 228-234).

[Per96]   Perry, T. S., & Geppert, L. (1996). *Do Portable Electronics Endanger Flights?* IEEE Spectrum. Vol.: 33 (9). (pp. 26-33).

[Pet79]   Peters, L. (1979). *Software Design: Current Methods and Techniques.* Infotech State of the Art Report on Structured Software Development. London. Infotech International. (pp. 239-262).

[Pet96]   Peterson, I. (1996). *Comment on Time on Jan 1, 1996.* Software Engineering Notes. Vol. 19 (March 1996). (p. 16).

[Pol95a]   Poledna, S. (1995). *Fault-Tolerant Real-Time Systems, The Problem of Replica Determinism.* Kluwer Academic Publishers. Hingham, Mass, USA.

[Pol95b]   Poledna, S. (1995). *Tolerating Sensor Timing Faults in Highly Responsive Hard Real-Time Systems.* IEEE Trans. on Computers. Vol. 44 (2). (pp. 181-191).

[Pol96a]   Poledna, S., Mocken, T., Schiemann, J., & Beck, T. (1996). *ERCOS: An Operating System for Automotive Applications.* SAE International Congress. Detroit, Mich. SAE Press. (pp. 1-11).

[Pol96b]   Poledna, S. (1996). *Lecture Notes on "Fault-Tolerant Computing"* Technical University of Vienna, A 1040 Vienna, Treitlstrasse 3/182.

[Pol96c]   Poledna, S. (1996). *Optimizing Interprocess Communication for Embedded Real-Time Systems.* Proc. of the Real-Time System Symposium, Dec. 1996. Washington D.C. IEEE Press.

[Pow91]   Powell, D. (1991). *Delta-4: A Generic Architecture for Dependable Distributed Computing* In: *Research Reports ESPRIT (Vol. 1).* Springer-Verlag. Berlin, Germany.

[Pow95]   Powell, D. (1995). *Failure Mode Assumptions and Assumption Coverage* In: B. Randell, J. C. Laprie, H. Kopetz, & B. Littlewood (Ed.), *Predictably Dependable Computing Systems.* Springer Verlag. Berlin. (pp. 123-140).

[Pro92]   Profibus (1992). *The Profibus Standard* In: Profibus Nutzerorganisation, e.d., Hersler Strasse 31, D-503689 Wesseling.

[Pul96]   Pullum, L. L., & Dugan, J. (1996). *Fault-Tree Models for the Analysis of Complex Computer-Based Systems*. 1996 Annual Reliability and Maintainability Symposium. Las Vegas, Nevada. IEEE Press. (pp. 200-207).

[Pus89]   Puschner, P., & Koza, C. (1989). *Calculating the Maximum Execution Time of Real-Time Programs*. Real-Time Systems. Vol. 1 (2). (pp. 159-176).

[Pus93]   Puschner, P. (1993). *Zeitanalyse von Echtzeitprogrammen*. PhD, Technical University of Vienna.

[Ram89]   Ramamritham, K., S., J.A., , & Zhao, W. (1989). *Distributed Scheduling of Tasks with Deadlines and Resource Requirements*. IEEE Trans. on Computers. Vol. 38 (8). (pp. 1110-1123).

[Ram96]   Ramamritham, K. (1996). *Dynamic Priority Scheduling* In: M. Joseph (Ed.), *Real-Time Systems*. Prentice Hall. London. (pp. 66-96).

[Ran75]   Randell, B. (1975). *System Structure for Software Fault Tolerance*. IEEE Trans. on Software Engineering. Vol. SE-1 (2). (pp. 220-232).

[Ran94]   Randell, B., Ringland, G., & Wulf, W. (Ed.). (1994). *Software 2000: A View of the Future of Software*. ESPRIT. Brussels.

[Ran95]   Randell, B., Laprie, J. C., Kopetz, H., & Littlewood, B. (1995). *Predictably Dependable Computing Systems*. Springer Verlag. Heidelberg.

[Rec91]   Rechtin, E. (1991). *Systems Architecting, Creating and Building Complex Systems*. Prentice Hall. Englewood Cliffs.

[Rei57]   Reichenbach, H. (1957). *The Philosophy of Space and Time*. Dover. New York.

[Rei95]   Reisinger, J., Steininger, A., & Leber, G. (1995). *The PDCS Implementation of MARS Hardware and Software* In: B. Randell, J. L. Laprie, H. Kopetz, & B. Littlewood (Ed.), *Predictably Dependable Computing Systems*. Springer Verlag. Heidelberg. (pp. 209-224).

[RMS96]   Reliability and Maintainability Symposium, Proceedings are published annually by the IEEE.

[Rod89]   Rodd, M. G., & Deravi, F. (1989). *Communication Systems for Industrial Automation*. Prentice Hall.

[Ros93]   Rosenberg, H. A., & Shin, K. G. (1993). *Software Fault Injection and its Application in Distributed Systems*. Proc. of 23rd Fault- Tolerant Computing Symposium. IEEE Press. (pp. 208-217).

[Rus93a]   Rushby, J. M., & von Henke, F. (1993). *Formal verification of algorithms for critical systems*. IEEE Trans. on Software Engineering. Vol.: 19 (1). (pp. 13-23).

[Rus93]   Rushby, J. (1993). *Formal Methods and the Certification of Critical Systems* (Research Report No. SRI-CSL-93-07). Computer Science Lab, SRI, Menlo Park, Cal.

[SAE95]   SAE (1995). *Class C Application Requirements, Survey of Known Protocols, J20056* In: *SAE Handbook*. SAE Press, Warrendale, PA. (pp. 23.437-23.461).

[Sah95]   Sahner, R. A., & Trivedi, K. (1995). *Performance and Reliability Analysis of Computer Systems: An Example Based Approach Using the SHARPE Software Package*. Kluwer Academic Publishers. Hingham, Mass.

[Sak95]   Sakenas, M., J., S., & Agrawala, A. (1995). *Design and Implementation of Maruti-II* In: S. H. Son (Ed.), *Advances in Real-Time Systems.* Prentice Hall. Engelwood Cliffs, N.J. (pp. 73-102).

[Sal84]   Saltzer, J., Reed, D. P., & Clark, D. D. (1984). *End-to-End Arguments in System Design.* ACM Trans. on Computer Systems. Vol. 2 (4). (pp. 277-288).

[Sch83]   Schlichting, R. D., & Schneider, F. B. (1983). *Fail-Stop Processors: An Approach to Designing Fault-tolerant Computing Systems.* ACM Trans. on Computing Systems. Vol. 1 (3). (pp. 222-238).

[Sch88]   Schwabl, W. (1988). *The Effect of Random and Systematic Errors on Clock Synchronizatin in Distributed Systems.* PhD Thesis, Technical University of Vienna, A 1040 Vienna, Treitlstrasse 3/182.

[Sch86]   Schneider, F. B. (1986). *A Paradigm for Reliable Clock Synchronization.* Proc. Advanced Seminar Real-Time Local Area Networks. Bandol France, published by INRIA, (pp. 85-104).

[Sch90]   Schneider, F. B. (1990). *Implementing Fault-Tolerant Services Using the State Machine Approach: A Tutorial.* ACM Computing Surveys. Vol. 22 (4). (pp. 299-319).

[Sch93]   Schütz, W. (1993). *The Testability of Distributed Real-Time Systems.* Kluwer Academic Publishers. Boston, MA.

[Sch96]   Schedl, A. V. (1996). *Design and Simulation of Clock Synchronization in Distributed Systems.* PhD Thesis, Technical University of Vienna, A 1040 Wien, Treitlstrasse 3/182.

[Seg88]   Segall, L., Vrsalovic, D., Sieworek, D., Yaskin, D., Kownacki, J., Baraton, J., Rancey, D., Robinson, A., & Lin, T. (1988). *FIAT - Fault Injection based Automated Testing Environment.* Proc. FTCS 18, IEEE Press. (pp. 102-107).

[Ser72]   Serlin, O. (1972). *Scheduling of Time Critical Processes.* Spring Joint Computer Conference. AFIPS. (pp. 925-932).

[Sev81]   Sevcik, F. (1981). *Current und Future Concepts of FMEA.* Reliability and Maintainability Symposium. Philadelphia, USA. IEEE Press. (pp. 414-421).

[Sha89]   Shaw, A. C. (1989). *Reasoning About Time in Higher-Level Language Software.* IEEE Trans. on Software Engineering. Vol. SE-15. (pp. 875-889).

[Sha90]   Sha, L., Rajkumar, R., & Lehoczky, J. P. (1990). *Priority Inheritence Protocols: An Approach to Real-Time Synchronization.* IEEE Transactions on Computers. Vol.: 39 (9). (pp. 1175-1185).

[Sha94]   Sha, L., Rajkumar, R., & Sathaye, S. S. (1994). *Generalized Rate-Monotonic Scheduling Theory: A Framework for Developing Real-Time Systems.* Proc. of the IEEE. Vol. 82 (1). (pp. 68-82).

[Shi87]   Shin, K. G., & Ramanathan, P. (1987). *Clock Synchronization in a Large Multiprocessor System in the Presence of Malicious Faults.* IEEE Trans. on Computers. Vol. C-36 (1). (pp. 2-12).

[Shi91]   Shin, K. G. (1991). *HARTS: Distributed Real-Time Architecture.* IEEE Computer. Vol. 24 (5). (pp. 25-35).

[Shi95]   Shin, K. G. (1995). *A Software Overview of HARTS: A Distributed Real-Time System* In: S. H. Son (Ed.), *Advances in Real-Time Systems.* Prentice Hall. Englewood Cliffs, N.J. (pp. 3-22).

[Sim81]   Simon, H. A. (1981). *Sciences of the Artificial.* MIT Press, Cambridge.

[Son94]   Son, S. H. (Ed.). (1994). *Advances in Real-Time Systems.* Prentice Hall.

[Spr89]   Sprunt, B., Sha, L., & Lehoczky, J. (1989). *Aperiodic Task Scheduling for Hard Real-me Systems.* Real-Time Systems. Vol.: 1 (1). (pp. 27-60).

[Sta88]   Stankovic, J. A., & Ramamritham, K. (Ed.). (1988). *Hard Real-Time Systems.* IEEE Press.

[Sta91]   Stankovic, J. A., & Ramamritham, K. (1991). *The Spring Kernel: A new Paradigm for Real-Time Systems.* IEEE Software. Vol.: 8 (3). (pp. 62-72).

[Sta92]   Stankovic, J. A., & Ramamritham, K. (Ed.). (1992). *Advances in Real-Time Systems.* IEEE Press.

[Sta95]   Stallings, W. (1995). *Operating Systems.* Prentice Hall. Englewood Cliffs, N.J.

[Sur95]   Suri, N., Walter, C. J., & Hugue, M. M. (Ed.). (1995). *Advances in Ultra-Dependable Systems.* IEEE Press.

[Tan88]   Tanenbaum, A. S. (1988). *Computer Networks.* Prentice Hall. New York.

[Tan95]   Tanenbaum, A. S. (1995). *Distributed Operating Systems.* Prentice Hall. Englewood Cliffs, N.J.

[The95]   Thevenod-Fosse, P., Waeselynck, H., & Crouzet, Y. (1995). *Software Statistical Testing* In: B. Randell, J. L. Laprie, H. Kopetz, & B. Littlewood (Ed.), *Predictably Dependable Computing Systems.* Springer Verlag. Heidelberg.

[Tin95]   Tindell, K. (1995). *Analysis of Hard Real-Time Communications.* Real-Time Systems. Vol. 9 (2). (pp. 147-171).

[Tis95]   Tisato, F., & DePaoli, F. (1995). *On the Duality between Event-Driven and Time Driven Models.* Proc. of 13th. IFAC DCCS 1995. Toulouse France. (pp. 31-36).

[Tok89]   Tokuda, H., & Mercer, C. W. (1989). *ARTS: A Distributed Real-Time Kernel.* ACM Sigops Operating Systems Review. Vol. 23 (3). (pp. 29-53).

[Tok90]   Tokuda, H., Nakajima, T., & Rao, P. (1990). *Real-Time Mach: Towards a Predictable Real-Time System* In: J. A. Stankovic & K. Ramamritham (Ed.), *Advances in Real-Time Systems.* IEEE Press. (pp. 237-246).

[Tra88]   Traverse, P. (1988). *AIRBUS and ATR System Architecture and Specification* In: U. Voges (Ed.) *Software Diversity in Computerized Control Systems.* Springer-Verlag.(pp.95-104)

[Ver93]   Verissimo, P. (1993). *Real-Time Communication* In: S. Mullender (Ed.), *Distributed Systems.* Addison-Wesley--ACM Press. Reading, Mass. (pp.447-486).

[Ver94]   Verissimo, P. (1994). *Ordering and Timeliness Requirements of Dependable Real-Time Programs.* Real-Time Systems. Vol. 7 (3). (pp. 105-128).

[Vet95]   Vetter, R. J. (1995). *ATM Concepts, Architectures, and Protocols.* Comm. ACM. Vol. 38 (2). (pp. 30-38).

[Vit60]   Vitruvius (1960). *The Ten Books on Architecture, written 0027 B.C., translated by M.H.Morgan.* Dover Publications. New York.

[Vog88]   Voges, U. (Ed.). (1988). *Software Diversity in Computerized Control Systems.* Springer-Verlag. Wien.

[Vrc94]   Vrchoticky, A. (1994). *The Basis for Static Execution Time Prediction.* PhD Thesis, Technical University of Vienna.

[Web91]   Webber, S. (1991). *The Stratus Architecture.* Proc. FTCS 21. IEEE Press. (pp. 512-519).

[Wen78]   Wensley, J. H., Lamport, L., Goldberg, J., Green, M. W., Levitt, K. N., Melliar-Smith, P. M., Shostack, R. E., & Weinstock, C. B. (1978). *SIFT: The Design and Analysis of a Fault-Tolerant Computer for Aircraft Control.* Proc. IEEE. Vol. 66 (10). (pp. 1240-1255).

[Wil83]   Williams, T. W. (1983). *Design for Testability--A Survey.* Proc. of the IEEEE. Vol. 71 (1). (pp. 98-112).

[Wit90]   Withrow, G. J. (1990). *The Natural Philosophy of Time.* Clarendon Press. Oxford.

[Woo90]   Wood, S. P. (1996). *The IEEE-P1451 Transducer to Microprocessor Interface.* Sensors. Vol. 13 (6). (pp. 43-48).

[Xu90]   Xu, J., & Parnas, D. (1990). *Scheduling Processes with Release Times, Deadlines, Precedence, and Exclusion Relations.* IEEE Trans. on Software Engineering. Vol. 16 (3). (pp. 360-369).

[Yan93]   Yang, Z., & Marsland, T. A. (1993). *Global States and Time in Distributed Systems.* IEEE Computer Society Press. Los Alamitos, Cal.

Index